ANIMALS!

ANIMALS!
ENGLAND v ARGENTINA

Neil Clack

KNOW
THE
SCORE

Know The Score Books is an imprint of Pitch Publishing

Pitch Publishing
A2 Yeoman Gate
Yeoman Way
Durrington
BN13 3QZ

www.pitchpublishing.co.uk
www.knowthescorebooks.com

Published by Know The Score Books 2010

A CIP catalogue record for this book is available from the British Library.

10-digit ISBN: 1848184084
13-digit ISBN:9781848184084

Picture credits: PA Photos, Colorsport and Action Images
Every effort has been made to identify the owners of the copyright of all illustrated material.

Printed and bound in Great Britain by Cromwell Press Group

CONTENTS

"I doubt very much whether today's game in Geneva will be played as if the result is of secondary importance. This just does not happen in games between these countries. Different cultures, different styles, different mentalities somehow mean these games have a badge of honour about them and that does not apply in other internationals.

In one half of the pitch there will be England, who, for whatever reason, have lagged behind at international level for many many years, but we must remember did give the game to the world. Is it that arrogance over such a long time which has upset the likes of Argentina, who, in the other half, think that there is a European prejudice against them? Do not talk about this being *just* a game of football. There is too much history to dismiss it as easily as that. Pride and honour are at stake."

Ex-England manager Graham Taylor before England faced Argentina in a friendly in November 2005.

"The English attitude is, 'we taught them to play like this and now they want to beat us' – the teacher denying the superiority of the pupil. This provokes annoyance. To win against England would be a homage to Ernesto Grillo and Diego Maradona and all those who have ever played against England. Always something memorable happens."

Robert Perfumo, ex-Argentina captain and TV analyst before the same match.

FOREWORD

BY RICARDO VILLA

WHEN I first signed for Tottenham, I struggled in the beginning to adapt to a different style of play – of course, the language is always a barrier as well.

The main problem was that my position didn't exist in England. I was an Argentinian no.10, an *enganche* (hook or link) as it's called in my country – the free man who plays behind the strikers. But English football demanded I tracked back and ran harder in a standard 4-4-2 midfield. That was tough.

Before I established myself in the Tottenham midfield, the manager Keith Burkinshaw said to me one day, "Ricky, you're a tall lad, have you ever played as a striker?" So, they put me up front in a training session, and played all these crosses and high balls up to me, but I couldn't head a ball. That wasn't my role, nor how I was used to playing.

We have these little differences in our football, differences that were there right from the beginning, in the first match between our two countries in 1951, and, amazingly, considering all the changes football has been through, can still be seen today. We have a different football background in terms of style of play, and yet we share the same football culture in so many other ways. Are there two more football-obsessed nations in the world than England and Argentina?

This is the story I always wanted to read. It's the complete story and the truth, or as near as one can get to it. Some of the misunderstandings and anecdotes made me laugh, but it is a rich and serious analysis as well, and the great thing is that it lets the players tell the stories themselves. For me, reading the book brought back to life so many memories of classic matches.

Of course there have always been the controversies too. But somehow they have added to this remarkable tale rather than detracted. Now the whole world cannot wait for the next instalment of England versus Argentina. Because it just might be as good, if not better, as those that have gone before.

ACKNOWLEDGEMENTS

FIRST AND foremost, I would like to thank all the players and ex-players who took part in this book. All of them embraced the idea with enthusiasm, gave sparingly of their time, and none asked for money. Memories of being plied with second and third helpings of caramel flan with cream by Carlos Roa, being shown around the Estudiantes training complex by Juan Veron and his father, sharing an after-meal *limoncheri* (vodka digestif) with Ardiles and Villa, and having my notebook filled with tactical arrows and diagrams by Silvio Marzolini will remain among my favourite memories of Argentina. I wouldn't want to single out one player more than any other, as all were so friendly and helpful, but ex-England goalkeeper Gil Merrick's memory of the 1953 matches was so sharp that he even remembered which horse had won the Derby that year. But then, just a few weeks after we spoke, in January 2010, news reached me that he had passed away, eight days after his 88th birthday. However, I was pleased to see that he received so many fitting tributes from the world of football. A true gentleman.

In Argentina, I would like to metion the staff of El Taller Bar, where a lot of the manuscript was written; Celeste, Gustavo, Claudio, Valeria, Cesar, Iris, Federico, and the incredible Mario provided me with numerous cups of tea (plus the odd glass or two of red wine), and plenty of humour during my late night vigils with pen and paper. Also Marina Castaño, Patricia Gonzalez Schepers, and Alan Moir, for their help and friendship during the writing process, and the Boca Seniors – Eduardo Sen, Juan Carlos Miranda, Pedro, Jaime, Cacho, Marta, Matius – for making me feel so welcome and part of the clan!

To my good friends and colleagues, Juan Pablo Mendez at Olé, Ezequiel Fernández Moores of La Nacion, EricWeil of the Buenos Aires Herald, Marcela Mora y Araujo of the Financial Times and author JonathanWilson for their expertise and advice, and to Klauss Gallo for checking the text for errors and introducing me to the Wednesday night 5-a-sides.

In England, much appreciation goes to Richard Drury for his encouraging attitude, in the initial stages, a decade ago, and to my Publisher, Simon Lowe of Know The Score books, for allowing me the freedom to write the book I wanted to write. Thanks too, to Nobuko Yokoyama for taking an interest in my first published pieces back in the late 90s and for helping me during difficult times, and to Gary Firmager for letting me write in Over Land and Sea during all these years.

This book would never have been possible without the dedicated round the clock work of Paul Camillin in the final design, the night before we were due to go to print! I'd also like to mention Graham Hales for his professionalism and help regarding the photo section.

No thanks to Darren Cooper, Robert Saggers, Andrew Giddings and Kevin Chapman who kept trying to drag me down the pub and distract me from the task at hand, and who could only manage two e-mails between them (consisting of jibberish nonsense) during all my years away, and no thanks either to the Iguazu Police who arrested me for 'molesting dogs' and threw me in a stinking cell for the night, right at a crucial stage, when I had a deadline to meet (please note, 'molest' has a different meaning in Spanish, the equivalent of 'disturb' or 'bother' – all I did was bark back at some guard dogs through a fence, honest guv).

Last but by no means least, thanks to my mother, for putting up with my outlandish schemes and numerous disappearing acts over the years, and to my father for always taking an interest in whatever I was up to. This book is dedicated to my grandmother and grandfather, who both died within a month of each other, at the grand old age of 95 and 96 respectively, while I was working in Argentina. They are dearly missed.

PREFACE

BUENOS AIRES, MAY 1997

AN ENGLISHMAN with an out-stretched arm: "Taxi, Señor."

El Taxista: "Adonde vamos?" (Where we goin'?)

"El centro."

"Che, de donde sos?" (Hey, where you from, mate?)

After previous guises as an Australian and a Canadian had exposed an embarrassing lack of knowledge of basic geography and population size of both countries, and having established that, 16 years on, there was generally no ill feeling towards British citizens over the Falklands (providing, of course, you agreed immediately that it was a stupid war), the passenger knew that it was actually quite safe, and certainly a lot easier, to tell the truth.

"Ah, London!" exclaims the taxi driver. "Beautiful, so clean; the River Thames, the bridges, so ordered, no crime or violence like here." El Taxista was conjuring up, as many Argentines do, an image of England that was outdated by at least half a century, if it had ever truly existed at all.

"Tell me, is it right that men wear bowler hats on their way to work?" he asks.

By now an experienced cab-rider, the passenger anticipated the next question and the nature of the conversation that was likely to follow.

"So, what team do you support, el Liverpool, el Manchester?"

Argentina is, as they say, *un pais futbolero* (a footballing country). *Muy futbolero* (very footballing) in fact. With the not-so-changeable weather ruling out that avenue of everyday conversation, more space is freed up to talk about football than even in Britain. Whenever men, and often women, shout loudly in Buenos Aires bars or restaurants, looking as if they are about to hit one another, the chances are they are merely discussing the latest match, and are actually, despite evidence to the contrary, best of friends. "On every street corner there's a football manager," runs the refrain.

Taxi drivers, especially, enjoy imparting their tactical nous. Not that there's anything new there. But so much so that you wonder if some sort of football test is a requirement of gaining the licence. Most demonstrate good historical knowledge of the game ... better than their knowledge of the streets of Buenos Aires, anyway.

"No, no, Liverpool and Manchester are not in London. I support West Ham United," replies the passenger.

"Oh, I'm sorry, I don't know them. Small team, is it?"

"Well, you know when England won the World Cup in '66, three of the players, including captain Bobby Moore and the goalscorers in the final, Hurst and Peters, all played for West Ham, so we always say we won the World Cup!"

"Ah, yes, 1966, the strange World Cup. You realise that was all a fix, don't you? They organised it all so the English would win," starts the Taxista.

"Ha, ha, I've heard that before, but I don't believe it," the passenger counters.

This time the conversation veers off on a slightly different tangent. Instead of the usual banter, 'well, if we fixed '66, then you fixed '78', this taxi driver-come-football-expert was a very serious one. Like an evangelical preacher eager to spread the word, it was imperative to him that the lost English soul in the back of his cab should see the light. So when the black vehicle reached its destination, the passenger was not allowed to leave. Head turned 180 degrees, the lecturer was in full flow, speaking of conspiracies; the Argentine captain Rattin's sending off, an English referee for Uruguay v Germany and a German referee for England v Argentina, all arranged by Stanley Rous, the English president of FIFA.

"And what about that son of a bitch English manager calling the Argentines a bunch of 'Animals'?! He should look at himself, the bloody gypsy ... he wasn't a proper Englishman, anyway," rants the middle-aged man, revealing a remarkable knowledge of Sir Alf Ramsey's ethnical background. He stops short of vowing to wipe the streets of the trash and the scum, but it was clear that the events of 1966 still had a traumatic effect on this taxi driver, who could not have been more than 10 or 12 at the time of the controversy to which he referred.

It irked the passenger. This particular conspiracy theorist may have been the most forthright in his views, but he could not be dismissed as a one-off loony. It was a familiar story that the Englishman had heard many times before, from Argentine journalists, friends, strangers in bars, and even the 60-year-old woman who ran the little *Pension* where he was staying. They were all adamant that 1966 was a fix.

"But how do you know for sure?"

The question was always met with the same response, "Oh, c'mon, don't be so naïve."

❖

You take your knocks in life. It's all part of growing up; discovering Father Christmas isn't real, the failed job interview, your Sunday morning pub team getting turned over 15-0, despite the change of tactics and formation you introduced, losing your new bicycle after leaving it outside the shops unlocked, losing all the rough copy, the only copy, of a book on the history of England v Argentina matches that you've been trying to write – all punches that hit you squarely in the face. Getting dumped, now that's a tough one, especially when it's a right hook that you didn't see coming, but in the middle of life's slings and arrows, you learn to cling on to the little comforts that make you happy, things that remain constant and true throughout life, like all that great music out there to make you smile, family and friends, and that picture of Bobby Moore holding the World Cup aloft in 1966.

They have erected a statue of Moore, Hurst and Peters outside West Ham's stadium, though it has to be covered in tarpaulin whenever Millwall are the visitors. The fans may joke that West Ham won the World Cup, but for the uninitiated tourist wandering around the club's museum, they would think they really did; over half the floor space and memorabilia is dedicated to that great summer of '66.

No doubt a lot of rubbish has been talked and written about 1960s England, and the reality was very different from the romantic nostalgia my generation have been fed, but, for us, the baby-boomers from that era, the ones who did not live it, the Swinging Sixties has always held a mythical attraction. The figure of the late Bobby Moore is symbolic of that period, a role model from a time when people were apparently more positive in their outlook and more respectful towards one another. Over time, Moore has come to represent something deeper than just winning the World Cup. The world, or England anyway, was a less cynical place back then, with some great music and fashion thrown in on top. So, when some Argentine taxi driver tells me England winning the World Cup was all a fix, I'm just not havin' it.

It's not in my nature anyway. I don't believe September 11th was anything more than a terrorist attack, I don't believe there was anything more sinister to Princess Diana's death other than a tragic accident, I do believe they put a man on the moon, and I don't believe the 1966 World Cup was all a big conspiracy.

But no matter how I tried, El Taxista had introduced a nagging doubt to the back of my mind. I had to admit that there was a ring of believability in all that he, and others, said. There were certainly a lot of unanswered questions and I did not know the full story. Even in Brazil, I had heard the rumours. "The strange World Cup," they said, "and the funny thing is, the English don't realise it."

I had learnt that South Americans have a tendency to believe in conspiracies, and who can blame them? Having suffered brutal dictatorships that manipulated information and fooled the majority of the populace it is no surprise that Argentines are one of the most authority-distrusting nations in the world, which is healthy to a degree, but I would regularly find myself protesting on a typical footballing Sunday afternoon "not every match is lost because the referee's been bought".

So, after promising myself for years, I finally took the plunge and decided to delve into the reasons why Argentinians believe England fixed the 1966 World Cup. At least it would be good to know what I'm talking about whenever I'm defending Bobby Moore's honour.

It must have been the 1978 World Cup. Your first World Cup is always the best and as I have ventured through life I've come across many of my generation who share memories of sneaking downstairs in the middle of the night to turn on the TV. The volume had to be kept low so as not to wake the parents, but just audible enough to hear the commentator, with that kind of echo on his voice that you do not get on satellite transmissions anymore, and the fervour of the crowds – that catchy, repetitive, haunting chant of 'Ar-gen-tin-a, Ar-gen-tin-a'.

I can remember our maths teacher wondering why so many of his 11-year-old pupils were falling asleep in class. There was something exotic about it – the World Cup, not the maths class – screened from the other side of the world, in a different time zone. The football was good as well; the total football of Holland, great players like Platini, Boniek, Krol, Kempes, and a plethora of long-range goals.

During the 2006 World Cup, Paul Jewell, manager of Premier League side Wigan at the time, admitted to having had similar experiences. In his column in the *Guardian* Jewell had this to say: 'It is just as well this is a column and not a podcast as you would be suffering my rendition of the 1978 World Cup theme. It was a great tune and whenever the World Cup comes around there are always moments when I am transported back to '78, Argentina, ticker-tape, Archie Gemmill and late-night vigils by the TV.

I would be sent to bed early, then called back down by my dad, Billy, to watch football from the other side of the planet in my pyjamas. Remember what it was like to be a teenage boy in love with football? That was me. 30 years ago there was barely any live football on TV and so the World Cup, especially one as visually spectacular as Argentina, thrilled me and everybody I knew in Liverpool.'

But if Argentina '78 was our World Cup awakening, then four years later came our political one.

"Sir, sir, look at the map, those islands are right next to Argentina, so why don't they belong to them?" We were winding the young history teacher up, knowing that he was probably against the war, but, of course, he would never be allowed to say that in front of the class, no matter how much we provoked him. Again, this faraway country had become the focus of attention during a crucial age of adolescence. The Falklands conflict came to a head during the 1982 World Cup. Fellow 15-year-old classmates and myself carried our books in the *de rigeur* 'Bulldog Bobby' sports bags of that summer. While the mascot for España '82 was an orange with a smiling face, the official England team mascot, sanctioned by the FA, was a snarling bulldog in an England shirt, which had gone down well with England fans and schoolkids alike.

We were asking a lot of questions about politics for the first time as well. I remember catching a late night documentary about the war and the dictatorship in Argentina and being fascinated by the amount of chanting and jumping up and down in the city squares, the same songs and flags that we had seen during the '78 World Cup. The programme ended with a catchy tune by Leon Gieco, the words in subtitles and a melody which has always stuck in my mind. Then, a couple of years later, on holiday in Spain, I met a group of Argentines who were very funny and friendly, and the girls were beautiful. I suspect that may have left an impression as well.

Of course, it took me years to get round to it, but I finally made it to Argentina in 1997, as a backpacker for a few weeks, and, by chance, landed some work as an English teacher, or, better said, cowboy English teacher, as the only qualification required was that you were a native English speaker. I'm not sure the pupils learned much about the basics of English grammar when they opened their books, but the teacher most certainly did.

So, I stayed for a few months longer than expected, and it was a good time to be there. Sixteen years after the dictatorship had fallen, but before the economic crash of 2001, people were going out at weekends, arriving home at 7am. It felt like being part of some sort of movement, young people enjoying themselves at non-pretentious clubs. DJs would happily mix dance music with 1970s rock that probably would have been laughed at in trendy London during 'Cool Britannia', but who is to say this wasn't cool when the women are pretty and the city breathes football? Buenos Aires, along with Montevideo, across the river in Uruguay, contains the highest concentration of teams in the world, and is a home from home for those who grew up on the terraces in Britain; cheap, noisy and smelly, with that unmistakeable whiff of hot dogs and urine as you enter the stadium. Nobody moaned if you talked about football at parties or weddings; in fact you were expected to.

Good times. But, of course, there's a downside to all that. You find it very hard to settle again back home. You begin to see both sides. Begin, even, to consider the possibility that there might have been something crooked about '66.

My quest for truth would manifest itself rather differently to the initial single task I set myself. It grew into uncovering the tales surrounding all 15 of the matches between two sporting enemies who had so many other issues between them, many of which neither really understood. It fascinated me, pulling me in to the web of intrigues, conflicts and personalities which over nearly 60 years have made England versus Argentina compulsive, and sometimes repulsive, viewing.

INTRODUCTION

MASTERS AND PUPILS – A BRIEF POTTED HISTORY

IT WAS the English who gave Argentina football. All Argentinians know that. They learn it at school; how a group of sailors were the first to put down jumpers for goalposts and started kicking a round-shaped object around the port of Buenos Aires sometime in the 1860s.

Legend has it that those *Ingleses locos* played in their lunch breaks, in the heat of the midday sun, but when the locals began to copy them, a new style of football developed – the rock-hard pitches of Buenos Aires demanding tighter ball control and dribbling, the opposite of the long hoofs of the English. The first football cultural difference exposed. Well, that's how the story goes – part true, part myth?

Then came the English railway workers. They always say English in Argentina, but really they mean British, as there were plenty of Welsh and Scots among them, building Argentina's infrastructure, digging ditches, laying down the tracks, and, of course, spreading the game of football inland. The British built the meat packing factories for all that succulent Argentinian beef, developed the leather trade, set up their own banks, businesses and schools, and that's why so many top Argentine teams today have English sounding names: Rosario Central is a railway station, Banfield and Lomas were British suburbs of Buenos Aires, and Newell's Old Boys were formed by Mr Newell, the headmaster of a British school in Rosario. Current Argentina First Division side Arsenal are innocently and affectionately referred to as 'El Arse' by both fans and press alike.

But that's not all Argentines learn about the English. They also know that, before the railways and the football, the British Empire tried to conquer and colonise their country. Twice. Failing on both occasions, they were defeated in 1806 and 1807 by women pouring boiling oil from the top of high buildings onto 'the English pirates' below, while their men fought off the invaders with their bare fists in the narrow Buenos Aires backstreets of San Telmo. It's all become part of Argentinian legend, much like Henry V and Agincourt to us Brits.

The English, or British rather, may have failed to colonise Argentina, but they did take over, in all but name, economically. Neo-colonialism is the term historians use. The rich

Estancieros (landowners and ruling classes) were happy to agree to bilateral deals with the British government, exporting raw materials, mainly Argentinian beef, in return for British manufactured goods, and that's why those British sailors and railway workers arrived midway through the century.

The English community grew to such an extent that by the 1890s there were 40,000 expats living in the wealthy Buenos Aires suburbs of Hurlingham, Lomas, Wilde, Claypole and Temperley, a confident affluent community that played cricket, rugby, tennis and polo, and rowed on the river Tigre, with bridge clubs and afternoon tea for the ladies. However, it was only their sport of football that captured the imagination of the native Argentinians, the other pastimes remaining the preserve of the British elite.

So, there has always been this confused mixture of admiration and resentment for the English in Argentina. Respect for their organisation, punctuality and ideas of sportsmanship, but tainted with a touch of animosity for the way they did the deals with the landowners, and controlled the raw materials. And for being a bunch of pirates who tried to invade in the first place...

The first ever registered football match in Argentina took place at the Buenos Aires Cricket Club in 1867, Colorados (colours) versus Blancos (whites), a strictly all-British affair, with only eight players on each side. However, it is Scotsman Alexander Watson Hutton who is generally considered as the founding father of Argentina football. He arrived from Edinburgh in 1882 to teach at the prestigious St Andrews school, but soon fell out with his employers over their reluctance to spend money on playing fields. He left St Andrews in 1884 and formed his own English High School where a higher priority was given to football.

Hutton founded the Amateur Argentine Football Association (AAFA) and the first Argentine league in 1893, only six years after the English league was formed and long before any other European country had taken such steps. There were five original teams: Lomas Athletic, Buenos Aires Railway, Flores, Quilmes Rovers, and Hutton's own English High School team. The original meetings of the Association were carried out in English, but switched to Spanish in 1903. The league expanded rapidly. By 1905 there were 77 clubs affiliated, the largest association outside Great Britain.

The old boys of Hutton's English High School formed a team called Alumni (Latin for pupils), and they dominated Argentine football in the first decade of the 20th century, winning nine league titles between 1900 and 1911. Alumni were as respected as much for their corinthian spirit as their success on the field. Their aim was to uphold the British ideals of fair play, and they disliked those who put success before sportsmanship. Moustachioed and peak-capped, old pictures of the team are often accompanied by captions explaining how gentlemanly they were. Legend has it that in one important match they even owned up on the spot to a goal which had been scored with a hand, and asked the referee to disallow it. The comparisons with the events of 1986 do not need any more emphasising.

Argentina's first international match took place in 1901 against Uruguay in Montevideo, where a similar football development had taken place. All the names on the teamsheet of both sides were English. 'Argentina' won 3-2. Their second international, the following year, was also against Uruguay in Montevideo, and this time Argentina won by a much bigger margin, 6-0.

Then came the visits of English club sides. Southern League Southampton were the first to make the month-long boat trip across the Atlantic in 1903. It was a grand social occasion for the British community, who enjoyed hosting to the first professional team on Argentine soil. They took the players and officials on meat factories tours, tram rides, polo matches, golf, and theatre trips, wine and beef banquets, providing the visitors with "an endless round of entertainments", as the Southampton chairman described it, during their three-week stay.

Saints were the reigning Southern League champions and beaten FA Cup finalists in 1900 and 1902, and their results in Argentina reveal the difference in the standard of football being played at that time. The touring English professionals beat Britanicos 10-0, Belgrano 6-0, and Alumni, Argentina's best side, 3-0. According to local press reports, Southampton 'received great applause for their speed and heading ability.'

Next to visit were Nottingham Forest in 1905. They attracted crowds of around 8,000 for their matches which were big events in Argentina, and clearly, from the figures, it was not just the British community in attendance. Forest had beaten Peñarol of Uruguay 6-1 on their way to Buenos Aires, and were too good for the Argentine teams as well, beating Rosario 5-0 (there was a special fête held after the match), Belgrano 7-0, Britanicos 13-1, and for the big match against Alumni, a record crowd of 10,000 turned up, including the President of Argentina, General Julio Roca. Forest won 6-0.

It was from these first visits of English clubs that the concept of 'masters and pupils' arose. The English clubs, the masters, showed their Argentinian pupils how to play. Newly formed Independiente were so impressed with Nottingham Forest that they adopted the club's red shirts, the kit they still wear today.

In the last decade of the 19th century the last great wave of Spanish and Italian immigration had come. Part of Argentine football legend is that some of the early, exclusively all-British, football clubs, didn't let locals, or these other Hispanics, join in. The roots of some of today's big Argentine clubs may bear witness to that suggestion. In Rosario, for example, the central Argentinian railway company had two teams: one for the British managers, Rosario Athletic, and one for the workers, Rosario Central. Only the latter has survived.

In the working-class Avelleneda district of Buenos Aires, Independiente were formed when a group of local factory workers wanted to form a team independent from the factory's English management's team. Seventy years later, in the 1970s, Independiente, in their Nottingham Forest kit, won the Copa de Libertadores, the South American equivalent of the European Cup, four times in a row, and overall, have won the trophy a record seven times, as well as winning the world club championship twice, against Ajax in 1973, and Liverpool in 1984. The original factory managers' team sunk without a trace.

By the turn of the century groups of young Argentines were beginning to form their own clubs and they generally developed around neighbourhoods. Out of respect for the game's founders, and because it was fashionable, many of the new clubs gave themselves, at least in part, English names.

Racing Club were formed in 1903, a couple of years before their arch rivals and Avelleneda neighbours, Independiente. (The stadiums of these two clubs are only one hundred metres apart, even closer than Anfield is to Goodison Park, similar to Dundee and Dundee United.)

River Plate were formed in 1901 in the dock area of Buenos Aires, their name a bad Anglicisation of *Rio de la Plata* (River of Silver), while River's neighbourhood rivals, Boca Juniors, were formed in 1905 by a group of young college friends who took the Spanish name of the area *La Boca* (the mouth – of the river), and added the English 'Juniors' because they wanted to show they were young students, the sons of the original Italian immigrants. Fortunately the founders of the now world famous club decided against anglicising both words; 'Mouth Juniors' doesn't have the same ring to it.

Boca Juniors wore a kit of blue and white stripes in their early days, but there was another team, Almagro, that had identical shirts, so they challenged each other to a match for the right to wear the colours, a common event between clubs in those times, and the reason why none of the teams in the top divisions have the same shirt design today. The young Boca lads lost and could not decide upon the new kit, so agreed to adopt the colours of the flag of the next ship that came into the dock. It was Swedish and gave rise to the club's blue and yellow shirts.

River Plate, known as *Los Millonarios* (the millionaires), moved away from the Boca area to a more lucrative part of the city in the 1940s, but the *superclasico* of Boca versus River is still considered the most passionate derby, elected the greatest sporting event in the world by England's *Observer* newspaper in 2001.

In 1905 British entrepreneur Sir Thomas Lipton donated a trophy, The Lipton Cup, as the prize for an annual match to be played between Argentina and Uruguay, with all the proceeds given to charity. From 1907, there was also a Newton Cup to be contested between the two countries. In fact all of Argentina's first 14 internationals were against Uruguay. They met 35 times between 1901 and 1914, the most frequently played international in the world, more so even than England versus Scotland.

A similar football development was also occurring amongst the smaller British communities in Brazil, and the Argentine team travelled to Sao Paulo for a series of six games against them in 1908. Argentina won five and drew one. The name Brown features heavily. From just one family, four Brown brothers, the stars of Alumni, played for Argentina in one of the matches against Brazil, an international record. Their cousin, another Brown, was also in the team. Curiously, in another link to 1986, a Brown starred in the team which defeated England and lifted the World Cup in Mexico – defender José Luis Brown.

The next English teams to visit were Everton and Tottenham, arriving together in 1909. Both were strong First Division teams, Everton having finished as runners up in the league that year. Both were visiting Argentina because there were healthy profits to be made. The matches against Alumni in particular attracted the masses. Everton beat the Argentinian champions 4-0, while Tottenham thumped them 5-0, although it is reported that the Alumni players were far from happy with some of the challenges and physical play of the English teams, especially their use of the shoulder charge, which was deemed unlawful in Argentina. Neither did the crowd like it and, at times, became rowdy – the first small sign of a breakdown in the respect for English football perhaps.

However, upon arriving home, an Everton director told the *Liverpool Echo* that the tour had been good for breaking down prejudices towards foreigners. He also remarked that the British community had provided "one long continuous round of pleasure" (Walter Ball of Tottenham stayed on for two years to coach football, reinforcing the idea of the masters teaching the pupils).

In 1910, the first South American international tournament was held in Buenos Aires between Argentina, Uruguay and Chile. Reports say that none of the sides committed any fouls and, on one occasion, when a penalty was awarded to Argentina they turned it down as they didn't think there had been an infringement. Argentina won the tournament and Mrs Ferguson served the teas. How very nice.

By the time Swindon Town visited in 1912 more and more Argentine names were appearing on the team sheets of local sides, and a couple of significant changes had occurred. First, in 1910, time was called on the traditional Britanicos v Argentinos annual game. The Argentines won the last match 5-1, and the British felt they could no longer field a team of equal strength.

Secondly, in 1912, Alumni, the all-British peak-capped bastions of fair play and corinthian values, disbanded. Argentine clubs had outgrown them. Alumni had always maintained their amateur philosophy, but league football was becoming more competitive. While Alumni were giving all their profits to charity, other clubs were investing in stadia and infrastructure, increasing their supporter bases.

The famous Brown brothers, all Alumni players, joined the still-British-controlled Quilmes club, who won the league the following year. Alumni had played their part in the evolution of Argentinian football and are always respected for that, but events were moving quickly forward.

Rather apt, in light of what was ahead in the distant future, was that even back in 1912, the same year as Alumni were winding up, a team from the small town of La Plata called Estudiantes, who had originally formed in 1896 and wore Alumni's red and white striped shirts as a tribute to the sporting English team, were now in the news for causing problems. Their supporters had assaulted the referee and two of their players were suspended for a season for inciting the fans to attack. Estudiantes de La Plata would feature later in the history of England versus Argentina.

Swindon Town drew 2-2 with a best of northern suburbs team in front of 15,000, and also drew 2-2 with a southern suburbs team in front of 20,000 – both record attendances. The Robins won all their other games, but not by the same margins as the earlier visiting English teams. Swindon also played in Uruguay and manager Sam Allan remarked that the standard of football he had seen on both sides of the River Plate was much higher than he had been expecting. Quite a few of the players could earn a living as professionals in England he reckoned, and he noted that there was a similar, rabid passion for football in both countries.

Allan also explained that a distinct style of play was developing in South America, different from England. As they played on rock hard pitches, the Argentine and Uruguayan players had great ball control and liked to dribble, always keeping the ball on the ground, although Allan did detect a reluctance to shoot (a neat description, which would be repeated with regular frequency in future reports of Argentina v England matches).

There are many theories as to why Argentina developed its own style of football. Some say it's because kids had to learn their ball skills in narrow back streets and confined spaces, with a need for tight control, but it was more than that, as Jorge Valdano, the 1986 World Cup-winning Argentina international and former Real Madrid manager explains: "The style is called *la nuestra* which means 'our way of playing'. The idea is to keep the ball from your opponent, to hide the ball with trickery." In Argentina, they compare football with tango dancing, an artistic performance with quick steps from the movement of the hips. It is, therefore, both an art form and an expression of passion.

1978 World Cup winner Ricardo Villa distinguished himself as a footballer in both Argentina and England, scoring a famous winning goal for Tottenham in the 1981 Cup final; a slalom past three Manchester City defenders, voted the best Cup final goal of all time by the BBC. He believes that even today you can see a distinct style: "The difference between English and Argentine kids is that the English youngsters are always looking for the goal, thinking only in the goal, whereas in Argentina we think more about the ball."

In a nutshell, the Argentinian game was always based on the *gambeta* (dribble). The dream goal, the most beautiful goal, would be to dribble around your opponents before placing the ball in the net, and the most dreamt of goal of all would be to do it against the English, the traditional 'masters of the game', the ones who had come to Argentina and taught them how to play. But in England, football was never meant to be so beautiful. It was originally played in the public schools (private, fee paying establishments) and universities as a healthy, virile, manly sport that encouraged the virtues of stamina, discipline and teamwork. However, it had fast become the abiding passion of the working-class male, who espoused ethics such as commitment, work-rate, excitement and physical challenge on the field, as much as they did off it.

Exeter City, the next English club to visit Argentina, were not amongst the best. They had only turned professional when replacing Football League-bound Tottenham Hotspur in the Southern League six years before they visited South America in 1914. By then, the two styles of play had diverged to such an extent that there was bound to be conflict. Again, the visiting English team attracted good crowds, and Exeter won five and drew one of their seven matches, including beating Argentinian champions Racing 2-0. However, for the first time, an English team was criticised in the local press. 'Exeter have no style and just hit long balls,' they complained. Argentine players were particularly unhappy with Exeter's physical approach, and what they considered excessive and unfair use of the shoulder charge. And they were even more upset that the travelling English referees allowed it! Even the British community were disappointed in Exeter. The ex-pats had always seen sport as a way of upholding and asserting traditional British middle-class values on Argentinian society, when, in reality, back in England football was now a rough, working-class game.

Following the hiatus caused by the Great War and the global influenza epidemic, the now extinct Scottish side Third Lanark (bankrupt in 1962) and England's Plymouth

Argyle were next to tour in 1923 and 1924, and results show the Argentinian teams were now competing on an even keel with the British professionals – an equal amount of wins, draws and defeats shared out between the hosts and their visitors. Third Lanark left a good impression and gave rise to the expression 'Scottish style' in Argentina, which meant short passing and dribbling with the ball on the ground. In the 1920s Scottish football was renowned as a more skilful passing game than the English, culminating in the 1928 'Wembley Wizards' who thrashed England 5-1 on their own turf with a dazzling display of passing and footwork, all with a forward line of five men, none of whom were any taller than 5 ft 7 ins.

English Third Division side Plymouth, however, didn't leave such a good impression. Like their south-west cousins Exeter, their physical play and shoulder charging caused problems. Argyle drew 0-0 with Argentine champions Boca Juniors, but in a niggly match against Rosario, the referee awarded a penalty to Plymouth, and the opposition players left the field in protest. Then, angry hordes from the stands invaded the pitch.

Crowds across South America, but in Argentina in particular, were becoming bigger, noisier and more excitable. In 1924 Argentina challenged their old rivals and Olympic champions Uruguay to a match. They drew, but the replay in Buenos Aires was brutal, with reports of the crowd throwing stones at Uruguayan players. Uruguay, losing, walked off with four minutes remaining amidst a shower of pebbles. The match was abandoned and the fences went up for the first time in Argentine stadiums. They have never come down.

Football was still very much an amateur game in Argentina in the 1920s, unlike in the UK where the four Home Nations had now voted to withdraw from FIFA at the governing body's insistence that teams entering the Olympic football tournament were solely amateur. Argentina first entered the Olympics in the tournament following the mass withdrawal of British sides in 1928, defeating the United States 11-2 (Domingo Tarasconi 4 goals, Roberto Cherro 3, both of Boca Juniors), Belgium 6-3 (Tarasconi 4 goals again) and Egypt 6-0 (just the 3 for Tarasconi this time) on the way to meeting the old enemy, and reigning Olympic champions, Uruguay, in the final. There was enormous expectation about the game in Europe as word had got around about the silky skills and dribbling of the South American sides. Around 250,000 tickets were in demand, but the Amsterdam stadium only held 40,000, the black market doing a roaring trade for the 102nd meeting between Argentina and Uruguay in just 27 years.

In Buenos Aires crowds gathered around loudspeakers on the corners of all the main squares, rigged up especially for the live commentary from Holland. They sang and chanted as if they were actually in a football stadium. Replica scenes were taking place across the Rio de la Plata in Montevideo. The match finished 1-1, with Tarasconi and Cherro shackled by the opposing defence. Uruguay won the replay 2-1.

While the best players were away at the Olympics, Motherwell from Scotland visited Argentina, achieving mixed results and then, in the following summer of 1929, came the infamous visit from Chelsea.

Argentinian crowds, behind the fences, were large and noisy, and they didn't like losing. Nor did they like the shoulder charge. Chelsea, who were a Second Division side, beat Provincials, Independiente and San Lorenzo, but in a match against a Buenos Aires XI at Boca Juniors' stadium, the Chelsea players became incensed with the Argentinian referee for penalising their charges. The game turned rough, players started fighting, and the match was abandoned with Chelsea leading 3-2. The police advised the Chelsea players to leave the stadium as soon as possible, but they were unable to because the tyres on their coach had been slashed. There were no more tours from British clubs.

The size of the crowds in Amsterdam had demonstrated that football was growing too big for the Olympics. However it was the political pressure applied by the British which finally forced FIFA's hand. Their walkout finally forced a vote on the inevitable and FIFA President Jules Rimet, prompted by French FA President Henri Delauney, proposed to his members the idea of a separate World Cup, one which would allow professionals to participate and thus be the best tournament in the world.

Uruguay, an affluent country and Olympic champions for the past two tournaments, were elected ahead of Spain, Italy, Holland and Sweden to host the first World Cup in 1930, which would also coincide with their celebration of 100 years of independence. The Uruguayans promised to build a new 80,000 capacity centenary stadium especially for the occasion, as well as offering to pay travelling expenses for all the European teams. Although England were now not a member of FIFA, Rimet sent the English FA a special letter inviting them to take part in the competition. The offer was declined.

In the end, the South Americans were quite bitter about the indifference shown by other European nations as well. Spain, Italy, Germany, Holland, Austria and Hungary had all intimated that they would make the journey across the Atlantic, but, one by one, they all pulled out. France, Yugoslavia, Belgium and Romania did make the trip and received an enthusiastic reception upon their arrival in Montevideo, crowds and bands gathering to serenade and cheer the Europeans off their boat.

Argentina reached the first World Cup final, but none of their group games were without incident. They had just taken the lead against France when the Brazilian referee inexplicably blew the final whistle with six minutes still remaining, just as the French were on a breakaway attack. Argentina fans invaded the pitch to celebrate, while the French protested furiously. Police horses cleared the crowd and an Argentinian player fainted in the chaos, before the final six minutes was eventually played without further score.

In their second match, Argentina beat Mexico 6-3, Guillermo Stábile scoring a hat-trick on his international debut. But the controversy was provided by the Bolivian referee (actually the coach of the Bolivian national team), who awarded no fewer than five penalties, three for Argentina and two for Mexico – all of them dubious, at least as far as the teams were concerned. In their final match, against Chile, the police again had to step in, this time to stop players fighting. Argentina won 3-1. Monti, the centre-half responsible for punching Chelsea players the previous year, and who had injured two French players in Argentina's opening game, was again the catalyst for the brawl.

In the semi-final Argentina beat USA 6-1, the North American team consisting of English and Scottish ex-professionals. So, it was the two old rivals, Argentina and Uruguay, who met once again in the final. There was already enough bad feeling between the two countries before the match, as Argentinian supporters, arriving in their thousands (estimated at 15,000) in boats across the Rio de La Plata, had been searched for weapons, placed under armed guard, and generally treated badly by the Uruguayan police (according to the Argentinian embassy). Argentina's government threatened to pull their team out of the tournament but eventually relented.

Then, there was a problem with the ball. The Uruguayan ball, which the entire tournament had been played with thus far, was bigger than the Argentinian one. After some heated discussion a compromise was found and the two teams agreed to play one half with one ball and the other half with the other. Considering the two teams had met each other 110 times over the previous 29 years you would have thought this issue would have been dealt with by this time.

The impressive 80,000 capacity, concrete-reinforced, Centenario stadium had just finished being built in time for the World Cup, and legend has it that the Argentina coach, Francisco Olazar, explaining his tactics in the team talk before the final, drew lines and crosses in the drying cement that can still be seen on the dressing room wall today. Logic says it can't be true, but don't try having that argument with an Argentinian football fan.

The first half, with the Argentinian ball, finished 2-1 to Argentina, but, in the second half, with the Uruguayan ball, the hosts came back and won 4-2, sealing the victory with a last minute goal from Castro. Celebrations went on all night in Uruguay, and a national holiday was declared, but across the river in Buenos Aires there were public demonstrations and the Uruguayan embassy was stoned. The Argentinian FA broke off relations with the Uruguayan FA.

Argentina entered the 1934 World Cup in Italy, but sent a team of reserves for fear of their best players being poached by professional European clubs. Juventus had already signed Orsi and hatchet man Monti, who had become naturalised and were now playing for Italy in this tournament. After travelling 800 miles by boat, the Argentina second string lost 3-2 to Sweden in their first match and so were out, as the tournament took a knockout form only, with no groups.

The holders Uruguay, like the British nations, did not enter the 1934 World Cup as a protest at the way hosts Italy and other European countries had snubbed their own World Cup four years earlier. Much to the delight of Mussolini, Italy won the tournament as he had planned, boosting nationalist sentiment at home.

Argentina pulled out of FIFA in 1936, and didn't return to World Cup competition until 1958. They were unhappy as they had wanted to host the 1938 tournament, but it was decided at FIFA's 1936 congress that the competition would be held in France. The South Americans felt that there should be rotation, and it was their turn to be hosts. FIFA were fixing things to benefit the Europeans, they claimed. This is significant; even in 1936, the South Americans felt that FIFA were favouring European countries.

The Italians also won the 1938 World Cup, although only Brazil from the South American contingent were present. England, despite having received invitations to take part in all of the first three tournaments, did not enter any of them. The Second World War would mean no more World Cup football until 1950.

---------------- ❖ ----------------

At the end of the 19th century, Argentina had been on the brink of becoming a major economic power. The Italian and Spanish immigrants, and indeed many of the British, had arrived full of hope. The country was rich in natural resources, and the beef produced on the Pampas was considered the best in the world. British engineers had built Argentina's infrastructure and, with an able and willing workforce, all the necessary factors were in place for the country to succeed. It did for a while. Buenos Aires during the 1920s was dubbed 'the Paris of South America'. However, the expected continued economic growth never materialised. The reasons for its failure are a matter for economists to argue over, which indeed they do. The 20th century became a struggle for many of the 40 million Argentinians: political instability, military dictatorships, and poverty. Only one thing prospered: football. The opium of the people, the great distraction from daily life, became an obsession.

The 1940s were the first golden age of Argentinian football. The masses migrated to newly-built stadiums every Sunday as attendances reached an all-time high. There was blanket media coverage, pages upon pages of newspaper space devoted to match reports, and Sunday afternoon radio was given over almost entirely to live football. (As in other Catholic countries like Italy and Spain, Sunday has always been the traditional football day, whereas in Protestant Britain it is Saturday, as football was not allowed on Sundays for religious reasons.) An indication of the game's popularity, weekly sports magazine *El Grafico* had a circulation of 200,000.

President Juan Peron (elected with an 11 per cent majority in February 1946) and his wife Evita encouraged football, and the government helped pay for some of the biggest stadiums, which still stand today. It was a means of holding the country together, a national sport, and perhaps a way of diverting the masses away from political interests, which included strikes (3 million days lost in 1947), and a billion-dollar foreign debt.

The great River Plate side of the 1940s was known as *La Maquina* (the machine), with the young Alfredo Di Stefano leading the attack. 'The best team in the world,' they exclaimed in Argentina, 'it was like a ballet.' "The idea was to score first and then, having established the lead, to toy with the opposition and turn on a show for the crowd," Di Stefano explained years later.

But how did they know they were the best in the world? River Plate and the national team had won South American championships, but it had been a long time since any British clubs had visited. San Lorenzo did tour Europe, and beat the Spanish national side 6-1 in 1946, but, still out of FIFA, Argentina did not enter the first World Cup after the war, in 1950. One theory is that Peron did not want the team to enter in case they would lose and have a devastatingly damaging effect on national pride which had been restored thanks to his many reforms and peaceful diplomacy abroad.

What Argentine football really wanted was to test themselves against English sides. The British embassy in Argentina, however, did not think it was a good idea and wrote a letter to London in 1945 advising against the visit of British clubs, explaining that, 'it would do our football reputation more harm than good'. The embassy's letter highlighted the issue of shoulder-charging. 'Local rules differ considerably from English rules,' it said. 'Argentinian fans are very excitable, and charging into the goalkeeper could start a battle.'

And anyway where was the English national team during all this time? In splendid isolation. Out of FIFA, and not entering those first World Cups, England still believed its football to be the best in the world, and their record does support that claim to some extent. England remained unbeaten by foreign opposition at home, and had beaten World Cup winners Italy 3-2 at Highbury in November 1934, Germany 6-3 in Berlin in 1938, Portugal 10-0 in Lisbon in 1947 and Italy again 4-0, but this time, significantly, in Milan. Those results served to increase the nation's sense of footballing superiority (Scotland, Wales and Northern Ireland, who England had played every year since 1882 in the Home International Championships, did not count as foreign opposition).

However, away from home, England had suffered some defeats in Europe, losing 4-3 to Spain in 1929, 5-2 to France in 1931, going down to both Hungary (2-1) and Czechoslovakia (2-1) in 1934, and losing the first international after the war 1-0 to Switzerland in Zurich in 1947. But overall England's record was good, with far more victories than defeats.

By now England had finally woken up to the global nature of the game and signed up to FIFA in 1946, entering the first post-war World Cup in Brazil in 1950, where they got the shock of their football lives: England 0 USA 1. Humiliation. Those cigarette card heroes of Wright, Mortenson and Ramsey lost to a bunch of part-timers, a country that did not even play football. It is widely considered the worst ever result in England's football history. Although England beat Chile 2-0, the so-called 'masters of the game' lost 1-0 to Spain, and so calamitously went out of their first World Cup at the group stage.

The football world, much like world order in general, was in the process of being turned on its head.

THE MATCH OF THE CENTURY

WEMBLEY STADIUM, WEDNESDAY 9 MAY 1951

ISRAEL AND Syria were going to war, as were the Koreans, and British Prime Minister Clement Attlee was warning against the build up of Russian arms. 'Mockin' Bird Hill', sung by Mary Ford and Les Paul, the inventor of the electric guitar, and pioneer of multi-track recording and amplified sound, was selling in bucket loads. One hundred years on from the historic 1851 Great Exhibition – a puffed-up Victorian celebration of British colonialism and pride – the toned down 20th century version was merely a display of British art and culture. A 'festival of football' was part of the events.

"Our football will be exhibited before all the world; it's the best thing we've ever done," said Stanley Rous, the general secretary of the English FA and president of FIFA. "It will give our clubs the opportunity to return the hospitality we've received abroad."

During the month of May, one hundred games were to be played between British and foreign teams, including two full internationals, the first of which was England versus Argentina, the first South American country to play on English soil. Wembley was sold out in anticipation.

Whether Rous's "best thing we've ever done" line refers to Britain giving the world the game of football, or simply organising the festival, isn't clear, but behind his proud words, the first seeds of doubt in English superiority were being sewn. Still reeling from the shock events at the World Cup in Brazil the previous summer, England needed a moral-boosting victory to restore confidence. After all, that defeat to the USA was just a fluke, wasn't it? A good win against Argentina would put to bed those first few whispers emanating from abroad that perhaps English football was not all it was cracked up to be.

England had still not been beaten at home by a nation from outside the British Isles (the 0-2 defeat at the hands of the Republic of Ireland in September 1949 didn't really count as they were British after all, it seemed). In the days before World Cup qualifying groups and the European Championship tournament, any England international was taken very seriously; all the best players made available to manager Walter Winterbottom, or coach Walter Winterbottom rather, as the team was chosen by an FA selection committee.

England would line up with their traditional WM system, so called because when the points of the defenders were joined together they formed a W, while the points of the attack formed an M. Legendary winger Stanley Matthews was injured, so Tom Finney would switch from the left wing to the right, with Vic Metcalfe of Huddersfield playing on the opposite flank in tandem with club wing-partner Harry Hassall. The wingers hoped to supply crosses for Jackie Milburn of Newcastle, a classic English centre-forward and strong header of the ball. 'Beware of the shoulder charge,' Argentine goalkeeper Miguel Rugilo was told before the match, advised to punch clear rather than try to catch the ball. Centre-half Jim Taylor of Fulham was making his England debut at the age of 33.

If the first international between the two countries was a big event in England then it was considered an historic occasion on the other side of the Atlantic. 'We have been waiting 50 years for this', cried *El Grafico* magazine, dubbing the fixture, 'The Match Of The Century'. The build up in Argentina began weeks in advance, with every news-paper, magazine and radio programme making constant reference to the analogy of the pupils taking on their masters; relentless coverage involved graphs, diagrams, player profiles and tactical analysis, including minute-by-minute accounts of the Argentina team's training sessions and what they had for breakfast (orange juice, cakes and coffee, generally).

In direct inverse to those first seeds of doubt in England there was a growing feeling in Argentina that their football had progressed to such an extent that they were now ready to take on, and possibly even beat, their instructors: 'those that boast to be the fathers and masters of our football; those that came to our soils to show us that one plays football like so,' said *El Grafico*.

As I walked up the steps of the *Casa Mutual de Futbol*, headquarters of the Argentinian Footballers' Cooperative Association in the centre of Buenos Aires, I had already decided that eccentric goalkeeper Miguel Rugilo was the player from that first match in 1951 I would most like to speak to if it was possible. A local journalist had advised me that the Union might be a good place to start for tracing old footballers, especially as their presi-dent, Rodolfo Micheli, had played in the second international between England and Argentina, in 1953.

"Oh, I'm sorry, he's passed away," said the secretary when I enquired about Rugilo.

"That's a pity, how about the striker, Mario Boye, my second choice, do you have any means of contacting him?"

The Union secretary opened up a big file. "Oh, I'm sorry, he passed away as well."

"The captain, Yacono?"

"He's dead," called out a voice from behind a typewriter across the office. I handed the secretary a piece of paper with the names of the 11 players who appeared at Wembley in 1951 and she put a little cross beside the names of Rugilo, Boye and Yacono.

Reminiscent of a rather sad version of Monty Python's cheese shop sketch, we went through the list of all 11 players: Mendez, dead; Labruna, died of cancer 1986; Loustau, passed away 1990; Faina...

"Oh yes, I think he's still alive. Hold on a minute while I look him up … oh no, sorry, he's dead."

In the end, the Players' Union were right out of footballers who had played at Wembley in 1951. I stared at the piece of paper, each player now with a little cross beside his name. The basic idea of speaking to at least one player from each England v Argentina match had fallen at the first hurdle. I was surprised, and quite disappointed. I thought most of the problems would come later, trying to contact modern players, or persuading players to agree to talk, especially about the rivalry and the major contentious moments, but it had never even crossed my mind that so many of the older Argentina players would be dead, especially as many of the English players from 1951 were still alive. Only recently, I had seen a sprightly Tom Finney open up the national football museum in Preston.

"When would you like to speak to Mr Micheli?" asked the secretary.

"As soon as possible," I replied, fearing the Union president, who played in the second match in 1953 might be at death's door. I need not have worried. When he arrived, Micheli was clearly a healthy and active man. Besides his duties as president of the footballers' union, he also runs his own *Kiosco* (small shop), and still finds time to coach youth football. During our conversation, he happened to mention that he did the coaching sessions in partnership with River Plate legend Santiago Vernazza.

"Now, there's someone you could talk to about the 1951 match," said Micheli. "He was one of the young reserves who travelled to England." Game on. I had my '51 player after all. Even if he had just been sitting on the bench, Vernazza had still travelled with the team and lived the experience, hopefully with a few tales to tell.

I found 81-year-old Vernazza very much alive, coaching kids on a series of municipal pitches on the outskirts of the capital. His memory was sharp and he began rattling away immediately. "I travelled to England as part of the Argentina squad in 1951. I was the reserve striker for Boye, so watched from the side. What a stadium! I remember the Wembley pitch was so green, like a carpet. In Argentina we were used to playing on dry dust pitches, full of holes."

In 1951, Vernazza had just joined the great River Plate *La Maquina* side. With Labruna, Loustau, and a young Alfredo Di Stefano, they had dominated Argentine and South American football in the mid-to-late-1940s, playing to a fast attacking rhythm. Di Stefano; quick, fluent, skilful, played as if the ball was stuck to his feet. With his *gambeta* (dribbling) and *pase corto* (short passing), he encapsulated everything Argentinian football wanted to be, but Di Stefano would not be playing at Wembley. He had left River Plate in 1948, attracted by the big money of the independent Colombian league, outside of FIFA's jurisdiction, and therefore not eligible to play for his home country anymore, to add to his tally of seven goals in seven games. Five years later, in a complicated transfer involving Spanish politics and General Franco's ministers, Di Stefano moved to Real Madrid, where he famously won five European Cups. Argentina's greatest player of the 1940s and 1950s acquired Spanish nationality and has since featured in many a trivia quiz as the only footballer in history to have played for three different national sides (Argentina, Colombia and Spain).

River Plate legends Labruna and Loustau *would* be playing at Wembley though, and all other news was relegated to the inside pages in Argentina as pictures of the players waving goodbye at the airport filled the headlines. For most of the players, it was their first time on a plane. They were excited: "there would even be some time for some shopping as well," they told the press.

The visitors were greeted by British foreign minister, George Canning, upon arrival, and driven by bus to their hotel at Hendon, before being whisked off to Buckingham Palace to watch the Changing of the Guard.

"Buckingham Palace was amazing," says Vernazza, "and the shopping! – Oh boy, we bought clothes, vacuum cleaners, washing machines, an enormous quantity of things. I was about to get married, so I bought lots of things for the house including a big fridge. We all bought fridges because you couldn't get fridges like that in Argentina, and I remember there were some problems at customs when we returned because we had all bought too much!"

On the morning of Saturday 5 May, the Argentina players trained at Arsenal's training ground, before going to White Hart Lane to watch Tottenham Hotspur clinch the English league championship with a 3-1 win over Liverpool.

Guillermo Stábile, top scorer at the 1930 World Cup, was now Argentina's manager. Asked his opinions on Tottenham's victory by the English press, he said, "It was a most pleasant game and it had lessons for us. We saw the British make the ball do the work rather than our style of the man using his speed and ball control to make the openings. The British know how to mark and tackle, but we are hoping to find some answers to the British style when we play at Wembley."

Mendez, the Argentine inside-right said, "without wishing to boast, we consider ourselves skilful players. We know that we're coming to confront the masters of football, but we want to utilise our skill to neutralise the scientific English play. We come with great expectations of doing well."

Vernazza remembers the Tottenham versus Liverpool match clearly. "It decided the championship and we reached the conclusion that we could beat them. Of course, once you're on the pitch it's very different from watching in the stands. We saw the way they pushed the keeper into the goal, so Rugilo, our goalkeeper, decided he was going to punch it rather than catch if he wasn't sure."

It was not only Argentine journalists who attended Arsenal's training ground for their squad's full practice session the day before the big match. Quite a crowd of English journalists and coaches gathered together there as well. As did all the Arsenal first-team players. Many had come out of curiosity, to see the South Americans play.

Vernazza's memory has not been withered by time as he recalls every detail of the training session. Argentina played a full match, first team against reserves (blues against whites). Simes had an injury, so Norman Smith of Arsenal took his place on the right wing, and Smith's Arsenal team-mates and all the journalists and coaches watching from the side were fascinated by the play.

'It's incredible that the Argentinians don't want to modify their way of playing; they stick to their mode without trying to adapt to the British style of play,' Charles Buchan wrote in the *News Chronicle*. British reporters thought this might prejudice the Argentines, but they did recognise that South American play was 'rapid and brilliant', although they had detected a reluctance to shoot when in good positions.

Ex-England international Bernard Joy wrote a piece in the *Star*, commenting upon the 'marvellous players' he had seen at the Arsenal training ground. He not only predicted an Argentine victory, but also that 'we would see big changes in the concept of English football; the Argentinians are of a very high quality, much higher than other national teams that have ever come to London.'

The Argentine players were taken to Mansion House to have lunch with London Mayor Dennis Lawson, while a reception for the directors and diplomats was held the night before the match. In his speech, Argentina's ambassador in London, Señor Carlos Leguizamon, gave thanks to President Juan Peron and his wife Evita who had given great support to Argentine sport and had helped fund this journey. The Perons themselves had sent a typically diplomatic message; they were sure the Argentina players would leave a great impression of Argentina on our 'English friends', but 'victory in the sporting field is not as important as the manifestation of the great friendship between the people of Britain and Argentina'.

On the morning of the big match, Argentine newspaper *La Nacion* spoke of 'two styles of play completely different; the long passes, the strict marking and the counter attack that distinguish English football from what they'll see in front of them; the excellent dribbling and speedy movement of the Argentines'.

The *News of the World* described it as, 'The most vital match of the season – on the result of this game our international prestige, buried beneath the soil of Brazil last year, will either be resurrected or dragged through the mire once more. The contrast in style with the Argentinians relying on the speed of the man while England rely on the speed of the ball could produce a classic.'

A boat carrying Argentinian beef to London for the players to eat did not make it on time as it had had to unload all its frozen meat in Hamburg. It also had on board 40 supporters with tickets for the match and the captain sent a telegraph lamenting the 'delay that impedes attending the game'. Luckily though, the Hendon hotel served beef steaks twice a day, with meat delivered from the Argentinian embassy as it demanded. The British press picked up on this little story and labelled the Argentinian team 'The Beef Boys'. "No, that's not true," says Vernazza, "we ate English food."

After inspecting the Wembley pitch the day before the game (they were allowed to walk on the turf but not allowed to play on it), captain Norberto Yacono remarked that it was very damp. "It won't allow players to run with the ball and the ball doesn't bounce as high as in the dry Argentinian stadiums." However, the players decided against modifying their light and short studded boots, best suited to the rock hard pitches.

A few hours before kick-off, a light rain began to fall from the grey London skies, just what the Argentinians did not want. The surface of the Wembley turf would be more slippery now, but, despite again being offered English-style boots, the South Americans opted to stick with familiarity, and not only the lightweight footwear, for when they took to the pitch the English players were shocked to see that none of their opponents were wearing shin pads and two of them, Pescia and Loustau, were not even wearing long socks, just short ankle socks.

"That's right, the kits were so different," says Vernazza. "The English kit made them look like giants. We didn't want to change boots because we didn't want to change what we were used to, but the rain and the grey skies gave the English a big advantage. We were used to the sun and a dry pitch, but it was a marvellous stadium, with an incredible pitch. All teams wanted to play at Wembley."

In a marked contrast to future receptions their team would receive at Wembley, Argentina were applauded onto the pitch by the crowd and their national anthem cheered. England wore red shirts for the first time ever, so as not to clash with Argentina's blue and white stripes. The match kicked off at 7.30pm, and it became immediately apparent that the English crowd were about to witness something very different from the type of football normally served up on a Saturday afternoon. Although the Argentines also employed the standard WM system, they sat back in their own half, seven or eight players in the last third of the pitch, but when they gained possession of the ball, they proceeded to play short intricate passes between themselves.

England attacked down the wings with Finney and Metcalfe, but they hit a defensive wall. Occasionally Argentina centre-half Faina would bring the ball out from the back, dribbling in his own half, a football crime in England, and the crowd were aghast by this perceived dangerous strategy. But when Faina moved forward, the right-back Colman would move across to the vacant centre-back spot and mark Jackie Milburn to cover.

On 18 minutes came the first serious attack. Labruna controlled goalkeeper Rugilo's clearance perfectly and sent his River Plate team-mate Loustau away down the left. The winger moved swiftly into the open space behind full back Alf Ramsey (making his first of many significant contributions on the England versus Argentina saga) who had pushed upfield. Loustau side-stepped the advancing goalkeeper Bert Williams and lobbed the ball across the open English defence for Boye to head the ball into the empty net.

"GOOOOOOL," screamed the loudspeakers across the plazas in Argentina, sending the crowds into a frenzy, hats thrown into the air by the thousand. Old black and white newsreel footage shows Boye turning around after scoring with a look of disbelief on his face. Incredulous, for a split second he doesn't seem to know how to react, but then proceeds to run, and leap, and jump, and run, back to the centre circle, laughing and grinning all the way. Geoffrey Green in *The Times* described the celebration thus: 'Boye, flushed with the excitement ran back to the centre as if he had conquered the world.' Boye later declared it to be the greatest moment of his life.

The English crowd were stunned, but continued to encourage their team, waving Union Jack flags and urging their men forward. The players responded. England's centre-half and captain Billy Wright assumed responsibility, and began to push forward, with the full backs, Ramsey and Bill Eckersley, joining him. They moved across the halfway line, playing the ball up for the forwards, but the Argentina defenders were quick in their tackling. With a comment that would be churned out with frequency over the years, Geoffrey Green observed, 'England still have not discovered the way to penetrate this defensive screen. Generally they were not quick enough in their release of the ball in attack, and too much lobbing into the danger zone, some of it, it seemed, in an almost desperate hope that something might happen.'

When England did manage to break through the defensive wall, they found Miguel Rugilo behind it, Wembley's introduction to madcap South American goalkeeping. Half Chaplin, half Groucho Marx, the man with the large moustache and tight shorts, far too short for the era, played to the crowd. He made diving saves from Milburn and Mortensen, and sprang elastically to stop two headers from Harold Hassall, before bowing and milking the applause. Wembley was Rugilo's stage.

When half-time arrived Argentina had only had three attacks, but were a goal to the good. Surely, the clown in goal's luck would run out in the second half? But the first 45 minutes had just been the opening act of the Rugilo show. After the interlude he treated his audience to an even greater display of theatrical dives, waves, shrugs, bows, comical acrobatics and forlorn frowns that a silent movie actor would have been proud of. He even swung from the crossbar at one point.

'Danny Kaye, Bob Hope and the Marx brothers have nothing to compare with this colourful artist, surely the best ever individual spectacle given in a football stadium. Three times he stunned the crowd, receiving ovations by holding his hands up like a boxer', the *Daily Herald* declared.

England continued to attack, Billy Wright the inspiration. The captain linked with Finney, also coming into his own now by running at the substitute left-back Allegri, who had replaced the injured Colman ten minutes before half-time. "It was like an avalanche," explains Vernazza, "the English constantly attacking; lots of long balls, deep balls, right into our penalty area, and they hit the ball so strongly from every part of the pitch while we were trying to play our '*futbol bonito*', the short passes and dribbling. It was very impressive, the way the English played – the strength, the force, the heart and soul. The one who really impressed me the most was the right winger, Finney."

Crosses were fired in from all angles, but each time Rugilo came to Argentina's rescue. His goalmouth was under siege. Milburn hit the post twice, once from a free kick outside the area and then from a powerful shot after Wright and Finney had carved out an opening. Allegri cleared from Milburn with a spectacular overhead scissors kick, and in the middle of the mêlée Rugilo continued to dive around making acrobatic saves. 'Give both sides their due, there was plenty of entertaining football and a lot of excitement, most of it under the Argentina crossbar', Geoffrey Green wrote.

Backed by the Wembley roar, England kept pushing forward. Williams in goal was a virtual spectator, but time was passing, rapidly. England's proud record of never being beaten at home was in serious jeopardy, but, with 11 minutes remaining, England won a corner. Finney swung the ball across the goal and Mortensen headed home. "YEEEEESSS," cried the relieved Wembley crowd in unison. Caps were once again thrown into the air.

The spectators chanted, "England (clap, clap, clap), England (clap, clap, clap)", and with just four minutes left on the clock, Ramsey took a free kick inside the Argentina half. Another high ball bombed into the box. Mortensen headed it across the goalmouth and Milburn fired home from close range. "YEEEEESSS," roared the Wembley crowd again. Silence across the squares of Buenos Aires.

England had finally been rewarded for all their attacking play. Finney on the right wing had been the outstanding player and Argentina had succumbed to two set pieces; a corner and a free kick, which revealed a weakness to high crosses.

'ENGLAND WINS MATCH OF THE CENTURY' – 'WEMBLEY THRILLS TO RUGILO'S BRILLIANCE' – 'LAST MINUTE GOAL SAVES THE TRADITION' were some of the headlines in Argentina. Rugilo was crowned 'The Lion of Wembley' in Argentina, and 'Lord Moustache' in England, with photos of him in all his poses and gestures.

The *Daily Herald*'s opinion was: 'The dextrous Rugilo reduced the English goal count … Moustachioed and theatrical, he saved at least six sure goals.' The *Daily Mirror* agreed: 'He dived at the feet of the forwards and launched himself with formidable leaps and jumps from one post to the other.' The *Daily Express* was equally descriptive, and equally fixated on Rugilo's facial hair: 'The moment he touched his hair in desperation, Laurence Olivier could have learnt something from this fantastic Argentinian keeper. Moustachioed and magnificent, he didn't miss an opportunity to show his agility, entertaining all those present at Wembley.'

Only the *Daily Mail* flew the English flag higher than the rest, Roy Poskett declaring: 'Argentina had been disappointing in attack but their funnel-shaped defence with every man magnificently covering his team-mate baffled England who surely have had enough practice against it for a counter plan to be blueprinted. The Argentinians were very clever in possession of the ball but showed little semblance of team work. Only the acrobatic Rugio saved them from a greater defeat.'

Argentina's *La Nacion* produced a match report that covered three pages, with a description of every single minute of the game and sports magazine *El Grafico* opined that Argentina had played with too much fear by fielding eight defenders, but that all the psychological factors had been against them from the start. 'The passionate Wembley crowd and the wet pitch, always a great leveller, suited the English. It was 90 minutes of emotion after half a century of waiting, and all played out in a cordial manner, with perfect organisation and sportsmanship from the crowd.'

Argentina manager Stábile remarked that the ball was very heavy and his players were not used to the wet pitch, but admitted that his forwards had tired quickly and were disappointing. "Williams had little work to do in the English goal, but we should praise the two teams because there was not one disagreeable incident or moment of ungentlemanly play," he said. If only that had set the tone for a longstanding friendly rivalry. The relieved England coach Walter Winterbottom said, "we've never seen a defence so difficult to pass", while Welsh referee Mervyn Griffith remarked that the match had "still not resolved the old dispute between the two schools of thought".

An after-match banquet was held for the players. Valentin Suarez, president of AFA, thanked the English for their hospitality and promised they would return the pleasure when the English team came to Argentina in 1953. (A return match two years later had been part of the deal.) Argentina would not be receiving any of the £38,000 Wembley gate money, but would retain all the takings from the return match in Buenos Aires.

The cordiality continued with long speeches made by officials from both sides. Norberto Yacono, the Argentina captain, held up his engraved glass. "Each time I have to toast England I will do it with this glass," he declared.

There was one unsavoury incident. Mr J. Hubbard, honorary treasurer of the English FA, collapsed during the banquet. He was taken from his chair and a doctor called. Valentin Suarez, the president of AFA, had been in the middle of a long speech when the 75-year-old Hubbard fell. Suarez stopped for an instant, but continued while Hubbard was taken out.

"Oh, yes, yes, I remember that, an old fellow," says Vernazza. "The problem was that no-one could understand the speeches as there wasn't an interpreter. The English officials would speak for a long time and none of us could understand what they were saying, and then the Argentina directors would speak, and it was vice versa. The English didn't have a clue what was being said, and Suarez did love speaking for a long time."

The détente was completed by an interchange of souvenirs. The hosts gave their guests an engraved plaque and inscribed glasses, while the visitors presented the English with a golden *mate bombilla* (a typical Argentinian herbal tea drinking mug) and objects of art and craft. "I've still got my glass at home," says Vernazza proudly. "It's made of porcelain and says, 'Match of Wembley, England v Argentina'. It's a marvellous and special souvenir, and probably the only thing I have left from the trip. I can't remember what happened to the fridge."

Three days later Argentina played Ireland in Dublin. 'None Shall Pass' was the headline in the *Dublin Evening Herald* on the day of the match, with a picture of Rugilo holding his hands aloft. "We played much better in Dublin," reckons Vernazza. The drier pitch and better weather helped his side in their 1-0 victory over the Irish.

The Argentina players returned to London for more shopping before flying home, to be met at Buenos Aires airport by flag-waving, cheering fans; an emotive reception that caused traffic jams. The biggest cheers were for goalkeeper Rugilo who raised his hands like a victorious boxer as he came through the arrival doors.

Valentin Suarez made another long speech at the airport, but nobody collapsed this time. "We can't compete with the extraordinary preparation of English football and the collective attitude of their players, its precision and planned details. For me, the right winger [Finney] gave them the triumph, but after observing English football first-hand, I still believe Argentinian football is better to watch, and if we can adopt some of the virtues of the English game like playing the ball first time it would be a template for all the world."

Rugilo said he was impressed with the way the English players shoot all the time, "from all angles and places – even the halves shoot!"

"I think the crowds turned up at the airport because they were proud of the team," says Vernazza. "We had gone there to look for experience and we weren't really accustomed to the pitch. Argentina had never played matches like this before, against this type of opponent, matches of a completely different nature. It was Rugilo's big moment, and they christened him 'The Lion of Wembley'. He was a showman."

In 1956 Vernazza transferred from River Plate to Palermo in Italy, where he scored over 50 goals in 4 seasons, earning a move to AC Milan in 1960. He spent two seasons at Milan and won a championship runners-up medal, but Jimmy Greaves's arrival meant Vernazza's departure. "Italian teams were only allowed two foreigners, so when Milan signed Jimmy Greaves from Chelsea I had to move on, but he ended up only playing seven games for them." Vernazza spent two seasons at Vicenza and retired in 1963 at the age of 35.

The kids are now arriving for training. "I coach all ages from 11 to 15," says the sprightly 81-year-old. "It's organised by the local council and just something I enjoy doing."

Back in England in 1951, the match against Argentina had put another slight dent into the idea that English football was superior to the rest of the world. *The Times*, in the opening paragraph of its match report said, 'The proud record all but disappeared yesterday. Until 81 minutes of an entertaining match, Argentina held a lead of 1-0. This seemed to be a mark in history. The old world was about to bow to the new. But in those remaining minutes England arose to their full duty, scored twice to gain the victory by two goals to one and sent 100,000 people home hoarse with cheering and happy that justice had been done in the end.'

England 2 (Stan Mortensen 79' Jackie Milburn 86')
Argentina 1 (Mario Boyé 18')
Wednesday 9 May 1951, Wembley Stadium, London. Friendly. Attendance: 99,000
Referee: Mervyn Griffiths (Wales)

England: Bert Williams (Wolves), Bill Eckersley (Blackburn), Billy Wright(c) (Wolves), Jim Taylor (Fulham), Henry Cockburn (Manchester Utd), Tom Finney (Preston), Stan Mortensen (Blackpool), Jackie Milburn (Newcastle), Harold Hassall (Huddersfield)
Manager: Walter Winterbottom

Argentina: Miguel Rugilo (Velez Sarsfield), Juan Colman (Boca Jnrs, sub 35'), Juan Filgueiras (River Plate), Ubaldo Faina (Newell's Old Boys), Natalio Pescia (Boca Jnrs), Norberto Yácono (c) (River Plate), Mario Boyé (Racing), Rubén Bravo (Racing), Angel Labruna (River Plate), Félix Loustau (River Plate), Norberto Méndez (Racing), Sub: Ángel Allegri (Velez Sarsfield, on 35')
Manager: Guillermo Stábile

THE IMPOSSIBLE GOAL

MONUMENTAL STADIUM, BUENOS AIRES, THURSDAY 14 MAY 1953

THE KOREAN war was at its height, Egypt invaded Suez, and Prime Minister Clement Attlee's Labour party had just won the local elections. Frankie Lane's 'I Believe' was enjoying 18 weeks at number 1 as the England football team set off for their first ever tour of the Americas, with games arranged against Argentina, Chile, Uruguay and the USA. First port of call: Buenos Aires.

The young Queen Elizabeth II's coronation, which would take place while the players were away, represented a new era for Great Britain, and the Football Association were not exempt from the new post-war mood. Previously, the men in blazers at Lancaster Gate would have scoffed, or at least failed to see the worth, of a month-long tour in the southern hemisphere, but the world was modernising swiftly, taking along with it international football.

Travel was easier and quicker. A trip to South America was no longer the three-week voyage those early visiting English clubs had endured, just a 36-hour flight. But there was something else behind the FA's decision to tour – the humiliation in Brazil in 1950. With two defeats out of three – one of them, embarrassingly, against the part-timers of the USA – England's first appearance at a World Cup had been a wake up call. A year later, Argentina had run England close at Wembley, 'perhaps too close', as the *News of the World* had said. If England were to do well at the next World Cup then some much-needed practice against different styles of play was necessary. Due to the good relations forged at Wembley in '51, England agreed to play two games in Argentina. The first was billed as a Buenos Aires League XI versus a Football Association League XI, the second, a full international. England were taking a squad of 18 on the tour, so the first match would be an opportunity to give some of the reserves a run out.

Photos of the smartly dressed England players arriving at Buenos Aires airport adorned all the front pages in Argentina. Immaculate in stylish 1950s suits and ties, with all the top buttons done up despite having just landed from a long-haul flight, the English players were feted like Hollywood film stars. 'Giants From Another World' and 'The

Masters of the Game', said *Clarin* on 9 May, the morning after their arrival. 'The first impression of the English stars is that they are true athletes, tall and strong, true professionals.' At this distance it feels like servants admiring their masters' almost superhuman appearance and aura. Indeed, throughout the tour, the 'masters versus pupils' analogy cropped up with regularity in the Argentina press, alongside photos, career statistics, weights and heights of the English players. Readers knew the details of them all, whereas in England it is unlikely that even the most ardent football fans would have been able to name just one of the Argentina players.

Argentine newspapers lamented the absence of Stanley Matthews, who had starred in the famous 1953 FA Cup final, 'The Matthews Final', just the week before. They explained to their readers that Matthews, at 38, was considered 'too old' and 'excessively individual for the English FA's tastes', but, after his performance in the Cup final, the selectors had changed their minds. Matthews, with dignity, had turned down the belated offer of joining the tour as a matter of honour, it was claimed. Nat Lofthouse, 'the man with the powerful boots', another star of that classic Cup final, was on the tour though.

The English players were stunned by their reception. Over a thousand people greeted them at the airport; cheering, clapping and waving a big banner saying 'welcome'. Surprised by all the fuss, captain Billy Wright spoke a few words: "We prefer to make the ball run and do the work instead of using uncontrolled physical force. Our only fear is that we have to play on hard pitches, but we know the capacity of our football and hope to achieve a good result."

President of AFA, Valentin Suarez, met the English players and officials at the airport and made another speech, but kept it brief and nobody collapsed. The players boarded the bus to their training camp, and according to the *Buenos Aires Herald*, 'engaged in a good old fashioned sing song along the way.'

"It was a fantastic reception at the airport," remembers Gil Merrick, the England goalkeeper, whose memory, like Vernazza's, is still very sharp. "There were photographers everywhere, and you could sense the enthusiasm of the crowds." Probably many of the welcoming party at the airport were expats. The British community in Buenos Aires was a large one, but their influence was waning in Peron's new nationalistic Argentina.

Like his mentors, Mussolini in Italy and Franco in Spain, President Peron recognised the importance of football as the passion of the working classes and he encouraged it. He considered football a healthy leisure pursuit that brought people together, and a useful tool in his vision of uniting the populace under the national flag.

Peron had been whipping up nationalism since coming to power through the ballot box in 1946, and both the working-class trade union movements and the middle classes lent him their support. He had confronted the *Estancieros*, the rich landowners who previously held power in Argentina and were reluctant to share their wealth. Peron was in the process of renegotiating what he considered to be one-sided trade deals with Britain, while trying to develop Argentina's own industry and infrastructure, instead of relying on the import of manufactured goods in exchange for beef, which was too dependent on fluctuating world markets. Also, for the first time, the issue of the sovereignty of the Falklands Islands was being raised, diplomatically of course, with Britain.

However, all these issues were put to one side when the England football team visited. There was no animosity felt towards the English in Argentina at that time, only respect for 'the Masters of the Game', and the following four days saw constant press reports on all the England players' movements and training sessions, including how they spent their free time.

England coach Walter Winterbottom allowed his men to sleep in on their first morning until 'the time they considered prudent' and captain Billy Wright, 'a model of discipline was the first to rise at 10.30am, according to *Clarin*. Later, there was a round of golf between Wright, Jimmy Dickinson and the Froggatt cousins, Jack and Redfern. *Clarin* even supplied its readers with a golf report, explaining, 'how intriguing it was to watch the way the Englishmen carefully selected their clubs and all of them were very adept on the links.'

Later in the evening, the players attended a reception at the British embassy, but 'nothing too late', Winterbottom had stressed to the diplomats. The first training session was not intense, just some shots and stretches, and a chance to get used to the hard ground. It was supposed to be behind closed doors, but this does not appear to have prevented a crowd of around a thousand turning up. All of Argentina's First Division matches had been postponed to allow the national team to prepare. 'A Sunday without football is like a Sunday without a girlfriend,' mourned *Clarin*, so it was the England training session that dominated the Monday morning sports pages, the press giving remarkable detail considering the training session was meant to be out of bounds. *Clarin* explained that, 'The forwards crash into the keeper and the spectators will be surprised to find this is not considered a foul, and it's not just the forwards, the defenders shoulder-charge as well. Above all, the English stars demonstrated exceptional athleticism, united with great speed and violence in the shot.' The newspaper could not reveal any more 'out of respect for the agreement not to declare the details of the training session, but we can say they didn't mark strictly man for man, but marked in zones and this is how they'll try to negate our forwards.' A lot of information from 'behind closed doors', begging the question of which aspect of the English play they didn't reveal out of respect for the agreement?

Curiously, throughout numerous pages dedicated to the first of the two matches, there was not any reference in Argentina to the fact that it was not a full international, but a Buenos Aires League XI versus a Football Association League XI. Judging by the coverage, the first match was being treated as a proper international in Argentina, but Gil Merrick is adamant that, as far as the English were concerned, the first match was "the reserve match – a chance to give some of the lads on the tour a game."

When the English players went to watch an Argentinian Second Division match – Argentinos Juniors versus Quilmes – on the Sunday afternoon, they were given a standing ovation by the crowd, and the following days saw them touring the city as privileged guests; sightseeing, theatre, horse racing at the San Isidro racetrack, and a reception as President Peron's guests of honour at the Government house. Peron's wife Evita had died the year before. The English players laid wreaths at her grave and each was presented with a copy of her autobiography, *The Reason For My Life*.

Peron spoke of his great memories of previous visits of English teams, Everton and Tottenham in 1909, Chelsea in 1925, and Valentin Suarez again gave a speech (longer this time), paying tribute to the 'masters of football'. Stanley Rous thanked the AFA for their 'efficient organisation and lavish hospitality' and FA secretary J.H.W. Mears hoped the English players 'would be able to stand up to the strain of all the rounds of events and entertainments planned.' As they joked together, relations between Rous and Suarez, the heads of the two Associations, were clearly good (things would not be so friendly between the two men when Argentina came to England in 1966).

Before meeting Peron, England had trained at River Plate's Monumental stadium, the venue for the two matches. Tickets for both games had completely sold out. Like many stadiums in Buenos Aires, the Monumental had been built in the 1940s with the aid of government money. 25 years later it would host the 1978 World Cup final. "It looked like a large opera house to us," says Gil Merrick. "It was completely round and open – very different from stadiums in Britain – with what looked like lots of boxes around the top."

In full reports of England's last training session (again, all the details – they played half an hour of football, 3 periods of 10 minutes, 8 versus 8, reds against whites, but the teams were changed around a lot and it was also noted that coach Walter Winterbottom was dedicating a lot of time to defensive organisation), the Argentine press were surprised to see that every single player practised shooting and noted that, 'in the precision of the long passes, the English players demonstrated why they are the true masters of the game.'

The English players had brought special lightweight rubber boots with them, but still complained that the pitch at the Monumental was too hard. The bounce of the ball was very deceptive and they couldn't control it properly.

Perhaps because the local players did not hold the same novelty value as the English, Argentina's training sessions were not afforded as much newspaper space as the visitors', and the English press hardly mentioned the Argentinians at all, but they had been quietly training every day for more than a week at Ezeiza, near the international airport, the same training ground that the national team uses today. Manager Guillermo Stábile was putting together a very different team from the one he had fielded at Wembley two years earlier. Not one of the players who made the trip to London would be in the starting line up.

"The 1951 team were all big names and established players, but two years later, we were in the middle of the Argentinian league season and the AFA wanted to play players who were in form at that moment, especially in attack," explains Rodolfo Micheli, the ex-Independiente striker and current president of the Players' Cooperative.

"Three months beforehand we had some trials, just meeting up one evening a week, but it wasn't practical as some players couldn't make the sessions due to club commitments, so Valentin Suarez said to Stábile, 'Look, forget the trials, why not put the complete attack of Independiente out there. They score an average of two goals per game, at least we'll be guaranteed goals.'"

Micheli himself was one of the famous five – Lacasia, Ceconato, Micheli, Grillo and Cruz – names that still roll off the tongue of the older generation in Buenos Aires today. Indeed Independiente would tour Europe at the end of the year, beating Real Madrid

6-0 in a famous match in Madrid's Bernabeu stadium. "It was the great Real Madrid side of Di Stefano and Gento," Micheli is keen to inform.

Fifteen days before the match against the Football League XI, the team was formed. The five-man Independiente forward line was welded onto the Boca Juniors defence and Racing's midfield.

There wasn't even a place for 'The Lion of Wembley'. "Ah, Rugilo," smiles Micheli, "he was a good goalkeeper but that game at Wembley was the easiest he ever had in his life. They were shooting from all sides, but they weren't low shots. They were all from outside the area, goalkeepers love those, and it looked like he was a goalkeeper from another galaxy, but he wasn't really, it got exaggerated. He was a good goalkeeper, but not great, and two years is a long time in Argentina football. It's still like that today, the national team changes a lot in two years."

Did manager Stábile have any special tactics in store? I asked Micheli. "England for us were the inventors of football. We knew they were more advanced than us, but we had never seen them play. We knew they were strong and played long balls – dah, dah, dah," Micheli points with his fingers, "and ourselves, the complete opposite, short passes. It would be a game unlike any other. We were playing against people completely different from ourselves.

"But Mouriño, the captain and Boca Juniors defender, came to us, the five Independiente attackers, a week beforehand at training and said, 'the English, they play all these long passes, so we have to be attentive to them, but we'll give them the problems if you five use your great ball control. You're all young and quick with a good first touch.' That's effectively what Mouriño told us, and with our goal average of two goals a game added to the Boca and Racing defence, it gave us security and confidence that we would play well."

❖

Clarin did not hold back on the morning of the match. 'The town lives in intense expectation. In a few hours' time the most sensational match in our capital will take place. Argentinian football versus English football, maximum expressions of two concepts of play, an extraordinary duel, which will interest all the world.' And even on the society pages: 'The match, the match … in the house, in the street, in the office, in the bar. The subject is the match of this afternoon.'

Ironically, considering future events, *Clarín* chose to put a large picture of Alf Ramsey on its back page. 'The famous full-back is one of the best English players, a serious stopper for our attacks.' But Ramsey would not be playing in the first match. Neither would Lofthouse, nor Finney. They were being rested for the second game, the official game. Captain Billy Wright *was* playing though, and Tommy Taylor, who had just joined Manchester United from Barnsley for £29,999, was leading the attack.

Just how aware the Argentinian fans were that the first match was not to be a full international is a matter of debate. River Plate's stadium was packed to its 52,000 capacity hours before kick-off. Gates had opened at 10am for the 3pm start (Independiente v Racing provided the pre-match entertainment), and the protocol certainly had the feel of a full international. Both teams emerged from the tunnel dressed in their traditional kits, both national anthems were played and cheered by the crowd. When President Peron entered the stadium he received a prolonged ovation before proceeding to his balcony.

The match referee was Arthur Ellis from Halifax, who had flown in with the England team, but his two linesmen, A. Bradley of Chesterfield and R. Lynch of Blackburn, were English referees based in Argentina as part of an exchange whereby English referees spent two years in Argentina. However there were no cries of foul at the officials coming from the visiting nation. "For me, and for Argentines generally, English referees were the best," explains Micheli. "They gave the sensation of being serious, authoritative and correct. I imagine it was felt that this was what the match needed to be considered a correct match. Bradley, Caswell, Lynch, five or six of them refereed in our league. They were good referees and I always remember what Lynch said to us once, 'for me to referee well means to not send anyone off. If I have to send a player off it means I haven't refereed well, even if the player deserves it.' That always stuck in my mind, those words."

'With English punctuality,' remarked *Clarin*, 'the match began at 3pm prompt.' 20-year-old Tommy Taylor tapped the ball to Roy Bentley of Chelsea, who tried to turn and play the ball out to the wing, but Garcia Perez, the Racing midfielder, immediately intercepted. Perez successfully passed to Grillo on the left wing, who ran at the English defence, cutting inside and crossing for Ceconato to head towards goal. Ted Ditchburn saved. It was a dangerous move, right from kick-off, a sign of what was to come.

On 4 minutes, Lacasia, from the centre of the pitch, sent a long ball for Ceconato to chase, and Ditchburn did well to run out of his penalty area to beat the Argentine striker to the ball, but the English goalkeeper's hurried kick fell to Cruz with an open net to aim for. A brilliant tackle from Malcolm Barrass of Bolton prevented a certain goal.

The Argentinians were dominant, comfortably breaking through the English rearguard, pushing them back into their own half. Micheli had a shot saved by Ditchburn, and Grillo struck another which was deflected off a defender for a corner.

"It was a hard match," recalls Micheli. "Eckersley was marking me. He was as short as me, but, boy, was he strong, but we were a young and very quick forward line, all between 20 and 23, and we kept the ball from them. We had Grillo, who was a very good dribbler. We knew they were big and strong in defence, so we had to be quick, not give them a chance to get near us – quick release of the ball, short passes and then moving; pass and move, pass and move, quick, quick, quick. That was the plan." Conversely, most of England's moves were breaking down due to 'deficient passing', according to *La Nacion*.

It was ten minutes before the first English attack arrived. Ray Barlow of West Bromwich Albion passed to Tommy Taylor, who played a delightful long through ball to his Manchester United team-mate Johnny Berry, but the whistle had already gone for offside when Berry put the ball in the back of the net.

That near thing spurred Argentina on to greater heights. They dominated the next 20 minutes with the English goal leading a charmed life at times. Grillo took a powerful shot that rebounded off the post and Lacasia hit another that whistled wide by mere centimetres, with the sprawling Ditchburn beaten. Immediately afterwards, Grillo produced one of his typical dribbles down the left wing, going past three defenders before crossing for Cruz, but Tom Garrett of Blackpool just managed to intervene and kick the cross clear. Lacasia then hit the bar with a header. England were suffering under the pressure. 'Playing a type of football resembling that of Brazilians, the Argentinians kept the ball off the ground and juggled with it at tremendous speed. The English defence were hard pressed to intercept the crisp waist-high passing among the forwards,' *The Times* worried.

The domination of Argentina, or the Buenos Aires XI rather, deserved a goal, but crossbar and post had each saved the English twice. Mussimesi, the Boca Juniors goalkeeper, had hardly been called into action but, on 41 minutes, Jack Froggatt of Portsmouth ran into the box and Dellacha intercepted for a corner. Froggatt took the kick himself, swinging the ball over to the far post. Mussimesi misjudged the flight of the ball, Taylor swivelled, extended his bullish neck muscles, and scored. 'A magnificent header,' said *La Nacion*. Against the run of play, England, or the Football Association XI, had taken the lead. As in '51, it was that English strength, and Argentinian weakness on corners and crosses that had exposed the defence.

"I'll never forget Tommy Taylor," says Micheli. "What a player. He was tall, blonde, a real handsome lad. He really impressed me. Right up to today, I still talk about him. He was such a good player and then it seemed like just such a short time afterwards we heard he had died in a plane crash [the Munich air disaster of February 1958].

The lead, however, would not last long. Just one minute after England had scored came the famous 'Impossible Goal', the first of several moments of genius which would pockmark matches between the two sides, just as moments of controversy would also come to be associated with this fixture. Lacasia opened the way, picking up a loose ball in the centre of the park, feeding a short pass to Ceconato, who played the ball out to Ernesto Grillo on the left wing. Grillo ran at the English defence as he had done throughout the first half. He eluded Billy Wright by going outside him, then Garrick, the right-back, by turning one way and then the other, before sprinting towards the bye-line. Barrass, the English centre-half, moved across to make a challenge, but fell to the ground, fooled by Grillo's dummy. Ditchburn, the English goalkeeper, moved forward, anticipating the cross, but two-footed Grillo flicked the ball up with his right foot and smashed it into the roof of the net like a rocket. The angle had been so tight that nobody was expecting a shot, but somehow Grillo had squeezed the ball between the keeper and the upright. Old men in Buenos Aires bars still talk about the goal today. Better than Maradona's in '86 they say.

In the reception of the Players' Union hangs a panoramic photo of Grillo's *Impossible Goal*, so called because of the angle it was scored from. Micheli re-enacts the whole move with relish, taking to his feet and doing little dummies as he shimmies around the room. "The ball was here *mucha cintura, Grillo* [a lot of hip movement from Grillo]." Micheli draws Grillo's route to goal on a note-pad, demonstrating the angle with his thumbs on the table. "The goal was here, Grillo was here, the goalkeeper Ditchburn was there, the goalkeeper moved forward a metre, logically. Ditchburn was correctly positioned as nobody thought Grillo would shoot from there, but he hit the ball with such tremendous force between the keeper and the post." Micheli clearly enjoys reliving this goal and shakes his head incredulously as if he's just seen it for the first time.

The stadium shook. Not only had Grillo scored, but it was a beautiful goal, the type of goal that Argentinian football had always dreamed of. Grillo had produced a scoring *gambeta* against the English. He had left three English defenders trailing. He had turned 'the masters of football' inside out, forcing them to go one way and then the other. It was the perfect goal.

Mendez had replaced Ceconato, who was injured, just before half-time. Each team was allowed one substitution, but only to replace an injured player, and only in the first half. The second half was like Wembley 1951, but in reverse, as the Buenos Aires XI continued to attack and apply relentless pressure. The English were struggling to cope with the mobility of the Argentinian formation. Centre-half Dellacha, who was marking Berry, would often abandon his defensive duties and bring the ball out from the back with one of the full backs moving across to cover him, a prototype for the modern sweeper. "The centre-half was outstanding," recalls Gil Merrick, who, with the rest of the England squad, was watching from the side. "He was an older player and the one I remember most. He must have been at least a couple of stone overweight and he didn't move that much, but he had excellent control and was supplying the passes for the forwards."

Lacasia and Mendez combined well in the centre and sent Cruz away on the left. Cruz had swapped wings with his Independiente team-mate Grillo, and he centred for Micheli, whose shot was saved by Ditchburn. In the very next attack, 13 minutes into the second half, the same players carved out virtually the same move again, except this time, Grillo's cross rebounded through a group of crowded players to Micheli who hit a low drive past Ditchburn into the left-hand corner of the net. 2-1 to the home side. Micheli turned away with arms aloft to receive the ovation of the crowd.

"It was like a release for the crowd," says Micheli. "Until then they had been quiet. I've got a tape of the radio commentary of the first 15 minutes of the second half at home and the commentator says, 'we're in the presence of an interesting match' and you can't hear anything from the terraces. It was a match where the crowd watched with fascination and concentration, silently studying, because it was more than just another match, it was very special."

Micheli talks through his goal but without quite the same passion as he had in recounting Grillo's. Perhaps he's just being modest, or maybe, in a country where so much emphasis is placed on style, he genuinely feels so much admiration for Grillo's spectacular first goal.

"I've got a big photo of my goal in my shop, two metres by one, and the notable thing about this move is that any coach looking at this photo today would say, 'Eckersley, what the hell are you doing there?' He's nowhere near me, but back in the area playing everyone onside."

Three minutes later, a carbon copy of the same move yet again ended with Micheli scoring, but this time the goal was disallowed for offside. "The strange thing is that, for me, it was exactly the same. I was in the same position. I don't think I was offside. Maybe Eckersley had moved up this time or I'd advanced a bit too far, I don't know, but really I believe I was onside."

A goal down, the English team abandoned attempts to play short passes, resorting to launching more long balls deep into the Argentinian half. On 71 minutes Froggatt crossed for Taylor but Perez headed clear, and then on 76 minutes Mussimesi beat Berry to a high cross, but that was about it from the English attack.

A minute later, the confirmation. Micheli took a low short corner to Lacasia, on the edge of the penalty area, who swivelled and hit a powerful shot on the half-turn, beating Ditchburn. Eckersley miraculously cleared off the goal line only for Grillo, sprinting into the six-yard box, to fire home for his second goal of the match.

The home side were in total ascendancy. 'Argentina were controlling, England were trembling', said *El Grafico*. One brilliant move between Grillo, Lacasia, Mendez and Cruz finished with the ball flying over the bar. England had one last chance five minutes from the end when Dellacha fouled Taylor. The Argentinian players lined up a wall expecting a piledriver from Billy Wright, but instead he floated over a hanging cross to Jack Froggatt at the far post, but his header went wide. Mendez forced one more good save from Ditchburn in the last minute, but then Arthur Ellis called time: Buenos Aires XI 3 English Football Association XI 1.

Seven English journalists had flown out with the English team and none of them objected to the result. 'BEATEN! BEATEN HANDS DOWN', cried Bob Ferrier in the *Daily Mirror*. 'We were outclassed and outplayed. Our fellows were punch-drunk oxen compared to gazelles.'

'There was no doubt about South American superiority,' said Desmond Hackett in the *Daily Express*. 'The FA XI were completely dazzled by the quick accurate Argentinians and our defence at the end was almost at panic stations.'

Charles Buchan wrote in the *News Chronicle*, 'There can be no excuses, Peron's boys were superior in all respects,' and Roy Poskett in the *Daily Mail* opined, 'for much of the time the FA XI were like carthorses chasing ballet dancers. England must play better.'

England manager Walter Winterbottom said, "We just didn't play well, the opposite of our adversary who played with skill and speed. My players and I are disappointed with our labour. Perhaps the climate has been inconvenient for our lads, who normally play in colder temperatures on a softer pitch, but the truth is that the Argentinian team were very skilful. We hope to improve on Sunday in the match that counts for us."

AFA president Valentin Suarez was very emotional and gave a long speech. One snippet sums it up neatly: "We've beaten one of the most powerful sides in the world. I'm full of pride. Our young lads played with great heart and deserved the tremendous ovation they received when leaving the field."

His English counterpart, Stanley Rous, did not want to say much. "The team didn't play the way we hoped, but we're confident we'll play better on Sunday."

Photos of 'The Impossible Goal' covered the front page of most Argentinian papers. 'We've never seen an Argentinian team play with such fight and heart,' said *Clarin*, and *El Mundo* dedicated the whole of its front page to pictures of the match with the big masthead headline, 'A BRILLIANT DAY'. Indeed the Argentine people were so jubilant that President Peron declared that, henceforth, 14 May would be Footballers Day. "We say it's the day football was born," says Micheli.

Coach Stábile was perhaps the only Argentinian not completely happy with the outcome. "Perhaps one more goal for us would have been a clearer reflection of our domination of the match. Grillo's first goal was magnificent, he placed the ball in the only place it could enter the goal. As for the English team, I'll reserve my judgement until after Sunday but today, it's true, they did very little and were not the masters of football."

Buenos Aires League XI 3 (Grillo 41', 77' Micheli, 58')
English Football Association XI 1 (Taylor 40')
Thursday 14 May 1953
Monumental Stadium, Buenos Aires. Friendly. Attendance: 52,000
Referee: Arthur Ellis (Halifax)

Buenos Aires XI: Julio Mussimesi (Boca Jnrs), Pedro Dellacha (Racing), Jose Garcia Perez (Racing), Francisco Lombardo (Boca Jnrs), Eliseo Mouriño(c) (Boca Jnrs), Ernesto Gutierrez (Racing), Rodolfo Micheli, Carlos Ceconato (sub 42'), Carlos Lacasia, Ernesto Grillo, Osvaldo Cruz (all Independiente), Sub: Norberto Mendez (Racing, on 42')
Manager: Guillermo Stabile

English Football Association XI: Ted Ditchburn (Tottenham), Thomas Garrett (Blackpool), Bill Eckersley (Blackburn), Billy Wright(c) (Wolves), Malcolm Barrass (Bolton), Ray Barlow (WBA), John Berry (Manchester Utd), Roy Bentley (Chelsea), Tommy Taylor (Manchester Utd), Redfern Froggatt (Sheffield Wednesday), Jack Froggatt (Portsmouth).
Manager: Walter Winterbottom

MATCH 3

RAIN

MONUMENTAL STADIUM, BUENOS AIRES, SUNDAY 17 MAY 1953

SATISFIED WITH the performance of the Buenos Aires XI, manager Stábile retained the same line-up for the full international. The only change was Mendez, the substitute in the first match, for the still injured Ceconato. There was no place for the disappointed Boye, scorer of the goal at Wembley in 1951, as Stábile did not want to alter his winning team. The Buenos Aires League XI simply became the Argentina national side, making it difficult for any Argentinian to distinguish the difference in stature between the two matches. Same team, same kit, same stadium, same sell-out crowd, same referee.

Conversely, England made seven changes, bringing the team up to full strength. While this had always been the plan regardless of the performance in the first match, it is also true to say that neither coach nor selectors were satisfied with the performance of the team in the previous match.

Tom Finney, remembered by the Argentines for his brilliant dribbling at Wembley, replaced Froggatt on the right wing. Nat Lofthouse would play at centre-forward, with Tommy Taylor switching to inside-left. Ivan Broadis of Manchester City came in at inside-right and Berry moved out to the left wing to complete the forward line. Alf Ramsey of Tottenham was at right-back, the highly-rated Jimmy Dickinson of Portsmouth at left-half, and Harry Johnston of Blackpool made his England debut at right-half. Gil Merrick replaced Ditchburn in goal.

Walter Winterbottom said he recognised that the characteristics of the Argentinian play, the short pass and unexpected movement, had created problems, so he spent the intervening three days working with the team on ways of combating it. This time the training sessions were kept closed and reporting was at a minimum. Somehow, after the glory of that victory, the Argentine obsession with 'the masters' had reduced. All of Argentina wanted to see the rematch and this time the gates opened even earlier, at 8am for the 3pm start. By 1pm the stadium was full, some estimates putting the attendance at well over the 52,000 supposed capacity.

Sunday 17 May had started just like any other day in Buenos Aires. Legend has it that England captain Billy Wright, mindful of how conditions could aid his side, looked up at the sky and said, 'oh, for a little rain'. At 1.25pm his wish was granted as the first drops began to fall on the massed heads of the crowd, and most importantly for England on the pitch. Half an hour later, the sky had opened up. Flashes of lightning and a full scale rainstorm ensued. By 2.30pm, the pitch resembled a lake and the pre-match entertainment had to be abandoned. Much to their credit, the military band still came out and played some bubbly tunes. They were applauded for their stoicism. Juan Peron and his ministers arrived at exactly the same time as on Thursday, 2.35pm prompt, but this time the cheers were more subdued due to the crowd being soaked through in the open stadium.

At 2.40pm the Argentinian team entered the pitch and received a grand ovation from the public, as did the following English team. The band played both anthems to the best of its ability in aquatic conditions and both were applauded. "It rained, and it rained, and it rained," remembers Gil Merrick. "It just wouldn't shift."

Some Argentinian journalists had been allowed into the English changing rooms and were fascinated by the players' preparation, and the English kit. 'It's as if the long shorts and heavy shirts have not been changed since the beginning of century', one wrote as if peeling away another layer of the veneer of superiority the English held over his countrymen. They were intrigued by the way the English players wrapped their feet in bandage before putting on thick socks, and then they rubbed 'some special kind of grease' into their legs. The English also wore boots with long studs on the heels. The special lightweight boots with short rubber studs they had brought with them for the hard pitches would not be needed in today's conditions.

"We wore shorter shorts because it made it easier to move," says Micheli, "and we had tighter, lighter shirts as well, but the advantage of the English kit is that it made their players look so big," he laughs.

"One comical incident I remember quite clearly," says Gil Merrick, "is that, in the warm up, I put my gloves on, but took my cap off and placed it in the back of the net. Just as the ref blew the whistle to start the match, some little urchin, who could only have been six or seven years old, ran on from somewhere, and stole the cap. It was quite funny really, because it was an old tatty cap that had belonged to my father. If that kid had taken it home and shown his parents, or friends, it wouldn't have looked very impressive, the England goalkeeper's cap."

By 3pm the whole of the pitch was covered in great puddles. The rain was intense. England kicked off. Taylor knocked the ball to Lofthouse, who played the ball out to Finney on the wing. Finney advanced, trying to dribble, but the ball got stuck in the mud, so he passed back to Ramsey instead. Ramsey swung in one of his typical crosses and Taylor slipped as he blasted the ball over the bar. It was obvious from the very first move that the conditions were going to make it difficult, if not impossible, to play.

England gained two corners in quick succession. The Broadis–Finney combination was trying to move the ball quickly on the right, with Finney making his runs down the wing, but the ball wasn't moving well. There were pools of water all over the field and passing quickly became impossible. In fact, the match quickly became a farce. Great splashes of water accompanied every kick. Some of the players were having difficulty standing up. It soon became dangerous, with players colliding into one another. Gutierrez caught Finney, and the Preston man took the free kick himself, hitting a cross into the penalty area where at least three players slipped over in the box.

Eric Weil, a Blackburn supporter, and sports editor of the *Buenos Aires Herald*, was at the match and his lasting memory is of the hapless Eckersley trying to make a tackle, then sliding all the way across the bye-line on his backside, unable to stop himself until hitting an advertising hoarding. Some of the crowd became irritated with the way England were just kicking the ball out of play in defence, but to try anything else would have been too risky.

On 22 minutes, referee Arthur Ellis took the players off the pitch. Ten minutes later, Ellis came out and inspected the pitch, before returning to the changing rooms. An announcement was made over the tannoy: "Given the impossibility to practise football, the match is suspended," Ellis explained. "While the ball rolls you can continue playing, but when it floats you have to stop. Also I couldn't see the lines of the pitch."

The *Buenos Aires Herald* praised 'the wise, courageous and correct decision' of the referee and lamented 'the uncharitableness of the weather gods who deprived the public the opportunity of witnessing what would have been a grand spectacle.'

'The match should never have started but the referee wanted to avoid the irritation of the public,' Charles Buchan wrote in the *News Chronicle*. It was an enormous disappointment for the huge gathering, many of whom had been waiting for up to seven hours for the match to start.

"The crowd went barmy," says Gil Merrick. "They started throwing oranges at anybody. Like bombs they were, these oranges coming down. It was dangerous, and I remember one of them hit Jimmy Trotter, the trainer, on the shoulder. Then, when we left the dressing room and got on the coach to go back to the hotel, the crowds were still throwing these oranges at us."

'It was a farce from the beginning,' bombasted Desmond Hackett in the *Daily Express*, before adding arrogantly, 'England would've won'. A touch presumptuous perhaps, although there was unanimous agreement in both countries that for the 22-minute duration of the match, England had played much better than on Thursday. Taylor had been more effective at inside-left, while Berry and Finney had looked dangerous down the wings.

"It would have been a good match, no doubt about that," says Gil Merrick, although Mouriño, the Argentine captain, reckoned his side had created the more chances. *Clarin* was less committal, stating that 'the 22 minutes of play didn't open the doors for any fair and definitive judgement.'

However another Argentine has a different view. "In this match, I always say, England had a much better team," admits Micheli. "Finney was really impressive and this team, on this pitch, in these conditions would have beaten us. Yes, yes, in those 20 minutes that we played you could see they were much stronger," he adds honestly. "I wouldn't say England were more aggressive, but they adapted better. They were employing the body more, but not with bad intention nor roughness, and when you got touched in those conditions it was impossible not to fall to the floor. But they were playing fairly. Anyway, you couldn't play on a pitch like that, but if the match had lasted 90 minutes they would have won because we couldn't play our way."

Not reported anywhere before, Micheli claims the players actually knew they were only going to play 20 minutes. "It had all been agreed beforehand," he claims. "We knew it was impossible to play but the AFA delegates came into the changing rooms and said, 'Lads, it's been agreed with the English, we're going to play 20 minutes because there are people out there who've been waiting since 7am, so we're going to give them something. Twenty minutes and then we go home.' So we put on yellow plastic bibs under our shirts and went out there." Gil Merrick says the English players were not aware of that.

The following day the two associations were locked in frantic negotiations to try and organise another match. The problem was that the English party had a tight schedule and were due to fly to Chile on the Thursday to play on the Sunday. The English FA suggested playing the next day, Tuesday, but the AFA said it would be impossible to organise at such short notice. England suggested free entrance for all those that were there on Sunday, but Argentina said that would be impossible to police and would cause chaos.

England refused to play at night, so Argentina proposed that if England agreed to play on the Thursday afternoon they would lay on a plane to take them to Chile immediately after the match, or early Friday morning if they preferred, but the English felt that would not give them enough time to prepare for the match against Chile, and, besides, they did not really want to change their travel plans and organisation. On agreeing to leave things as they were and move on to Chile, England promised they would try to come back another time. They never did. Well, not until 1977.

So 1953 ultimately produced an inconclusive ending – if you're English. In England, official records of international matches say 1953, Argentina 0 England 0 (match abandoned after 22 mins), with no mention of the first match. In Argentina, it's the opposite; official records state Argentina 3 England 1, with no mention of the second match. With FIFA it's the same as in England. Only the second, abandoned, match was classed as a full international, something which does not go down well with Argentinians.

Micheli had been so helpful and spoke about the first match with such enthusiasm that I did not want to destroy all his illusions, but he is fully aware of the situation. "We know that for the English the first match was a friendly and the second was the official one, but that's not important for us because we played against an English national team. For us, it was two official matches."

Clarin was saying as much on the morning of the second match: 'Though this second match has the character of the official Argentina v England that they include in the international calendar, we understand that it is purely a formal difference, that doesn't alter at all the authenticity of the first match.'

Despite not having appeared at the 1950 World Cup – nor applying to enter the 1954 tournament for obscure reasons – Argentina were confident now that their way was the right way. An article in *Clarin* the morning after the first match summed up their new attitude and confidence that, arguably, would contribute to their downfall and the disaster of the 1958 World Cup. 'Yesterday we played football how it should be played. We won the match with a demonstration of quality. The *criolla* [South American] style can always overcome the English method, we know how to counter European tactics, our way is best for our character, we don't need foreign ideas, the Argentina supporter wants virtuosity, beauty and glamour.' One of the journalists travelling with the England team, ex-player Vernon Morgan, head of sports for *Reuters*, sounded out a warning after the first match in Buenos Aires: 'Argentina were superior in all aspects, they made quick and slow play when the circumstances required, their defenders were mobile and switched positions and the individual skill, especially that of Grillo, easily overcame the rigid English defence. We must learn from this or it won't be long before we lose our invincible home record.'

Argentina 0
England 0 (match abandoned after 22 minutes)
Sunday 17 May 1953. Monumental Stadium, Buenos Aires. Friendly. Attendance: 52,000
Referee: Arthur Ellis (Halifax)

Argentina: Julio Musimesi (Boca Jnrs), Pedro Dellacha (Racing), Julio Garcia Perez (Racing), Francisco Lombardo (Boca), Eliseo Mouriño (Boca Jnrs), Ernesto Gutierrez (Racing), Norberto Mendez (Racing), Rodolfo Micheli, Carlos Lacasia, Ernesto Grillo, Osvaldo Cruz (all Independiente)
Manager: Guillermo Stabile

England: Gil Merrick (Birmingham), Alf Ramsey (Tottenham), Bill Eckersley (Blackburn), Billy Wright(c) (Wolves), Harry Johnston (Blackpool), Jim Dickinson (Portsmouth), Ivan Broadis (Manchester City), Tom Finney (Preston), Nat Lofthouse (Bolton), Tommy Taylor (Manchester Utd), John Berry (Manchester Utd)
Manager: Walter Winterbottom

ARGENTINE BUTCHERS

WORLD CUP GROUP MATCH, ESTADIO BRADEN COPPER CO., RANCAGUA, CHILE, SATURDAY 2 JUNE 1962

BANFIELD IS a suburb in the south of Buenos Aires named after Edward Banfield, a British executive of the Southern Railroad Company that built the network that is still used today. In 1897, English language newspaper *The Standard* printed the names of players from the two sides in a match that took place at the newly formed Banfield Football club: Goole, Moffat, Brown, Watson, Hunter, Enright, Woodwell, Sharenburg, Rangey, and two others (sic) are one team, and Harriman, Rugeroni, Morgan, Patter, R. Wilson, Dunn, Hunt, F. Wilson and two others (sic) make up the other. The 'two others' in each team could have been Argentines, brought in to make up the numbers, and the reporter perhaps forgot their names as he didn't speak Spanish.

There can be no doubt about Club Atletico Banfield's British roots, but today they are a strong Argentine First Division side that won the Argentine championship for the first time in their history in 2009. Much of Banfield's success has been due to their youth policy – players like Javier Zanetti and Gabriel Paletta have come through their academy, which is run by the legendary Silvio Marzolini.

Tall, handsome, blond Marzolini made 366 appearances for Boca Juniors, winning five Argentinian league championships, and was Argentina's left-back throughout the 1960s. He was selected alongside greats like Di Stefano, Puskas, Eusebio and Lev Yashin to star for the Rest of the World team at Stanley Matthews's famous testimonial at the Victoria Ground, Stoke in 1965. As manager of Boca, he won the league championship in 1981, with Diego Maradona in the team.

"You can't just turn up in Germany and ask to see Beckenbauer," I was told by Stefan, the German backpacker at the friendly *pension* where I was staying. Stefan was right, nothing like a bit of Anglo-Saxon realism to keep your feet on the ground.

After a hard day's night in the Buenos Aires newspaper library, swotting up on reports and comment from old England v Argentina matches, I did question my sanity. The newspaper library was an eye opener, though. Open 24 hours, the poor and homeless sought refuge in its warmth at night, sleeping crouched over the tables. I arrived back at the *pension* tired, but humbled, and full of self doubt.

"I can't believe it," said Dora, the middle-aged landlady, when I walked into the lounge. "Silvio Marzolini phoned here. I spoke to Silvio Marzolini! Do you realise just who he is?" She was excited. "He was like Beckham for us; all the teenage girls were crazy about him. I can't believe I spoke to him on the phone." Dora was soon reliving her youth and we listened to teenage tales from 1960s Argentina. "He left a number for you to contact him," she finally told me.

Marzolini is an Argentinian football legend and he was phoning the *pension* to return a call from some English bloke who had left a message on his club's answering machine. I liked him already. He did look a bit like Beckham as well, back in his day. I realised Dora wasn't exaggerating when I saw a photo of the 1962 Argentina World Cup squad, although, with his narrow suit and sixties haircut, he looked more like David McCallum from *The Man from UNCLE*, the '60s spy series. The picture did cause quite a discussion among Dora and the females staying at the *pension*. If he had been playing today, Marzolini's marketing potential would be an advertiser's dream. Still recovering from Marzolini's call, Dora was flabbergasted the next day when Antonio Roma, legendary 1960s Boca Juniors and Argentina goalkeeper, called. "Micheli told me you want to speak to players who played against England in the past, is that right?" Dora, more used to answering the phone to Scandinavian backpackers, was beside herself.

"Oi Stefan, I've got another of the 'Animals' – doesn't matter if I don't get Rattin now; I'm going to speak to two of his team-mates," I announced proudly. Stefan still hadn't got over the weekend and the fact that people in Buenos Aires don't go out for a meal until midnight, and that arriving home at 6am is considered early. "You can't just turn up in Germany and ask to see Beckenbauer," he repeated resignedly, but, it seemed, things are different in Argentina!

Banfield's training complex is outside town and only accessible by taxi from the train station. The *taxista* wanted to talk about football, as usual, and when he realised we were going to meet Silvio Marzolini he too was starstruck, although he recovered quickly enough to give me a comprehensive rundown on Argentine football in the '60s, making sure that I realised I was about to meet one of the greatest players of all time.

Once through the security checks, we were shown to the reception and a big man in his football gear, covered in mud, appeared. Marzolini is 60 years old but I would not like to play against him even now. We went to the canteen area, ordered some coffee and bade farewell to the taxi driver, ecstatic that he had been able to have his photo taken with one of his heroes.

June 1962. Russia and USA were arresting and releasing spy pilots in a forerunner of the Cuban missile crisis that would come to a head later in the year, three Air France Boeing 707 planes crashed that month, two US army officers were killed in Saigon, Vietnam, and Elvis was number 1 with *Good Luck Charm*. The 1960s had arrived, but Silvio Marzolini, along with the rest of the England and Argentina squads, was cut off from the world, holed up in a small mining town in the heart of the Chilean Andes.

"Rancagua was cold," says Marzolini. "Our conditions weren't good, but we went for some mountain walks and saw some nice scenery."

England were staying down the road in a posher complex, complete with golf course and cinema, although that didn't stop Jimmy Greaves complaining about it in his newspaper column during the 1998 World Cup when he compared conditions in Rancagua to the luxury today's molly-coddled footballers are afforded. 'We had to endure cramped bunk beds with mosquitoes and insects,' wrote Greaves.

"Bunk beds and mosquitoes! – that would've been like a palace to us," jokes Marzolini. The Argentines were not quite living in a shoebox in the middle of a road, but, unlike the English, there was no golf course or cinema at their digs, so they had to make do and provide their own entertainment, which they did with the aid of guitars, maracas and sombreros as photographs in Argentine papers prove.

Although skilfully disguised as romantic Latinos with maracas and silly hats, Argentina '62 were a tough team; big men (an average height of 6ft) who went to Chile with the most negative tactics their country had ever seen, as far removed from the spirit of '53 and the attacking flair on display against England in Buenos Aires, as Claudio Gentile is to Pelé.

"The manager [Juan Carlos 'Toto' Lorenzo] was obsessed with the opposition," says Marzolini. Argentina's tactics were based upon man marking and stifling their opponents. What on earth had brought about such a different approach, just nine years on from Grillo's *Impossible Goal*?

"It was the disaster of '58 that did it," replies Marzolini instantly. To understand the *disaster* in its full context you have to appreciate what had happened in the intervening years. Remember those quotes from the Argentinian press after the first match in '53; 'we don't need to learn from European football ... our way is the best for us', etc. Simply put, they had gone to the footballers' heads. Argentina had won the 1955 *Copa America* (South American championship), with some outstanding attacking play and a record number of goals, Micheli scoring four in one game. In 1957, they won the same competition again, thrashing Brazil 3-0 along the way. Argentina were unbeaten in years. The country loved it, rejoicing in its team's attacking, joyful, dribbling style as much as the results.

But, for unknown reasons, Argentina had not entered the 1954 World Cup in Switzerland, just as they had not in 1950. "There are two theories," explains Marzolini. "One is that Peron asked the Argentina Football Association 'will we win it?', and the AFA said 'no', so Peron said 'don't enter then'. The other theory is that the AFA had problems with FIFA." The first theory is plausible as, after General Peron's regime fell in 1955, overthrown by the military he was supposed to be the head of, Argentina entered the next World Cup, Sweden 1958.

After so much success in South American competitions, expectation was high in 1958, and the public were not prepared for what followed. "Disaster," says Marzolini again, unconsolably shaking his head, although, at 18, he was too young to be part of it.

"When Argentina won the *Copa America* in 1957 there was a new generation up front; Maschio, Angelillo and Sivori, 18, 20, and 21 years old. They were known as the *Angels with Dirty Faces*, but all three of them were signed up by Italian clubs and it was considered shameful to play them at the World Cup as they had, to all intents and purposes, defected from the country," he continues.

Shorn of its young forward line, some old faces were recalled, including Labruna, now 40 years old, one of the stars of the great 1940s River Plate side, and a veteran of Wembley '51. Grillo, author of the 'Impossible Goal' in 1953, was also now playing in Italy, but as he had left Argentina at an older age, it was not considered such a disgrace if he was selected. Dellacha, the podgy centre-back, now 32, was another survivor from the 1953 matches against England.

Perhaps complacency had set in, over-confidence from their South American triumphs, perhaps they thought they could just turn up in Sweden without any preparation and win? Whatever the case, this ageing Argentina team tried to play their neat little passing game, but this time it didn't work. They weren't fast anymore. They lost their opening game to West Germany (3-1), beat Northern Ireland (3-1) as expected, and then came the humiliation. Czechoslovakia 6 Argentina 1.

To a proud country, especially proud of its football, 6-1 was a shock and an embarrassment. This time, the Argentina team were booed by crowds when they arrived home at the airport, and just to rub salt in the wounds, Brazil won the tournament.

Not only that, Brazil won the 1958 World Cup using modern techniques. The clips of 17-year-old Pelé acrobatically turning the Swedish defence in the final may give the impression that those free spirited Brazilians had just turned up fresh from the beaches, but the truth is that Brazil, an ever present at World Cups, had learnt and developed. Brazil's first World Cup victory had as much to do with solid preparation, fitness and tactical nous as it had to do with Pelé and Didi's individual skill.

"The 1958 World Cup opened up serious debate in Argentina," explains Marzolini. "We'd been humiliated, and it was the catalyst for change. Players in Europe were different; they were stronger and fitter. We didn't have the facilities in Argentina, and, mistakenly, we hadn't played the European-based players out of a sense of shame."

In the post mortem, out went Stábile after 18 years as manager, and out went the idea of beautiful football, played with joy and honour. In came new manager Victorio Spinetto and Argentina won the Copa America again in 1959, but Spinetto did not last long, and Jose Moreno took over for a couple of months before he was sacked. Then, amazingly, Stábile and the old ways were brought back, but two heavy defeats to Brazil saw him sacked and any thoughts of those old ways returning ever again consigned to the dustbin. The spinning wheel spun and Spinetto was handed the job again, but a disastrous European tour saw him sacked once more and Jose D'amico took over for a few matches.

Clearly there was some sort of a crisis going on at the AFA. Instability, presidential power struggles, rapid hiring and firing of managers and arguments over style of play. Despite all the chopping and changing, Argentina managed to qualify for the 1962 World Cup in Chile, where they were drawn in the same group as Hungary, Bulgaria and England. Juan Carlos Lorenzo was put in charge of the team just four weeks before the tournament.

"Lorenzo was obsessed with tactics," says Marzolini. "He'd played in Spain and managed Atlético Madrid, so he had a European outlook. For the first time ever Argentina players were encouraged to think about the opposition, not just themselves. For the first match, Lorenzo took us down to watch the Bulgarians train. We hid behind a wooden building, a sort of shed-like construction." Marzolini smirks and shakes his head at the thought of it all. "We sneaked behind this shed thing and tried to watch the Bulgarians through holes in the fence but it was a waste of time as we couldn't see anything. What a farce!"

Today every manager studies reams of footage of the opposition, aided by computers showing players' movements, but back in 1962, Argentinian players were sneaking behind a shed to try and form some sort of inkling as to how the opposition would play. In a World Cup. It was indeed the kind of mission on which one might expect UNCLE to dispatch Illya Kuryakin. Mind you, this took place at the height of the cold war when spying was all the rage and the Russians, as you would imagine, were at it as well. Ahead of the rest in fact. The Soviet Union had been caught secretly filming all World Cup matches to show their players the movements and tactics of opposing teams. "This has to stop," said FIFA president Stanley Rous. Times were so very different then.

Stanley Rous was by now a 'Sir'. The head of the English FA had succeeded another Englishman, Arthur Drewry, as president of FIFA in 1961, and had just been re-elected on the eve of the 1962 World Cup. Not bad for the leader of an association that had not wanted anything to do with the World Cup or FIFA before the war. This upset some in world football, who felt Rous had come to power too easily, considering his country's lack of support for FIFA in the first 35 years.

Peeking a snoop from behind wooden sheds may have been a waste of time, but Argentina won their first game against Bulgaria all the same. Marzolini made the only goal of the game after four minutes, one of his typical runs down the left, feeding Facuno to score.

After the goal Argentina shut up shop for the remaining 85 minutes, much to the frustration of their fans, who had trekked across the Andes, and much to the ire of the press corps who felt their team could have annihilated the Bulgarians if they had wanted to. There were simply no more attempts to attack after the goal, but this was the new approach, the modern way, just as manager Lorenzo, with his 'European' tactics, dictated.

'Not satisfied', said *Clarin*. 'We understand that results count but the manner in which you achieve them does as well.' *El Grafico* agreed: 'Triumphs like this leave a bitter taste.' Lorenzo defended himself against the accusations that he was betraying Argentina's football traditions: "I didn't give the order to play like that. What else could the players do once Rossi and Facuno got injured?" Substitutes were not allowed.

Not only had Argentina v Bulgaria been a poor spectacle, but there had been some very hard tackling from both sides. Too hard for some sections of the English press. 'The referee will have to be strong when England play Argentina,' warned the *Daily Mail*. 'Navarro and Saachi use a violence we don't know in England.'

"Ah, Navarro … he wasn't a footballer," says Marzolini, "he couldn't play." Peter Lorenzo in the *Daily Herald* counselled England about their next opponents: 'Despite their brilliant footballers, the Argentines look for streetfighting triumphs. It will be a hard match.'

Desmond Hackett in the *Daily Express*, the man who nine years previously had drooled over Argentinian skill, describing them as a 'ballet', now called them 'Butchers' and 'Hatchet Men'. He then claimed that his comments had caused Argentinians to come looking for him, incensed by what he had written. It didn't seem to stop Hackett, though. On the eve of the match with England, he wrote, 'Their soccer skulduggery put the Bulgarians' two best players out of the World Cup, but now the Argentines tearfully complain and manager Lorenzo whines, "I have the most injuries because the Bulgarians were so crude and brutes."'

Are we here, with Hackett the Hack, seeing the first signs of a breakdown in the friendly relations between Argentina and English football, and moreover, the English press? Remember Hackett was one of the seven journalists that had been wined and dined, and well-treated, in Buenos Aires in 1953, but here he is nine years later rewarding his generous hosts with headlines of 'Butchers'. Hackett must have been aware of how offensive those headlines would have been to members of the Argentine press who understood English. He must have realised they would get reported back home. He surely cannot have been so naïve to think his own style of butchery would not get up the noses of England's forthcoming opponents, that he would not be igniting the fire beneath a diplomatic incident?

The social and sexual revolution of the 1960s had arrived in England, if not yet the rest of the world and, it would appear, it included newspaper reporting throwing off old, stuffy styles and ushering in the first headlines of modern tabloid journalism; jingoism that would manifest itself to ridiculous levels in future England v Argentina matches. Any humour in those headlines was lost on those abroad, particularly in Argentina where overtones of colonial rule and control still hung over the nation. They did not understand and were insulted. Weren't the English supposed to be gentlemen?

However, that is not to say Argentina v Bulgaria was not a brutal match. It seems to have been the trend of the time. Chile '62 is widely regarded as the most violent World Cup ever, the tournament where negative tactics came to the fore. Only three teams, Hungary, England and Brazil, made any real attempt to play open and attacking football. *Clarin* described West Germany 0 Italy 0 in Santiago as 'Stalingrad … it wasn't a match but a battle, it wasn't football, but a war and it didn't deserve a goal. These two ex-champions played to see who could be the most violent.'

'BISH BASH ITALIANS DRAW', exclaimed the *Daily Express*. 'Italy and West Germany thumped their way to a brawling draw that proved this World Cup will be decided more by destruction than soccer ability. Players had to leap away from the ball to survive. Football was forgotten as players tried to destroy each other.'

But Italy v Germany was just the prelude for the real *Battle of Santiago*, which took place between hosts Chile and Italy on the same day as England v Argentina. With his trilby hat and clipped accent, young David Coleman's impassioned introduction on the BBC newsreel footage is a classic: 'What you are about to see is the most stupid, appalling, disgusting and disgraceful exhibition possibly in the history of the game.'

Italy and Chile introduced rugby tackling, punching, and kung fu kicks to the game of Association football. Noses were broken and blood was spilled. At one point, two separate boxing bouts took place, pugilists holding up their guards and delivering right hooks as if professionals in the ring. The initial reason for the bad blood between the sides was that Italian journalists had been reported as questioning the appeal and morals of local Chilean women.

English referee Ken Aston sent three players off in the *Battle of Santiago*, but was widely criticised for losing control of the match. Appalled at what they had seen, the Swiss team informed Sir Stanley Rous that they no longer wished to take part in the World Cup. The peaceful Swiss had been unfortunate enough to have been drawn in the same group as all the worst offenders of violent play: Italy, Chile and West Germany. A crisis meeting was called and Rous instructed referees to clamp down hard on the bullies.

'Poor Football', said *Clarin*. 'In three rounds of World Cup brutality, fighting, and, logically, injuries and expulsions, we've seen nothing, absolutely nothing, of football. With a couple of exceptions, we are in a chapter of war.' Armed police were on the field three times during the *Battle of Santiago*, and after the match armed air force police protected the Italian team at the school where they were staying. Restaurants, bars and even some shops in Santiago bore notices reading 'NO ITALIANS ADMITTED'.

Marzolini attempts to explain the Argentinian formation against England to me: 4-2-2-2. His memory is sharp and he seems very clear about it. Like Micheli before him, he takes a pen and paper and draws the system to explain how it works. "To be honest the players didn't really understand what Lorenzo wanted," he says. "Of the two sitting in front of the back four, Rattin was to mark Johnny Haynes, and Vladislao Cap was to mark Bobby Charlton. If you could stop those two you could stop England, it was felt."

Reading through the reams of Argentine newspaper coverage during the build up – all those arrows and diagrams, pages of tactical analysis – I'm not so sure the journalists understood Lorenzo either. However, who would not find it confusing when he announced to the press the day before the match against Bulgaria that 'Rattin would play if it didn't rain, but would not if it did.' It must have rained as Rattin did not play.

Argentina did not need to sneak behind a shed to watch England as Lorenzo had made sure all his players had seats in the stands when England lost 2-1 to Hungary in their opening game. "An excellent match," says Marzolini. Maybe for the neutral, but the English press were quite critical of their team, accusing England of bad passing and hitting too many long and hopeful balls.

English football had not fared well in the nine years since they had last played Argentina. If the warning signs had been there on that South American tour in '53, then the wheels finally came off England's grand design six months later, and they did not just slip off their axles quietly, but came flying spectacularly off, when Hungary visited Wembley in November 1953 and blew the idea of English invincibility into oblivion forever. With mesmerising movement off the ball and an exquisite touch on it, Puskas and company enthralled the Wembley crowd as Hidegkuti, a deep-lying centre-forward, something never seen nor heard of on British shores before, bamboozled the England defence, who simply didn't know who to mark. Billy Wright, for so long the symbol of English solidity in the centre of the park, was given a particularly torrid time, being left on the seat of his pants for the visitors' third and most iconic goal. Puskas dragged the ball back with the sole of his left foot and fired it high past Gil Merrick's left hand into the roof of the net while Wright chugged past, outwitted 'like a fire engine late for the fire' as one newspaper put it. The Hungarians certainly knew how to shoot as well. Three of their goals came from outside the penalty area. The final score was 6-3, a great match, but England were clearly no longer the 'masters of the game'. It was official and the confirmation came the following May when the still hungry Hungarians hammered England 7-1 in Budapest.

But England did reasonably well at the 1954 World Cup. Expectations had been drastically lowered after the Hungarian demolitions, the public aware that England were just another team now, but England won their three-team group by beating Belgium 4-0 and hosts Switzerland 2-0, before losing to Uruguay, 4-2, in an exciting quarter-final. Walter Winterbottom remained as coach, using the same tactics, the WM formation that had not changed since the '60s, and at the 1958 World Cup England drew all three of their group games, versus Russia (2-2), Brazil (0-0), and Austria (2-2), before losing to Russia (2-1) in a hastily organised play-off match (the two teams had finished in the group with exactly the same points and goal average).

Mitigating circumstances must apply to England in 1958. If the Argentina team had been shorn of its forward line by defections to Italy, then England had lost four of its best players in much more tragic circumstances. The Busby Babes: centre-forward Tommy Taylor, David Pegg, England captain Roger Byrne, and the brilliant 21-year-old Duncan Edwards were among nine Manchester United players killed in the Munich air crash just four months before the World Cup. Considering the situation, the England team, featuring future England manager Bobby Robson and Munich air crash survivor, 18-year-old Bobby Charlton, did as well as could be hoped.

But four years later, going into Chile '62, there was realistic hope for a good performance. England had some skilful players: Jimmy Armfield was as good a right-back as he is a commentator on the radio today; solid, reliable and accurate with a splash of panache. The youngsters, Ray Wilson of Huddersfield, Bobby Moore of West Ham, Bobby Charlton and Jimmy Greaves of Tottenham all showed promise. In light of Hungary '53, English players had worked harder on their ball skills than the generation before them, the result of recognition among some enlightened British coaches that English players needed to spend more time developing technique with the ball at their feet. Greaves had already firmly established himself as a phenomenal goalscorer in the English league, scoring 124 league goals in four seasons at Chelsea before moving to AC Milan in the summer of 1961, where he scored 9 goals in 12 games. However, he failed to settle in Italy and transferred back to Tottenham just five months later for £99,999, a British record transfer fee. Manager Bill Nicholson had insisted on not paying a penny more because he did not want Greaves to carry the burden of being the first £100,000 footballer.

Argentina offered incredible coverage of the 1962 World Cup; separate supplements every day in most national papers, charts, squad profiles and analysis of all the teams, whereas, in England, the coverage was sparse, just short match reports and some limited comment on the England team, with very little information on the other countries. Horse racing, tennis and cricket took priority over the World Cup, including England matches.

This was the summer, after all. It was not until England hosted (and won) the tournament in 1966 that the nation, as a whole, embraced World Cup football.

Argentines, like their latin ancestors, the Italians and Spanish, have always been more interested in the tactical side of the game, or at least discussing it as if it was a game of chess. (Or, putting it another way, depending on how you see these things, the latins have always had a tendency to fill their newspapers up with realms of useless statistics and information.)

La Nacion wrote of England manager Walter Winterbottom's 'elastic WM', which was not a reference to his choice of underpants – even Argentinian papers are not that detailed – but the term they preferred to use to describe England's formation, 'By sticking with the "elastic WM", Winterbottom remains loyal to his theory that the men are more important than the tactics. The universal 4-2-4 invented by the Brazilians and used by most countries today has left the old WM behind, because 4-2-4 is less rigid, more flexible, and allows players more movement and more fantasy. The WM closed the pages of an era but incredibly the English are still using it.' (The article claims 46-year-old Winterbottom insists the best method for football is to repeat specific moves on the training ground over and over again, and that he had been criticised 'for lacking spontaneity and being too conservative' ... 'he writes in newspapers, always about physical fitness and psychology. he is not an academic and is unlikely to change'.)

'How the English play' was the title of an article in *Clarin*, basing its analysis on England's first group match. 'The Hungarians were more skilful and intelligent, better at passing and keeping the ball. England, at times, play too fast and lose possession, but they are infinitely fitter than our players. They are strong and good in the air; Springett comes out of his goal well and collects crosses and Armfield, the right-back, is very strong. He brings the ball out of defence and attacks in the style of Silvio Marzolini. The full back Wilson is two-footed, and Maurice Norman is a "none shall pass" centre-half.' They identified 'ambidextrous' Bobby Charlton as one of the danger men, 'he plays and makes play', and also Greaves, who 'plays with his head up, a virtue of all good players'. The weakness according to *Clarin* was Greaves's striking partner Gerry Hitchens, 'an awkward element, who just crashes into people, nothing more.'

In fact Winterbottom dropped Hitchens and handed Middlesbrough's Alan Peacock his England debut against Argentina. Maybe the Argentine weakness for crosses and high balls could be exploited. Peacock, a traditional British centre-forward, was tall and powerful in the air, and in a rare outbreak of an English newspaper dedicating some space to a World Cup match, the always understated *Daily Express* ran a piece entitled 'Peacock Chases Glory Against Butchers'. Desmond Hackett explained that the 'virtually unknown handsome young husky from Middlesbrough' had not even been a regular for his club that season until they had sold Brian Clough. Although 'bitterly criticised' Peacock was in fact one of the best headers in world football, according to Hackett.

Clarin carried a large photo of the England squad, standing in a relaxed line at their training camp. Two things stand out. First, Bobby Charlton has got hair. The other striking feature of the photo is Bobby Moore. He is standing on the end with Jimmy Greaves, the pair of them a little aloof from the rest. It's almost as if Moore knows his destiny. Whilst most of the other 22 England squad players are looking down, or laughing in the line, Moore is standing upright, shoulders back, chest puffed out, with a serious face, as if he's taking on the role and responsibility of being his country's greatest sporting icon already. Also Moore's shorts are shorter than everyone else's. He looks like a player from another era, superimposed onto the end of an old photo.

In the late 1950s, under the influence of captain Malcolm Allison, who was obsessed with Continental football, the West Ham players changed to shorter shorts to allow easier movement. They also drank cappuccinos at an Italian coffee bar next to the ground, discussing tactics with salt and pepper pots, and were further encouraged in their new thinking when the innovative and future England manager Ron Greenwood took over.

West Ham used lighter boots and tried to play a passing game, with Moore bringing the ball out from the back. 'Where's yer handbag Bobby Moore?' was one of the insults the young England player would receive, especially as he had an uncanny knack of keeping his shorts and socks pristine white, even in the muddiest of conditions. However, Greenwood's methods, whilst only bringing mixed success in English league football, served England well, as his young prodigy would demonstrate over the next few years – although one presumes the aero-dynamic shorts proved to be pointless, as with so much emphasis placed on sports science today, modern players take to the pitch with shorts the size of tents wrapped around their legs.

Argentina were forced to make changes for the match against England, which would be the first competitive meeting of the two sides, as no fewer than four players had been injured during the brutalities with Bulgaria. This time Rattin would be playing, rain or no rain, with specific instructions to mark England captain Johnny Haynes. Vladislao Cap was to mark Bobby Charlton. "We spent as much time discussing the opposition as ourselves," recalls Marzolini, "and I remember Lorenzo telling Cap that Charlton was left-footed, so not to let him shoot with his left, but move him onto his right whenever you can." The Argentinian coach also had another device up his sleeve. "Lorenzo confused the press with his shirt numbers," says Marzolini. "It was the first time they didn't correspond to the positions as we all had squad numbers. This was something he'd picked up in Italy and Spain. The old left-half was now a marker. That wound the press up a bit," he says, laughing, "but Holland really blew it away in 1974 when they deliberately gave their best players numbers like 14 and 21."

England, in an all-white strip, kicked off at 3pm. Cap fouled Charlton immediately and, heedful of the brutality of the tournament thus far, the Russian referee gave him a strong warning. Ron Flowers of Wolves hit the free kick hard, but Roma saved. Most of the play in the opening 15 minutes took place in the middle third of the pitch. England tried to move the ball forward, but Rattin, Cap, Sosa and Oleniak, Argentina's midfield, sat deep and waited for them.

England's right-back was Jimmy Armfield, who remembers what happened next: "It was a must win situation, against a team desperate to succeed on their own continent and one with a ruthless streak running though them. They would try and get away with things and this game was not going to be different in that respect. They would stand on your heels and nip you. It was nasty, petty stuff really and it set the tone for four decades worth of contests between the countries as World Cup rivals. They got up to all sorts of stuff. One guy tapped me on the shoulder, I turned around and he went to spit in my face, but didn't. It was like that. Little things. They were that sort of team."

When Paez fouled Haynes, the referee again blew for dangerous play and issued a stern warning. It was clear England had the strong official their press had been calling for. Argentina, in their change kit of all navy, knocked short passes between themselves, but with a lack of urgency and no penetration. This was the new breed of defensive football that was Chile '62.

However, on 17 minutes, that all changed. Charlton, on the left, escaped Cap's guard before cutting inside and crossing high for Peacock. Roma, the goalkeeper, left his base and, together with Paez, jumped to challenge Peacock, who did exactly what he was brought into the side to do. Peacock's header was goalbound, but Navarro dived to stop it on the line ... with his hand. The referee whistled for handball. Penalty. There were no protests.

There appears to be some disagreement as to who exactly was responsible for the handball. Without the benefit of action replays, a couple of reports say the ball deflected off Paez's hand when he went up for header, but the majority say it was Navarro's hand on the line which prevented the goal that the spot-kick was awarded for. Our friend Desmond Hackett in the *Daily Express* must have had a better view than everyone else as he was in no doubt that 'tough guy Navarro punched the ball away'. However, Hackett also wrote that Peacock had shot with 'veteran calm' whilst every other report says the centre-forward headed it.

Flowers shaped up to take the penalty, Roma dived to the left, Flowers placed it to his right. There were a few cheers from the English press contingent and some polite ripples of applause from the Chilean crowd who were supporting England, or, to be more precise, not supporting neighbouring Argentina.

A goal down, Argentina had to at least think about going forward, but "we weren't really set up for attack," says Marzolini. "Suddenly we had to change our tactics, but it's difficult to change after 15 minutes. It was all very confusing." There was little action compared to the previous England v Argentina matches. 'Much of the rest of the play in the first half was sluggish and unrewarding,' wrote *The Times*. In the Argentine midfield, Antonio Rattin was having a quiet game, marking Johnny Haynes and practically going unnoticed. He would not be quite so inconspicuous the next time England and Argentina met in the World Cup.

Finally, at the end of first half, something worth writing home about. Charlton, bursting through the middle, escaped Cap's attention for the second time, and from 30 yards hit a scorcher past Roma. It was the type of Charlton goal we've seen footage of many times, but this time he did it with a full head of hair. It was his 25th goal for his country, leaving him just five behind Tom Finney and Nat Lofthouse on 30 goals for England.

Roma received the blame for the goal in Argentina as he had been beaten from so far out, but he had been taken by surprise because Charlton had shot with his right foot.

"Always move him onto his right, so he can't shoot Lorenzo had told Cap, and what happens, Charlton scores a cracker with his right foot," laughs Marzolini. Instead of listening to their manager, the players should have read *Clarin*'s 'How to beat England' article before the match. 'Ambidextrous Bobby Charlton is the danger man, adept with both feet, shooting with equal power with either', it had warned.

In the second half, Argentina, two goals in arrears, had to attack, but they did not trouble the England defence until the last 15 minutes. 'The Argentina team installed in the England half was like a polite guest that doesn't disturb you,' *Clarin* sighed. They hit high balls and crosses, a grave error against the likes of Maurice Norman, the big Tottenham centre-back, and especially as Sanfilippo, the Argentina centre-forward, did not feel like chasing long balls. *Clarin* reckoned the English back four could have afforded to leave him completely alone for the amount of threat he caused.

Just how physical the match was is difficult to gauge. There are no references to brutal challenges nor dirty play in either country's reports. However, Belen had to leave the field after receiving a blow in the stomach and Peacock complained afterwards that Navarro, the man that wasn't a footballer, according to Marzolini, had kicked and punched him all match.

Halfway through the second half, Argentina broke free from their self-imposed shackles and began to press. Cap, on the right, centred for Sanfilippo and, 'a novelty', according to *Clarin*, 'he actually moved and managed a header'. Another cross appeared to be handled by the young Bobby Moore who was playing at left-half. Argentina protested, but it was not given.

On 72 minutes, Argentina tried to attack down the right through Sosa, but Ray Wilson intercepted and played the ball down the line to Bryan Douglas, who, finding himself in acres of space for the first time in the match, went charging upfield and hit a low shot. Roma blocked, but spilled the ball in front of Greaves; a fatal error. Greaves with lightning instinct buried his chance to make it 3-0 with his 20th goal for his country. Desmond Hackett's match reports with their unusual metaphors are most enjoyable. 'Instead of trying to batter through, Douglas peeled off gracefully like a fighter leaving his squadron and there, doing his old appearing act – and don't ask me how he did it – was Jimmy Greaves, who tapped the ball in and scampered away like a small boy knocking on the door of a house for mischief.'

England were cruising now and came close to a fourth when Jimmy Armfield got forward to good effect. Armfield takes up the story: "We had too much for them, particularly down the flanks. Walter always encouraged me to overlap and that day it was effective. I got forward a lot and even hit the post with one shot. I came in from the right and saw the keeper had left a space and hit it. My shot struck the woodwork. That was probably the nearest I got to scoring for my country."

With only ten minutes remaining and the game effectively over, Haynes tried an audacious run down the middle of the pitch, but Federico Sacchi caught him in possession and advanced into the open space that the England captain had left behind. With nobody challenging, Sacchi played a neat through pass to Sanfilippo who beat Norman to the ball. Springett sprang out of his goal but failed to spring at Sanfilippo's feet and the previously static centre-forward dispatched the ball into the net. 'The only thing Sanfilippo had done in 180 minutes of play', bemoaned *Clarin*. Any thoughts of a late, dramatic Argentinian comeback were misplaced and the game finished 3-1.

Reports are unanimous that England deserved their victory. 'England's strength and speed were the decisive factors,' said *Clarin*. '[Their] system of play was simple and structural, employed with order and a clear formation they deserved their win.' Maybe Walter Winterbottom and his old elastic WM wasn't so bad after all.

Argentine match reports were critical of their team, some using a self-deprecating irony, normally the reserve of the English. 'The English defensive curtain was strong and effective especially when confronted by players with no speed. We've regressed', said *Clarin*. But manager Lorenzo was absolved of some of the blame: 'he can't change lazy types, or convert tortoises into speed – a team that moves with the slowness of Argentina can't come back from behind confronted by a rival with a demonic velocity that makes the ball run as if it is a mad firecracker.' *Cronico* whined, 'The English players always moved into open spaces while the Argentina attack were stuck on their own bases.' Quite a turn-around from 1953, almost identical comments, but in reverse.

Desmond Hackett, whose 'Argentine Butchers' headline had made me gulp earlier, was by now fast becoming my favourite jingoistic reporter: 'This was the most flowing, lucid win in the World Cup so far. Football will not be fair if England fail! And so say all of us.'

Strangely, it was not the English but the Argentine press which carried post-match quotes from England, reflecting the greater coverage they dedicated to the World Cup. Walter Winterbottom said, "I'm very happy with the marvellous reaction of my team. We're in condition to reach the quarter-final now. I'm very happy with Peacock, he worked hard, didn't misplace any passes and his aerial play gave Navarro a hard time."

Jimmy Greaves said, "I was worried before the match but as the minutes passed we felt comfortable. I find it more difficult to control this Chilean ball than the ones we use in Europe, but I'm not trying to make excuses. I think it's difficult for attackers in general to shine in this World Cup against the impeccable defensive systems used by the majority of teams."

Two days later Hungary beat Bulgaria 6-1, which left a tangled situation in the group. The last round of group games did not kick off at the same time, which gave a distinct advantage to the teams playing last as they would know the exact result required. Argentina needed to beat Hungary, although a draw would suffice if England should later lose to Bulgaria. Now that they had to attack, and with the four players who had been injured against England back, Argentina played their best football. They were unlucky not to win, but had been confronted with a nine-man Hungarian defence, who only needed a draw. Argentina had a couple of penalty shouts turned down, but the final score remained 0-0. Therefore, England needed only to draw their last game against the already eliminated Bulgarians as their goal average was better than Argentina's. The two teams played out a terrible 0-0 stalemate. 'A feeble, insipid match,' said *The Times*, 'the last 15 minutes' play featured aimless passing and retention of possession on both sides in turn. The Bulgarians had memories of brutal treatment by Argentina in their first match and did not want them to qualify. The public booed both teams.'

This time, all the English papers tore into the England team for this dreadful and unsporting performance. Desmond Hackett demonstrated all his dramatic qualities, switching from one extreme to the other in just two days. 'It was a depressing performance – Haynes had his worst game ever in an England shirt and Greaves continued to dismay.'

Three days earlier hunky, husky Peacock had been one of the best headers of the ball in world football, but now Hackett criticised the tactic of 'launching high balls' up to him. 'The only reminder that we were watching a World Cup match was Jimmy Armfield, to whom we should be grateful for small mercies, but the small mercies were so small I needed a star-gazing telescope to make them even look lifesize.'

'And Where Is The Fair Play?' was the headline in *Clarin*. 'We knew it would be a draw. The Bulgarians didn't even try to take their chances. They want Europeans through in place of South Americans. This way of regulating a match in favour of another team is inevitable and FIFA must take measures. Where is the fair play that the old world is so proud of? If you fix a result it's not a sporting fight. Even Hungary's 6-1 win over Bulgaria looks suspicious now.'

Here it is then. For the first time, there is talk of conspiracy in Argentina. They felt, perhaps with some justification if the English match reports are anything to go by, that something had been arranged, even if it was just an understanding between the players of either side. There is a whiff of victimisation in the Argentinian remarks that European teams were favoured over South Americans. They urged FIFA, which was run by an English president, to do something about it. Nothing happened.

Incredibly FIFA didn't change the system for another 20 years. It finally took a blatant piece of match fixing between West Germany and Austria in Gijon, Spain at the 1982 World Cup – playing out a 0-0 draw to ensure both teams went through at the expense of Morocco – for FIFA to finally see sense and ensure the last round of matches within the same group kicked off at the same time.

England went on to lose to Brazil 3-1 in a quarter-final universally acknowledged as the best match of the World Cup. According to *The Times*, 'an immensely thrilling quarter-final, England's best performance, and a place in the last eight is probably a fair reflection of our standing in world football at the moment.'

However, despite honourable defeat against Brazil, the reigning world champions, who would go on to win the trophy again, sections of the English press turned on the team. Desmond Hackett really did have a good World Cup. 'No Class – That's Why England Flops Fly Home' was his headline. 'While the England players had the ball bouncing away, often yards, and were compelled to getting the ball under control before passing, the Brazilians simply flowed.'

And then remarkably, considering how little players in the past earned compared to today's millionaires, Hackett concludes his rant with, 'I say Winterbottom's duty is to stay here and keep the pathetic, homesick, complaining players right with him to the final. They might then appreciate how far down in the class of world football they are.

In my view, things were too easy for top players. There is too much money, too little effort.'

The *Daily Express* invited its readers to write in with their opinions on 'What's wrong with the England team'. Some of the letters are fascinating:

'English footballers are a yard slower than overseas players,' G. Robinson, Stafford.

'The home countries are too small for World Cup games, they should unite,' H. Hammond, Newton Abbott, Devon.

'Train the players to use both feet, teach them to back heel and body swerve to pass a ball with the instep. Sack Winterbottom,' T. Johnson, Southampton.

'The people in charge are not competent to see what's wrong and correct it. Main trouble lies in defence – not in defending but in the inability to initiate attack,' K. Dawson, Berkshire.

'The England players were smashing, as good as any. Biggest flops were the so-called critics and experts,' F. Fowie, High Road, SW7.

One man who I doubt ever gets so wound up about football, and who can always see the funny side of things, is Silvio Marzolini, who provided a final anecdote before he left. "After the match against England, we all went down to a bar that was well known for where some of the local girls hang out. You know how it is, you're a long way from home, and some of the Chilean girls are very nice, but when we got there, all the England players were already there, chatting up all the available girls – there weren't any left for us. They'd beaten us on the pitch and off it as well!"

England 3 (Flowers 17' (pen) Charlton 42' Greaves 72')
Argentina 1 (Sanfilippo 80')
Saturday 2 June 1962. Braden Copper Company Stadium, Rancagua. World Cup Group Match. Attendance: 9,794
Referee: Nikolai Latyschev (USSR)

England: Ron Springett (Sheffield Wednesday), Jimmy Armfield (Blackpool), Ray Wilson (Huddersfield), Ron Flowers (Wolves), Maurice Norman (Tottenham), Bobby Moore (West Ham), Bryan Douglas (Blackburn), Jimmy Greaves (Tottenham), Alan Peacock (Middlesbrough), Johnny Haynes(c) (Fulham), Bobby Charlton (Manchester Utd)
Manager: Walter Winterbottom

Argentina: Antonio Roma (Boca Jnrs), Vladislao Cap (River Plate), Silvio Marzolini (Boca Jnrs), Federico Sacchi (Racing), Rubén Navarro(c) (Independiente), Raul Paez (San Lorenzo), Juan Carlos Oleniak (Argentinos Jnrs), Antonio Rattin (Boca Jnrs), Rubén Sosa (San Lorenzo), José Sanfillipo (San Lorenzo), Raúl Belen (Racing)
Manager: Juan Carlos Lorenzo

THE NATIONS CUP

THE NATIONS CUP, RIO DE JANEIRO, BRAZIL, SATURDAY 6 JUNE 1964

JUNE 1964. Three civil rights workers are murdered in Mississippi, United States by members of the Ku Klux Klan, South Africa sentences Nelson Mandela to life in prison, six days later Malcom X forms the Organization of Afro-American Unity, and US President Lyndon B. Johnson announces the goals of his Great Society social reforms to bring an 'end to poverty and racial injustice' in America. In the Vietnam War an explosion sinks the USS Card while docked in Saigon and there is social conflict in Argentina as the CGT general union calls for strikes.

The Beatles' 'Can't Buy Me Love' and 'All My Loving' were both flying high in the British pop charts, while, in Rio de Janeiro, the melancholic Bosa Nova beat of newly released 'Girl from Ipanema' drifts across the beaches. Brazil were hosting La Copa de Naciones (The Nations Cup), an interesting interlude between the 1962 and 1966 World Cups; a four-team tournament featuring England, Argentina, Portugal, and hosts Brazil, all preparing and experimenting for 1966.

England had a new manager. Walter Winterbottom had stood down after Chile '62, and Alf Ramsey was appointed on the strength of his remarkable success at Ipswich Town. The ex-Tottenham and England international full back had taken the Suffolk club from the Third Division (South) to the First Division in six years, and then his team of journeymen, having been tipped for relegation by virtually all pundits, won the 1961/62 championship in their first season in the top flight. An incredible feat, never achieved before, and only once repeated since, by Brian Clough's Nottingham Forest in 1978.

Ramsey, who had played at right-back in the first England versus Argentina match in 1951, and in the rain-abandoned 20 minutes in Buenos Aires in 1953, had gained 32 international caps as a player, and was familiar with the machinations of the Football Association. The cut of the FA blazer fit Ramsey well, but some said he was a 'yes man', a backward appointment, and not the innovative coach English football needed. This criticism was based upon the pragmatic and unimaginative style of Ipswich Town, where Ramsey had to get the best out of limited players. At international level, with the pick of the crop, it was hoped his England team would play with more flair.

Ramsey knew exactly the requirements of the job; to produce a good performance at the 1966 World Cup, which England would be hosting, having been awarded the championships in August 1960 thanks in no small part to the influence of Arthur Drewry in his role as FIFA president. The new manager immediately caused a stir when he took charge in April 1963 by predicting England would win the tournament.

Winterbottom's '62 World Cup team had been a blend of ageing, established players and promising youth, and those youngsters now formed the spine of Ramsey's team. Bobby Moore, at 22, was chosen as captain in May '63, Bobby Charlton was now the chief playmaker as well as a consistent goalscorer, while Jimmy Greaves, who was taking the First Division by storm and scoring a welter of goals, was first choice striker.

Upon his appointment, one of the first things Ramsey did was finally dispense with Winterbottom's WM formation, and bring England in line with the rest of the world by playing 4-2-4. He also insisted that he should have the right to pick the team, without interference from an FA selection committee. That was a condition of his taking the job and signalled the final severing of the old ways which had so held England back since the Second World War.

One problem Ramsey had inherited, though, was on the wings. Bryan Douglas, Terry Paine, John Connelly and Peter Thompson had all been tried but could not produce consistent performances. They, more than anyone, were on trial at the Nations Cup. As preparation for 1966, Ramsey wanted his men well-rehearsed against different styles of play. The mini-tournament in Brazil provided a perfect testing ground, and as events turned out, his young players could not have asked for a greater baptism, a better insight into the workings of Latin American football, complete with much of its madness.

On the way to Rio, England made a brief stop in New York and beat the United States 10-0. When asked if this victory served as any consolation for the 1950 World Cup defeat Ramsey had played in, the England manager replied stone-faced, "Nothing will ever be a consolation for that."

The first serious test of England's ability was their opening match in Rio against the hosts. Bearing in mind that Brazil had won the last two World Cups and the 200,000 capacity Maracana stadium was full, rocking to a pulsating samba beat, and that Pelé was at his peak, by now considered the greatest footballer on earth, the odds were stacked against England, but, even so, the 5-1 beating was not a good result.

Ramsey tried to put a brave face on the thrashing: "The ability to get goals as they did makes them world class, but the margin of the result is unfair. We were matching them until they got three from nowhere." If that smacks of 'the ninth goal was offside' syndrome, then in Ramsey's defence, the score had still been 1-1 after an hour – Greaves having equalised Rinaldo's first half goal – but then Pelé had taken over and Brazil scored four times in the final half hour.

Our old friend, *Daily Express* soccer correspondent Desmond Hackett, drooled over Pelé in a way that only he could. Under the headline 'VOODOO', he wrote, 'England were shattered and destroyed by the black magic of a dark prince called Pelé. He cast his spell which must have been evoked by the ancient voodoo of this country. I looked for sulphur smouldering from his feet as he imperiously performed his magic.' Maybe Hackett had got his religions mixed up? There is a lot of spiritualism in Brazil, but not much voodoo. It's unlikely that Pelé was sticking pins into dolls of England players. Jimmy Greaves put it very simply – and more accurately – after the match: "That Pelé's on another planet to everyone else." Pelé had made fools of the English defence by putting the ball through Bobby Moore's legs, and then doing the same to Maurice Norman, before curling in a shot for Brazil's fourth goal. Workmanlike England could not compete with such genius.

Argentina beat the Eusebio-led Portugal 2-0 in their opening game with goals from Rojas and Rendo. Their defensive unit, first seen at Chile '62, was still in place, but had been developed and improved. The slow-coaches up front had been replaced with speed. That made a big difference. Also Antonio Rattin, the young central midfielder who had been criticised for going missing two years earlier, was now the fulcrum of the midfield. At 6 ft 4 ins, he cut an imposing figure. The breaker and creator of play, Rattin was a natural leader, although the captain was his Boca Juniors team-mate, Carmelo Simeone, known as *El Cholo* (the Dark One, and not related to his namesake who would famously cause David Beckham to be dismissed at France '98).

Silvio Marzolini was not in Brazil as he was injured, and neither was Juan Carlos Lorenzo as the AFA had continued their penchant for changing managers rapidly. Now, it was the turn of Jose Minilla, but Lorenzo's defensive system remained; a deep lying, double padlocked defence, numbering eight at times, but capable of breaking out in swift counter-attacks. The new forwards, Onega, Rojas, and Telch, all had pace, and were more dangerous than their predecessors.

Then came the match that shocked Brazil. Argentina comprehensively beat the world champions 3-0 in their own back yard. How did they manage that? There was a simple answer – they stopped Pelé. More than that, they frustrated him to such a degree that he was provoked into committing his most disgraceful action on a football pitch ever. The match and incident are part of Argentine folklore. It was a tactical triumph on the Argentinians' part. Unlike the English, who had let Pelé roam at will, Argentina assigned a man marker. Mesiano followed Pelé all over the pitch. Wherever the Brazilian genius ran, strolled, or sloped in frustration, his shadow went with him. On 30 minutes, with the score at 0-0, Pelé had had enough; he swung round and headbutted Mesiano in the face. The crowd were stunned. Blood poured profusely from Mesiano's broken nose. Pandemonium. The Argentinian bench – coaches, physios, reserves – all rushed onto the pitch, as did photographers, radio commentators and police. 'For more than five minutes the pitch resembled a boxing ring at the end of a world heavyweight title fight,' *The Times* reported.

Desmond Hackett, never one to understate, saw it like 'a centre of a revolution', and 'for six terrifying minutes lives were in danger until at last, crippled, half-conscious Mesiano was carried off'. The Brazilian crowd were shocked by what they had seen. Pelé, their hero, a supposedly sporting gentleman, had just delivered one of the most vicious assaults seen on a football pitch. But the referee had missed it. Pelé stayed on the pitch. It would appear that some of the reporters did not see the incident either as there is some discrepancy over whether it was a butt or a punch. What is certain though is that it took over five minutes for the Argentinians to calm down, and play to resume. When it did, Rattin assumed responsibility and took over the role of marking Pelé. He did equally as good a job of subduing the legendary Brazilian as the departed Mesiano. Perhaps Pelé himself was so stunned by what he had done it put him off his game.

Argentina's goals were scored by Onega, and two by substitute Telch, who had come on for Mesiano. Argentina had played defensively for most of the game, but broke out in sudden bursts through Rattin and Rendo's perfectly weighted through balls. Now that there was real speed up front, they were a dangerous unit. Although he was not there to witness it, this improved version of Lorenzo's system in 1962 was paying dividends. 'Brazil ran in circles into the deep Argentina fisherman's defensive net where pragmatism defeated attempts at poetic play. It was like a canvas being despoiled,' said *The Times*.

Alf Ramsey and his England players watched from the side of the pitch trying to observe and learn, but, in reality, they spent more time trying to dodge missiles thrown by the Brazilian fans. The atmosphere had turned nasty after Argentina's first goal, and the Pelé incident. Unfortunately for the England players they were seated behind the Argentina bench, directly in the line of fire of bottles and other flying objects that were hurled down from the steep Maracana terraces. Ramsey's young men were receiving their initiation into South American ways. *The Times* reporter described the atmosphere during the match as 'dramatic' and 'theatrical'; 'the football bore as much resemblance to the English game as a daisy to a palm tree.' The teams' arrival had been greeted with fireworks and explosions, cueing another Desmond Hackett metaphor: 'the stadium was buzzing continuously like a wasps' nest planning a revolution.' Each time Argentina scored, the missiles came raining down. Fans had been frisked before entering the stadium, but some had got through with bottles, which were duly thrown, often hitting the English party.

In the second half, with the score at 2-0, Brazil were awarded a penalty when Pelé fell in the area, apparently without being touched by Rattin. It caused uproar amongst the Argentines. Pandemonium again, with all the usual pitch invaders rushing into the mêlée, again followed by photographers, radio commentators and the police. According to Hackett, some of the furious Argentina players threatened to strike but, 'an uneasy calm was restored when Rattin threatened to crack his players' skulls if they did not behave.'

When Gerson's penalty was saved by Carrizo, the missile throwing reached its crescendo. Alf Ramsey was hit on the back of the head with a piece of fruit and many of the English press and players wanted to move from their vulnerable position, or even leave the arena altogether. Ramsey stood firm and told his men to stay put because to do otherwise would be cowardly, undignified and un-British. Johnny Byrne, the cheeky West Ham forward, began throwing missiles back at the Brazilian crowd, winding them up even more, and when Argentina scored their third, all the English players cheered.

Pelé, the fallen idol, was made to attend an emergency football court the next day. He was fined heavily for his actions, but the real damage had been to his reputation. *The Times* correspondent observed that Argentina had suffocated Pelé and thus suffocated Brazil. 'Even Brazil and Pelé can be contained by a ruthless deeply laid defensive plan.' Other teams also took note for 1966.

England versus Portugal finished 1-1 the following night. It was another tempestous affair, again the crowd in ugly mood, according to English reports, with the Brazilians supporting their mother country. Again, *The Times* reported that 'the press invaded the pitch like locusts at the slightest pretext.' Seeking to avenge the previous month's 4-3 friendly defeat in Lisbon in which Johnny Byrne had won the game by completing his hat-trick two minutes from time, Portugal took the lead on 41 minutes through Perez after a bad mistake by Flowers. England equalised when Byrne and Greaves combined well at the beginning of the second half, with Greaves finishing the move. Overall, England did not create many chances. Gordon Banks, replacing Tony Waiters in goal, was England's best player.

Portugal finished with nine players. Torres was sent off half an hour from the end after fiercely disputing a disallowed goal. He tried to hit the referee, and only the wire fences of the Maracana prevented violence. 'The disallowed goal caused ugly scenes and protests,' said the upright *Times*, which noted that England, in the first half, had also had 'a couple of goals, by Hunt and Byrne, disallowed for offside, but, in their case, each decision had been taken calmly and sportingly, underlying the difference in attitude and temperament.' After the match, the Dutch referee said, "We're in enough trouble in Europe, but this is worse. We ought to stay in our world and let them live in theirs." Presumably he was referring to the Brazilian crowd and not the Portuguese players.

Bobby Charlton did not play against Portugal. Whether he was dropped after the 5-1 defeat against Brazil, or Ramsey wanted to try out some new faces is not clear. Hackett certainly thought he had been dropped. 'CHARLTON SACKED IN BIG ENGLAND SHAKE UP', ran his headline. 'Charlton looked very unhappy, sad-faced and depressed.'

Dropped or not, Charlton was back to face Argentina for England's final match of the competition. He would play on the left wing with Liverpool's Peter Thompson on the right. Jimmy Greaves and Johnny Byrne continued their partnership up front, while George Eastham of Arsenal and Gordon Milne of Liverpool were the two central midfielders in Ramsey's 4-2-4 (both back in the side having been left out against Portugal). Gordon Banks of Leicester City kept his place in goal, Bobby Thomson of Wolves made his debut at right-back, but the rest of the defence was the established three of Maurice Norman and Bobby Moore in the centre, with Ray Wilson at left-back, veterans from the '62 World Cup.

Argentina fielded the same 11 that had played against the Brazilians, except Mesiano, Pelé's victim, who was replaced by Telch. The English press had been confused by Argentina's numbering against Brazil. They could not understand why Mesiano, a number 11 who usually played left-half, was marking Pelé. Other numbers were clearer; Rattin, the central midfielder, wore 5, a number that still represents that position in Argentina today, and Ermindo Onega was a classic South American number 10, playing as 'El Enganche' (the Hook).

The Argentina number 10 shirt is loaded with significance. It is reserved for 'the free man', who plays behind the strikers and links play. With his socks rolled down, the distinctive Onega was the first in a long line of prestigious Argentina number 10s: Kempes, Maradona, Ortega, Riquelme. A reflection of different football cultures, there has never been a satisfactory name given for the *enganche* position in English football parlance, probably because rarely is a British player given the role. Some coaches refer to it as 'playing in the hole', but that expression also gets confused with the movements of a second striker, so hardly serves as an adequate translation of a position that is as much part of South American football fabric as the right-back or centre-forward.

The magnificent Maracana stadium was less than a sixth full for England v Argentina, but the 29,000 Brazilians who did turn up were supporting the English, the very men they had been throwing fruit at a couple of days earlier. Besides Argentina being the traditional enemy, Brazil now needed their neighbours to lose in order to win the competition.

Sir Stanley Rous, the president of FIFA, met up with his old friend Valentin Suarez, president of the AFA, and Teobilo Salinas, the Peruvian head of the South American FA. The three men greeted each other, but it would be the last time they smiled and laughed together, as the events of 1966 would sour relations.

England wore red shirts and white shorts, Argentina their traditional blue and white stripes, with black shorts. Kick-off was at 8pm Brazilian time, four hours behind England, which meant no reports in the English press until Monday morning. The referee was Leo Hoen, the Dutchman who had opined that "we ought to stay in our world and leave them in theirs."

From the off England attacked and Argentina, needing only a draw to win the tournament, defended in numbers. As early as the second minute, Peter Thompson skilfully beat Vidal on the right wing, and centred, but Rattin cleared. Vidal, standing in at left-back for Marzolini, was considered the weak link. 'Thompson right from the start unhinged the Argentina left-back in a beautifully expressive display of controlled dribbling,' declared *The Times*. The Brazilian crowd cheered Thompson every time he received the ball and ran down the wing. '*Garrincha, Garrincha,*' they cried. England were playing for Brazil.

After 10 minutes, the now receding-haired Bobby Charlton let fly with one of his specials, but Carizzo, still without his net breached in the tournament, saved comfortably. Charlton later hit the post, but as the half progressed, Argentina gradually moved into the ascendency. A good pass from Rattin sent his speedy Boca Juniors team-mate Rojas away. Norman intervened with his hand, but the referee did not see it. The incident did not cause ructions, but it wasn't long before the violence erupted. Thompson committed a 'violent foul' on Rendo, 'so Rattin went over and punched him', said *La Nacion*, matter of factly. Rattin had his name taken, the 6ft 4 midfielder standing looming over the referee as it was written down. Rattin's looming over the referee routine would feature in much more dramatic circumstances in 1966 when the events of this match would come home to roost for all concerned, but in particular the hulking Argentinian midfielder.

In the last minute of the first half, Onega, the number 10, received the ball in a deep position, and advanced without opposition, before unleashing a firecracker of a shot that Banks did well to parry. The ball fell kindly for Chaldu, the substitute who had just come on for the injured Prospetti, but he put too much back lift on his shot, which sailed over the bar.

Argentina's defence was solid, eight or nine deep at times, as against Brazil, but eight minutes into the second half, a slick England move saw Thompson clear. However,

Greaves failed to turn the ball in after it had bounced around in the goalmouth. The striker had not been on form during the trip.

For Argentina, Onega was performing the *enganche* role perfectly, roaming horizontally from left to right flank, taking up deep positions, and confusing the English defence, who were not quite sure who should be picking him up. Ten minutes into the second half, Onega put Chaldu through again. He shot from 30 yards, but Banks saved well.

Argentina were advancing, but without taking risks, as a draw would suffice. But then came their moment. Chaldu picked up a loose clearance on 73 minutes, and as everybody was expecting him to shoot again, he showed great vision by cleverly putting Rojas clean through on goal. 'The Tank' placed his shot, giving Banks no chance. Silence, and the beginning of a mass exodus from the Brazilian crowd. The *Daily Express* said the English defence had 'gifted the goal'.

Argentina played out the rest of the match by passing the ball between themselves, the disorganised English attacks rarely bothering them. A few minutes from the end, a drab rain began to fall and the stadium was virtually empty as the final whistle blew.

'We left the great Maracana stadium sadder, but, we hope, wiser, as moths flickered in the floodlight beams and a gentle drizzle fell as if nature itself was in tears.' Colourful prose from the anonymous *Times* football correspondent. The following night, when Brazil beat Portugal in the last match of the tournament, he described the Maracana as, 'shining like a jewel in the sunshine as Brazil rounded off the gala with a lazy careless rapture, a 4-1 victory over Portugal.'

Perhaps momentarily losing himself in his world of words on a Brazilian beach, caught up by the sensuous pull of the Brazilian sunshine and culture, temporarily forgetting how the local crowd had behaved during Brazil versus Argentina, the sensitive anon wrote about the differences between European and South American football and their respective outlooks, a piece as relevant today as it was then: 'The differences in the game are hard to explain but here football has an air of carnival, a breath of freedom, of emancipation. Music and dancing. Much of this is typified by the explosive movements of Pelé, the idol of Brazil, who intoxicates the crowd with his shining, powerful, poetic rhythm. Progressively, football is becoming the province of the negro and mulatto races. Their players ripening in the sun, provide a rich crop.' Whoever the mystery man in *The Times* was, at least he managed to pull himself away from the beach to watch the final match which is more than can be said of some of England's players.

Back in England, the inquest had begun. 'We must learn to be more flexible,' said *The Times* editorial, citing how Argentina had adjusted their defensive planning and formation to the needs of the situation. Against Portugal they had used 4-2-4, against Brazil 5-3-2 to blanket Pelé, and against England their shape was 4-3-3 (4-3-1-2) with Onega playing the free role. 'Argentina played neat little triangles in midfield with the tall, powerful, but subtle Rattin suddenly hitting telling through balls, the players running into the gaps. We must learn to explode in a sudden flair of attack, turning situations of nothing into everything.'

Even though WM was no longer the system, *La Nacion*, as it had done in 1962, claimed English football was dated. 'They have strong lads trying to move within schemes, but they do not believe in imagination or improvisation. It's a football with a lot of vigour but little beauty. They repeat mathematical schemes; boring and lacking in variety, and even worse, they defraud at what we always thought they were good at, shooting. They have shown themselves less capable than our own players at shooting, which traditionally has always been our weakness.'

Typically Desmond Hackett was more damning in his criticism. 'Too many players have no pride in wearing the England shirt. The triple lion badge could be three tabby cats as far as they are concerned … international matches have become one more pay day in an era when living is too easy,' he ranted before weighing in with another of his choice metaphors: 'England looked like a bunch of yokels trying to puzzle their way out of a maze.'

Even back in 1964, the same accusations. Whenever my generation heard this mantra repeated time and again in the 1970s, 1980s and 1990s, we were always led to believe that the 1960s was a golden age for English football, but it appears the same comments about lack of passion and skill existed back then as well.

Roger Hunt was among those pelted with fruit on the bench at the Maracana, but he remembers that game more as a seminal moment in the thinking of Alf Ramsey who was as aware of the deficiencies shown by his team as the watching press men. "Those defeats against Brazil and Argentina further persuaded Alf that he needed to change the side's tactics before the World Cup," Hunt says. "Alf started to experiment and settled on that 4-3-3 system and I was concerned. If you imagine I'd always had two good wingers knocking the ball in from either side, which was how my goals had come, but now they've gone. All of a sudden I was thinking, 'Where's the ball going to come from?' It was so different. Alf encouraged the full-backs to overlap and we did have good players such as Cohen, Wilson and Armfield who could do that, but it took some getting used to. The fans were finding it hard to get used to the new system too. You can understand it. They were used to seeing the likes of Tom Finney and Stanley Matthews flying down the wings before floating in perfect crosses for centre-forwards to leap majestically and head home. That wasn't happening anymore and many of them weren't happy. By the time it came to our next meeting with Argentina Alf had converted to a 4-4-2 formation with Alan Ball going out onto the right. I am sure he was aware of how physical things would become and was compensating for that."

So confident was he in his thinking after those chastening defeats in Brazil in 1964 that Ramsey chose the moment to set himself up for a huge fall if he failed to live up to his prophecy: "I'm not so convinced that England were such second raters and I still believe England have a chance of winning the 1966 World Cup." He was laughed out of town for that one.

Worse was to follow for Ramsey. A scandal. Some of the England players were unable to pull themselves away from the joys of Copacabana beach and did not turn up for the last match of the tournament between Brazil and Portugal, missing the prize-giving ceremony. FA officials were stunned by the players' absence, and felt let down by Ramsey, who had been given control over the organisation of the tour. Sir Stanley Rous stood grim-faced and embarrassed during the closing ceremony in the Maracana.

Now it was the English officials who were convening a hastily arranged emergency court. Manager Ramsey and his captain Bobby Moore had some serious explaining to do.

The *Daily Express* said that certain players, assured of their places in the team, had broken the rigid discipline. It was expected that Moore would be sacked as England captain.

The press, throughout the Brazilian tour, had been close to the players who had been staying in a hotel on the Copacabana beach, and there were alleged stories of players regularly sneaking out for a late night drink. England's arrangements were compared to the professionalism of the Brazilians who, in preparation for 1966, had already sent officials to London to check out hotels, food and training facilities. 'In comparison to this efficiency, England's approach looks sloppy and shows up the lack of interest in some of our players and the absence of stern disipline by the manager,' came the damning indictment.

That last sentence would have hurt Ramsey, as he was hauled up before the FA to explain why the players were on a beach when they should have been wearing their blazers and attending a football match, representing their country. However, one of Ramsey's great strengths was to always defend his players as a matter of principle. He never criticised them in public. In the event, Ramsey stood by Bobby Moore and his team-mates, taking responsibility for their actions himself. Moore was not sacked as captain, but the message had got through. Things would be different from now on.

Back in Buenos Aires, the team that had left with little hope returned triumphantly, with the Nations Cup trophy. Some 5,000 noisy fans turned out at the airport, a sea of flags and celestial blue and white inflatable footballs, the biggest reception the national team had ever received. Mesiano, for the umpteenth time, gave his version of events on the evening he had spent as Pele's shadow, and confirmed that it had actually been a headbutt and, of course, no Argentine homecoming would be complete without the obligatory speech from an emotional Valentin Suarez: "From the bottom of my heart I've been waiting for a long time for happiness like today for our football."

The tournament had been an undoubted success for Argentina; Rattin had been impressive, dominating in the middle of the pitch, as had Onega, playing behind the front two. The system was working well; a packed defence, retention of the ball, and quick speedy counter attacks. This team was superior to that of Chile '62. There was new blood, and speed, and they looked forward with quiet confidence to the World Cup in England in two years' time, knowing they had once again bettee their masters.

In stark comparison, English football was at an all-time low, and things had never been so bad – if all was to be believed in the English press. The players had no skill, no passion, no discipline, and their football was backward, unimaginative, boring and out of date.

An article written a couple of days after the Nations Cup tournament caught my eye simply because it concerned my team. 'West Ham Back League Chiefs' was the headline. The 1964 FA Cup winners were one of the few clubs prepared to back the league management committee's proposed 'Pattern of Football' report, which demanded that managers and coaches must do something to brighten up the game. The report showed how attendances in English football had dramatically fallen over the previous ten years. It condemned players' salary increases and the raising of entrance fees that were driving crowds away. Over five million fans had been lost to the game, it said, but the report was rejected by the majority of clubs.

All these damning reports of the England team and the state of the national game in 1964 are so similar to all that was being said about English football in the late 1980s and early 1990s, especially when England failed to qualify for the 1994 World Cup and English clubs were regularly beaten in European competitions. But Euro '96, the European Championships held in England, changed all that, bringing the fans back, heralding a new era, boosted by Sky's coverage of the revamped Premier League and assisted by rebuilt or new stadia around the country which were more family friendly. In 1964, the saviour was just around the corner too, in the shape of the 1966 World Cup.

Argentina 1 (Rojas 73')
England 0
Saturday 6 June 1964. Maracana Stadium, Rio de Janeiro. Nations Cup . Attendance: 29,000
Referee: Leo Hoen (Holland)

Argentina: Amadeo Carrizo (River Plate), José Ramos Delgado(c) (River Plate), Miguel Vidal (Huracan), Carmelo Simeone (Boca Jnrs), Antonio Rattin (Boca Jnrs), Abel Vieytes (Argentinos Jnrs), Ermindo Onega (River Plate), Alberto Rendo (Huracan), Predo Prospitti (sub 44', Independiente), Alfredo Rojas (Gimnasia y Esgrima La Plata), Roberto Telch (San Lorenzo), Sub: Mario Chaldú (Banfield, on 44')
Manager: Jose Minilla

England: Gordon Banks (Leicester), Bobby Thomson (Wolves), Ray Wilson (Huddersfield), Gordon Milne (Liverpool), Maurice Norman (Tottenham), Bobby Moore(c) (West Ham), Peter Thompson (Liverpool), Jimmy Greaves (Tottenham), Johnny Byrne (West Ham), George Eastham (Arsenal), Bobby Charlton (Manchester Utd)
Manager: Alf Ramsey

MATCH 6
ANIMALS
WORLD CUP QUARTER-FINAL, WEMBLEY STADIUM, SATURDAY 23 JULY 1966

JULY 1966. London was swinging, the mini skirt was at its highest, and World Cup Willie, a lion in a Union Jack shirt, smiled down from England's advertising hoardings. 'Paperback Writer' by The Beatles and 'Paint it Black' by the Rolling Stones were in the charts, although Frank Sinatra's 'Strangers In the Night' had pipped them to number one, closely followed by the Kinks' 'Sunny Afternoon'.

In election year, the Labour government were having problems with a series of strikes. Prime Minister Harold Wilson remarked that the Seamen's dispute was being masterminded by a "tightly-knit group of politically-motivated men". Within their ranks was a young John Prescott. In Argentina, a bloodless coup d'état known as Revolución Argentina (Argentine Revolution), on 29 June had seen military dictator General Ongania assuming control from the democratically elected president Arturo Illia (Radical Civic Union, UCR) immediately before the tournament began, at a time when economic decline was beginning to set in. Since Peron's overthrow in 1955 six presidents had taken office, but only two of them had been elected, although both elections were 'overseen' by the military.

There was another kind of battle taking place in England, supposedly a sporting one – although this would see plenty of blood spilt, both real and metaphoric. For so many people the 1966 World Cup was the big one. England manager Alf Ramsey had predicted his team would lift the trophy in the final on 30 July, a move calculated to heap pressure on himself, rather than his players. Pelé's Brazil were seeking to become the first team to lift three consecutive World Cups and thus keep the Jules Rimet trophy outright. The FA were frightened to death when the trophy itself was stolen from an exhibition display in Westminster on Sunday 20 March sparking a nationwide hunt. A ransom note was delivered to FA chief Joe Mears demanding £15,000 for the return of the 35 cms high 3.8 kgs solid gold trophy. While the search continued the FA commissioned a replica in case it had already been melted down, but a week later a dog named Pickles eventually sniffed out the £30,000 trophy's whereabouts, discovering it wrapped in newspaper on

Beulah Hill, south-east London. Sighs were heaved across the world, not least at Lancaster Gate.

FIFA had already fought one battle. The tournament had been boycotted by 16 African nations after the qualifying format required the champions of their zone to play-off against either the winners of Oceania or Asia zones. The Africans believed winning their continent's qualifying tournament should be enough to earn a place in England. Stanley Rous, elected as president of FIFA shortly after the tournament was awarded to England, was seen as responsible for Eurocentric policies which annoyed the Africans.

If England's sway in winning the right to host in 1966 had annoyed other countries (Arthur Drewry, an Englishman, was head of FIFA when the decision was made in 1960) that was nothing compared to what was to come as the tournament progressed, especially concerning the South American contingent. First Brazil were kicked out of the tournament and then came a quarter-final encounter between the hosts and Argentina which proved to be the straw that broke the llama's back. The until-now generally friendly Anglo-Argentine football relations would collapse in a heap of accusations and cries of conspiracy.

England's World Cup started slowly, a bore draw with Uruguay sparking questions in the press about how negative tactics would ruin the tournament and in the House of Commons as to whether it was morally acceptable for so much football to be on BBC TV.

However what none of the pundits would admit was that it was the England manager who was developing a new system (arguably mainly on the evidence of the 1964 Nations Cup) that placed a greater emphasis on stopping others, as much as instigating their own flowing football. Unable to find two consistent wingers (his patience with Peter Thompson had finally run out the previous year), Ramsey had switched from 4-2-4 to 4-3-3, copying the Brazilians, who were responsible for most of the game's major innovations during the era. But this was no copycat system designed to mimic Brazil's samba football which had won them the last two World Cups. 4-3-3 helped Ramsey sort out his problems with the wingers, with the formation requiring only one wide boy instead of two, but also allowed him an extra midfielder who would be utilised to man mark the tournament's playmakers: Pelé of Brazil, Eusebio of Portugal, Uwe Seeler of West Germany, Ermindo Onega of Argentina, Jaques Simon of France. And in Nobby Stiles, Ramsey had just the man for the destruction job.

Not only had England played poorly in their opening game – with Wembley a disappointing three-quarters full – but, also, the organisers had managed to upset some of the South American journalists by failing to find them seats among the empty 25,000. The Uruguayans had been refused entry to watch their team play and were quite upset about it, as were the Mexicans and Chileans. It all got reported back to South America.

'All this way and we can't watch our team – terrible organization,' cried the Uruguayans, 'we just got told over and over again by a man in a suit with a robotic voice, "sorry, there are no more tickets, you can't come in … sorry there are no more tickets, you can't come in." Can you imagine what they would have said if this had happened in Uruguay or Chile? But this occurred in England.'

Prime Minister Harold Wilson did his best to raise spirits, turning up at FIFA's traditional eve of World Cup conference in jovial mood. "You've more delegates than the United

Nations," he told the floor, before explaining that his was the only government in the world with a qualified referee in the Cabinet (sports minister Dennis Howell). Wilson went on to inform the delegates that he was the only world leader who carried a picture of the best team in the world in his wallet, upon which he pulled out a photo of Huddersfield Town.

However, probably without realising it, Wilson's most poignant remark of the evening was his opening gambit about the number of delegates. The quip may have been greeted with a guffaw of laughter from the floor, but it also hit a raw nerve with the South Americans. FIFA did indeed have a lot of delegates and most of them were, pointedly, European. Not that South Americans believed in slim line associations. Argentina had no less than 12 club presidents in their entourage on the pre-World Cup tour of Denmark, Italy and Austria. Juan Santiago was the head of the delegation, but the roles of the other 11 were not very clear. 'A lot of chiefs of tourism and days out,' remarked *Clarin*.

Sir Stanley Rous also addressed the conference. A former grammar school teacher and international referee, who, in 1938, had been given the task of rewriting the Laws of the Game into the 17 Laws we know today, he had been appalled by the cynicism of the 1962 tournament and now warned that such brutality and downright cheating would not be tolerated. Rous told the assembled managers, coaches, referees and delegates from every participating country that, "We will do all we can to assure that this World Cup will be the most correct ever. We ask for no time wasting, nor coaching from the side … we want the World Cup to be played in a sporting spirit and the disciplinary committee will adopt measures against any disruption of order." Each referee was presented with a whistle at the conference, and told to "use them wisely and sensitively."

Despite the presence of 12 club presidents, Argentina's warm up tour had not gone well. There had been a lot of organisational problems, not least due to a lack of clear definition over who exactly was in charge of what. Players were arguing with delegates, who were arguing with the coaching staff, and the tension reached a nadir when team captain Antonio Rattin punched Omar Pastoriza, a reserve who had taken his place in one of the matches.

When news of the in-fighting got back to that old soothsayer, and legendary speech maker, Valentin Suarez, still head of the AFA, he immediately flew from Buenos Aires to Austria to sort things out. Suarez locked all the players into a room for a long 'clear the air' meeting. None of the other delegates, nor the manager, were allowed to enter. Everybody said what they felt, especially captain Rattin.

"When Rattin speaks, Rattin speaks clearly," Rattin told the press upon the squad's arrival in England, referring to himself in the third person and explaining that everything had been patched up with Pastoriza and that all the problems on the pre-tour were a result of the "total disorganisation of the trip". The team had "badly slept" and been "badly trained" according to Rattin. They had flown from Argentina and spent a whole day mooching around in the airport in Paris before going to Denmark and playing, having done no training at all. They had changed hotels three times in one day in Italy, and were constantly eating their main meals on planes.

"Do you now consider yourself the leader of the group?" asked *La Razon*. "With respect," replied the intense skipper. "I always was."

In the rest of the interview, *El Caudillo* (the governor), as Rattin is known in Argentina, remarked that no team was favourite to win the World Cup, and that he felt it would be a very open tournament. He revealed that he had a cassette tape of his wife and two children that he listened to ten times a day. "If I could draw up my own contract for football at this level, I assure you I would put a clause in it that says I can only play in Buenos Aires and would never leave my country again." He did not come across as a particularly happy man away from home.

However, *El Caudillo* looked contented enough on 9 July, smiling for the cameras, when, as captain, he was assigned the task of raising the national flag to celebrate Nation Day. All the Argentine players wore their blazers and ties for the special ceremony, in which they were joined by the Spanish team who were in the same Birmingham-based first round group. The two Spanish speaking squads celebrated together with sherry and orange juice while the head of the Argentine delegation, Juan Santiago, headed off to Wolverhampton to present a special marzipan cake to handicapped children at a hospital. The cake was a football pitch with two teams lined up in Argentina and, group opponents, West Germany kits, complete with referee and linesmen. "We have come here on a sporting mission," Santiago told the local Birmingham press. "We've shown our gentlemanliness outside the stadium, and now we must show it inside the stadium" – famous last words in light of all that was to come, although one journalist did note that someone had squashed the marzipan referee.

"Everything went smoothly after the clear the air meeting in Austria," Marzolini tells me. "Everyone had their say and it produced a great team spirit that we took to England. The truth is we were still not very organised as a group and, in terms of preparation, we were still a long way behind the Europeans, not as strong as them in the upper body, for example, but at least we had good spirit now."

Marzolini reveals that, following the meeting with AFA president Valentin Suarez in Austria, it was actually a group of leading players who were picking the team. That might explain why Diego Simeone and Irueta, Boca Junior team-mates of Rattin, Marzolini and Roma, flew into England at the last moment, arriving on the day the final squad of 22 was announced, while Rojas 'the Tank', who was injured, and some disappointed reserves flew the other way.

Juan Carlos Lorenzo, the tactically-obsessed coach of Chile '62 had re-appeared again, appointed manager only one and half months before this World Cup. Lorenzo had spent the intervening four years as manager of Roma, and then Lazio, in defence-minded Italy, and so would inevitably revert to the same system that he had first introduced in Chile; the packed defence that suddenly breaks and counter attacks, tactics which had been fine-tuned by Minelli at La Copa Naciones in '64, which Argentina had won.

The Birmingham police headquarters was converted into the Argentina training ground and they were joined by Mr Aldridge, an old friend of Lorenzo's, and one of the English referees who had officiated in Argentina in the 1940s. The first practice was a special session dedicated to European refereeing. Eighteen of the twenty-five referees officiating at the World Cup were European, and ten of them were British.

"My players will have to get used to the system of refereeing that they apply in Europe," Lorenzo told the assembled press pack on that first day of training. "The players in Europe charge with the shoulder for high balls, and leave you lying on the floor. I hope my players will know how to obey the whistle without complaining and comply in every moment with what the referee orders." More famous last words.

After the training session with the English referee, 32-year-old goalkeeper Antonio Roma was given intense shot-stopping practice. He saved shots from four forwards, all pinging multiple balls at him at once, and then saved eight consecutive penalties before finally letting in the ninth, receiving an enthusiastic round of applause from a group of watching British policemen.

Roma, like Marzolini, had returned my call and I met him at the ArgentineFootballers' Cooperative. He's the same height as myself, but when we shook hands, I understood that I could never have been a goalkeeper. His hands were twice the size of mine. Roma confirmed that a group of leading players were picking the team in 1966, but that Lorenzo was in charge of organising the training and tactics, and that he stuck to his well-worn defensive guns. However Roma also confirmed other of Lorenzo's habits had died hard. Although the Argentine manager had not arranged any sneaking behind sheds this time, he was worried, arguably obsessed with the notion, that others may have. Hungarian espionage was well-known, according to La Razon, which claimed they had spies at every training ground, and Lorenzo was concerned that group opponents, Spain and Germany, might be at it as well, so he thought up a cunning counter-espionage plan.

Curiously, all the Argentine contingent – players, delegates, journalists, and even supporters – were staying together in the same hotel, the Albany in Birmingham. At breakfast, two days before the team's opening game, the players and journalists were given some secret information by Lorenzo and told to keep it hush hush. The training session that day was not going to take place at the police centre as planned, but had been switched to a secret location 50 kilometres away to avoid Spanish spies. "Not a word to anyone outside the Argentine circle, OK?" Lorenzo had told them. 'We didn't know whether to laugh or cry,' wrote the reporter in La Razon.

Lorenzo explained to the Argentine reporters that he had befriended an Aston Villa left-back who had informed him of a training ground called Lilleshall, and the player was turning up with a coach to take the Argentina players there. Again, the journalists and players 'didn't know whether to laugh or cry' when the (unnamed) left-back turned up, not with a coach, but a rickety old bus, 'the sort you would see in Buenos Aires about 30 years ago,' said La Razon. They all squeezed into it, players, journalists, and delegates. A horrendous journey around housing estates and winding roads followed. They got lost twice before finally arriving at their destination two hours later.

It was raining and cold but the players made for the Lilleshall changing rooms to prepare for the practice match. Lorenzo was going to run through the tactics for the opening game against Spain but, to the general incredulity of everyone, the manager announced that there was a snag. They had forgotten the kit. 'We didn't know whether to laugh or cry, again,' said La Razon. 'Two hours of travelling to disorientate the spies, Villalonga and Schön [the Spanish and German managers]. We were going to make a great secret game using the tactics to be used against the Spanish, and the result was that after so much detail we lacked the fundamental, and now it was decided that we would return to the police centre where the whole of the FBI would be watching us.'

Rattin was furious and vented his anger. "This is a result of the general disorganisation," he screamed at Lorenzo. "If you want to escape from the spies you should have done something serious and got the utility man to come here in the morning with the kit and get everything prepared." Just at that moment, the Aston Villa left-back came running along, shouting, 'I've got some kit, I've got some kit, it'll be here in 15 minutes." The players silently reboarded the bus to avoid the rain and waited for their kit to arrive. It was not ideal. Hired from a local gym, it was more like an assortment of items used for various sports. 6ft 4 Rattin played in a green vest with a pair of luminous long white boxing shorts that probably belonged to a heavyweight, and his socks were so small they were not worth wearing. 'It was comical,' commented *La Razon*.

The mock Spanish team featured manager Lorenzo pretending to be Spanish play-maker Luis Suarez in midfield, but he was also the match referee, and the Aston Villa left-back was at centre-forward. A group of English adolescent teenage girls arrived and watched, 'but we don't think they were spies,' mused *La Razon*, adding that, 'it was the worst possible image for our football.' Even more comical, the mock Spanish team won 1-0.

At 8pm, everybody boarded the cramped bus back, 'cold, tired and defrauded'. However, sometimes out of adversity comes good. The players started singing on the bus home, with the physio, at the back of the bus, leading the ruder numbers. The players sung their hearts out for the whole journey and many of the songs were directed at Lorenzo, who sat at the front of the bus, smiling. It may not have been a great day out for counter-espionage, but it had worked a treat for team bonding. Everybody arrived back at the hotel laughing.

"How did the training go?" asked AFA President Valentin Suarez.

"Very well, very well," everybody told him, "but where were you?" The AFA president explained that he had not made it to Lilleshall because the taxi he was in, which was trying to follow the bus, got lost somewhere on the journey. 'We didn't know whether to laugh or cry,' said *La Razon* for the umpteenth time.

Later in the evening, one of the delegates, the president of Banfield, spilled the beans, and told Valentin Suarez the truth; the lack of proper kit, the Aston Villa player, and the rude songs aimed at Lorenzo. According to *La Razon*, Suarez and the Banfield president sat up all night, drinking brandy and shaking their heads in despair.

But Argentina won their first match. They beat much-fancied Spain, the European champions, 2-1 at Villa Park. Spanish playmaker Luis Suarez had limped out of the game, but not, as has been erroneously reported since, because he was brutally fouled, but because he was already injured and doubtful to play before the match began. The defensive system Lorenzo had first introduced in '62, honed and tweaked by Minelli in '64, was now reaching perfection. Rotation, rhythm and speed. Argentina had impressed. Both goals were scored by the speedy Luis Artime, both made by the clever *enganche* Ermindo Onega. 'Argentina could be champions,' said the local press in Birmingham. The bookmakers changed the odds. The Brazilians were still favourites, but England and Argentina were joint second now.

Argentina's second group game was against West Germany at Villa Park in front of a 45,000 crowd: two strong teams, both candidates for the trophy. "That was a very hard match," says Marzolini. Lorenzo had said beforehand that his team would be happy with a draw. They achieved their aim, 0-0. It was either a fascinating tactical study, or an appallingly violent match, depending on which reports you read. Maybe both. The young German defender Franz Beckenbauer caught the eye. He marked Onega well, but when Germany attacked he would join the midfield, getting involved with Rattin on more than one occasion, and displaying a great range of passing.

Halfway through the second half, Albrecht, the Argentina central defender, became the first player sent off at the 1966 World Cup after chopping down Weber. "It was a bad one," admits Marzolini, although Lorenzo and some of the Argentinian bench disagreed, running onto the pitch to protest at the dismissal. Argentina had shown their cynical side. "What we saw today borders on the limit of the tolerance," claimed German manager Helmut Schön, adding that he was "pleased with the way [his] players maintained their cold blood and didn't respond to any irregularities."

Bert Trautman, the legendary German former Manchester City goalkeeper, a spectator at Villa Park, said, "I was a footballer for 15 years and I've never witnessed anything like what I saw today."

Tom Holley in the *Sunday People* described the match as 'a disgrace. Not just the sending off, but all the other fouls that were taking place in the match. If our players used the same methods, British football would die. Both teams, especially the Argentines, were prepared to go to the limit to maintain their goals intact.'

However, Billy Wright reckoned the Germans were more responsible for the fouling. "They were less skilful, and their clumsy challenges provoked the Argentinians," said the ex-England captain. Danny Blanchflower agreed: "Argentina could consider themselves unlucky to be a man down as Overath had committed a far worst foul on Gonzalez in the first half."

The *Sunday Telegraph* said, 'it was as if the two sides had made an agreement to act like each other and the only miracle was that no-one was maimed for life.' Coupled with the Uruguayan bore draw against England, *The Times* had taken offence to a certain style of play: 'The legend has grown up here that South Americans were gay, uninhibited players, colourful artists who shun physical contact. Uruguay and Argentina have dispelled that myth. So long as they do not lose, they do not worry whether spectators or opponents are bruised by their play.'

After the match against West Germany, the whole of the Argentina team received a warning from the FIFA disciplinary committee for 'unethical tackling'. They were offended and Lorenzo travelled to London to protest. He took a document containing a list of all the German fouls. "Why were Argentina being singled out?" asked Lorenzo. "Why were they being made scapegoats? Other teams had been just as bad, if not worse. What about the Bulgarians against Brazil – they had kicked Pelé out of the match. Albrecht's foul was nothing intentional, just an accident, the two players collided while going for the ball."

It is true that Weber had also tugged Albrecht down, but the German escaped punishment. Perhaps it was the behaviour of the Argentine bench that had most upset the disciplinary committee, not to mention Stanley Rous. While encroaching onto the pitch in the heat of the moment to contest a decision may have been common, and indeed tolerated, in South America, it was just the kind of affront to order that Rous abhorred and was determined to outlaw from international football following all the problems in Chile '62. The Englishman just would not allow such behaviour.

The first half of England's second match, against Mexico, followed the same pattern as the opening game versus Uruguay; the Central Americans sitting back, shunning attempts to attack, with the host country unable to break them down, offering very little excitement and goalmouth action.

The restless Wembley crowd were just beginning to voice their frustrations when, seven minutes before half-time, Bobby Charlton broke the deadlock with an angled shot from outside the penalty area. Roger Hunt made it 2-0 in the second half, but it had been another unconvincing performance. Ramsey's team selections were seriously questioned, especially the role of Jimmy Greaves.

Ramsey was having none of it though and reiterated his belief that England *will* win the World Cup. "Note I said will and not can," Ramsey told reporters, irritably. There was a certain arrogance about Ramsey that was not going down well abroad, or, at least, it was not fitting in with their stereotypical idea of how an English gentleman ought to behave. Weren't the English supposed to be polite and modest? Ramsey was anything but.

Sports minister Dennis Howell denied reports that the British public were not enthused by World Cup football. "They try to make a scandal because not every match is sold out, but that doesn't mean we're not enjoying it." Howell reminded reporters that there were only 5,000 people at England's matches in Chile, and Sir Stanley Rous said he was satisfied with the way the tournament was going. His only criticism was that the play was based on defence more than he had hoped.

Argentina cruised through their third and final group match, a 2-0 victory over Switzerland, in front of 30,000 at Hillsborough in Sheffield, with goals from Artime and Onega. They finished second in their group behind West Germany and so would play the winners of Group 1, England's group. English commentators observed that Argentina were the dark horses of the tournament, who had shown that when they want to play they can. Who would they meet in the quarter-final, England or Uruguay? There was a growing feeling that any of the remaining teams could win the competition, but Argentina were realistic contenders, especially now the Brazilians were out.

The holders had lost 3-1 to Portugal in their last group game, in which Pelé was singled out for special treatment for the second time in the tournament. He had been kicked badly in Brazil's opening 2-0 win against Bulgaria, forcing him to miss the 3-1 defeat to Hungary, in which he was sorely missed. Pelé returned for his team's final group game, only to be repeatedly kicked again. Vicente deliberately whacked his boot into Pelé's weakened ankle after half an hour, and, limping badly, Brazil's most important player continued until just before half-time, when Morais put him out of the match completely, with a brutal two-footed, jumping challenge.

Perhaps aware of his over-reaction against Argentina at the Nations Cup two years earlier, Pelé took it all in an extremely dignified manner, thus building his image as one of sport's true gentlemen. One of the lasting, and saddest, images of the '66 World Cup is the photo of Pelé being helped off the Goodison Park pitch by two medics, injured, with an overcoat draped over his shoulder. He showed no anger at the time but, after the match, declared that he would never play in a World Cup again, nor indeed, any other FIFA organised competition.

The president of the Brazilian federation, Joao Havelange, watched events from the stands with disgust. The Brazilians had been unhappy with the English referee in their opening match, who, they claimed, had let the Bulgarians kick Pelé at will. The events of the Portugal game would make Havelange determined to fight and change things at FIFA and he would eventually succeed Rous as president of FIFA in 1974, being in post until 1998. Back home, Brazilians took to the streets in protest, and there were a couple of suicides. Thankfully, Pelé later changed his mind about never appearing in a World Cup again and gave the football world the beauty of Mexico 1970, four years later.

In Birmingham, Silvio Marzolini was voted player of the group by the local press, and presented with a trophy and engraved tankard. He told me he was "surprised" to receive the award, but put his good performances down to how calm he felt when he played away from Argentina. "I always felt more nervous and under pressure playing in front of the Boca Juniors' crowd as they all know me." Back in '66, before the quarter-final opponents were known, Marzolini told the press, "The only team that can beat us is Germany," and added, tellingly, "England can't beat us if there's a good referee. The public and the conditions don't bother us, but the referee is fundamental." Already, before it was even known whether Argentina would play England or not, the emphasis was on the referee.

England beat France 2-0 in their last group game, so it would be England v Argentina after all in the first knockout round, the quarter-final, although manager Lorenzo, watching England at Wembley, misheard the West Germany score read out over the Tannoy, thinking they had drawn. The Germans had actually beaten Spain and therefore finished top of the group on goal average, meaning second-placed Argentina would face hosts England. Lorenzo spent the two-hour car journey back to Birmingham planning the tactics, with his assistant, for the quarter-final. When he arrived at the hotel, he announced to the players that they had an after dinner meeting in which he would reveal the plan to beat the Uruguayans. 'We didn't know whether to laugh or cry,' said *La Razon*, again.

England had beaten France with two goals from Roger Hunt, but again lacked flair. 'Stupid tactics – Greaves does not fit the system and he keeps getting caught offside', said the *Daily Mail*. Three up-front called for hard graft from all three men in the forward line, but there was a feeling that Greaves was not pulling his weight. This time Ramsey agreed with the criticism of his players. The next day he called them in for a showdown. In no uncertain terms the England players were told that their effort and performance was not good enough. Only hard-working Roger Hunt was exempt from criticism. The others were reminded just what it meant to wear an England shirt. Ramsey accused his players of complacency and letting the country down.

England versus France had not been without controversy either. While the English players and crowd were celebrating Hunt's first goal, Jacques Simon, the French play-maker, lay concussed on the Wembley turf. "It had been a bad one," admitted perpetrator Nobby Stiles to his team-mates afterwards, according to Geoff Hurst, but the referee had not seen it.

Stiles was hauled up in front of FIFA's disciplinary committee the next day, the first individual player in the 1966 World Cup to be cautioned by the committee for violent play. Ramsey was told by the English FA to leave Stiles out of the team, for the good of the game and the image of the country. Not a good public speaker, Ramsey was never at ease with the media. Hailing from working class Dagenham, and always slightly ashamed of his roots, he had been taking elocution lessons in an attempt to sound more posh, but they left him with an odd, ventriloquist's-dummy sounding voice that opened him up to ridicule – especially when he kept telling everyone England would win the World Cup. However, away from the media spotlight, Ramsey was always comfortable on the training ground, and during four years of precise preparation for 1966, the England manager had built up considerable respect from his players. Ever loyal, as a rule he defended them in public.

"If he goes I go," Ramsey told the FA. "I've asked Nobby if he meant it and he said he didn't. It was an accident, he caught him late, that's all, I'm not dropping him." Stiles, the toothless little hard man with plenty of bite, who wore contact lenses, stayed in the team.

But there would be other changes. Big changes. Despite the four years of prepara-tion, Ramsey had still to find a settled team. Or formation. Unlike their quarter-final oppo-nents, Argentina, who had been playing the same 4-3-1-2 formation, with virtually the same players in every match, England had been chopping and changing at every turn throughout the group stage.

In the first match, Ramsey had used John Connolly on the left wing, with Alan Ball on the right of midfield. For the second match, Terry Paine played on the right wing with Martin Peters in midfield and, in the third match, Ian Callaghan took the place of Paine on the right wing, but none of them had created many openings. This time, instead of changing the winger, Ramsey changed the system and, this time, it was not a copy of the Brazilians, but something completely new. Against Argentina Alf Ramsey introduced 4-4-2 to the world of football for the first time. The so-called 'wingless wonders', it is a formation that has outlasted any other.

4-4-2 meant Alan Ball and Martin Peters could play together for the first time, accom-panying Stiles and Bobby Charlton in the midfield. Although Ball and Peters would play on the right and left, respectively, they would move inside and back much more than out and out wingers. Peters had a sweet left foot and could cross a ball as well as any wide man.

England had experimented with the 4-4-2 formation before, with success, in friendlies against Poland and Germany in the autumn of 1965. Whether it was always Ramsey's inten-tion to use the system at some point in the World Cup, against the more difficult opponents, like Argentina, for example, or whether it was only introduced as a result of England's lack-lustre performances in the group games, is a secret Ramsey took with him to the grave.

Also, another significant change; the much questioned Jimmy Greaves had picked up an injury against France and was out. Whether Ramsey was considering dropping Greaves or not – he took that secret to the grave as well – Geoff Hurst came in to make his first World Cup appearance in the quarter-final.

Throughout all the changes, the defence had remained the same. Goalkeeper Gordon Banks behind right-back Ray Wilson, now of Everton, left-back George Cohen, with Jack Charlton of Leeds and Bobby Moore of West Ham in the middle. The two central defenders complemented each other. Charlton, the tall no-nonsense stopper, was the natural successor to Maurice Norman, while Moore, the cultured reader of the game, was responsible for starting as many of his team's own attacks as he was breaking down the opposition's.

Ramsey explained why England would beat Argentina: "Our defence is as good as theirs, but with fewer players – we will win the World Cup." AFA president Valentin Suarez was equally adamant why Argentina would win: "England never have more than three players in the adversary's box." Not that his own side piled forward in numbers very often.

Argentina coach Lorenzo had his two-pennorth, saying: "England only have three good players, the two Charltons and Bobby Moore, the rest play without intelligence. We'll have to be careful with Jack Charlton because he's dangerous on corners, and Stiles because he starts incidents. What we really hope for is a referee who won't be pressured by the Wembley crowd."

Again, pressure being applied to whoever the poor mite might be who was appointed as referee.

---- ❖ ----

Reading through the reams of articles published in Argentina before the quarter-final clash at a distance of over 40 years, it is almost uncanny – as if they were pre-empting what was going to happen. The Argentine reporters, just like the players, coaches and officials, were, to a man, very concerned about the choice of referee, and how the appointment would be made.

At a meeting at the Royal Gardens Hotel in Kensington, Sir Stanley Rous and five other European FIFA delegates decided upon a German referee, Rudolf Kreitlein, to officiate England v Argentina at Wembley, and an English referee, Jim Finney, for West Germany v Uruguay at Hillsborough. Smelling more conspiracy theories than the *Daily Express* on a slow news day, the South Americans cried foul. 'This is most unusual,' said *La Razon*, 'it should have been done by lottery.'

Clarin ran an article saying that they did not think it was right that the quarter-finals should be officiated by referees whose teams were still in the tournament and questioned 'why were there not any South American delegates present when the referees were chosen?' Good question. The practice has now been ended by FIFA.

Juan Santiago, the head of the AFA delegation, claimed they were told the meeting began at 1900 hours, but when they arrived, on time, they were informed by Rous that it had been changed to 1700 hours, and the selection had already been made. Marzolini shrugs when asked for his opinion: "They probably just arrived late," he says resignedly. This is interesting. Marzolini did not appear to be toeing the standard Stanley Rous/FIFA carve up theory that the Argentine press, and most football people in Argentina, adhere to – even today.

Many Argentinian reporters were also unhappy with the way Wembley had been chosen as the venue. However, it appears they had been wrongly informed by reading in an unofficial pre-World Cup brochure that the winners of Group 1 would be playing runners-up of Group 2 at Goodison Park, when, in actual fact, the decision was to be made by a FIFA committee after the quarter-finalists were known. Stanley Rous explained that the committee had chosen Wembley for England v Argentina simply because it had a greater capacity. This does seem to be a misunderstanding rather than a conspiracy, not that you can ever convince any South American of this. However, there doesn't seem to be any reasonable explanation why the Argentines were not allowed their allocated 20 minutes' practice on the Wembley turf the day before the match, which was their right according to the competition rules.

The day before the game, the entire Argentine squad were called to a special meeting about the referee. Valentin Suarez made a speech, but it wasn't his usual 'thank you' number. He told his players not to react to anything abnormal. If they lost, they must accept defeat with dignity. This seemed unequivocal and hardly likely to cause what was to happen the following afternoon, however, at the meeting Rattin was told by some of the twelve Argentine delegates that he had the right to an interpreter – on the pitch.

"That's what they said to him. They told him he had the right to an interpreter, but it was wrong," says Marzolini. There's an underlying theme to his comments. The delegates arrived late, and gave out wrong information to Rattin about an interpreter. He did not say it directly, but was he not implying that all those 'chiefs of tourism and days out' did not know what they were doing?

One English player also had a 'special' meeting the day before the quarter-final. According to Geoff Hurst, coaches Les Cocker and Harold Shepherdson "pinned Nobby Stiles against the dressing room wall – 'don't let Alf down – he's stuck his neck out for you,'" they told the little Manchester United player.

Again, creating and pre-empting a situation, rather than preventing it, Ramsey began his Wembley dressing room team talk with, "Gentlemen, I think we all know what kind of match we're in for this afternoon." Like Suarez, Ramsey also warned his men to stay calm, not to get involved, nor become provoked.

Striker Roger Hunt recalls, "Alf was wary of any South Americans. We knew they were technically very gifted, but also very cynical and would resort to all sorts to get their way. They would be difficult to beat, they weren't very ambitious and that meant we would have to work very hard to break them down and that proved exactly right."

At last, Wembley was completely sold out. Just as the Kinks song in the charts described, it was a sunny Saturday afternoon in summer time. World Cup fever was gripping the English nation for the first time. Group games over, this was the first of the knockout phase, and Argentina were a fancied team. It was going to be a tough, do-or-die contest.

On the morning of the match, *La Razon* alleged that there was an orchestrated campaign against the Argentina team and the English public were being fed a distorted image. 'You get the impression our men had accidentally got out of caravans to devour the blonde angels who make a pink ballet on the pitch.' They complained that, in England, 'whereas the brusque Germans are described as athletic, the Argentines are ruffians.'

Gone completely were the days of the 'masters v pupils' analogies in Argentina; that had not been mentioned once, and the great respect for English football that accompanied the coverage of the first matches between the two countries was by now conspicuous in its absence.

There is a classic photo: Bobby Moore in all-white, and Antonio Rattin, wearing Argentina's traditional blue and white stripes, the two captains smiling in the sun, exchanging pennants, in the centre of the Wembley pitch before the game. Between the pair, about half the size of Rattin, is the short, balding German referee Rudolf Kreitlein. He has a stern face.

It was hot, but there was a nervousness in the air. Union Jack flags were flying and the crowd were chanting. "Eng-land (clap, clap, clap), Eng-land (clap, clap, clap)." At 3pm, Argentina kicked off. Solari moved forward, but Peters intercepted, and Solari blatantly obstructed the England midfielder. The first foul of the match, in the very first seconds.

Roger Hunt remembers that foul set the tone for what was to follow: "They were physically imposing, but also very skilful. Everybody thought these were going to be our toughest opponents. They had won the mini-world cup in '64, their players had been around and were experienced, they could mix it and were right up there among the favourites.

"The game began and immediately I was conscious of their somewhat mischievous tactics. A defender called Marzolini was at it. I was strolling out of the penalty area when I felt a right whack on the back of my leg. The ball was nowhere near us and so I've spun around and he's looking at me with his arms outstretched as if to say, 'That's what we do.' I couldn't believe it."

The England left-back was George Cohen recalls that it didn't stop there: "Hard tackling is fine, but it was some of the snidey things they were doing – the spitting and pulling the short hairs on your neck, pulling your ear. They were trying to intimidate us. The trouble was when they found out they weren't going to get their way they fell into some of the worst excesses I've ever seen. We were trying to play push and run two-touch football, but they wouldn't allow it. They just fouled us immediately. One foul after another. It was a very physical game, but we were a strong side when necessary and stood up to it."

Watching footage of the match now Rattin is easy to spot. He cuts an unmistakable figure in the centre of the park, 6 ft 4 ins, with the captain's armband. The kingpin of his team, most of the Argentine play goes through him, subtle passes, often sideways and backwards, as the South Americans play neat triangles between themselves. Rattin points and shouts. When England move forward, he picks up Bobby Charlton. Likewise, it is clear that this time Nobby Stiles is going to track playmaker Ermindo Onega, who had been left to roam at will by England, with damaging consequences, in the Maracana, two years previously.

What little flow there was in the game quickly disintegrated; a few innocuous chal-lenges here and there, but the referee blew his whistle for every single one of them. Stop-start, the game lacked fluidity, became nigglesome, difficult to watch, and tough to play in. The first bad foul came from Nobby Stiles, who scythed down Ferreiro. The referee gave the free kick, but did not book Stiles, although he did book Ferreiro a few minutes later for a foul on Peters – fuel to the Argentine belief that the Europeans were out to get them.

Gonzalez and Solari produced some good play in the middle of the pitch, but the ball always ended up back with the Argentine full backs or goalkeeper. It was frustrating and the English crowd did not like it. They began a slow hand clap. "I wish they wouldn't do that," remarked Jimmy Hill, the BBC match summariser.

A long ball forward was intercepted by Moore, who jumped up and caught it with both hands. It looked comical and would be an automatic yellow card offence today, but at that time this was not considered worthy of a booking. The free kick was given, without the England captain even being spoken to by the referee. Then Hunt and Rattin collided tamely, but the referee, 'inexplicably', according to *La Razon*, gave a free kick to England. Next Perfumo fouled Ball and the referee took Perfumo's name. 'Fussy' and 'authori-tarian' are words that have been used to describe the German official, and not just by South American journalists. 'He collected names in his notebook like a schoolboy collecting train numbers,' said Maurice Smith in the *Daily Mail*.

Within the first half an hour, the names of Solari, Perfumo and, strangely, Bobby Charlton were all in Kreitlein's book. We think, although it is not clear. Charlton did not realise he had had his name taken until 32 years later when he looked up his player profile during the 1998 World Cup in France. He thought the computer was wrong, but upon enquiry was shocked to learn he did not have a clean record. FIFA confirmed that Charlton's one and only international booking came in the 1966 quarter-final.

On 37 minutes an Argentina attack broke down. England cleared the ball out to Cohen and Artime caught him. It was not a bad challenge, but the Argentine striker was added to Kreitlein's list. Moore took the free kick, short to Bobby Charlton, who shot wide. The camera followed the ball and, as it zoomed back, it found Rattin talking to the referee in the middle of the pitch, the giant Argentinian pointing to his captain's armband. There appeared to be a breakdown in communication. Rattin continued pointing at his armband, although it was not clear what was going on. Then suddenly the referee raised his arm, and, to the general astonishment of all, sent Rattin off.

The imposing figure of the Argentine skipper loomed over the tiny referee. With arms open and a look of disbelief on his face, he made the classic latin shoulder-shrugging gesture – *que pasa?* (what's going on?). Rattin's team-mates surrounded the referee. Their captain was still pointing at his armband, the Argentina players were pointing at the referee, but the official continued to point his finger firmly in the direction of the changing rooms.

Manager Lorenzo came onto the pitch, as did the physio, and then all the Argentine reserves. FIFA officials were next onto the field of play, and then the police. It was a mêlée. A mess. A South American football scene was being played out at Wembley. Rattin had been sent off, but he was simply refusing to go.

At one point it looked as if the whole Argentina team were going to leave the field. Albrecht marched them off in protest, but FIFA officials and the head of referees, Ken Aston, the man who had been in the middle of the infamous Battle of Santiago in 1962, talked, in turn, to referee Kreitlein and then to Rattin. None of them understood one other, but Aston indicated to Rattin that he must leave the pitch.

The English players were not involved as the arguing and gesticulating continued. They just talked amongst themselves, stretching, keeping their cool in the sun, the importance of which Ramsey had stressed earlier. The Wembley crowd burst into song, "Oh, why are we waiting, why are we waiting?" Roger Hunt stood and watched the incident unfold over its 11-minute duration. "Rattin wanted the game abandoned, they all did," he says. "One of the FIFA guys came on and got the message across that very soon, we would be awarded the game. That got things moving a bit."

Hunt recalls a sideshow occurring around this point: "Some of us were sitting around waiting for the game to get going again when suddenly a roar went up around Wembley. I looked up at the scoreboard and it read, PORTUGAL 0 NORTH KOREA 3. The crowd went berserk. Here's the Argentinian captain refusing to walk and the crowd are cheering on the Koreans. That was surreal."

Finally, Rattin reluctantly left the field and began his slow walk around the side of the pitch. The official film of the '66 World Cup entitled *Goal* followed Rattin's every step. Accompanied by the physio, he was led along the touchline, occasionally stopping and looking back to watch some of the restarted match, before continuing on his way again. The crowd shouted and threw things at him, chocolates and fruit. Rattin stared back.

When he arrived at the corner of the pitch, Rattin stopped and wiped his hands on the Union Jack corner flag, or, rather, gave it a twist, considered an action of disrespect in Argentina. He watched some more play before recommencing the slow dramatic walk. In front of the royal box he sat down on the royal red carpet and nonchantly watched the end of the first half rather than retiring to the dressing room as the Laws of the Game required him to do. Was this meant to be an insult to the Queen?

"It wasn't a dirty game," Marzolini tells me. "The referee kept breaking the game up. Rattin wanted an interpreter. His gesture to the referee had been misunderstood." Marzolini shakes his head at the ridiculousness of it all. "It's funny, they threw chocolate at him and he ate it," he says, laughing.

"The sending off was strange because Rattin was dismissed not for fouling but for talking to the referee and trying to run the game," says Cohen. "It was a shame in a way because there's no doubt he was an outstanding player. In fact they were a very, very good technical side, wonderful really, maybe the best we played at that World Cup."

"We knew we couldn't win now," Marzolini says. "Our only hope was to keep it at 0-0 through to the end of extra-time, and then it would be decided by the toss of a coin." Incredible as it may seem, in 1966, before the penalty shootout had been conceived, drawn matches were to be decided by heads or tails.

In the second half, with Rattin now removed from the pitch side, England made heavy work of the extra man – that old football cliché, 'It's more difficult to play against ten men' proving true. With every Argentina player sitting deep, protecting their goal, England were reduced to long range shots from Charlton, Hunt and Ball. Even without Rattin marking him anymore, Bobby Charlton was having an off day. The crowd were getting more and more frustrated.

"We were playing well with ten men," says Marzolini. "We kept the ball and played good possession football. Roma the goalkeeper would roll the ball out to me ... I'd knock it inside to Gonzalez ... he'd play it back to me ... and I'd knock it back to Roma again. The England players would come over to my side of the pitch, on the left, to mark me … so Roma would roll it out to Ferreiro on the right. The home crowd didn't like the way their team was playing, and what impressed me was that it felt like the English crowd were with us, applauding our play." A partisan English crowd were applauding the Argentinians? Has he got that right?

Goalkeeper Roma agrees: "It was like a training workout and we were playing well. The crowd were with us, applauding our possession. The more we played possession and kept the ball moving, the more the Wembley crowd were with us and applauding our play."

Suddenly it dawns on me. I had worked in Spain in the early '90s. The game was slower out there. Teams built from the back more than they did in England, and, as they did so, the crowd responded with a flamenco clap as the players passed the ball around. It is a slowish clap, with six beats, the emphasis always on the sixth beat. That rhythm would be known in Argentina too, and sometimes they chant 'ole' in the build up.

But the pace and rhythm of the latin clap is similar to the British slow hand clap, and the British slow hand clap is most definitely not a show of appreciation, but a rather rude and noisy demonstration of intense displeasure. The more I thought about it the more I thought there was no way the English crowd would have been applauding the Argentina players constantly playing the ball back to their own goalkeeper in a World Cup quarter-final against England at Wembley! It is ludicrous to even think they would. I did not have the heart to tell either Roma or Marzolini the truth. It did give me pause for thought about the gulf of understanding between the two peoples.

Fouls continued to break up the play. Roma claims that on a corner, at the beginning of the second half, Jack Charlton stamped on him while he was on the ground, ramming his studs into his stomach: "I was winded for the rest of the match," he says, wincing at the memory. Charlton was booked, but several England players have also spoken of things going on off the ball from the Argentines.

Twenty minutes into the second half there was a good chance for Argentina. Onega, socks rolled down, played a precise through ball for Mas to sprint onto, but his shot flashed past the post. Surely, ten-man Argentina could not win it?

Perhaps sensing they could, they set up another rare attack as the match entered the final 15 minutes. Ferreiro, the right-back, moved forward, deep into the English half, the first time he had crossed the halfway line in the second half. But he pushed too far forward and got caught offside. The ball went out of play. Wilson took the throw-in quickly to Moore, and the captain side-footed it back to Wilson, who played it down the line to Peters on the left, while Ferreiro was still up the other end of the pitch. Peters had space for the first time in the match. Perfumo, the centre-half, moved across to cover for the missing

Ferreiro, but, as he did so, Peters curled over a first time cross. Hurst ghosted in at the near post and glanced the ball past Roma with his head. "YEEEEESSS!" The crowd let out all their pent up frustration. At last a breakthrough. The Argentine players appealed in vain for offside.

It was a goal straight off the training pitch, as Geoff Hurst explains: "The near post cross – we'd worked on that move time and time again under manager Ron Greenwood at West Ham, who took the idea originally from the Hungarians in '53. One day Ron put down cones as full backs and the wingers had to run and cross the ball before they reached the cone, bending the ball around the cone so it landed in the space between the goal-keeper and his back line of defenders. It was the task of the forwards to anticipate the cross and attack the ball before the goalkeeper or defenders could reach it. When we got it right, there was little the opposition could do about it."

Roma disagrees: "I swear to this day, he didn't head it properly. As the ball came over I shaped up for the header and had the right side of the goal covered, but Hurst was stretching and didn't connect properly. It sort of skimmed off his head and went into the other side of the goal."

Perhaps not surprisingly, Hurst does not agree with Roma's version of events. For the England striker, it was a well-rehearsed glancing header. Roma recalls that the Argentina players were a little disappointed with Ferreiro for pushing up so far and getting caught out of position. The instructions had been to stay back.

Argentina had no choice but to attack, and only 15 minutes to rescue something from the game. They nearly equalised towards the end. Marzolini, for the first time in the match, moved forward on the left flank, and Mas's shot brushed past the post. However, with ten men against a strong England defence, and with a team so set up to defend, Argentina were unable to create any other openings.

Final Score, England 1 Argentina 0. And now the madness really begins. As the referee tried to leave the pitch, he was surrounded by Argentinian reserves and staff. Pastoriza, the player who had fought with Rattin on the warm up tour, now showed his support for his captain by taking a swipe at Herr Kreitlein. The police were quickly on the scene and surrounded the official. 'Police escorts and riots frequently occur in South America, but this was one of the most disgraceful exhibitions seen on a football pitch,' said the *News of the World*.

Not all the Argentina players were involved in the fracas. Some did their best to remember Valentin Suarez's words, "if we lose, we must lose gracefully". They shook hands and tried to swap shirts, but Alf Ramsey, in a school-masterly fashion, prevented them from doing so. In one famous picture, which adorns the front of this book and has come to symbolise the enmity between England and Argentina, stern-faced Ramsey is tugging on a bare-chested George Cohen's England top as the full-back tries to hand it to Mas.

"I remember it really well," Cohen tells me. "When the famous picture was taken at the end of the game I was about to change shirts with this guy. He was insisting on having it. Alf saw what was happening and rushed over and told me, 'you're not changing shirts with *him*.' Or words to that effect. By which time the sleeve of that shirt must have been about three feet long. Alf was incensed by the way Argentina had played and would not allow any of the usual post-match niceties."

However, Marzolini managed to successfully exchange shirts with Bobby Charlton. "It's a lovely shirt, quality material," he says. "I wore it in bed as a pyjama for years. Full of holes now, but I've still got it up in my attic somewhere."

There are so many different versions of what happened next, and none of them correspond much. It is almost impossible to gauge what actually went on once all the arguing players, referee, officials, and police went down the tunnel, like a whirl of hot air in front of the bemused Wembley crowd. It seems that a group of Argentinian journalists went down the tunnel with the players and skirmishes broke out. *La Razon* and *Clarin* both claim the police would not let them near the dressing rooms to interview the players, and that the police were excessive in their use of the truncheon.

George Cohen remembers this clearly, although he didn't actually see any of it. "There was a lot of commotion in the tunnel after the game. Nobody was allowed out of our dressing room, so we didn't see it. The door was shut and with Alf, Harold Shepherdson and Les Cocker in with us, there was no way we were going anywhere. There was banging on the door, but I can't say who it was. The police were out there anyway, so no-one was getting in."

Another culture clash? In South America it was, and is, standard procedure for the press to swarm around the players upon the final whistle, shoving microphones and cameras in their faces, chasing them down the tunnel for want of a word. In England that would never have been allowed. Even so, the Argentine journalists seem to have been able to get the immediate post-match thoughts of virtually every angry Argentine player.

Solari: "Who can win against a referee? It's impossible. We were the better team."

Gonzalez: "The expulsion of Rattin has no justification. All match, the referee was sentencing our players and pardoning every England foul."

Roma, the goalkeeper: "I don't want to say anything. It's unjust, a lack of etiquette, I don't want to speak."

Mas: "It's incredible, I never thought they'd eliminate us in this manner. I never thought this could happen in a World Cup."

Ferreiro: "I really can't believe it. The Germans kicked us all the time and nothing happened, but they sent off Albrecht, and now they sent off Rattin because he's correctly questioning a foul that only exists in the imagination of the referee. I think we played well. If Rattin had not been sent off, we would have won, for sure."

Albrecht: "Until Rattin was sent off we were controlling the game. They could only shoot from distance. They were no danger to us. Even with ten men we were the better team."

Onega: "Our plan was working to perfection. I'm sure we would have won if we had continued with eleven."

The England players obviously see it differently. Although official post-match conferences were not part of World Cup football in those days, and no English newspaper carried quotes from England players the following day, later, various members of the team have claimed things were going on off the ball; repulsive things like spitting, kicking and the pinching of the upper arm disguised as a handshake. Geoff Hurst also claims the Argentina players tried to smash the English dressing room door down after the game. "They all wanted to fight afterwards and threw a chair through our dressing room door. Jack Charlton, Nobby Stiles and Alan Ball were standing behind the door, shouting at Ramsey to let the Argentines in. "I'll fight them all," stormed Charlton.

Marzolini and Roma, as you would expect, deny this. "No, that's not true at all. We just went straight to our changing room and sat dejected." Maybe it was the journalists trying to smash the England dressing room door down.

Whatever was going on, it was in the tunnel, in the middle of the mayhem, that BBC commentator Kenneth Wolstenholme thrust a microphone under Alf Ramsey's nose. It was in the middle of the whirlwind that Ramsey said *it* – the word that would echo around South America for years to come, never quite forgotten. Not the most diplomatic of men, what the England manager actually said, word for word, was, "England's best football will come against a team that come out to play football and not act as animals." But only the most naïve man could not expect the press to pounce on that feed line.

'ANIMALS', cried the Sunday papers the next day. The *News of the World* plastered the single word headline over its back page: 'England are through to the semis but only after a World Cup quarter-final against wild bulls of the pampas, who reduced football to a disgraceful soccer fandango.' However, the same paper was also very critical of Kreitlein. Reg Drury wrote, 'Football was reduced to an all-in wrestling brawl for which I place much criticism on the ref who was too authoritarian and fussy.'

'IS THIS REALLY FOOTBALL?' asked the *Sunday Mirror* in its back page headline, although it also stated that the referee was to blame.

The *Sunday Express* spoke of the most shameful scenes ever seen at a match. 'Butchers of Buenos Aires,' said the *Sunday Telegraph*. 'They converted football into a farce.' Their correspondent David Miller said, 'The Argentinians had cultured feet mixed with an infant school mentality.'

Rattin and his men did receive support from some surprising quarters. Maurice Smith in the *Sunday People* said, 'The play wasn't so brutal as the ref made out. If we're honest England also fouled, but they weren't punished so strongly.' The foul count showed that England had in fact committed 11 fouls to Argentina's 9 in the first half, and England had made 10 to Argentina's 8 in the second. Indeed Rattin was not dismissed for any kind of physical or free-kick offence at all. He was sent off for arguing with the referee.

Clarin put a large picture of Kreitlein on its front page, under the headline 'THE CULPRIT – A Broken Dream And An Unjust England Success'. Referring its readers to an article written two days before the match about the appointment of the referees, *Clarin*, as indeed did all the Argentine papers, claimed they had predicted what was going to happen, and, to be fair, they had. They had all complained about the way Stanley Rous had chosen the referee, warning there would be problems.

'SCANDAL IN WEMBLEY', said *La Razon*, who told their readers, 'we had said this would happen.'

'It was an abnormal match', said *Clarin*. 'Argentina was prejudiced by a bad referee. Wembley had no fair play. There is a mafia of European referees that fix everything.' *La*

Razon vented its anger: 'The England team is in ridicule. We applaud Rattin. The German referee favoured the English, expelling Rattin without reason, and the English referee favoured the Germans by sending off Troche and Silva.' This referred to events that same afternoon at Hillsborough, where the West Germans had defeated Uruguay 4-0, although they had only led 1-0 at the time of the two dismissals. English referee Jim Finney had also denied Uruguay a penalty when a shot was handled on the line and the game turned nasty after that incident. All match reports state that the Germans were fouling as much as the Uruguayans and indeed sparked the dismissals with their foul play. Emmerich kicked Uruguayan captain Troche, who retaliated by kicking him back, but only Troche was sent off. Five minutes later, Silva was ordered to leave the field for a retaliatory foul. The nine remaining Uruguayans held on remarkably well, keeping the score at 1-0, and still clinging on to hope with occasional counter-attacks, until 20 minutes from the end when the floodgates opened and Germany scored three. The police had to escort the players off the pitch.

The conspiracy theory was complete. In the eyes of South America, it had all been orchestrated, a 'complot', to ensure England and Germany would go through. Joao Havelange, the Brazilian football president, already incensed by the way his team had been kicked out of the competition, spoke of "political referees, hand picked by Stanley Rous" and vowed to start putting the wheels in motion to oust the Englishman. In the Uruguayan capital Montevideo, the British embassy was surrounded and stoned by an angry mob.

The Times, naturally, had a different perspective on events and was very strong in its condemnation of both the Argentines and Uruguayans, not in its sports pages, but its main editorial. 'The exemplary behaviour of the sporting Brazilians aside, the South American effort in this World Cup has been dismal. Their whole attitude has been negative. They are killing the game in more ways than one, not least in certain instances by undisciplined, cynical behaviour and flaunting of authority.'

Interestingly, the BBC world service sided with Argentina: 'The referee notably favoured the English, giving them fouls and booking Argentinians, leaving them with inferior numbers after the unjust and suspicious sending off of Rattin. The partiality of the referee gave the victory to England.'

Unlike Ramsey, the old smooth-talking president of AFA, Valentin Suarez, tried to be as diplomatic as he could in the immediate aftermath. "Without wishing my words to be interpreted as a protest," he began, "the referee was decisive in the English triumph. We must accept defeat with the same modesty as if we triumph, but it wasn't an impartial referee. I don't think Argentina would have lost if things had gone normally; our team played slowly because the game was developing and they were saving their legs."

'What exactly did Rattin do?' asked *La Razon*. Rattin himself explained, "In the chat before the match, it was pointed out to me that if a problem arose, then as captain, I had the right to ask for an interpreter, and that's what I did, but the first time I asked the referee, he pretended to be deaf, and the second time he just showed me the way to the changing rooms."

The next day, a sunny Sunday afternoon in London, the Argentine press tracked down Kreitlein to a deck chair in Kensington Park. There is a photo of him, sitting alone, reading a book. "I don't want to talk about it," he said, but after some persistence, no doubt disturbing his reading, he informed the journalists that Rattin had been sent off for "violence of the tongue". "I didn't understand what he had said, but I didn't need to because I could read it on his face. He followed me all over the pitch and I got angry. I had no choice but to send him off. They banged on my door and were insulting me after the match. I really don't want to talk about it anymore."

As the Argentinians finished packing their bags at their hotel in Birmingham the following day, things took a turn for the even worse when news of FIFA's strict disciplinary committee's sanctions came through. Rous had kept to his pre-tournament promise: Rattin was suspended for four games, Ferreiro three, and Onega three for spitting in the face of a FIFA official. AFA were fined 100 Swiss francs for the behaviour of the whole team, and Argentina would not be allowed to compete in the 1970 World Cup unless AFA could give assurances over the conduct of its players and officials.

Now the Argentinians were livid. Juan Santiago, the head of delegation, the man who had delivered the marzipan cake and spoken of gentlemanliness when the squad first arrived in England, said Stanley Rous was a "modern pirate Morgan" and described FIFA as "a dictatorship". The only thing they wanted to do now was "leave this country as soon as possible."

"They've really stuck the knife in now," said Lorenzo, "but as manager of the team, I must stress the only one to blame for all that happened is the German referee who used two different criteria – one, the worst, for us, the other, much smoother, for the English. I don't blame the England team in any way, but the incapacity of Kreitlein to referee a match that was too big for him. Not one English player was injured; they were all fine after the match, although you'd think differently if you heard some of the things that have been said. How many players have been injured by the actions of our lads against Spain, Germany, Switzerland and England? None."

Valentin Suarez, as ever, appealed for calm. "We must analyse all this carefully and calmly," was his contribution. The following day the executive committee of the South American football federation, including delegates from Brazil, Uruguay, Chile, Peru, Bolivia and Venezuela, rejected the ruling that Argentina should be suspended from the 1970 World Cup. They issued a statement: 'We think that asking assurances from Argentina cannot be given by that commission because it exceeds their powers.' They also declared a special meeting of the South American Confederation in Buenos Aires to discuss 'all our difficulties in the World Cup.' This row would rumble on and on.

As if rubbing salt into already open and stinging wounds, a copy of an English newspaper with the 'ANIMALS' headline was lying in the lobby of Argentina's Birmingham hotel. "Ramsey is an abnormal man," muttered Lorenzo. "His comments are not worth responding to."

The FIFA disciplinary committee agreed, also making Ramsey apologise for his remarks. He did so reluctantly, issuing a statement that I am not really sure constitutes an apology or not: "I was under pressure at the moment to say something, and was unfortunate in my choice of words." If ever any Argentinian acknowledges FIFA's telling off of the England manager they will immediately, and possibly rightly, point to how poor Ramsey's apology was and how FIFA failed to ensure a proper one was elicited. Indeed, in Argentina, not one reporter, nor columnist, doubted the conspiracy theory. Photos of

Stanley Rous, whose name was rarely mentioned in the English press, appeared in most Argentina newspapers alongside explanations of how the whole World Cup was fixed. 'Rudolf Kreitlein, a German referee, was the simple executor of a sinister plan that leaves the England team with a free road to the final,' said *Clarin.* 'It was the culmination of a plan devised in the offices of FIFA a long time ago.'

Some of the stuff written in Argentina is very strong. *Clarin, La Razon, La Nacion,* the three biggest selling newspapers, let loose. Here is a medley of some of the abuse: 'FIFA is a dictatorship' ... 'the World Cup is a fraud' ... 'FIFA are fascists' ... 'the referees are like the women of the night who do it for money' ... 'there was a gentlemen's agreement – an Anglo-German agreement to ensure the final will be between blond Bobby Charlton and blond Uwe Seeler' ... 'Argentina is victim of a scientifically pre-meditated exercise by FIFA' ... 'God save the Queen and God save us from FIFA.'

The anger was increased, and the conspiracy theory further enhanced, by the fact that nobody in the English press had bothered to mention how the referees were chosen, too busy concentrating on their 'Butchers of Buenos Aires' headlines. 'In not one English daily have we read about the shameful collusion between the English delegates and FIFA, not one criticism of the way they are manipulating the tournament, nor a word about the way they hand-picked referees when it should be done by lottery,' moaned *Clarin.*

In a rather novel thought, *Clarin* informed its readers that the English public were in shame over what had happened. 'The English papers are delinquents, thieves, but we don't have that opinion of England or the English people. Despite this distorted image of Argentina, given to the British public, and the orchestrated insults, the typical Englishmen, the sane public opinion, the sensitive English people that we meet in the street every day, have not been fooled by its gutter press which is rotten by bribes from FIFA delegates.' 'England,' *Clarin* concluded, had been 'sunk in the mud of indecency by its football manager, a seller of lies, a terrorised individual who will lose his job if his team doesn't become champions. The country recognises this and England celebrated its victory timidly yesterday. The true England is in shame, the public celebrate with a bitter taste.'

Picking up on Ramsey's ethnical background, *Clarin* rounded off its rant with, 'Ramsey is a gypsy dressed as an Englishman.'

The Argentina players were treated like heroes when they landed in Buenos Aires, dubbed as 'Honourable Winners' and feted by thousands at the airport. The biggest cheers were for Rattin. The new president, General Ongania, sent a message to the players congratulating them on their brilliant campaign, carried out with "courage and fighting spirit." It was the military government who had called for the public to greet the returning players. General Ongania was desperately keen to have his photo taken with Rattin.

When the 1966 Cabinet papers were made public in 2006, Foreign Office files report how England's victory against Argentina in the 1966 World Cup provoked an anti-British backlash in Buenos Aires. A dispatch from the British embassy in Buenos Aires describes how, while the Argentines were given a 'tumultuous' heroes' homecoming welcome, the British embassy was receiving 'hundreds of abusive phone calls', annoyed that the World Cup had been snatched from their team by the German referee whose appointment was part of a 'blatant conspiracy to defraud the South Americans and keep the trophy in Europe.'

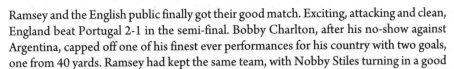

Ramsey and the English public finally got their good match. Exciting, attacking and clean, England beat Portugal 2-1 in the semi-final. Bobby Charlton, after his no-show against Argentina, capped off one of his finest ever performances for his country with two goals, one from 40 yards. Ramsey had kept the same team, with Nobby Stiles turning in a good performance as well, keeping Eusebio, the tournament's top scorer, quiet.

Ramsey kept the same line up for the final as well, another sunny Saturday after-noon, one week on from the match against Argentina. England's famous 4-2 victory over West Germany after extra time arrived thanks to three goals from Geoff Hurst and one from Martin Peters. Needless to say, the 'was it over the line or not' controversy of England's crucial third goal suited the South American conspiracy theorists down to the ground.

After the hot-tempered shouting in print the week before, the Argentinian press had now calmed down considerably, revising their opinion of the English and actually praising the new world champions. Impressed with the way England had played against Portugal and West Germany, *La Nacion* concluded that this style of play 'produces a lot of goal-mouth action which is what the British public want. We admire the way they all fight for each other and their spirit.' There were, however, still a few digs about the way Nobby Stiles protested a lot in the final, but, unlike Rattin, without being so much as cautioned. They also noted both sides' lack of skill, which ignored their side's wholly negative approach to football. But by now truth and proportionality had divested themselves from bombasticism when it came to England versus Argentina.

England 1 (Hurst 77')
Argentina 0
Saturday 23 July 1966. Wembley Stadium, London. World Cup Quarter-Final. Attendance: 90,000
Referee: Rudolf Kreitlein (West Germany)

England: Gordon Banks (Leicester), George Cohen (Fulham), Ray Wilson (Everton), Jack Charlton (Leeds), Bobby Moore(c) (West Ham), Alan Ball (Everton), Nobby Stiles (Manchester Utd), Bobby Charlton (Manchester Utd), Martin Peters (West Ham), Geoff Hurst (West Ham), Roger Hunt (Liverpool)
Manager: Alf Ramsey

Argentina: Antonio Roma (Boca Jnrs), Roberto Ferreiro (Independiente), Silvio Marzolini (Boca Jnrs), Roberto Perfumo (Racing), José Albrecht (San Lorenzo), Antonio Rattin(c) (Boca Jnrs), Jorge Solari (River Plate), Alberto Gonzalez (Boca Jnrs), Ermindo Onega (River Plate), Luis Artime (Independiente), Oscar Mas (River Plate)
Manager: Juan Carlos Lorenzo

WITH THE ANIMALS

NOT FOR want of trying had I been unable to find the truth. Both the English and Argentinian Football Associations had kindly allowed me into the archives, to look through their files; maybe the first time those old documents had been dusted down since they were written in 1966, but I was none the wiser. There were no clues, just pages of accounts and minutes of meetings regarding the organisation of the World Cup, but no mention anywhere of the crucial meeting at the Royal Gardens Hotel where the referees were chosen, or drawn from a hat, or hand-picked by Stanley Rous, whichever you choose to believe.

All the European delegates present at that infamous meeting, and the South American ones not present, were dead now.

I did not expect a reply when I sent a letter to the Argentine Congress, but there was no harm in trying. A week later I was surprised to receive a phone call from Eduardo, a secretary at the Congress, informing me that if I could send a fax with a list of questions, then the senator would be happy to discuss past matches between Argentina and England.

The Argentinian Congress is an impressive building; a dome on the roof and a large square in front, that looks down to 'La Casa Rosada' (The Pink House), the presidential building, scene of many triumphs and stirring speeches. Juan and Evita Peron, General Galtieri and Diego Maradona have all whipped up the fervour of the crowds from the presidential balcony.

Outside the Congress, there was a noisy demonstration; old age pensioners banging drums and chanting against cutbacks in their allowances. A frail old woman with a walking stick staggered up to the microphone. She looked as if she would barely be able to speak, but from somewhere in her lungs, produced a powerful oration. Addressing her audience as "comrades", and with a delivery not too dissimilar to Evita Peron, she covered everything, from the war in Iraq to cuts in pensions, and she spoke of conspiracies.

I met Eduardo the secretary in the lobby as arranged, and after a series of security checks, was escorted into the lift, and along the corridors of power, to an office on the sixth floor. "Come in," said the senator as he stood up from behind his desk. He was a very tall man, immaculately dressed, and looking very healthy, much younger than his 67 years.

"I love London. It's my favourite city in the world," he said as we shook hands, "and I enjoy watching English football too. It's different, perhaps a bit naïve defensively, but good to watch. You can watch a match in England and the home team can be winning by two or three goals, and then the match finishes 3-4. That never happens here, 2-0 to the home team and you might as well go home." He loomed over me, just as he had loomed over the German referee at Wembley in '66.

Sitting back behind his desk, Senator Rattin explained how he had spent three months in England in the late 1970s, studying English football and, at one time, was Sheffield United's representative in South America. "In those days, English football didn't allow agents. They would fine a team, or dock points, if they were dealing with an intermediary, so Sheffield United gave me a work permit, and I was officially their representative in South America. I recommended Alex Sabella of River Plate to them for £160,000 because I could see he had the characteristics to adapt to English football. Two years later, they sold him to Leeds for £400,000. So, for my vision, they gained £240,000. They gifted me a load of steel for my work," he says, laughing.

"My big error, though, was not learning English. If I had studied the language perhaps I'd be living in England today as an agent or representative of a club. Imagine that, Rattin the Englishman!"

The really big error though, was surely Sheffield United's. The Second Division side nearly bought the teenage Diego Maradona in 1978, but, in the end, manager Harry Haslam thought the £200,000 asking price was too high for an unproven player.

Rattin could talk all day about his love of England's taxis, parks and shops, but the idea is to talk about the matches he played in against England. He responds obligingly, starting with the 1962 World Cup. "That was the worst Argentinian team I ever played in. There was no expectation for us to do well in Chile. It wasn't a serious team. It was all improvised in that era. The coach Lorenzo arrived from European football a couple of weeks beforehand with different ideas that we'd never heard of before, and one little anecdote I can give you is that, during a practice match, he told us about the idea of the *libero* [sweeper, or free man behind the defence]. We'd never heard of it. He gave one of the players a different coloured bib from everyone else so we could see the movements of the *libero* around the pitch, but it was all a bit late to be trying out new ideas, just before the World Cup was about to begin."

"Against England in '62, Lorenzo told me to mark Johnny Haynes. Those were my instructions, follow the number 10 all over the pitch, and I remember Bobby Charlton, he was only 21, but he was phenomonal even then – he won the match for England that day."

Without any prompting, Rattin moves on to the 1964 Nations Cup match against England in Brazil. "Did you know that we were invited to that tournament at the last moment in place of Italy? We didn't do any training, but just met up at AFA's headquarters a few days beforehand, took a coach to the airport, and ended up winning all three matches without conceding a single goal – so much for preparation, ay! It was a prestigious tournament. We beat Portugal in the Maracana, then Brazil 3-0 in Sao Paulo – boy, what a merry dance we led them that day, and then we beat England 1-0 in the Maracana. Everything had been prepared for the Brazilians to win the tournament. They were commemorating their victories at the '58 and '62 World Cups, and everything had been planned for a big celebration, but we won it and ruined their big party!

"I remember the prize-giving ceremony; even though we won the Brazilian players were all given a gold medal with their names engraved on it, but they just gave us a pen each, like this one," he says, holding up a biro.

He remembered the incident with Peter Thompson, just before half-time. "He clattered into Rendo, a bad foul. There was a bit of a scuffle, and Rendo was only small, so I went over to sort it out." *La Nacion* says that Rattin hit Thompson. "Thompson had a very good game that day, England's best player, and I remember Banks. It was the first time I'd seen him play, and I realised he was very good, then there was Greaves, of course – we knew about him because he had played in Italy, and Moore, the blond kid, good player. I remember the Maracana wasn't full against England, so there wasn't much atmosphere compared to when we played Brazil. The stands are a long way from the pitch. I played in La Maracana with Boca Juniors and it's divine for the away team as the crowd are so far away, unlike at Boca where the spectators are so close to the pitch."

Rattin continues talking about football, little stories and anecdotes, but then he winds up and stops – as if it was a natural end and there were no more matches against England to talk about.

Trying to raise the subject as subtly as possible, I reminded Senator Rattin that he played in a third match against England, in 1966. He leant back on his chair. The expression on his face changed. Suddenly he was not an ex-footballer telling funny stories about his time as a player, but a politician with a serious point to get across. "That team in '66 was the best Argentina side I ever played in," he said, "and that World Cup was very open. Any team could have been champions. Perhaps Germany were a little better than the rest, and then there were the English who had a tremendous advantage as hosts."

His tone became more formal, like a university lecturer explaining a theory. In fact, he explained that just the night before he had given a talk at a college, and the audience had asked him about 1966. His answer was well rehearsed.

"When we talk about the '66 World Cup, there are two themes to consider. The first is that it was the last World Cup without satellite television. If you see footage of '66, or any tournament before it, there is no advertising around the pitch. Before 1966, the host country had always reached the final – Sweden were runners up in '58, Chile finished third in '62, Uruguay won it at home, as did Italy, and Brazil were in the deciding match in 1950. Why? Because FIFA used to help the host team as the only way they made money at the World Cup in those days was from the sale of tickets on the gate."

He explained why, in his opinion, it is different today. "At the 2006 World Cup in Germany, for example, all the money from television, advertising and sale of tickets was made in advance. If Germany had fallen in the first round, it was covered, but before satellite TV, if the host team went out early, the public would lose their enthusiasm for the World Cup, and money would be lost as they wouldn't go to matches. That's the first point you have to consider."

Rattin's second point is, perhaps not surprisingly, the selection of referees. "When the delegates were invited to the lottery for deciding the referees, the Argentinian and the Uruguayan delegation travelled together as they had a natural affinity through speaking the same language. FIFA had told them to arrive at 1900 hours and they arrived 18.45, but, upon arrival, Rous told them, 'it's already done, we were waiting for you – we've already made the draw'."

"When the South American delegates asked to see the results, what a surprise. A German referee for England v Argentina, and an Englishman for Uruguay v Germany. And what happened? – the Englishman let a German handball on the line go unpunished, and then sent off two Uruguayans when the match was only 1-0, and the Germans went on to win 4-0. With us, they settled for 1-0, but if we had equalised they would have sent off Roma or Marzolini, or someone else."

Rattin is forceful and convincing, and had managed to give his thoughts on the '66 World Cup quarter-final without even mentioning his sending off. Was he sure the selection of referees was meant to be done by lottery? Yes, he was sure.

What did he remember about the match against England? What were the tactics?

Perhaps I was being a bit too diplomatic. Perhaps I should have just said, 'C'mon, Rattin, tell me all about the sending off and when you besmirched the Union Jack and sat on the royal carpet.'

He broke the silence.

"Let me tell you something," he said. "That World Cup was the most violent I've ever seen. There were lots of injuries. Eusebio got injured because they kicked him. Pelé was kicked out of the tournament. Ramsey called us the 'Animals', but really all the teams played like that, and a World Cup is only as violent as the referees allow. You didn't have yellow cards for fouls in those days.

"I don't have a lack of respect for referees, but I hadn't done anything. I didn't make any violent play, or even foul anyone, but I was the captain of the team and I asked the referee for an interpreter. I wanted to know what was going on. I wanted to know why he was giving everything in favour of the English. You had that big number 5 [Jack Charlton] using his elbows all the time, and that son of a bitch with the contact lenses [Stiles] kicking everyone. It was all prepared for England to win and that's what happened.

"The bad luck we had was that, due to goal difference, we had to play the hosts. It could have been different and we could have played Uruguay, and then England would have played Germany, and then I think you would have seen an England v Argentina final."

Time has not mellowed Rattin's opinions on the match. He is still convinced it was an injustice, and a fix, although he does just see it as 'one of those things' now.

Why didn't he leave the pitch?

"Because there was no reason for my expulsion. I hadn't done anything. If I had made a violent play then I'd accept it, and go. I carried on arguing for about ten minutes, and then the vice president of FIFA came on the pitch and told me I had been sent off and I had to leave the pitch, so I did.

"Later, I sat on the Queen's carpet, but it's OK, the Queen wasn't there, so it wasn't disrespectful and nobody was offended. I sat there for seven or eight minutes watching the match, nobody told me I had to move, and when the half-time whistle went, I just got up and went to the dressing room.

"Before that, the crowd were shouting insults and throwing chocolate and cans of beer at me. I had to duck out the way, so I twisted the Union Jack on the corner flag and stared back at them, and that's it, the story of my sending off. I think sitting on the red carpet has a greater significance here in South America than in England. It wasn't such a dishonour. I think sometimes the Queen is respected more outside of England than inside. In England it wasn't considered such a dishonourable act."

There is a picture on the wall of Rattin in his playing days, wearing the distinctive blue and yellow shirt of Boca Juniors, who he captained to three championships in the 1960s. The young Rattin reminds me of someone, but I can't think who.

Did he still feel angry about '66?

"No, no, not at all. England didn't win because they were the best team, but because it was all prepared. Naturally, you're angry at the time, when you play like we did for 25 minutes, and then you've got 60 or 70 minutes left with a man less, and you can't make changes. Moreover, I was the captain and leader of the group, an important player in the team. I watched the second half from the edge of the changing room. Don't forget also that in those days Argentina didn't carry the weight it does now at international level. It was very different then.

"But I like the English people. They're a special type. They want to win but they want to win fairly. The next day, the taxi drivers wouldn't charge me, and in the big shops everybody stopped and asked me for my autograph, and apologised to me for all that happened."

Rattin represents the right wing Federalist Union Party (Paufe) and works as the head of the commission for sport and tourism. Appropriate, as even during his playing days he was known as 'the governor'. As I left, I passed another picture on the wall, a team photo from the '60s, with Marzolini and Roma also in the line up. They were some team.

As I walked down the corridor I realised. Yes, of course, Rattin was a dead ringer for Eric Cantona.

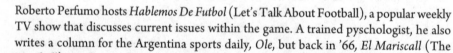

Roberto Perfumo hosts *Hablemos De Futbol* (Let's Talk About Football), a popular weekly TV show that discusses current issues within the game. A trained pyschologist, he also writes a column for the Argentina sports daily, *Ole*, but back in '66, *El Mariscall* (The Marshall) was the young centre-back at the heart of Argentina's defence.

His memories of the tournament differ slightly from his team-mates.' Knocked out by the fashions of the swinging '60s, which had yet to reach Argentina, he marvelled in a different world. "I was only 23, and everything that happened was brilliant for me. It's a pity I never got an England shirt. Ramsey came onto the pitch and told his players not to change shirts with these 'beasts'. But to come to England, to play at Wembley in a quarter-final of the World Cup was fantastic. It was impossible to eliminate the hosts, but I loved it all. London is my favourite city in the world, and it really was spectacular in that era – the clothes, the fashion, so different from anything I'd ever seen before."

Perfumo made 77 appearances for Argentina, captaining the side at the 1974 World Cup, and he remembers that against England in '66, he had a hamstring injury that he hid from Lorenzo and the physio. "I'd picked it up in the group match against Switzerland, and it was very painful, but if I had told the manager, he would have taken me out of the team, so I didn't say a word because I wanted to play at Wembley. I was worried when we entered the pitch because I wasn't able to run properly, and there were no substitutes in those days. If we had had a fitness test, like today, I would have failed it, for sure, but, curiously, once the game started, the pain passed. I had so much enthusiasm to play I just forgot about the pain."

I ask him what playing against England meant to him.

"It's a 'Superclassico'," he replies, drawing deeply on a cigarette. "The two most important matches, for us, are Argentina v Brazil, and Argentina v England. We've always been obsessed with the English as they arrived here, building the railways and the meat factories, and, of course, it was the English who first started playing football here and formed the first clubs. England and Argentina were always friends in football. English football was always respected because they played to win and never used defensive tactics, but that match in '66 changed everything. Before then, Argentina always looked to the English with admiration. It was always the 'masters v pupils' thing, but I think its fair to say we lost that respect for England in '66, and from then on it became like a form of war."

He talks of the selection of the referees, the same story as always; Rous hand-picking the German for England v Argentina, and the Englishman for West Germany v Uruguay, but Perfumo insists it was not a dirty match. "Things get exaggerated. There wasn't so much kicking as they say, and the atmosphere in the stadium wasn't as hostile as they say. Neither was it our plan to play so defensively as they say. Those words Ramsey used were very bad. It wasn't our idea to play as he said. The strategy of the Argentina team in all the matches in '66 was to keep possession of the ball. Our tactic was to break the rhythm of the opposition. We were a very difficult team to beat. England had a very good team, great players like Moore, Charlton, Hurst and Hunt, but we had a team with a lot of experience and a lot of quality."

He is also adamant that nothing untoward happened after the match.

Roma and the Argentina press believed Ferreiro, the right-back, was at fault for the goal for advancing too far up the pitch, but Perfumo blames himself for the only goal of the game. "We played four in a line," he says, drawing on paper. "Me here, Albrecht there, Hurst entered here, and I should've been here with him, but I'd moved out to the right to stop Peters.

"But the truth is Rattin has to take a lot of the blame for what happened; he protested a lot. We were all convinced that the referee had been bought and I think Rattin was very influenced by things that the delegates had said to him before the match. They filled his head a bit in my opinion. We kept telling him, during the game, 'don't protest anymore', but he carried on. He was asking for non-existent things, like an interpreter, but you can't ask for an interpreter, that was in the 1950s. If they'd had red and yellow cards, the referee would've shown Rattin the yellow and he would have shut up, for sure."

Perfumo also acknowledges that he and his team-mates did not cope well with their captain's dismissal.

"When they sent him off we were all angry. We lost our heads in the heat of the moment. We shouted and insulted the referee. We thought we had lost the match, and we were angry because we had been playing well until then, and it hadn't been a dirty match."

During the interview, which took place in a café in June 2003, members of the public recognised Perfumo, and came over to greet him, remarking upon what a good player he had been, and how much they enjoyed his TV programme. Two months later, Argentina president Nestor Kirchner announced a new Cabinet. In Argentina the legislature is separated from the Congress, so a minister does not necessarily have to be an elected politician. Roberto Perfumo was appointed Argentina's minister of sport.

So, I'd met the 'Animals' and survived to tell the tale. None of them had kicked me, bitten me, nor spat in my coffee. In fact they were all highly articulate, funny and affable. Alf Ramsey must be turning in his grave; all these 'Animals' holding respectable positions in society: Rattin, an elected congressman, Perfumo, minister for sport, Roma, active at the Players' Cooperative, and Marzolini, successful manager and academy director.

Their feelings on '66 had differed though. Marzolini had laughed it off: "the delegates probably arrived late," he'd said. Perfumo had admitted that the Argentina players had "lost their heads" and that "Rattin had protested too much." However, Rattin himself was still convinced his sending off was pre-arranged by FIFA. Roma and Perfumo also believed the story that the delegates arrived at the appointed time, only to find the selection of referees had already been made by Stanley Rous without them.

Questions remained unanswered. Were the referees meant to be chosen by lottery? Rattin insists they were, but in the absence of any information from the English FA, or FIFA, there is little way of ever knowing. Could it be that the South American delegates arrived late, as Marzolini has hinted? At the time, Rattin was complaining more than anyone about how unorganised the large Argentine entourage was. Another cultural difference; with all due respect to latin people, their time keeping is not always the best. Arrange to meet at 7pm and there is a general understanding that probably means around 7.15pm (ish). Even televised matches do not start on time in Argentina. In fact, it would be almost considered rude to turn up at a party at the given time. However, if it is true that the Argentinian and Uruguayan delegates did arrive late, then surely Stanley Rous and the European representatives should have waited for them? Especially if the South Americans were travelling to the Kensington Park Hotel from Birmingham, in a foreign country where they did not speak the language. Rous should have had the sense to realise that going ahead and making important decisions without their presence was not only a lack of respect, but would naturally invite suspicion as well.

Or did FIFA really fix it? Deliberately giving the South Americans the wrong time, and instructing their chosen referees to officiate in a partial manner? Senator Rattin puts forward a strong argument about satellite TV, gate money and the importance of the hosts reaching the final.

Did the Argentina captain have the right to an interpreter or not? It can hardly be believed that this was the case. However, having been told by his FA that he was, the captain had stuck to his guns. A case of friendly fire?

Whichever version is correct, there does seem a certain inevitability to the events that unfolded on the pitch, if not the actual specifics of Rattin's sending off. Everyone could sense beforehand that something was going to go wrong in this match, so much so that both England manager Alf Ramsey and AFA president Valentin Suarez were busy warning their players in the dressing room not to react. There had been a culmination of events, perhaps dating as far back as 1962, a smouldering build up of cultural clashes that finally ignited that hot July afternoon in 1966.

This series of three games in four years (1962, 1964, 1966) are only a decade on from the first matches between England and Argentina, but the intervening period had been one of football's most fast-evolving in terms of tactics and fitness. By the '60s, even the kits were completely different, an era away from the early 1950s, when those first meetings between the two countries had the feel of festival, or exhibition, matches, which indeed they were.

Little importance was attached to it in England in 1962, and it has rarely been mentioned since due to lack of footage and sparse reporting in a nation that only took a lukewarm interest in World Cup football at the time, but, by all accounts, including in the British press, England and already-eliminated Bulgaria played out a terrible 0-0 draw in Chile; an unwritten gentlemen's pact to ensure England's qualification? While the television era has borne witness to the suspicious Argentina v Peru of 1978 (discussed in chapter 8), and the blatant piece of match-fixing between West Germany and Austria in 1982, pre-satellite England v Bulgaria has long been forgotten. England deserved their victory over Argentina in Chile, in a non-controversial match, but later, the Argentine press were quite upset by the manner in which England progressed at Argentina's expense. 'Where's the fair play?' they cried.

As much as the brutal battles in that Chile World Cup tournament, it is also likely that events in Rio de Janeiro in 1964 had sharpened Stanley Rous's hardline refereeing stance. FIFA presidents did not travel around the world watching matches from other continents in those days. The Nations Cup was an eye opener into the ways and methods of South American football for Rous, who, it must not been forgotten, had been the game's lawmaker and a stickler for their application. In Brazil '64, the play was constantly interrupted by protests and encroachments onto the pitch by all and sundry on the sidelines, while the wild Brazilian crowds threw bottles and fruit. It was unedifying and primal. Rous disliked it intensely.

Aside from Pelé's headbutt in Argentina's 3-0 victory over Brazil, play had been held up for over five minutes as the Argentinians protested furiously over a penalty given against Rattin for an alleged foul on Pele, with all the usual suspects – coaches, substitutes, photographers – invading the pitch. Was Rous sitting in the stand thinking that he was not going to allow this form of anarchy at the World Cup in England?

Perhaps this explains why Argentina were singled out after their group game against West Germany in 1966. Manager Lorenzo went to the hearing with his document, listing all the German fouls, but the German bench had not invaded the pitch, as the Argentines had. Even today, pitch encroachment is not unusual in Argentina, often occurring without punishment, an almost unwritten acceptance that it is a natural reaction to moments of high excitement. A cooling down period is allowed as tempers subside. It is simply never tolerated in Europe.

Then there are the natural ball skills of the South Americans, and the cultural differences over what constitutes a foul. The Brazilians felt that an English referee had allowed the Bulgarians to kick Pelé and his team-mates at will, in their opening game of the tournament. Argentina manager Lorenzo spoke before the tournament of how his players would have to get used to the shoulder-charge, which has never been accepted in South America. He even hired an English referee to brief his players in the ways of European refereeing, such were the differences, but they were undone by failing to understand other crucial differences in football culture.

Even today, despite homogenised FIFA rules, elements of those differences still exist. Carlos Tevez in his first season at Manchester United remarked how in the Premier League, "referees wave play-on for tackles that would be a sending off in Argentina." Arsenal's manager, Arsène Wenger, made a similar point when his striker Eduardo's leg was broken by a dangerous challenge, even calling for the culprit to be banned for life. The Frenchman observed that the English get more upset by players diving and protesting than violent tackles that could seriously injure, or terminate a player's career. In South America especially, diving and protesting do not carry anywhere near as much negative stigma as in England. In fact it is almost as if it is accepted as part and parcel of the game, even admired in some quarters.

Before the 1966 quarter-final, England's Martin Peters observed that the atmosphere was different from the group games, with tension in the air as the fans made their way up Wembley Way. The English press referred to the Argentines as 'Butchers' on more than one occasion. But when the incident came, it was not as expected. There was no violence, no foul even, no protesting, nor encroaching onto the pitch, not initially, anyway, just a player speaking to the referee. TV footage only adds to the sense of nothingness. "Violence of the tongue," explained the referee the next day, but he did not even speak the same language as the player and admitted he did not actually understand what was said. And, the most risible element, after all the soaring tension? The captain was asking for an interpreter that his directors had apparently, erroneously, told him he had the right to demand. Since when had there been interpreters in international football? Was Rattin seriously expecting someone fluent in Spanish and German, perhaps dressed in a gown, to join him on the pitch, and instantly translate for him? Ludicrous. But then again, in World Cups, where drawn matches were decided by a toss of the coin, perhaps it is not surprising that ideas like this existed, even if only in the minds of a handful of South American delegates.

The doubt will always remain. We will never know the truth. Rudolf Kreitlein, alive and well, was a guest at the 2006 World Cup in his native Germany, but did not want to speak about 1966 and all that. He had said everything there was to say in an interview in Argentina's *El Grafico* magazine in the early 1970s, but that shed no more light on events than his original questioning by Argentine journalists as he sat in a deckchair in Kensington Gardens the day after the match.

Two things came out of England v Argentina in '66 that changed the world of football. First, on his way home from the match, referees' supremo Ken Aston could not stop thinking about all that had happened, the breakdown in communication and problems with the language barrier. Driving his sports car through Kensington High Street, he approached the traffic lights, and sped up because they were green, but the lights changed: *"Yellow, go easy, I thought, and then red, stop, you're off."* It gave him an idea. The next World Cup, in 1970, saw the introduction of red and yellow cards which are now in common usage at all levels of the game across the planet.

The second consequence of this match is that it is the turning point in the story. Two old friends had fallen out. Badly. There is a before and after 1966. From now on, England versus Argentina would take on a new dimension. It had become a grudge match, with feelings always running high in both countries, especially in World Cups. There would be far more controversy to come.

———————— ❖ ————————

Having grown up in England – and especially as a West Ham fan – with Bobby Moore and the legend of '66, it would be a great shame to learn that it was all a fix. In fact, I am not having it. Now, to any Argentine taxi driver, or waiter, who, upon hearing I am English, wants to tell me the 1966 World Cup was all a big conspiracy, and finds it laughable that I think England won fairly, I can confidently say, 'where's the proof? Maybe you are the gullible one? I can still watch that vintage footage of Bobby Moore lifting the World Cup, with pride. For me, the Jules Rimet trophy is still gleaming.'

But it was a different world then. The World Cup was a clash of cultures and a clash of playing styles, without a clear, universally-defined set of rules and directives. Ken Aston, the Englishman who was head of the referees' committee for the tournament, the man who finally convinced Rattin to leave the field, had this to say on his personal website before he died in October 2003: 'The 1966 World Cup was another big screw up and for that I blame FIFA.'

SONS OF THE ANIMALS

WEMBLEY STADIUM, WEDNESDAY 22 MAY 1974

THINGS COULD not get much worse. But they did. This time, it was the Intercontinental Cup, the annual fixture between the champions of South America and the champions of Europe that stretched Anglo-Argentinian relations to the limit.

In 1967, Celtic became the first British side to win the European Cup, and the following year Manchester United became the first English side to lift the trophy. When Racing Club won La Copa de Libertadores, the South American equivalent of the European Cup, in 1967, Argentinian football was evolving into two broad groups; those who still played the traditional 'Rosario game', with the emphasis on attack and dribbling, and those, generally more Buenos Aires-based clubs, applying more modern and cynical tactics. Racing fell very much into the latter group.

Celtic beat Racing 1-0 in the first leg of the Intercontinental Cup in front of 84,000 at Hampden Park. Roberto Perfumo and future Argentina manager Alfio Basile formed Racing's central defensive partnership. "That game in Glasgow was the best match I played in my whole career," says Perfumo. "Think about it, I played over 1,000 games, but I'm telling you I had a very good game that day. Celtic were a great team – Tommy Gemmell, Billy McNeill and the legendary Jimmy Johnstone on the wing. I was marking Johnstone and I did a good job. We were very happy to lose just 1-0."

Based in the working class Avelleneda district of south Buenos Aires, Racing play in a cylindrical concrete stadium, the moat and fences preventing passionate fans from invading the pitch. Celtic received a hostile reception. "We were worried about losing, so we set out to wind them up and get them angry," says Perfumo with brutal honesty. "When we play the Brazilians, or British teams, we know they're not used to it, and they lose their heads. Our plan worked a treat."

In the warm up, Celtic goalkeeper Ron Simpson was hit on the head by a missile from the crowd. Celtic claim blood was pouring from the gash, but Perfumo reckons he feigned injury. Either way Simpson did not play and reserve keeper John Fallon took over.

The match was littered with fouls. Celtic took the lead through a Gemmell penalty, but Racing won 2-1. There was no away goals ruling, so a third match was arranged in Montevideo, Uruguay, just across the Rio de la Plata. Hardly neutral territory.

"By the time we got to Montevideo, Celtic were so wound up that they fouled worse than us," says Perfumo. BBC footage of the third Racing v Celtic tie in Uruguay is on a par with David Coleman's "most disgraceful match ever" clips of the Battle of Santiago in '62. Rulli and Basile of Racing and Bobby Lennox and Jimmy Johnstone of Celtic were all sent off in the first half. Lennox refused to go and the police intervened with dogs and batons, several times, before he eventually left the pitch. Players squared up off the ball. The Paraguayan referee also sent off John Hughes and Bertie Auld of Celtic in the second half for throwing punches. In a classic piece of BBC newsreel footage, Gemmell can be seen chasing a Racing player across the park. Racing won 1-0, which meant they were champions of the world.

However, Racing were mere novices in the art of gamesmanhip compared to Estudiantes de la Plata, Manchester United's opponents the following year. After the violent incidents between Celtic and Racing, many in Manchester questioned the sense in sending a team to Argentina, but manager Matt Busby was all for the Intercontinental Cup. Ahead of his time, he wanted to spread the name of Manchester United globally, just as he had been a pioneer, in the 1950s, for English clubs competing in the European Cup, despite opposition from within the FA.

"We have two fundamental objectives," announced Busby upon his team's arrival in Buenos Aires for the first leg. "First, to leave the impression that football continues to be a sport of gentlemen, and second, to win. I refute the claim that we have come here looking for a draw."

Nice speech from Busby, but nobody understood it. Busby's strong Scottish accent was lost on the Argentine interpreter, so he had to go through it again, with club chairman Louis Edwards translating, or rather Edwards repeating Busby's words in English, with a more precise accent for the official interpreter to then translate into Spanish.

George Best and Nobby Stiles grabbed all the attention in Argentina, for differing reasons. Best, sporting a Sergeant Pepper moustache, was the famous 'Beatle footballer' the South Americans had seen on TV, destroying Benfica in the European Cup final. Best told them his favourite player was Pelé, his business affairs were looked after by his agent, and his one regret was that, instead of tapping the ball into the empty net after his excellent dribble against Benfica, he wished he had stopped the ball on the line and nudged it with his bum, something that had crossed his mind at the time, and he sincerely believed he could have done.

Stiles said he had no problems with Argentinian players and everything that had happened at Wembley in '66 was in the past as far as he was concerned. The United team stayed at the same Hindu club as the '53 players. They ate steak and chips every night, and their photos appeared in the press every day, *La Nacion* observing that 'virtually all the Manchester United players smoked during meals.' They played a lot of golf, strolled down the main shopping streets, and Bobby Charlton bought some shoes for his wife.

United trained at Boca Juniors' stadium, venue for the match, but were not impressed with the pitch, which was too hard, but they were impressed with the meals at the Hindu club: breakfasts of fruits juices, eggs and ham, coffee and cakes, and, the night before the big match against Estudiantes, an enormous chicken and chips supper with ice cream and champagne dessert. At a polo match, Paddy Crerand told the Argentinian reporters that he was having the time of his life.

So far so good for Anglo-Argentine relations, but then the match began. Denis Law claims he had his hair pulled in the first minute by his marker Carlos Bilardo, a qualified dentist, and future Argentina manager. Bobby Charlton needed stitches in his shin after being kicked by his marker Madero, and, according to the English journalists, United were kicked and spat at throughout the whole 90 minutes. Nobby Stiles was sent off by the Paraguayan referee in the last minute for remonstrating over an offside decision. He was escorted off the pitch by the Argentine police, much to the delight of the crowd who booed and threw missiles at him. Stiles had a gash over his eye from a headbutt in the first half.

The normally placid Matt Busby protested, "If Stiles had been bad, I'd be the first to recognise it, but there was a campaign against him the moment we got off the plane. We can accept hard play, but we're not accustomed to the things that took place in this match. I don't want to not play these games because of certain incidents, and I don't want to rush to condemn South American football – what better exponents of football in the last ten years than the Brazilians? – but really some of the things going on this evening were outside the laws of the game." United also had a perfectly good goal disallowed, according to Busby.

The English press were not so diplomatic or restrained. 'The Argentinians are killing international football, soon it will be impossible to play,' blustered *The Times*.

'The Night They Spat On Sportsmanship', gasped the *Mirror*.

'FIFA must prohibit Argentina from playing in the 1970 World Cup,' demanded the *Mail*, although the *Express* reckoned, 'worse things take place in the Engish FA Cup.' Alan Holy in that paper said, 'the problem between English and South American football, especially Argentina, is that there are occasions when they interpret the rules differently. The English "tackle" appears to be a bad word for South American referees, and they give a foul, but in South America they allow obstructions, pushing with hands, pulling arms, tugging ... Man United were robbed and received cruel treatment throughout the match. Moreover, we were insulted by 66,000 fanatics whose whistles and fireworks converted the stadium into a deafening storm.'

La Nacion retaliated: 'It's only a football match. We don't like the way the English press is judging Argentinian people; they're inventing a fantasy that we are a nation of ruffians, and we can not permit that.'

The second leg, at Old Trafford, got off to a bad start even before a ball had been kicked, with South American indignation over a programme on Granada TV that described Argentinians as "brutes", while George Best called for the United fans to be "aggressive". Estudiantes manager Zubeldia fought fire with fire: "We'll go out to play football, but if the English want to resort to violence, then we'll raise our arms."

Argentine journalists who had spoken so highly of Birmingham and England when they first arrived for the 1966 World Cup, had changed their attitude towards the country. It was constantly raining and grey, and the people in Manchester did not seem interested that there was such a big event on. 'Like a black and white film, it's a strange way to live,' whined *Clarín*.

El Cronico went further, the glamour of swinging '66 clearly gone. 'Since we arrived in London, we've been treated badly. Soho and Piccadilly Circus are full of dirty people, badly dressed, dangerous and aggressive. There are young girls, far too young to be wearing mini skirts. It's like a different planet, and their scandalous newspapers show a lack of respect. The country of gentlemen shows a poor image of ethics and morals.'

Football hooliganism was just beginning to develop in England. The Estudiantes hotel had to be cordoned off by police as Manchester United fans congregated outside. 'It's a brutal climate,' said Cronico, 'and all this aggressiveness has been created by George Best. It's like total war here; we can't leave our hotels without fear of being hit, and there is a defamatory campaign against Argentina in the press. It's a shock for us, the people here have long hair, and are drunk in the street – and we're supposed to be the Animals!'

Juan Veron, the Estudiantes forward, takes up the story. "It was a very hostile atmosphere, but that's normal, we knew it would be, but the clever thing we did is that we went out onto the pitch early, 10 minutes before the United players, and we took all the abuse. We let them boo us, throw things at us, insult us, so that when the match began they'd got it all out of their system, and things had calmed down."

After five minutes, Veron scored. "It was a set piece. I stood on the edge of the penalty box and knew exactly where the ball was going to be delivered. I timed my run late, and met it with a header. That put us up 2-0 up on aggregate, so what we had to do now was defend for the rest of the match."

Defend they did. "Jose Medina had an exceptional game marking George Best," says Veron. In the last 10 minutes, the tension exploded. Best hit Medina with a forearm smash after the Argentine fouled him. Medina was taken off the pitch with blood pouring from his face and the referee sent both players off.

With three minutes remaining, Willie Morgan scored a late goal for United, from Crerand's free kick, but Estudiantes were still ahead 2-1 on aggregate. On the stroke of full time, Brian Kidd slammed home Morgan's cross, but the Yugoslav referee had already blown the final whistle. 'Perhaps just as well,' remarked some of the English press, as a third match might really have been too much. Busby promised he would play again should United qualify, but Fleet Street saw little point in the competition. In 1977, the next time a British club won the European Cup, Liverpool declined to take part, against Argentina's Boca Juniors.

"We stayed up all night celebrating," says Veron. "You've no idea how incredible it was. We were a small team from La Plata, a small town just outside Buenos Aires, and we had beaten the mighty Manchester United to become champions of the world. They were good times, although the irony is that I scored the goal that beat Man United but later my son, Juan Sebastián, played for them."

Estudiantes won La Copa de Libertadores three years running in the late 1960s, which meant two more two-legged Intercontinental finals against European champions; AC Milan in 1969, and Feyenoord in 1970. They would prove equally, if not more, brutal as the Manchester United matches. Estudiantes lost both on aggregate, and after the second leg against AC Milan, Argentina's military government realised Estudiantes were becoming a serious blemish on the nation's reputation and ordered the arrest of the whole team. The Estudiantes players and management spent a couple of days in prison, and goalkeeper Poletti, who had punched a Milan player, was suspended from football for life.

Unsurprisingly, there was no great rush to organise any more matches between English and Argentinian teams, at either club or international level. Fortunately for FIFA, a 1970 World Cup confrontation between the two countires was an impossibility as Argentina failed to qualify. "We just weren't organised," says Silvio Marzolini, "as the manager kept changing the team and tactics every few months. There were so many different styles of play – the brutal anti-football tactics of Estudiantes on one hand, while other teams tried to play a more traditional Argentine game. Also, we were in the same qualifying group as the Peru of Cubillas, the greatest Peruvian side ever."

The nucleus of Ramsey's '66 World Cup-winning team remained for the 1970 tournament, and they finished second in their group, beating Romania (1-0), Czechoslovakia (1-0), and losing a very close match against Brazil (1-0). Then, after having been 2-0 up, they lost 3-2 to West Germany after extra time in the quarter-final. At 2-1 and with 20 minutes remaining in normal time, Ramsey substituted Bobby Charlton to give him a rest, thinking the game was won, but the substitution freed up Charlton's marker, Franz Beckenbauer, who ran amok, creating the two goals which won the tie for Germany. Ramsey was heavily criticised. He hung on to his job for another two and half years, another defeat – this time 3-1 at Wembley – by the Germans knocking his side out of the European Championships. But it was the failure to qualify for the 1974 World Cup which was the straw that broke the camel's back. A tortuous 1-1 draw against Poland in the final qualifier at Wembley, in which England converted just one of numerous chances, while conceding an easily preventable goal at the other end, meant Ramsey's time was up.

Argentina were in Europe in May '74, preparing for the finals which were to be held in Germany. Before arriving in London, they had beaten France 1-0 in Paris, with 19-year-old Mario Kempes scoring on the day Giscard d'Estang won the French presidential election.

England's failure to qualify for the World Cup led to all those pre-1966 quotes being churned out again: no skill, no imagination, English football was in the doldrums. Bobby Moore and Bobby Charlton had grown old, and there was not anybody with the same quality to replace them. But with the old guard gone there was also no hangover from the last meeting of the two sides. There could be no vengeance to be carried out, so surely it was safe to arrange a warm-up friendly?

England certainly needed the practice against top quality opposition. Four days before the game against Argentina, caretaker-manager Joe Mercer's team lost 2-0 to Scotland at Hampden Park in the Home International tournament. English football had not felt so low since the 1950 World Cup defeat to the USA. They were playing for pride against Argentina if nothing else.

Everything possible was done to avoid a repeat of the events of '66. The emphasis was on a 'friendly' match, a chance to heal the wounds and bury the hatchet of Ramsey's 'Animals' remark once and for all – hopefully not in someone's back. Argentina agreed to play on condition that the referee would be Argentine, and, in a gesture towards Rattin, it was agreed that an interpreter would be available to them, although quite why they needed an interpreter when the referee was Argentinian is rather puzzling. Surely it would have been the England team in need of assistance on that score.

However, the Argentine's arrival was disrupted by forces outside the FA's control. An IRA bomb was detonated by police 300 metres from where the plane carrying the touring party landed at Heathrow. Vehicles were destroyed, people injured, and the players held up on the plane for two hours before disembarking to be greeted with newspaper headlines such as 'The Return of the Animals'. Football might have been ready to forgive and forget, but the media were not. The Argentine ambassador sent a letter to the British foreign office complaining of the attitude of the England press. It was a futile gesture. The press were just getting into their swing.

Celtic had lost to Atletico Madrid 2-0 in the European Cup Winners' Cup final the previous week. Atletico's boss was Juan Carlos Lorenzo, Argentina's manager at the '62 and '66 World Cups, and two Atletico players had been sent off, including Argentine striker Ayala, who would be in the team to play against England. 'The Villain of Glasgow' and 'The Bad Boys of Wembley Are Coming', said the English papers.

"They called us the sons of the Animals," defender Francisco Sa, who currently runs AFA coaching courses, tells me.

Still unfamiliar with the concept of English tabloid jingoism, Argentinians once again took offence. 'It's an absurd, aggressive campaign,' complained *La Nacion*. 'They won't forget 66, and only talk about the brutality of Argentina football.' Argentina manager Vladislao Cap, who had marked Bobby Charlton in 1962, insisted to English journalists, "we want to look forwards not backwards." They didn't listen.

The IRA bomb and negative headlines were not the only problems for Argentina upon arrival. Some of the players were missing. "We had the usual organisational problems," said Perfumo, now captain and the only remaining player from '66. "It was difficult because some of the European based players had club commitments". Hector Yazalde of Sporting Lisbon was Europe's top scorer that season, but he phoned through to London at the last minute to say he could not make it as he was injured, and there was no sign either of Ramón Heredia and Rubén Ayala, the Atletico Madrid pair.

"I don't know what's going on," said manager Cap in the press conference on the morning of the match. "I've been assured they'll arrive at 7 o'clock, but we phoned Madrid and couldn't find them. This must never happen again. I've no idea what my team will be. This is an important match, we are preparing for the World Cup, and I really want to get a result here today." Asked about tactics, Cap said, "I'm not going to lie to you, we will probably play defensively. England always play up and down the wings and play high balls and crosses, looking for their forwards' heads, so we'll play with a lot of players deep and look for the counter-attack. If we can survive the avalanche of the first 15 minutes then perhaps we'll take some risks." These were the same tactics as both '51 and '66, Argentina's two other Wembley appearances.

The match was live on television in Argentina, but not in England, although there would be highlights later on BBC's *Sportsnight*. As usual, more newspaper space was afforded to the match in Argentina. Referring to some of the things written in England, *La Nacion* said, 'It's time to put out this absurd fire.'

The Times agreed: 'Whatever the outcome, let us bury once and for all the continued whispers of Argentine 'Animals' as expressed by Sir Alf after that 1966 shambles of a match ... the echoes of it should have died long since. Let us hope there will be no cause to revive them tonight.'

Some Argentine journalists went along to England's training session at the Bank of England cricket grounds, and found caretaker-manager Mercer rather rude, an odd assessment, as Mercer generally had an image of a jovial, avuncular figure. In a piece entitled, 'The Aggressiveness of Joe Mercer', Ernesto Muñiz of *La Nacion* claimed that when he informed Mercer that the Argentina team had come to play a good game without any incidents, Mercer had abruptly replied, "I'll believe that when I see it." Then, when asked about his team for the match, Mercer's response was, "What's it got to do with you?" 'Then he turned round and walked off without even saying goodbye,' complained Muñiz. Argentine journalists with pages of space to fill were used to structured pre-match press conferences with managers speaking openly and at length about their team selections. This was simply not the case in England, although no-one communicated this to either side, another case of cross-cultural breakdown.

The FA had already appointed Leeds United's Don Revie as the new England manager, but he was bound by club commitments until the end of the season, so Mercer was standing in for a month to cover the Home Internationals and end of season friendlies. Mercer's successful Manchester City side of the late 1960s had a reputation for attacking football, so he was a refreshing change from Ramsey. Mercer wanted to give England a bit of spark and his choice of players during his seven-game reign reflects that: three strikers – Mick Channon of Southampton, Frank Worthington of Leicester, and Kevin Keegan of Liverpool, the latter given freedon to roam and move out wide like an Argentina number 10, behind the front two. A brave move from Mercer, as few England players would be used to the tactics. Colin Bell would understand, though. The Manchester City midfielder was a prodigy of Mercer and the innovative assistant coach at Maine Road, Malcolm Allison. Having made his England debut in 1968, Bell was now the most experienced player in the team.

West Ham midfielder Trevor Brooking was making his first Wembley start, having gained his first cap in Ramsey's final match, a disappointing 0-0 draw in Portugal. Completing the attack-minded three-man midfield was Keith Weller of Leicester, on the right. Alec Lindsay was handed his England debut at left-back, Emlyn Hughes, also of Liverpool, was the established right-back and captain. Colin Todd of Derby County and Dave Watson of Man City were the centre-back pairing.

Heredia finally arrived from Spain on the afternoon of the match, but told Cap he did not want to play as he felt too tired having played for Atletico Madrid in the Cup Winners' Cup final the week before, and then at Sporting Gijon in the Spanish league on the Sunday. There was still no sign of Ayala.

"I remember the Argentina referee Arturo Irurate being very strict about time-keeping," says Perfumo. "He wanted everything to go efficiently as he wanted us to leave a good impression of ourselves in England. He told me the match must start on time. He knocked on our dressing room door and called me to lead the players onto the pitch, and

I signalled for everyone to follow me out of the dressing room. I walked alongside Hughes, the English captain, through the corridor, but just as we were about to walk onto the pitch, I looked behind me and no-one was there. All the England players were there, behind Hughes, but none of our team had followed me out of the changing rooms, so I had to go back and get them. A couple of them weren't ready so we went on to the pitch without them. Ayala had just arrived from Spain at the last moment, and he joined us on the pitch during the playing of the national anthems."

The Argentina national anthem was booed by the Wembley crowd for the first time. 'Lamentable,' decried *La Nacion*. England and Argentina both wore their traditional kits. "The atmosphere wasn't too hostile," says Perfumo, "certainly no worse than any English team could expect in Argentina."

It was a cool, spring Wednesday evening, free of the tension that filled that hot Saturday afternoon in '66. As expected, England attacked and the visitors defended. Argentina manager Cap had said as much, although Perfumo disagreees that Argentina set out specifically to close down the opposition. "We had Ayala and Kempes up front, that's not defensive. It was a free-flowing game and we contributed to that as well. We were trying to form a team for the World Cup, concentrating on keeping the ball, but I disagree that we were so defensive."

After eight minutes, Alec Lindsay took a free kick and Worthington hit the post. Then Bell centred from the left, but goalkeeper Carnevali beat Worthington to the ball and punched clear. "Those high crosses are always difficult for us to deal with. We were not used to that type of play," says Perfumo.

Argentina counter-attacked on 17 minutes. Telch to Ayala on the right, who crossed, but Shilton came out of his goal and caught. Kempes was a dangerous presence with his direct running; Hughes brought him down with a bad foul after 20 minutes and the referee warned the England captain. "That was the match in which I first realised just how good Mario Kempes was," says Perfumo. "I'd heard about this 19-year-old from Rosario, but, as I was playing for Cruzeiro in Brazil at the time, I'd never seen him play before. In that match at Wembley, he was phenomenal. He ran more than the English!

"Wembley was such a difficult pitch. So tiring. Every time I played there, I was tempted to just lie down on the turf and sleep because it's so energy sapping, but Kempes covered every blade of glass. He could run and run for the whole 90 minutes."

England continued attacking. Brooking and Bell made in-roads, playing the ball out wide to Keith Weller on the right and the overlapping full back Lindsay on the left. High balls and crosses rained in. Lindsay's centre created a scramble in the goalmouth, Carnevali eventually recovering the ball after shots from Channon and Worthington. Then, Channon hit the post with a shot that rebounded back off the goalkeeper, before Perfumo hooked it away. England were on top but had nothing to show for it. That, however, was about to change.

With 45 minutes on the clock, Watson cleared to Bell on the left, and his first time cross was met by Channon who cannoned the ball home, just reward for England's attacking play throughout the first half.

No England versus Argentina match would be complete without a little controversy, and on the stroke of half-time, it duly arrived. Watching live on television in Argentina, the public saw it all unfold. "What's going on?" asked the match commentators. "Hughes and Glaria are hitting each other in the centre of the park." For a moment it seemed as if another major incident was about to spark, but this time the choice of referee proved to be the dampener on any confrontation, rather than the catalyst. The Argentine official stepped in and separated the pair, simultaneously blowing the whistle for half-time. He briskly and brusquely led the players off the pitch without taking any action. The BBC footage and most reports seem to have missed what sparked the friction. Some say Hughes had caught Glaria with a bad challenge, others say the England captain went over and goaded him about the goal.

Clearly some diplomatic work took place at half-time as Glaria did not appear for the second half, substituted in favour of Quique Wolff. The Argentines and their referee were worried that Glaria might have sought further retribution. For the respective associations, peace was high on the agenda. *The Times* described the altercation as, 'a gentle punch up', and *La Nacion* called it, 'a minor incident, completely out of context with the friendly spirit the match had been played in so far.' Certainly it was handled superbly by Sr Irurate.

Mercer could hardly instruct his players to sit back on their lead as with such a bold and attacking choice of players it would have been suicidal for Mercer's team to try to play any other way. So they came out firing on all cylinders at the start of the second half, as they had done in the first. Eight minutes after the break, Bell strode forward and unleashed a blistering shot from outside the penalty area that ricocheted off the crossbar, landing invitingly at the feet of Frank Worthington, who coolly tapped home. Wembley cheered, and Worthington, Weller and Channon jogged back to the halfway line laughing. This was easy.

Perhaps, though, it was the English who could not resist the temptation to lay down and sleep on the hallowed Wembley turf as two minutes after Worthington's goal, Ayala and Kempes caught them napping. Long-haired Ayala broke away, sprinting down the left. Shilton could only parry his cross-come-shot, and the equally long-maned Mario Kempes was the quickest to react, gliding the ball into the net. Clearly things had changed in Argentina since *La Nacion* had remarked disfavourably about those 'long-haired Englishmen' in Manchester in 1968. Now, it was *The Times*'s turn to comment on hairstyles: 'Ayala clearly needed a ribbon or two.'

With Argentina sensing they could rescue the game, it became more open. Lindsay, who had spent the entire match moving up and down the left flank, floated in yet another cross, from which Channon's shot hit Carnevali and went wide. The referee booked Channon for a foul on Ayala, and Perfumo for a foul on Keegan. Up went the chant of Animals, Animals', from the Wembley crowd, stoked by all those reminders in the press over the preceding days. 'Lamentable,' decried *La Nacion*, again.

Rene Houseman, the nippy little winger from the shanty towns, replaced Brindisi and made a significant contribution straight away as Argentina came out of their shell, sensing an equaliser. Kempes escaped Hughes and fired a powerful shot, which Shilton blocked. Houseman kicked the rebound goalwards, but the omnipresent Lindsay stopped it on the line to save a certain goal.

As the match entered the final few minutes, with England heading for victory and the Wembley crowd happily singing, Hughes made a fairly innocuous challenge on Kempes, who rolled around on the ground, and the referee awarded a penalty. Now we had controversy.

'Clear penalty, Kempes was chopped down,' declared *La Nacion*. 'Dubious decision, Kempes made a song and dance of falling over Hughes's sliding tackle,' opined *The Times*.

No matter. It was given. Albeit by an Argentinian referee. Kempes coolly dispatched the penalty himself, and Shilton stood shaking his head over the decision. Some 12 years later Shilton would again shake his head in disbelief, but only after protesting far more vigorously, in the Azteca stadium, Mexico City, when another refereeing decision went Argentina's way.

"I remember, right at the end of that match in '74, I went up for a corner," says Perfumo. "I ran past the referee and whispered to him, 'Hey, Arturo, give us a penalty'."

"I've just given you one," he replied.

"'Yes, I know, but we brought you here to give us two!' I told him."

The 2-2 result suited everybody. Some of the England players were still complaining about the penalty as the teams left the pitch, but the players swapped shirts in a friendly enough manner. The match had passed off without major controversy thanks to Irurate's intervention at the crucial moment. There had been goals and plenty of attacking play, but nothing had got out of hand. Relations had improved, which was the aim. *The Times* described it as, 'kicking but in a friendly way.'

The press pondered the differences styles; 'a splendid contrast,' wrote *The Times*. 'Argentina's play was more finely woven, subtle and of a refined touch. England's play was open and recognisable with the ball moved in long and wide areas.' You could easily be reading a report from the first match between the two teams, 23 years earlier.

The Sun agreed: 'Anybody with half a neutral eye on Wembley could see that in terms of individual skill, expertise, technique and vision, we have fallen light years behind the world's best. Argentina had the aficionados drooling with envy at their instant control, their ability to shield the ball, their confidence and mastery in different situations.'

That England team was not to last long, nor given a chance to develop, though. Don Revie, a controversial choice given his Leeds team's reputation as the bad boys of British football, had other ideas once he took over from the caretaker Mercer, and his selections over the years revealed a penchant for chopping and changing, as well as a mistrust of maverick ball players. Frank Worthington, who Argentina's *La Nacion* had described as 'an exquisite player', only made one more full appearance for England, and one as a late substitute. Weller was never picked under Revie.

Argentina lost their final warm-up game for the 1974 World Cup to the Holland of Cruyff, Neeskens and Krol, 4-1 in Amsterdam. In the finals themselves they finished second in their group after losing to Poland (3-2), drawing with Italy (1-1), and beating Haiti (4-1), but in the second group phase they lost to Brazil (2-1), drew with East Germany (1-1) and were played off the park by Holland again, losing 4-0, in a rain soaked match featuring Cruyff turns on the slippery surface, and a perfomance that many consider to be the Clockwork Orange's finest ever.

South American football did win one famous victory off the pitch at the 1974 World Cup. At the eve of tournament FIFA conference, Joao Havelange's shuttle diplomacy of the previous eight years paid off. His lobbying for support, especially in Africa, with the promise of an extended 20-team World Cup, and extra places for Africa and Asia, secured the votes needed to finally oust Sir Stanley Rous.

Havelange's ideas had been bitterly opposed in Europe. The Belgian FA issued a warning before voting took place: "In the World Cup this year we have Zaire, Haiti and Australia. If we increase the number of finalists to 20 there will be only one extra place for Europe, but more for other parts of the world. Is this what you want? – a World Cup where the Soviet Union, Czechoslovakia, England, Spain, and Belgium are not taking part, but third-rate countries are? I would rather be a champion of Europe than champion of the world if that's the case."

79-year-old Stanley Rous had spoken to the European FIFA members before voting, saying, "I appeal for you to vote for me because its Europe versus South America, and Europe must retain the leadership of football. If I am elected for a further term you must look for a successor to me from Europe so that European leadership is maintained."

Rous went on to personally attack Havelange for not being a football man: "I'm an ex-player and an ex-referee, but Havelange is a water polo player." Havelange was also a successful businessman and it was that acumen, and the lobbying of the Asian and African confederations, that won the day for him, although, crucially, it was the latin votes of Italy, Spain and Portugal that swung the election in his favour.

Now he was president, one of Havelange's first decisions was to confirm that Argentina would now definitely be hosting the 1978 World Cup finals. The pendulum had most definitely swung.

England 2 (Channon 45' Worthington 53')
Argentina 2 (Kempes 55', 89'(pen))
Wednesday 22 May 1974. Wembley Stadium. Friendly. Attendance: 68,000
Referee: Arturo Irurate (Argentina)

England: Peter Shilton (Stoke), Emlyn Hughes(c) (Liverpool), Alec Lindsay (Liverpool), Colin Todd (Derby), Dave Watson (Manchester City), Keith Weller (Leicester), Kevin Keegan (Liverpool), Mick Channon (Southampton), Frank Worthington (Leicester), Trevor Brooking (West Ham), Colin Bell (Manchester City)
Manager: Joe Mercer

Argentina: Daniel Carnevali (Las Palmas), Roberto Perfumo(c) (Cruzeiro), Francisco Sá (Independiente), Oscar Glaria (San Lorenzo, sub 45'), Roberto Telch (San Lorenzo), Angel Bargas (Nantes), Agustin Balbuena (Independiente), Miguel Brindisi (Huracan, sub 70'), Carlos Squeo (Racing), Rúben Ayala (Atletico Madrid), Mario Kempes (Rosario Central), Subs: Enrique Wolff (River Plate, on 45'), René Houseman (Huracan, on 67')
Manager: Vladislao Cap

THE ANIMALS' REPRISAL

BUENOS AIRES, SUNDAY 12 JUNE 1977

'ANIMALES, ANIMALES!' The chant went up early at Boca Juniors' Bombonera (Chocolate box) stadium, so called because the stands go up and up, one on top of another, like layers in a chocolate box. The cramped 55,000 crowd are close to the pitch, an intimidating atmosphere.

La Boca is a dockside working class area of Buenos Aires, where the locals are fanatical about football. Eleven years may have passed since Alf Ramsey's infamous words, but no amount of diplomacy was going to allow them to forget 1966. Rattin was a Boca Juniors hero, captain of the 1960s team that won the league three times. Today, a sculpture of Rattin's head is carved into the outside wall of the stadium, alongside team-mates Marzolini and Roma, and other Boca legends. Diego Maradona looks down from the top.

Great Britain was one big street party in June 1977. Every road in the country was decked out in red, white and blue bunting for Queen Elizabeth II's Silver Jubilee; plastic hats and sausages on sticks had taken over in the last great outpouring of British post-colonial national pride. Virginia Wade was on her way to winning Wimbledon, but the Sex Pistols were sticking two fingers up at it all, sailing down the River Thames on a boat, blasting out their banned number 1 song 'God Save The Queen'.

In Argentina, it was much more than than just punk rock songs that had been outlawed – opposition parties, newspapers and anyone who had a different opinion for a start. The country was in the throes of a brutal military dictatorship. People were disappearing. Thousands of them.

La Bombonera was hosting a series of international matches against European opposition in preparation for the 1978 World Cup that Argentina would be hosting the following year, despite protests from Amnesty International. Hungary, Poland and West Germany had already visited, with Scotland, France, Yugoslavia and East Germany still to come, but it was the match against England that had captured the people's imagination. 'Of all the matches in the series, this one, without doubt, perhaps for reasons beyond football, is the one most eargerly awaited,' *La Nacion* declared.

England defender Trevor Cherry remembers the hostile reception the players received on arrival: "Looking back, I can't understand why we went to play a friendly there. It was anything but friendly. I don't know if it was an English thing or a football thing, but they really hated the British in Argentina. When we arrived there were banners saying 'You Animals' and 'Go Home English', things like that." Goalkeeper Ray Clemence felt the same, saying that it was "the most intimidating atmosphere I've ever played in. There was the army walking around with tear gas on their backs, and alsations everywhere, and they all had machjine guns strapped to them. We were all thinking is this a football match or what is it?"

When the names of the English players were read out over the Tannoy, the booing was so deafening that the words of the announcer could not be heard and when some of the English players came out for a pre-match warm up, the chant of "Animales, Animales!" went up again. The England players undestood that alright, especially as it was chanted at them in both Spanish and English, but the cry of *piratas* (pirates) would have been lost on them, and they would not have understood the banner behind one of the goals even if it had been written in English. 'Las Malvinas Son Argentinas', it proclaimed, a reference to a small group of islands in the South Atlantic that barely anyone in the UK, let alone internationals footballers, had heard of.

The wall of noise reached its crescendo when the two teams entered onto the pitch, together in two parallel lines. They were greeted with a 'ticker-tape' reception, a 'papering', thousands of pieces of white paper raining down from the terraces, covering half the pitch, and accompanied by that repetitive, inspiring, threatening chant that became so familiar during the '78 World Cup, "Ar-gen-tin-a, Ar-gen-tin-a!"

"The best acoustics in the world," Rattin says of La Bombonera. The military band played the Argentine national anthem and the crowd sang along, but 'God Save the Queen' was greeted with an incredible wall of piercing whistles that the Sex Pistols would have been proud of.

The England players had arrived for their two matches in South America in a poor psychological state. They had played badly in the Home International Championships the week before, losing at Wembley to both Wales (1-0) and Scotland (2-1), the latter a famous victory for the Tartan Army, who celebrated by invading the pitch, smashing down the goals and taking chunks of the Wembley turf back home to Scotland.

With news of Italy's 3-0 victory over Finland filtering through, the chances of England qualifying for the 1978 World Cup were increasingly slim. However, three days before this match in Buenos Aires, England earnt a moral-boosting goalless draw against Brazil in La Maracana which raised spirits, even if the Brazilians had, at times, outplayed them, missing a hatful of chances. Goalkeeper Ray Clemence had been in excellent form. It was the first time England had held the Brazilians on South American soil. Manager Les Cocker expressed himself satisfied with the result.

Yes, England manager Les Cocker. He was in charge of the team in Rio even though he was not a manager, but the FA general secretary. The real manager, Don Revie, was watching the Italians play in Helsinki, casting his eye over the opposition for the crucial World Cup qualifying match at Wembley in November. Well, that was the official reason given for his absence at the time. Actually, Revie, was not anywhere near Helsinki, but had donned long robes and a head scarf, so as not to be recognised at Heathrow airport, and taken a plane to the United Arab Emirates to negotiate a new job and a King's ransom of a salary.

The real England manager did make it to Argentina, though. He arrived in Buenos Aires alone, the day before the players arrived. Perhaps he should have continued with the Arabian disguise as a group of Argentine journalists were waiting for him in the lobby of the Sheraton Hotel. They tried to interview him whilst he still had his suitcases in his hands, but Revie politely informed them that the only thing he wanted to do was have a shower and go to bed as he had not slept for two days as a result of constant travelling.

One of the journalists was Ernesto Muñiz of *La Nacion*, responsible for interupting Joe Mercer's training session three years earlier. Revie, jet-lagged, but no doubt aware that one of the reasons for the match in Argentina was to try to build bridges, surrendered to the journalists' persistence and agreed to give a brief, improptu interview. In the lift.

The full transcript appeared in *La Nacion* the following day and makes interesting reading with hindsight. Revie may have been tired, a little irritable maybe, but his answers to the questions reveal an increasing disillusionment with the England job and the criticism that comes with the territory.

'How can you explain that Liverpool, are champions of Europe, but the national team are losing at home to the Welsh and the Scots?' Muñiz began.

'We've been trying out different types of tactics. Maybe the players don't understand them. I don't know, but, until now, we've not been getting the results. I'm getting heavily criticised and accused of managing badly, and people say the team lacks imagination, but what nobody ever points out is that the players I have to manage are nowhere near the level of those who won the greatest prize in football in 1966. Footballers with the personality of Gordon Banks, Bobby Moore, Bobby Charlton, Alan Ball, Jimmy Greaves and Martin Peters aren't born every day. We do have one great player now, though, and that's Kevin Keegan, who's just been sold by Liverpool to Hamburg for £500,000. Despite his transfer, he'll be with us against Italy in November and I hope here in Argentina next year for the World Cup.'

'Did you know that England played extremely slowly and defensively in Brazil with lots of back passes to the goalkeeper, and other defects of South American football?"

'I've just arrived and I don't know anything about that match, but our plan is to adapt our style to the teams that we meet in this part of the world.'

According to *La Nacion*, Revie now began to comb his hair in the mirror of the elevator, and signalled that he wanted to end the interview, but, 'we persisted,' says Muñiz. The England manager answered one last question. 'Do you realise that the pressure and noise from the public in the stadium on Sunday could have a big influence on both sides?'

'We've had a long chat with the lads about this. We've inherited that unfortunate expression of Alf Ramsey's and we must accept that. But the delegation of my country is composed of young people now, that only want to look forward, and one of the objectives of coming here is to regain the respect and sympathy of Argentina as we had 25 years ago in the stadium of River Plate...' The lift door closed before the journalists had time to reply.

It's a bizarre interview, laced with so many facts and figures it sounds unnatural. In those times of heavy censorship in Argentina, in which *La Nacion* was one of only a handful of newspapers allowed to publish, Muñiz's version of the interview may have been doctored to also provide a neat description of the England team and players, within the manager's answers.

Revie's reign had started brightly back in September 1974, in every sense. In his first match in charge, England, for the first time in a century, no longer wore plain white shirts, but carried red and blue stripes down the sleeves, upsetting purists. Not only did the manufacturer's logo controversially appear on the shirts and shorts, but Revie and the substitutes had the word ADMIRAL emblazoned across the front of their tracksuits.

New kit, new manager, new era – England beat Czechoslovakia 3-0 in Revie's first match but, from there, it went downhill. Overall, Revie's three years in charge had not gone well. England failed to qualify for the 1976 European Championships, and now their hopes of qualification for the 1978 World Cup were hanging on a knife edge.

The biggest criticism of Revie was that he chopped and changed the team too much. The period he was in charge (1974–77) contains many players with just one or two caps to their name. For example, Brian Little of Aston Villa, one brief appearence as substitute then discarded, Colin Viljoen of Ipswich, one full game, Charlie George, never picked by Ramsey during his peak years, called up for 60 minutes under Revie, then never considered again. Full back Terry Cooper received his first call up for three years, only to be left out again after one match, and names like Alan Hudson of Stoke, Steve Whitworth of Leicester and QPR full backs, Dave Clement and Ian Gillard, would come in for two or three games and then disappear off the England scene. After a 5-1 victory over Scotland in the Home Internationals, captain Alan Ball was dropped and never picked again, thus adding his name to the ever growing list of dissenters.

For the crucial World Cup qualifying match against Italy in Turin in November 1976, Revie made six changes, an obvious admission that he did not know his best team. England were beaten 2-0, and then outclassed by Holland 2-0 in a friendly at Wembley in February 1977. After the humiliating defeats to Wales and Scotland in the Home Internationals at Wembley, the calls for the manager to go were growing louder and louder. Little did anyone know at this stage that Revie was already planning his escape route.

Appointed immediately after the 1974 World Cup, and, crucially, two years before the 1976 military coup, Cesar Luis Menotti, like Ramsey in '62, was given the specific task of preparing a team for a World Cup on home soil in four years' time. For the first time, AFA had chosen a manager for the long term, giving him total backing, regardless of results.

Had the military coup come before 1976, Menotti would not have been appointed. In fact, it is more likely he would have disappeared. The long-haired, chain smoking intellectual had been a political activist in his youth, and not on the side of the military. The generals, though, had the good sense to retain Menotti, as they did not want to disrupt the carefully laid plans for 1978. A successful World Cup for Argentina would be to the government's benefit; an outpouring of nationalist sentiment could only serve to strengthen the dictatorship and help to hide the genocide beneath the flag-waving. It was a strange alliance, Menotti and the Generals.

Hailing from Rosario, the home of *La Gambeta* (the dribble), Menotti, 38 years old in 1977, had played his football in the late 1960s outside Argentina. During the era of the brutal Estudiantes team, and the negative tactics that prevailed, Menotti starred as a striker alongside Pelé at Santos, while studying Brazilian coaching methods. He burst onto the Argentinian scene in 1973, winning the championship in his first season as manager of modest Huracan. Not only did they win the league for the one and only time in their history, but Huracan played in a refreshing attacking style, the polar opposite of the 1960s club sides, and Lorenzo's defensive tactics at the previous World Cups.

Menotti may have had to keep quiet on politics once the generals took over, but he had no trouble in voicing his strong views on football. He wanted his teams to play in a way that, in his opinion, reflected the true character of the Argentine people; a team with flair, in the style of the tango dancers, a style associated with his home town Rosario, free from European influences and negative tactics – although that did not stop him selecting a rustic centre-back called Daniel Killer. Nowadays 'Menottism' is a philosophy in Argentina. For some, it's a beautiful, lyrical way of viewing football. For others, it is pretentious rubbish.

Traditionally, the national team had always consisted of players from Buenos Aires clubs, but Menotti wanted to change that. With the backing of AFA, he vowed to scour the interior in search of young, skilful ball players. Players like Ricardo Villa, Osvaldo Ardiles, Daniel Bertoni and Daniel Valencia fitted his criteria perfectly.

This series of games against European opposition in 1977 were a vital part of Menotti's World Cup preparations, athough he was without his star player, Valencia's Mario Kempes, the only European-based member of his squad. Argentina beat Hungary 5-1 in the first match in the series in February, then the team who had come third in the 1974 World Cup, Poland, 3-1. They then lost to reigning world champions West Germany 1-3. Against Hungary, Menotti had handed an international debut to a prodigious 16-year-old, bringing him on as a second half substitute, but, the following year, when Menotti named his squad for the World Cup, the young player did not make the final 22, and took the news so badly that he vowed never to play football again, opting for early retirement at the golden age of 17. However, a few weeks later, the curly-haired kid, whose name was Diego Maradona, changed his mind and said he would consider playing football again after all.

Midfielders Ossie Ardiles and Ricardo Villa were central to Menotti's plans and are great disciples of his football philosophy. They were in good spirits when we first met up in a downtown Buenos Aires restaurant to discuss England versus Argentina matches. "Don't show me the list of players, let me remember," says Ardiles, childlike, when asked about the match in 1977.

"I can tell you one name that isn't on that list," says Villa. "I had a hamstring injury and couldn't play."

The pair are eating huge steaks and drinking red wine. Racing Club, who Ossie was managing at the time (2003), with Villa as his assistant, had just gained a credible away draw at Estudiantes. Ardiles reels off all the names of the Argentina team from '77 perfectly; it is the basis of the World Cup team the following year – Luque and Ortiz up front, Ardiles, Bertoni, Gallego in midfield, Passarella and Tarantini at the back – but the two ex-Tottenham players are a few short when trying to recall the England line-up. They remember the attacking players, Keegan (who captained the side), Channon and Stuart Pearson, and, after a few guesses, the defensive midfielders Ray Wilkins and Brian Talbot, but, "there must be someone more creative in there," says Ardiles. "What about the blond guy who played for Leeds, Tony Currie?"

No, Currie was not there, and neither was Trevor Brooking, who was injured. In fact there was not another creative player. This was the Don Revie era and the midfielder they could not recall was Brian Greenhoff, probably because he was a defender, whom Revie played in midfield. I realise that the boot really had firmly transferred to the other foot in terms of both tactics and mentality.

They remembered Trevor Cherry, for obvious reasons, as we shall see later, centre-back Dave Watson and Ray Clemence in goal, but then are stuck. After ordering some more 'limoncheri', an after-meal vodka and lemon drink, Villa remembers full back Phil Neal, but they still can't get the last player and give in. It's defender Emlyn Hughes. Groans all round: "Aarr, my ankles, my ankles," says Villa bending forward and grabbing his feet in mock agony, "they still hurt to this day!"

"Hughes could kick the opposition better than he could kick the ball," says Ossie.

Ardiles, then of Huracan, was quoted (in *La Nacion*) in 1977, saying, 'Let nobody doubt that all these matches in this series have great importance. We're looking for progression. English football has decayed a lot, but that is not to say it won't be a demanding game.' The 'Famous Last Words' trophy for this match must go to Daniel Bertoni, who was quoted alongside Ardiles: 'I think we're in condition to shine and provide the public with a great spectacle.' Bertoni did indeed provide a great spectacle, but perhaps not in the way he had intended beforehand.

"Who is Pirate Morgan?" I asked. The head of the AFA delegation in 1966 had likened Stanley Rous to him years before and the crowd chanted his name at the English players before this match in 1977.

"It's a fictional character, isn't it? A typical pirate's name," says Ardiles. "The English were always seen as invaders in Argentina and Las Malvinas [the Falklands] was a much bigger issue here than it was in England at that time. I remember when we were negotiating our transfers to Tottenham in 1978 I asked Keith Burkinshaw [Tottenham manager] about the problem. 'What about Las Malvinas? Won't it be a problem, two Argentines playing in England?' But Keith, like the majority of English people at the time, had never even heard of the islands and didn't know what I was talking about."

In Argentina's heavily censored newspapers in 1977, the issue of Las Malvinas was being raised with more frequency than when the England team had last visited in 1953. "It was a hostile atmosphere," says Daniel Bertoni, who is also happy to talk about the match when I call him. "Without the politics, it's still a big match for us and the crowd always try to help us in the stadium, the twelfth man as we say, but now we had the politics on top. The newspapers influence people a lot and they spoke of 'our territory'."

Clearly there were undertones to this game which the English simply didn't understand. Similarly the Argentines did not realise that their visitors had no idea what all the fuss was about.

Unlike the previous visit in 1953, England wore red shirts when they emerged into the cauldron of the Bombonera, while Argentina sported their traditional blue and white stripes. The match kicked off on the Saturday afternoon to the roar of 50,000 passionate voices. The midfield trio of Ardiles, Gallego and Bertoni excited the crowd with some neat touches, but it was clear that England were going to deny them space. Greenhoff, Talbot and Keegan, the latter playing deep in midfield, snapped around them, allowing little room for Argentine manoeuvres. The 20-year-old Ray Wilkins of Chelsea had been handed the holding role, sitting in front of the back four.

The crowd greeted each Argentina touch with an olé and booed, like a pantomine audience, every time England gained possession. After three minutes of this noisy show, Talbot nicked a touch, a good interception, and played the ball forward to Pearson. Stocky Argentina captain Daniel Passarella let Pearson know he was there, committing the first foul of the match, just inside the Argentina half.

Greenhoff took the free kick quickly before the opposition could reorganise, stroking the ball out to Channon on the right wing. The Southampton striker swung over an excellent curling cross for Pearson, who ghosted in, Geoff Hurst style, at the near post, beating Daniel Killer to the ball. Goalkeeper Hector Baley was caught in no man's land as Pearson's header sailed into the top corner of the net. An excellent way to quieten the hostile crowd. 'The silence was uncanny,' said *The Times*.

Following the goal, Argentina tried to push forward, but England had nine men behind the ball, Pearson playing as a lone striker. Channon was wide right and Keegan virtually a defensive midfielder. Argentina responded by raising the pace. The handful of English journalists who had made the trip were surprised at the tempo. Menotti's team played with speed, more in common with the 1953 team of Grillo and Micheli than the defensive tactics of the 1960s and early 1970s. The English defence and midfield coped well, though.

Argentina had not had a shot on goal, when, on 16 minutes, Greenhoff fouled Bertoni just outside the penalty area. Goalkeeper Clemence organised the wall as Ardiles stood over the ball, studying the line of red shirts. He informed the referee he was ready, shaped up to shoot, but ran over the ball. Off a run of no more than two steps, Bertoni curled the ball beyond the stretching Clemence. 'GOOOOLL!' screamed the Argentine radio commentators as the crowd erupted. "It was an innovative set piece that we practised a lot in training," says Ardiles. "You don't see it too much these days because, like all new ideas, you can only use it for a while before defences cotton on."

Towards the end of the first half, Argentina retained possession, but the English defence was resolute, refusing to be intimidated by the crowd. "England were just sitting back and waiting for us, playing on the counter-attack," explained Bertoni. The roles had, indeed, reversed.

On 34 minutes Bertoni fouled Cherry and collected a booking from Uruguayan referee Ramón Barreto Ruiz. The pair of them had been having their own personal duel down England's left, and both had now been booked. Killer lived up to his name, making a bad foul on Pearson, who needed treatment.

Just before half-time Leopoldo Luque, the speedy, moustachioed centre-forward (who bears more than just a paassing resemblance to the *Spinal Tap* lead guitarist), shot from just inside the penalty area. Clemence spilled the ball, a mêlée of players running in to claim it, but Watson was first to the ball, and cleared off the line.

England made one change at half-time. Brian Greenhoff, the defender who had been struggling in midfield, was replaced by Ray Kennedy, giving England more shape as the naturally left-sided substitute allowed Talbot to move into the centre.

When Ray Clemence emerged for the second half, he was applauded by the Argentinian fans behind his goal. Brazil versus England, in which Clemence had been outstanding the week before, had been shown live in Argentina (but not in England). *La Nacion* observed that all the English players chewed gum incessantly, and that Clemence took his out of his mouth and stuck it to the side of his goalpost. The English substitutes had cameras and took photos of the crowd.

The problem for Argentina was that, despite all the possession of Ardiles, Gallego and Bochini in the middle, they badly missed Mario Kempes, the injured Ricardo Villa, or the 16-year-old Maradona; someone who could run at the defence and open England up. In an effort to mix things up, Menotti made a change, with a double substitution on the hour mark. Larossa came on for Bochini and Rocha for Ortiz, but it failed to change the pattern of the game. The impetus lost, the crowd quietened. In direct inverse of '66, England began playing the ball back to their goalkeeper with regular frequency, but there was no slow hand-clapping, just a chorus of boos from the crowd. No possibility of misunderstanding the watching audience's feelings there. Only Emlyn Hughes clapped each time an English player passed back to Clemence, 'including applauding himself', *La Nacion* noted. England were getting to their hosts.

After Killer was finally booked on 77 minutes for taking out Channon, the game was petering out into nothing when suddenly Bertoni provided the spectacle he spoke of beforehand. England left-back Trevor Cherry tackled Bertoni from behind. It was not a foul. At least, not in England, anyway – more one of those tackles that divided England from the rest of world: a two-footed challenge in which 1970s English defenders would specialise, sliding through the man from behind to take the ball. The ball went out for a throw. Bertoni pulled himself up from the floor, and Cherry retrieved the ball, brushing past Bertoni on the way. Without warning Bertoni spun around and punched Cherry in the mouth, knocking out his two front teeth. The Englishman did not retaliate, but the referee sent them both off. Cherry recalls: 'I'd had a brush with Bertoni in the first half. I'd probably caught him with a couple of tackles, and later in the game he just turned round and whacked me one. Unfortunately, the politics out there are that the ref sent us both off. I don't think he dared to send off just an Argentina player.' The crowd, awoken from their slumber, chanted 'Animales, Animales!' and on that sour note the match ended.

The incensed crowd booed both teams off, and the English players were advised to change quickly and leave. They boarded their coach and were given a police motorcycle escort back to their hotel.

"Trevor Cherry must be the unluckiest player to have been sent off ever," said Don Revie in the post match conference. "Not only was it not a foul, but he lost his two front teeth."

Menotti and Revie sat next to each other. This was meant to be part of the bridge building process, but the Bertoni–Cherry incident had thrown a spanner in the works. "It was a deplorable incident," added Revie, forgetting his cordiality.

All thoughts of bridge-building went out of the window back in England. 'SHAME OF THE ANIMALS', screamed the *Sunday Express*. 'Argentina throws a brick against its own World Cup window'. The *Mail on Sunday* spoke of, 'violence against the England team', and the *Sunday People* believed the Uruguayan referee was a coward: 'To compensate the sending off of Bertoni, he sent Cherry off as well'. The *News Of The World* neatly summed things up by stating, 'the match started well, but couldn't have finished worse.'

The *Daily Telegraph* rightly concluded that, 'the old and bitter history of the sporting incompatibility between England and Argentina returned to manifest itself again when the brutality exploded into violence and caused the sending off of Cherry and Bertoni.'

Speaking about the incident today, Daniel Bertoni is full of remorse: "It was a hard match and there was tension in the air. Cherry followed me for the whole game. He marked me well, and tackled very hard. I reacted badly and punched him. I regret my action so much. I was young, 22 years old, and it was a tough match, more like a World Cup qualifier than a friendly. We played to the death, but I was wrong, very wrong, and I received a four-match suspension."

Bertoni still has the scars on his knuckles from Cherry's teeth, but, despite the four-match ban, he returned to play a key role in Argentina's 1978 World Cup victory, scoring a goal in the 3-1 victory over Holland in the final.

Reaction to the incident was more muted in Argentina. The real story for the press there was not to provoke further animosity against the English, but how their team was going to win the following summer's World Cup. 'OPAQUE FOOTBALL', was the headline in *La Nacion*. It spoke of the 'unusual atmosphere' and how 'the tension had been the worst in the series so far'. The match reports are accompanied by photos of the generals in the directors' boxes, and finish with a long list of the members of the military junta present in the stands. Many papers were critical of Menotti and Argentina's performance. 'No sign of evolution, the team didn't function collectively, and offered an image of impotence,' said *Cronico*. 'Menotti is under pressure.' Maybe the generals were considering firing him at that point? (figuratively speaking). *Cronico* also criticised England for lacking imagination: 'We hardly saw the much talked about Kevin Keegan in this match of irritating monotony, a match to forget.'

Menotti defended his team's performance: "We've got a lot more time yet, we're still trying things out. England were very defensive, but the game showed we can compete against any team in the world." The following week Argentina also drew 1-1 with Ally McLeod's Scotland, also in La Bombonera, in a nasty encounter that saw winger Willie Johnston and Argentine right-back Pernia sent off for fighting. Argentinian historian and writer Klauss Gallo, who attended both matches, remembers that whereas 'God Save the Queen' had been roundly booed against England, the same national anthem was cheered a week later by the same noisy crowd before the match against Scotland. It seems it was only the English who riled Argentinian tendencies quite so much.

Back at the press conference, accused of negative tactics, Don Revie contested that his team had played 4-4-2, and that was not defensive. He expressed his love for "the South American style", but said "it works well here, but wouldn't work in the modern European game." Menotti shot him a puzzled look, and shook his head. Revie continued, "Bearing in mind my players have played ten months consecutively without a break, I have to be satisfied, especially that we've drawn away from home against Brazil and Argentina, two favourites for the World Cup."

Revie then predicted that the four semi-finalists at Argentina '78 would be Argentina, Brazil, Holland and Germany, a small faux pas, as the World Cup had not had semi-finals since 1970 – instead featuring a second group stage with the winners progressing to the final and the two second-placed teams contesting a third/fourth play-off match – and would not be having them in 1978 either. Not that it mattered that the England manager was not familiar with World Cup structure as his team would not be going, anyway.

The press remarked that Revie looked and sounded like a man under pressure, suggesting that the stress of World Cup qualification was taking its toll. They were wrong. Revie was now actually under no pressure at all to qualify for the World Cup. Not unless the United Arab Emirates were expecting to qualify, that is. He had spent the night before the game against Argentina sitting up with FA executives, negotiating the termination of his contract. Unbeknownst to them, he had already accepted a lucrative offer from the Emirates, for which he later received a year ban from English football when it came to light.

Three days later, England played out a dreary defensive 0-0 draw in Uruguay, Revie's last game as manager, and a fitting epitaph to this dismal period in English international football history. Ron Greenwood took temporary charge and went for all-out attack against Italy in November, with Steve Coppell and Peter Barnes on the wings. Brooking and Keegan combined perfectly for both England goals in a 2-0 victory, but it was too little too late. England failed to qualify for the World Cup on goal difference, having not scored heavily enough against either Luxembourg or Finland.

Under Menotti's leadership and with Kempes, Ardiles and Passarella as the kingpins, Argentina won the 1978 World Cup on home soil, but those images of Mario Kempes galloping through the ticker tape and the Dutch defence in the final will forever be associated with the country's dictators. When Passarella went up to collect the cup, it was General Videla, the commander of the death squads, who handed it to him, and how many times has it been repeated that while the team ran their lap of honour, the screams from the torture chambers could be heard just a few blocks down the road.

It must be difficult for the players who lifted the trophy. Imagine fulfilling your boyhood dream, only for it to become mixed up with stories of black Ford Falcons coming to take people away in the middle of the night. *El proceso* (the process) it was called; torture and genocide. Between 1976 and 1982 over 30,000 people disappeared in Argentina.

"What player doesn't want to play for his country?" asks Ricardo Villa rhetorically. "Yes, it's true, we were used by the military government. We were their little toys and in that sense I feel bad. I was a simple footballer and I thought only about playing. Honestly, I was not aware of what was going on politically. It was only when I went abroad that I began to hear things about the Disappeared. Today, with all the clarity we have about what happened, all I can say is yes, I feel bad about it, but what can I do? The only thing I can do is to hope 'never again'.

"They used the fervour of the people, the enthusiasm and passion of Argentinians for World Cup football. It's easy to fool the people, but it was a strategy that did not reach the players. We were normal people. If people say it's barbaric that we played for the national team at that time, well, with respect to all this, I don't want to defend the government in any way, but I will absolutely defend the football part to the hilt. A footballer only wants to play for his country and become champion of the world and if the president of the country is democratic or not that's due to non-related circumstances. We knew absolutely nothing about what was going on.

"Luckily for me, I didn't have any family disappear. There wasn't the technology of today, nor the internet, with all the information it provides. We were naïve, but I can look myself in the mirror. I was born a footballer, a long way from governments, with a different way of thinking. What footballer doesn't want to play for his country and become world champion?"

Mario Kempes is not known for his good memory. His only recollection of the friendly against England in 1974, in which he scored both Argentina's goals, is that Wembley Stadium was "very impressive", but obviously when it comes to reminiscing on 1978, things are clearer. Kempes had struggled through the group games without scoring, and the joke was that this was due to his moustache. It was captain Daniel Passarella who suggested a shave, and in the next match, Argentina beat Poland 2-0 with Kempes scoring both goals, setting him on the way to the Golden Boot award as the tournament's top scorer with six goals.

The real reason that many attribute to Kempes' and Argentina's better perfomances in the second round was the change of stadium. Having lost to Italy, Argentina were obliged to play their second round matches in Rosario Central's stadium, where Kempes had been a local hero before moving to Valencia in Spain. "The crowd are close to the pitch, and they love football," says Kempes. "The noise was incredible, and it had a very positive effect, not just on myself, but the whole team."

After beating Poland, Argentina drew 0-0 with Brazil in a very tight match. "Menotti kept reminding us we were playing for the people. In all the team talks he emphasised the people. It was nothing to do with the government," says Kempes, smoking a cigarette as if in honour of his manager of the time. It is a tribute well paid, as Ricky Villa agrees. "It was a new era for Argentine football," he says, "and Menotti got the players together both on and off the pitch. A coach is also a conductor in life; he forms people, customs and attitudes. He taught us how to manage the ball, to improve our defects and to repeat situations. Sincerely, I believe that any player who passes through the hands of Menotti will become a better player. He is the same now as ever, strong in his convictions, always preaching players to hold onto the ball and look for the spaces."

But besides the controversy of a World Cup being organised by a military dictatorship interested more in controlling their populace than pure sporting glory, there was also the suspicion of match-fixing. Brazil beat Poland 3-1 in a match that kicked off two hours before Argentina faced already-eliminated Peru, meaning Argentina knew precisely the result required to reach the final. The Brazilians had complained beforehand, but FIFA said they could not change the times due to contracts and arrangements with television companies. Argentina needed to beat Peru by four goals to reach the final. They won 6-0, with the Peruvians capitulating after only being one goal behind in the moments leading up to half-time. Rumours have always persisted.

"It's inevitable that people say these things," says Villa resignedly. "They say we paid money, that we fixed the match, but they're lying."

In Argentina there have been books and documentaries that have investigated the circumstances of the Peru match, but evidence is thin. Attention centres on Peruvian defender Manzo, who is arguably at fault on a couple of the goals, and who later played in Argentina for Velez Sarsfield, but, naturally, he has always denied any wrongdoing. What is a fact is that the Peruvians, who could not qualify for either the final or the play-off match, were an unhappy bunch before the game. The majority of the squad either played for Sporting Cristal or Alianza Lima, the two big Peruvian club sides, and were divided along those lines, bickering and disunited. The players have said that all they wanted to do was go home once they were eliminated. Peruvian goalkeeper Quiroga, who lived in Argentina and played for Rosario Central, at whose stadium the match was held, has always had the finger of suspicion pointed at him as well. But watching the game on video, it is difficult to fault him on the goals, apart from the fifth one, where his positioning could be better on a cross. Peru actually hit the post and could have taken the lead when the score was still 0-0.

Circumstantial evidence is equally flimsy. There has been much speculation over shipments of grain from Argentina to Peru, which was also under military rule. This is based on shipping invoices in Buenos Aires docks, but closer analysis shows that there was nothing unusual in these exports, as similar loads were regularly transported throughout the previous years. The *Sunday Times* produced a very inflammatory article on the day of England versus Argentina in the 1986 World Cup that claimed the Peru result had been arranged. It quoted an anonymous civil servant, who had served during the dictatorship, and two anonymous football officials. The author of the article, Maria Avignola, has always refused to reveal her sources, without which it is difficult to gauge its credibility.

Other conspiracy stories that have been written in English publications include the military forcing the Argentina players to have drug injections before the Peru match, and one of the Argentina players showing up as being 'pregnant' in the post-match urine analysis – a clear indication that they had given false samples. Mario Kempes and Alberto Tarantini were accused of being so high after the match that they could not stop running for an hour, but no sources or evidence are ever presented. To this investigator's mind, they appear to be tales invented from nowhere.

Needless to say, the idea, in England, of Argentina fixing the '78 World Cup in their favour, adds to the antagonism between the two countries, just as the thought of England fixing 1966 does in Argentina.

But are all the stories made up?

It is true, though, that President Videla, accompanied by former US secretary of state Henry Kissinger, did enter both dressing rooms and speak to both set of players before the Peru match. Rather than threatening the visitors, however, he was, according to Kissinger himself, merely wishing them 'good luck'.

Ricky Villa believes that rather than the president intimidating the Peruvians and motivating his countrymen, it was the crowd who performed those functions. Villa, who had came on as a substitute in the previous matches against Poland and Brazil, was an unused substitute against Peru. "The crowd in Rosario received us with a fervour, a force that motivated us, and it was there that we began to play this style of football that we claim so much. I honestly believe the crowd scared the opposition as well. It was complicated against Peru. The games were staggered for TV and the moment the final whistle went in the other match – Brazil 3 Poland 1 – the players took to the pitch knowing we had to win by four goals. Menotti delivered a very passionate team talk. He told us we had to play well and that if we played well the people would go home happy regardless of the result.

"We were very focused, and we were going to play in the same manner as always. Menotti had great conviction in his beliefs, and that evening was the culmination of his four years' work. We were going for all-out attack, but he stressed the need for calm and patience. We knew we needed two goals in the first half and we got them. We entered the changing rooms at half-time calmly, knowing we could do it."

The night turned into a demonstration of pure Menottism. Kempes (2), Tarantini, Luque (2) and Houseman scored the goals in front of a delirious home crowd. "Peruvian football is good but it lacks *garra* [balls]," states Villa. "They were already out and weren't playing for anything, and I think they gave up easily, but I swear I never saw anything unusual in that match." Manager Menotti has sworn on his daughters' lives that nothing underhand occurred that night and is always quick to remind the doubters that Argentina had won comfortably in Peru in a pre-tournament friendly. Perhaps it was simply that the Peruvians were tired and only wanted to go home.

"It was a normal match," says Kempes. "Three or four of the goals were moves we had worked hard on under Menotti, and we were very prepared and motivated. Somebody would have noticed if any of the players had fixed the match. I don't see how you could do it without anybody noticing."

Ardiles is more open to suggestion that the match could have been fixed and has even said that he would be prepared to return his World Cup winners' medal if anybody could demonstrate that fraud had taken place. "On our part, the players and the coaching staff, I can say for certain that there was absolutely nothing irregular. But, obviously over time a lot of doubts have arisen about this match. If you ask me if the military would be capable of doing that, well they were capable of doing anything. All I can say is I don't know. I hope they didn't do anything and the triumph has been a simple sporting one. If it wasn't I would feel bad and would give back my medal."

"In the end, I suppose it's just a question of whether you believe these things or not," says Villa. And perhaps he's right. In England we are as prepared to believe the conspiracy theories behind Argentina '78 as the Argentines are to shout about those behind England '66.

Watching a film in Argentina of the 1978 World Cup, it's the first time I've seen these images since sneaking downstairs after midnight as an 11-year-old to watch the matches live on TV. Memories come flooding back; the frenzied crowds, the ticker-tape reception, the smiling Gauchito mascot in his sombrero, that repetitive haunting chant of "Ar-gen-tin-a, Ar-gen-tin-a" and, of course, as the camera pans the crowd, the sinister image of the Generals presiding over it all.

Argentina beat Holland 3-1 after extra time in the final, with two solo goals from Kempes and one from Bertoni. There was no talk of match-fixing surrounding this game. Rensenbrink hit the post in the last minute of normal time with the score at 1-1 and nearly won the Cup for Holland. On the back of Argentina's World Cup triumph, Ardiles and Villa moved to Tottenham Hotspur, a transfer which caused a sensation in England.

"We Argentinians always want to play in Europe – today, yesterday, always," says Villa. "The money is abroad. After the World Cup, we returned to our clubs. I was at Racing and Ossie was at Huracan. Both clubs had financial problems, so when Tottenham came to search for players, the possibility of signing Osvaldo and myself was the most concrete for them. I don't think they knew me very well but they knew Osvaldo because he'd played more games in the World Cup. We just closed our eyes and went. We didn't know anything about England, nor what to expect, but our arrival was big news and at every match the people looked at us as if we were something strange, but nobody ever treated us badly. We were always given great respect."

Argentina 1 (Bertoni 16')
England 1 (Pearson 3')
Sunday 12 June 1977. Bombonera Stadium, Buenos Aires. Friendly. Attendance: 50,000
Referee: Ramón Barreto Ruiz (Uruguay)

Argentina: Hector Baley (Huracan), Daniel Killer (Racing), Vicente Pernia (Boca Jnrs), Daniel Passarella(c) (River Plate), Alberto Tarantini (Boca Jnrs), Osvaldo Ardiles (Huracan), Américo Gallego (Newells Old Boys), Ricardo Bochini (Independiente, sub 60'), Daniel Bertoni (Independiente), Leopoldo Luque (River Plate), Oscar Ortiz (River Plate, sub 60'), Subs: Omar Larossa (Independiente, on 60'), Juan Ramon Rocha (Newells Old Boys, on 60')
Manager: Cesar Menotti

England: Ray Clemence (Liverpool), Phil Neal (Liverpool), Emlyn Hughes (Liverpool), Dave Watson (Manchester City), Trevor Cherry (Leeds), Ray Wilkins (Chelsea), Brian Greenhoff (Manchester Utd, sub 45'), Brian Talbot (Ipswich), Kevin Keegan(c) (Liverpool), Mick Channon (Southampton), Stuart Pearson (Manchester Utd), Sub: Ray Kennedy (Liverpool, on 45')
Manager: Don Revie

MUTUAL RESPECT

WEMBLEY STADIUM, TUESDAY 13 MAY 1980

EVERY NOW and then a match comes along that is a joy to watch. In 1980 all the ingredients were there; world champions versus a resurgent England on their own turf. Managers Ron Greenwood and Cesar Menotti both preached open, attacking football, and in Kevin Keegan and Diego Maradona, the European and South American footballers of the year, both teams possessed a player who could genuinely live up to the hype. Throw in a relaxed spring evening, with little at stake, and an entertaining friendly was eagerly anticipated.

"I think it's going to be quite some game," said Greenwood. "I believe friendlies like this should be a platform for what football is all about. Certainly if we have anything to do with it, it'll be a game to remember, and Argentina's attacking attitude at the 1978 World Cup suggests they think the same way."

In 1966, delegates, managers, players, not to mention the press, had all sensed a bad match was on its way, and they willed it on in a self-fulfilling prophecy. In 1980, it was the reverse. "I like this current England team," said Menotti, "because they believe in attack. Every one of their players is capable of getting forward and scoring, and all the English players hit the ball very hard, a virtue not many teams have."

World champions Argentina flew into London on a Thursday evening, five days before the match, which was a tough workout for England a month ahead of the 1980 European Championships in Italy in which England would be taking on two Hispanic opponents in the host nation and Spain in their tricky-looking group.

Something had changed. Maybe because it was FA Cup final weekend, with finalists Arsenal also playing in the European Cup Winners' Cup final the following Wednesday, or maybe it was the refreshing way Argentina had played in the '78 World Cup, and the positive effect Ardiles and Villa were having on the English game since their arrival at Tottenham, but there was not a single adjective out of place in any English newspaper. For the first time since 1966, the word 'Animals' was nowhere to be seen.

Ardiles had decided not to play against his adopted country though, as he did not want "to risk my good relationship with the English people." Villa was injured and would not risk his reputation either. "It'd be a bad gesture if Ardiles plays," acknowledged Menotti. "Besides, I know everything about him already and his place in the 1982 World Cup squad is assured." Mario Kempes was also unavailable as he was playing for Valencia against Arsenal in the Cup Winners' Cup final the night after the international (Valencia won after extra time and penalties).

Despite not playing, Ardiles and Villa welcomed their compatriots to England. "I suspect it will be Wilkins who draws the short straw and has to mark Maradona," Villa told Argentine journalists who only wanted to know about England's plans to shackle the boy genius. Ardiles disagreed: "No, I don't think they'll assign anyone in particular to mark Diego. It's one of the peculiarities of the English game that they play in zones and don't man-mark. Wilkins may be the one who has to pick up Diego in the sense that he'll probably be the nearest to him for much of the game, but other times it will be the defenders, depending on whose zone he moves in. The English let you play. The English don't like the free man and that's what Maradona is. He starts from deep, but then comes through the middle and joins the attack. It's what I do at Tottenham and it drives the English crazy because they're not used to it. It's one of the reasons I've been successful here."

Ardiles explained how centre-forward Leopoldo Luque would drift out to the left wing, leaving the centre free for Maradona to dribble into from deep. But "watch out for Kevin Keegan," Ardiles warned. "Really, he's special. He looks like an awkward player who can't dribble, but he can. You think he doesn't know how to shoot, but believe me he does. He is a very intelligent player, who always plays the precise ball and takes up the right positions."

The British public had first witnessed Maradona a year earlier when Argentina had beaten Scotland 3-1 in a friendly at Hampden Park, Glasgow. The 18-year-old had created his team's first two goals, both scored by Luque, and then rounded off an absorbing display with a brilliant solo third, for which he was applauded off the pitch by the Tartan Army. "It's amazing how popular Maradona is here in Britain," said Ardiles, "and they've hardly seen him play."

The wonder goal against Scotland has only ever been seen by those who were in attendance at Hampden Park as there was a television strike. In the absence of any footage, Scotland goalkeeper George Wood recounted the goal (to Nick Harris of the *Independent*) 25 years later: "It's still clear in my memory. He picked up the ball, it seemed like on the edge of his own box, and went through everyone without stopping, leaving just him and me. First I forced him out wide, to my left. He shot anyway, but over-hit it. I thought 'I've got away with this' because the ball was heading away towards the flag. But then he chased it to the goal line and I went with him. I dived, to my right this time, thinking he was going to cut back another shot. But he just put his foot on the ball instead. That left a gap to my left, and I recovered to dive that way because he was shaping to shoot there. Except he didn't. As I dived left, he tucked it inside the near post. It was unbelievable skill, executed with so much confidence. Jock Stein said to me afterwards 'He's done you at the near post, George.' And I said, 'No boss, he did me three times actually.'

"For everything good that a goalkeeper can do, more likely is you'll end up one day as a souvenir in someone else's book. That's what happened to me. You look at Maradona's autobiography and there's me in the picture after he's scored his first Argentina goal. Me, on all fours in the goalmouth, helpless.

"There were some big-name players in the Scotland side that day, Alan Hansen, Kenny Dalglish, John Wark, Arthur Graham; and Maradona was just tying them in knots. He was only 18, but he was strong, mobile and had fantastic balance and ball control. Even when we tried to push him off the ball he was stocky and could stick with it. He was just a kid and yet he was able to take the Mickey.

"Of course, in our dressing room afterwards we were despondent, heads down because we lost the game. But everyone was talking about Maradona. I'd never heard of Maradona before that day. I don't think any of us knew much about him at all, apart from the newspapers on the day of the match that said Argentina might play this new wonderkid. We all knew who he was at the end."

In 1980, Argentina were staying at the Royal Gardens Hotel in Kensington, the same location in which Stanley Rous had chosen/drawn/hand-picked the referees for the 1966 quarter-final, but the Argentine journalists were more preoccupied with the on-off transfer saga of one of their players than reliving that particular controversy. The much talked about Diego Maradona had left Argentina 'mentally and spiritually exhausted' after several days in the spotlight. Argentinos Juniors had requested that their player be removed from AFA's list of 34 untransferrable players, so that they could sell him to Barcelona for an unprecedented £6 million dollars (£3 million), eclipsing the record of £1.75 million paid by Juventus to Vicenza in 1976 for the services of Paolo Rossi. The 19-year-old had arrived at the airport to join his team-mates travelling to England, hiding on the floor of his father's car.

There was opposition to the transfer in Barcelona. The Catalan communist party branded it 'shameful' at a time of crippling economic crisis and rising unemployment. Barcelona's Danish striker Allan Simonsen described the fee as 'madness'.

Upon arrival in London, the Argentine players slept in until 1pm the next day to recover from jet lag, before going to the Bank of England training grounds for an intense training session. A hastily arranged press conference had been convened to satisfy the world's media, camped on the doorstep of the hotel awaiting news of the world's biggest transfer. All the players came down to meet the journalists except the one they wanted to see. Diego Maradona had been advised to stay in his room.

The 19-year-old had actually signed for Barcelona a week beforehand, but the transfer had now been cancelled by the Argentina Football Association. A new rule introduced by the military dictatorship stated that no player under the age of 20 would be allowed to leave the country. The Spanish television crew wanted to speak to Maradona personally, but in his absence, Julio Grondona, president of AFA, explained the situation. "Resolution 37 exists for the good of Argentina, for the good of our football clubs, for the good of our players, and for the good of the national team, so we're going to stick to our country's rules," he stated.

"What would happen if Argentinos Juniors took the issue to court?" asked the Spanish press.

"They wouldn't," said Grondona, "because resolution 37 is one of the rules of AFA and they belong to AFA."

"What about Maradona? Isn't it unjust that you're denying him the right to gain an extraordinary sum of money? Couldn't he also take you to a court of justice?"

"No," said Grondona. "I know Diego well and he would never do that. Let me speak clearly, the rules are the rules, and they are to be obeyed, without exceptions. I believe we can find a satisfactory solution to all this. I believe we can find businesses in our country that can fund Argentinos Juniors and Maradona nearly as much money as Barcelona are willing to pay them."

So, there it is. Back in 1980, for the first time, a player had become owned, not by his club, but a third party; a consortium of agents and commercial interests. Barcelona president Josep Nuñez, who was in London to meet Grondona, asked how much it would cost to take Maradona's name off the list of the 34 untransferrable players, but, in the end, Maradona was loaned to Boca Juniors by the business consortium that now owned him (he finally joined Barcelona two years later, after the 1982 World Cup).

When he was 14, one of Maradona's friends from the shanty town where he grew up, Jorge Cyterszpiler, had offered to become his personal manager. Cyterszpiler, a year older than Maradona, had a bad leg and could never join in with their little games of *futbolito* on the dust pitches of Villa Fiorito, so stood watching from the side. Maradona had always felt sorry for Cyterszpiler and when his friend offered to become his personal manager, the adolescent Maradona put him in charge of accounts. When the Barcelona directors had flown to Argentina to broker a deal the week before the match against England, *Clarin* carried a photo of Maradona signing the now obsolete contract. That photo, published on 5 May 1980, shows Barcelona president Josep Nuñez and his powerful directors Nicolaus Caucaus, and Joan Gaspart, besuited, with serious faces, sitting around a table with the teenagers, Cyterszpiler and Maradona, while an assortment of scruffily-dressed family and friends stand in the background. The curly-mopped boys look like two mischievious kids who cannot believe what is happening. Cyterszpiler, wearing a leather jacket, is grinning from ear to ear, with a cigarette in his mouth, as Maradona puts pen to paper. In a cartoon he would have dollar signs in his eyes.

Many years later, attempting to explain why he was nearly bankrupt at 30, Maradona revealed that Cytzerspiler's accounting had not been the best over the years, and that everything had been done on trust, with no papers signed between them. "Cyterszpiler had had such bad luck with figures that quite a few noughts went missing from the accounts." (Cyterszpiler today is one of the world's top football agents, specialising in taking South American players to Europe, but is not on speaking terms with Maradona.) Might the collapse of his deal to move to Barcelona affect his performance against England?

After the Spanish TV crews had left the Kensington Gardens Hotel, without so much as a glimpse of the teenager, he did eventually come down from his room and spoke to Argentine journalists who were staying at the same hotel. "No, absolutely not; to lose the opportunity of earning 3 million dollars, well, I don't think anybody would like that, but football is my life and when I'm on the pitch money doesn't exist," Maradona told them. "At Wembley, I'm going to play the game of my life. I'm going to play to the death. First, because we are the champions of the world, and we've got to demonstrate that we're worthy of the title, and secondly, for what the stadium represents. In 150 internationals the English have only lost 3 times [to foreign opposition] at Wembley and you remember that match in '66, when they sent off Rattin and fixed the result? I was only five years old then, but, growing up, I heard so much about it and I've always dreamed about that match and that if I'd been playing that day I would've scored a goal. That's always been my big dream, to score a goal against the English."

An early example of Maradona's own particular brand of jingoism and fantasy.

Omnipresent Ernesto Muñiz, the intrepid reporter previously responsible for classic interviews such as 'The Aggressive Joe Mercer' and 'Don Revie In A Lift', set about his task of tracking down the new England manager, and duly pounced at the FA's head-quarters at Lancaster Gate the day before the FA Cup final. And he would not take 'no' for an answer.

"Mr. Greenwood, is it true that Trevor Francis is injured and will miss the match against Argentina? Is it true Real Madrid are not releasing Laurie Cunningham for the match? There are rumours that Kevin Keegan has an injury and might not play. Is this true or just pre-match mind-games on your part?"

It is unlikely that the gentlemanly Greenwood would have even heard of the concept of psychological mind-games, let alone contemplate playing them, and he responded to Muñiz's questions quickly: "Oh please, concern yourself with your own team and don't worry about ours."

According to Muñiz, the England manager smiled, turned his back, and walked off towards his car. Muñiz followed him.

Greenwood, perhaps remembering that one of the responsibilties of his position was to be courteous at all times, especially towards Argentinians, who had been so bitterly offended by Alf Ramsey in 1966, stopped in his tracks and apologised to Muñiz for his abruptness. He then proceeded to answer all of his interrogator's questions in full. "The only absentee for sure will be Trevor Francis, who is injured. The others we'll have to see, but don't worry, we'll still have 11," assured Greenwood.

The England manager then invited Muñiz for a beer, which was turned down on the grounds that the Argentine did not drink alcohol. All this was reported in *La Nacion* the following day; the public informed that Ron Greenwood was dressed in a grey suit with a blue shirt and red tie, drove a light green Rover and headed off in the direction of Hyde Park (good work from the non-beer drinking roving reporter in these times of heavy censorship and dictatorial control in Argentina).

Thanks to a *Daily Telegraph* journalist who was at Lancaster Gate to collect his press pass for the FA Cup final, Muñiz was able to obtain Kevin Keegan's phone number in Hamburg, but unfortunately, when he rang, Keegan was out walking the dogs, so the readership of *La Nacion* had to suffice with an exclusive interview with Keegan's wife. It was printed up in full in the country's best selling broadsheet. According to Mrs Keegan, husband Kevin loved the dogs but was having difficulty walking, a problem with his right knee, but he had a great desire to play against Argentina at Wembley.

Muñiz concluded his pre-match analysis by complaining about the scant amount of newspaper space dedicated to the big game in England. 'It's almost as if there isn't a match on,' he whined. He does have a point. There was far less information in England on the colour of the manager's clothes and cars, and not a single exclusive with any of the players' wives. The only interview with an Argentine player's wife of any interest to a Brit was with the store detectives at Harrods after Mrs Tarantini and some of her friends were caught shoplifting hats and scarves. They were arrested and fined £1,000 each.

Alberto Tarantini, who had already spent one miserable season at Birmingham City after starring as a 19-year-old in the World Cup triumph, protested his wife's innocence. "I am destroyed emotionally, not only because I can imagine the things they're going to publish and say in Buenos Aires, but because all this has been the result of a big misunderstanding. At no point did my wife try to take something without paying. I'm very bitter about this. It's one of the worst moments of my life." Could this be the equivalent of Bobby Moore being detained in Bogota, Colombia for 'stealing' a bracelet?

As in Argentina's first visit in 1951, the players attended an English match. This time, it was the FA Cup final. They were all supporting the underdogs West Ham against Arsenal, as they could not believe a Second Division team could be playing in the final of such a prestigious competition. 'Another eccentricity of English football,' said Muniz, and he wrote about his Cup final experience in a full report, clearly moved and fascinated by the 'infernal din that you couldn't imagine' and the 'aggressive interchanging of gestures' between supporters as they made their way to the stadium, but there was 'lamentably, a surprising quantity of people in a state of inebriation with bags full of cans of beer.'

The Cup final also gave Muñiz another chance to accost Ron Greenwood, and he did so at half-time. Considering Greenwood had been West Ham manager for 18 years before taking on the England job, it is unlikely he would have been over-enthused by the sudden appearance of Muñiz during the break, on one of his club's greatest days. But Greenwood had to be careful as every single one of his words was printed up in *La Nacion* the next day in direct quotes:

"Oh, not you again. I congratulate you on your persistence. I know, you don't need to ask me, you want to know if Keegan, Francis, Woodcock and Cunningham are all going to play. If they can't play I ask you to do me a favour – go to Madame Tussauds and get them to make waxwork replicas of those players so that I can place them on the pitch on Tuesday, just to keep you happy and stop you asking me about them. Please ask me something different."

"Does this mean you're not happy with my line of questioning?"

"Yes, yes, clearly yes," said Greenwood at the Wembley bar. "Let's draw a line under the subject. It's most likely that none of them will play: Cunningham and Woodcock haven't been released from their clubs, Real Madrid and Cologne, Francis is definitely out injured and, as for Keegan, we won't know until Monday, the day before the match. We really do not know. I'm not trying to hide information from you. Now, come with me, get yourself a beer and I'm going to give you a pound for each time you don't ask me about the English team."

Ron Greenwood was impeccably dressed in a dark blue blazer with the badge of the Football Association woven in gold onto the pocket. He wore grey trousers, a white shirt and a blue tie that was also emblazoned with the FA's three lions emblem. 'He measures around 1m 85 in height, is semi-bald with blonde hair, he is jovial, has a soft voice, pauses a lot, but speaks a slow perfectly understandable English without any strange idiomatic turns of phrase that many other English people have – although, during the beer and brief chat, he was still unable to clear up the situation regarding the team for Tuseday,' reported Muñiz, diligently.

Immediately after the Cup final, the Argentine players trained in Kensington Gardens; some stretching, others undertaking a spot of ball work amongst the general public, who lounged in deckchairs. They gave their opinions on the Cup final. "Really, I thought it was only in our country and Brazil that you had such a euphoric atmosphere like that," said Leopoldo Luque. "Honestly, it was fantastic. You realise immediately that the people here really do love football and Wembley, what an intimidating place. It must be scary to play inside there."

Captain Daniel Passarella said, "What impressed me was that although West Ham were the champions, both teams did the lap of honour. I've never seen anything like that before. The England players do look awkward, but I'm warning our young players, as I've played against England before, that they aren't as awkward as they look, and when you're on the pitch, they run and run. It's much more difficult than it looks."

In their last training session, arranged by Ardiles and Villa at Tottenham's stadium, Argentina worked on defending headers and crosses, the English speciality. Right-back Jorge Olguin said, "The problem is not how the English head the ball, but how they jump to reach it. The only one of us who can compete with them in this aspect is Passarella [5 ft 8 ins], but it would be ridiculous if he tried to stop them alone. Therefore, we've all been practising how to jump and make shoulder-charges that are within the rules."

Menotti gave one of his typical prosaic press conferences, which the *Daily Mirror* summarised into a single sentence: 'The way we play is more important than the result, and we have an important commitment to play attacking football.' A neat précis from the *Mirror*, as actually Menotti had waxed lyrical for over half an hour, providing the uninitiated in England with a blueprint of pure Menottism: "Although we practised defending headers we haven't come here to defend, nor to steal a draw. On the contrary, we have come here to try and create a spectacle because to close the defence and play for a draw without glory would be a betrayal of the true Argentinian football values. I cannot predict the result, but this team must not let anyone down with their style of play. Our team must show why they are the current world champions, and that they have achieved something important with respect to a style of play, a style so often betrayed in the past..."

England trained on the Sunday and Monday, but Greenwood had serious problems with player availability. Trevor Brooking, who had scored the winning goal for West Ham in the Cup final on the Saturday, now had to play in a rearranged Second Division fixture up at Sunderland on the Monday night. Due to tiredness, he would start on the bench for Tuesday's international.

Winger Cunningham was definitely out, Real Madrid refusing to release him, but the good news was that Woodcock had been made available by Cologne, and Keegan, who was negotiating his transfer to Southampton, also believed he had a chance of being fit. "Keegan will arrive the day before the match," revealed Greenwood. "I know he's desperate to play, but I've told him to rest and not try to train. We'll give him a late fitness test. His knee's bad, but sometimes when a player's desire to play is so strong it overcomes the pain."

Naturally Ernesto Muñiz was at England's training ground to get all the latest news. Greenwood and the Argentine reporter appear to have struck up a friendship now, with the England manager granting him a chat over a cup of tea in the training ground canteen. "The important thing in this profession is to know how to find the solutions to the problems instantly, and not to lose your calm, nor think that the war is lost," explained the England manager. "Of course, I'm disappointed to have lost Trevor Francis and Laurie Cunningham, but it's inevitable. You can't have your first choice players all the time, and now I've got to find the remedy for the situation." Greenwood presented Muñiz with a photo of the England team and signed it, 'to my Argentinian friend'.

Muñiz also managed to get an interview with every single one of the England players. Ray Kennedy applied Scottish logic to the match. "The public have been very happy with our recent performances, and now we face the world champions, so if we beat them, then we will be the champions."

Phil Thompson delivered one of the worst football interviews ever. He started reasonably well, "for every professional footballer, it's an honour to play against the world champions and I hope we'll enjoy the match." But then, considering he's speaking to an Argentine journalist, he tailed off badly: "From what I saw of Argentina in the World Cup, I liked Kempes the most, and errm ... sorry, I can't remember the names of any of the others."

Kevin Keegan delivered the archetypal Kevin Keegan interview, "My dad was a miner, I know what it means to work hard" being a typical excerpt. He also revealed that one of the biggest influences on his career was a nun. Unfortunately, he did not elaborate, if he did say it, but the heavily-censored *La Nacion* no doubt thought it would be a nice idea to mention it and show the European footballer of the year in that light.

England were on a good run. They had qualified comfortably for the 1980 European Championships with resounding victories over both Irelands and Denmark, and had recently outplayed Spain in a friendly in Barcelona, winning 2-0 when it should have been more. Greenwood's teams had created a lot of chances, especially down the wings, with Coppell, Peter Barnes or Laurie Cunningham, and the manager was getting the best out of the Keegan–Brooking combination, both at the peak of their careers. But it was a rather downbeat England manager who spoke at the press conference the day before the match. Like Revie before him, Greenwood was far from happy with many aspects of the job. Asked about the formation of his team, not by Muñiz this time, but English reporters, the manager responded with a sigh: "I don't know, really I don't know. I've always believed English football must change the structure of its leagues, and I've asked the FA for only 18 clubs in the first division. It's absurd that the season's finished and England have a big match against the world champions, and the European Championships to prepare for, but there are still league matches being played. Nottingham Forest play at Wolves tonight and West Ham are at Sunderland, and I don't know if my players will be with me tomorrow or not. Neither do I know what condition they'll be in. I've asked Cloughie not to play Gary

Birtles tonight, but is that fair? If the public and the press of this country really want the national team to do well, then first they have to respect it and treat it like a newly born baby. That's the only way we can return to what we were.

"We've achieved our aim of qualifying for the European Championships, but England's return to a major competition [England had not competed in the finals of a major tournament since 1970] doesn't necessarily mean that everything's well in our football. In many ways it's just papering over the cracks." Most of Greenwood's words were not reported in England, due to a lack of newspaper space, or perhaps because they were not deemed interesting enough. In fact they struck at the heart of the structural change which would visit English football over the coming decade. However, Argentine papers printed his discourse in full. *Clarin* reported how, with the appointment of John Cartwright and Dave Sexton as youth coaches, men who shared Greenwood's philosophy, the England manager was hoping to instil his methods and ideas across the whole of the English game. "Some of the things I hear that are being coached at league clubs are quite shocking," said Greenwood. His opinions fell on deaf ears in his own country. Yet, throughout the 1980s, English football regressed in the opposite direction to Greenwood's ideas, with the long ball game coming more and more to the fore, too many games being played and not enough priority given to the national team.

"I like this current England team," said Menotti, inhaling on a cigarette, "because they believe in attack. The English don't all move together as a block, as say the Dutch or the Germans, but every one of their players is capable of getting forward, and all the English players hit the ball very hard, another virtue not many teams have, including the Dutch.

"We also know how good they are in the air. I've been explaining to my defenders that the English don't all go up to jump for the ball, but some just jump for the charge and we've emphasised to our players how important it is to try not to give away corners." *La Nacion* noted that ultra-cool Menotti was wearing a new pair of brown leather boots, purchased the day before in a Carnaby Street boutique.

Greenwood returned the compliments: "Argentina have more flair, flamboyance and technique than any team in Europe, but they still have to apply some of the organisation, determination and spirit that an English or German team can bring into the game. Our two nations could borrow from each other to produce a perfect side. At Wembley tomorrow, our players will have to find the wit, wisdom and character to counteract the opposition's natural advantage."

❖

Keegan passed his fitness test and, in the absence of Brooking, would be playing in midfield instead of his usual striking position, but not the deep role Revie had assigned him in Buenos Aires in 1977, more as an attacking midfielder, very much like an Argentina no. 10, the shirt Maradona would be wearing.

Keegan was joined in midfield by Ray Kennedy on the left, and Coppell on the right, with Wilkins playing the holding role. Dave Watson and Phil Thompson, who had replaced the ageing Emlyn Hughes for both club and country, were the centre-backs, but Thompson had instructions to sit back in more of a sweeper's role to cover

Maradona's runs. Phil Neal of Liverpool was at right-back, Kenny Sansom of Crystal Palace left-back, Ray Clemence in goal, and up front David Johnson of Liverpool part-nered Woodcock. The manager had found the remedies he had spoken of. It was a balanced side.

The match at Wembley was transmitted live on Argentinian television, and afforded quite a build-up, but in England it would again only be highlights on *Sportsnight*. Argentina had six of their World Cup-winning team in their line up: Fillol, Olguin, Passarella, Taran-tini, Gallego and Luque. Wembley was sold out for the evening kick-off, but this time the referee, Mr B. McGinlay, was Scottish. Any Argentine doubts concerning the referee's neutrality were soon put to rest when it was explained that all Scots fiercely want England to lose. Always.

England had a new kit, and now the purists were really upset as the white shirt also had red and blue over the front, as well as down the sleeves. Argentina wore their traditional blue and white stripes with black shorts. 'God Save the Queen' was cheered, the Argen-tinian national anthem roundly booed, but this did not offend so much anymore, just an accepted part of Wembley formalities.

As expected, Maradona sat deep before moving forward into the spaces. He combined well with Valencia in the first minute, and moments later, Passarella, the centre-back and captain, demonstrated that Argentina had come to attack by sprinting the length of the field to head a cross metres wide. Without a chance to draw breath, and with Passarella still at the wrong end of the pitch, Keegan shot wide. Disappointing in Buenos Aires in '77, the now bubble-permed England captain was at the height of his popularity, the first foot-balling popstar. Literally. His single, 'Head Over Heels' was in the charts. No Argentine teenage upstart was going to steal his show, even if Maradona's hair was naturally more curly.

Argentina did exactly what their manager had instructed them to try to avoid, giving away a corner after 10 minutes. In contrast to Keegan, Dave Watson wore lank jet-black hair with a headband, and the sight of the 6ft 2 ins centre-back trotting up the pitch like an Indian chief on the warpath to take up his position in the opposition's penalty area, was a regular feature of England corners during this era. Argentina may have done their heading homework, but they were unable to prevent Watson leaping to meet Woodcock's curling corner. It was a strong header, but Fillol saved.

Shortly afterwards, Maradona sent Valencia away on the left as the game continued to be engaging and entertaining. The forward advanced towards goal, beat Clemence with a cross shot but, luckily for England, Sansom was on hand to anxiously clear off the line. Valencia hit the rebound against the post. It was an escape for England.

On 19 minutes came a very significant moment. Maradona received the ball on the right, just inside the English half, and set off on a speedy run. With turns and shimmies he evaded Kennedy and Wilkins, cutting inside Sansom on his left, sprinting past Watson on his right, the ball glued to his foot. Leaving four England players in his wake, and with only Clemence to beat, Maradona shot across the England goal, the ball going agonisingly wide of the far post. The Wembley crowd gasped and then stood *en masse* to applaud the little teenager – yes, back in 1980 the English public gave Maradona a standing ovation.

"I phoned my brother after the game," said Maradona a few years later. "We spoke about that run. 'Why didn't you go round the keeper?' he said. 'You should've placed the ball with your left, not shot with your right.' I always remembered my little brother's words." Maradona would not make the same mistake again when a virtual carbon-copy run presented him with the same situation in Mexico six years later.

Halfway through the first half, Santamaria crossed from the right, but Valencia, completely free at the far post, could not connect. Another chance had gone begging. At the other end, on 34 minutes, a strong header from Woodcock produced another fine save from Fillol. Fine, crisp play burst from both sides. While Argentina's build ups were more patient – waiting for the breaks, looking to send the strikers away with careful through balls on the ground – Keegan bossed and ordered, always demanding the ball be played forward quickly.

Two minutes before half-time, Phil Neal played the ball out to Coppell on the right wing. Maybe Tarantini's mind was on other things because Coppell beat him easily and took the ball to the bye-line, chipping in a high centre. Johnson jumped between Gallego and Passarella and headed goalwards, leaving Fillol with no chance. A classic piece of traditional English wing play with an old-fashioned centre-forward's header to finish off the move had brought the first goal. No amount of practice seems to have resolved the old Argentine weakness against the English strength of crosses and headers. It sent England into the break a goal up.

Five minutes after the restart, centre-halves Van Tuyne and Passarella hesitated, allowing Kennedy on the left to cross for an unmarked Johnson, who produced another rocket header. 2-0. 'The power he got in the header was so strong it was as if he hit it with his foot,' said *La Nacion*.

Johnson ran behind the goal and saluted the cheering crowd. Crosses against short centre halves were meat and drink to the Liverpool striker, who was making a rare international appearance thanks to the absence of Francis. Undoubtedly this was his finest hour in the white, with red and blue bits on the front, England shirt.

'Don't cry for me, Argentina', the hit song from the musical *Evita* rang around the Wembley terraces between chants of 'England, England', but two minutes after Johnson's second goal, Maradona began another run. He dribbled past Wilkins and Watson on the right, before entering the penalty area, where Sansom tripped him. Passarella hit the penalty high and strong. 2-1 in the blink of an eye. Could Argentina come back, as they had done in the last match at Wembley in '74?

End to end, a thrilling match ensued. From England's left, Kennedy crossed for Woodcock, who skilfully turned Van Tuyne to shoot low, producing yet another good save from Fillol. England made no attempt to close the game down and defend their lead, instead cavorting up the pitch in search of a third goal. Keegan did not want to stop attacking. He ran and ran, an innate desire to prove himself against the best after the opportunity had been denied him when England had failed to qualify for the World Cup. But, on 60 minutes, Luque shot narrowly over from Santamaria, wasting a good chance. The moustachioed World Cup winner was substituted two minutes later, replaced by Ramon Diaz, the 18-year-old wonderkid who had starred alongside Maradona in Argentina's 1979

Youth World Cup triumph in Japan, and bizarrely ended up managing Oxford United in 2004.

Coppell's direct running down England's right was balanced by Kennedy's deeper play on the left. On 69 minutes, Johnson demonstrated that he was more than just a battering ram by moving into open space on the left wing to collect a pass from Kennedy. Johnson's cross was instantly controlled on the penalty spot by Coppell, who laid it off perfectly for Keegan, who capped a marvellous personal performance by volleying past Fillol for England's third. The pop star saluted the crowd.

Even with a two-goal cushion, England did not try to close down the game. Brooking came on for Kennedy, Birtles for Johnson, and Cherry (exorcising demons) for Neal, attacking rather than defensive substitutions. Fillol was called upon to make more impressive saves, from Coppell and Woodcock, while Clemence stopped a shot from Valencia when the Argentina striker, after being put through by Maradona, should have done better than shoot straight at him. In the final minute, Diaz, dribbling in from the left, rounded Clemence, but his cross from a tight angle was cleared off the line once again by Sansom.

It had been a superb match, packed with entertainment and barely a niggly tackle. All the players swapped shirts. Keegan and Maradona hugged and walked off the pitch together wearing each other's tops to the sound of feverish applause.

'A game so good it's difficult to find an adjective to describe. We haven't seen a better match for years,' claimed the *Daily Mirror*. And they weren't alone in heaping plaudits on the performance of both sides and the spectacle they had served up. *The Times* said, 'Argentina had caused problems in the first half, showing marvellous talent for instant control and releasing the ball after an opponent had committed himself to the tackle, but by the second half England had learnt to deal with it.' *La Nacion* said, 'We fell with honour, it shouldn't be treated as a tragedy, and we mustn't forget how well Argentina played in the first half.'

This game was arguably Greenwood's finest as England manager, the night when all his ideals on football came together. Aside from providing an entertaining match and bringing footballing philosophies and understanding closer together, old wounds had been healed considerably between the two nations, 14 years on from 1966. What could possibly stand in the way of ongoing cordiality now?

The post match press conference turned into a virtual love-in between Greenwood and Menotti. "It was a lovely match," said the happy England manager. "Argentina didn't come to defend a title, they came to play a game. They played well in the first half, but tired in the second due to the great movement of Tony Woodcock and Kevin Keegan."

Menotti said, "We played against a great adversary, but we added to the spectacle and contributed to a game of great quality. We made bad mistakes defensively in the second half, and that surprised me, but really I don't want to take anything away from England. The goals had as much to do with their qualities rather than our mistakes."

On Maradona, Greenwood said, "A few days ago I said that if he's to be considered a star he'll have to pass this exam. After what I've seen today, I assure you he could be considered a superstar, and, as a man of football, I have to say it was a real pleasure to watch him out there today because only very rarely do players of this extraordinary level appear."

Is Maradona as good as Pelé?, the press wanted to know. "Well, he's yet to win three World Cups, or score 1,000 goals, but yes he had a good game today," replied Menotti, who had played alongside Pelé at Santos.

Mutual compliments continued. "Argentina played openly and loyal to their attacking ideals," said Greenwood, "and you have to bear in mind they were without players of the capacity of Kempes, Ardiles and Bertoni, the first of whom is at the same level as Maradona and Keegan when it comes to finishing, which is what Argentina lacked today."

Menotti countered, "I liked the English team because they never stopped coming forward, and I congratulate Ron Greenwood for consolidating his philosophy of attack. The English should never forget that when they abandoned that philosophy they suffered big disappointments."

Maradona, however, did not share his manager's views that entertaining was as important as winning. "I'm really disappointed. I so much wanted to win. That we played good football is not a consolation. I hate losing even when it's only a friendly."

Captain Passarella said, "I didn't realise the English players could jump so high. But it's incredible that we created eight clear chances at Wembley, and came away losing. The defeat hurts, but this will serve as a lesson that we must correct our aerial play."

Back at the hotel, Menotti held one of his late night *tertulias* (a social gathering, usually with artistic overtones), staying up until 4am smoking, drinking and analysing the match with journalists. "We created more chances than the English, but the problem was the high balls. We didn't have much time to practise them, but we can work on it and eradicate that deficit, but they'll never have our virtues on the ball. We can improve, but they'll never have our skill."

Argentina flew to the Republic of Ireland the next day. The *Irish Standard* had described Argentina's match against England as a 'supershow', but the *Irish Independent* was furious with Diego Maradona. It claimed his representative had asked for a large sum of money for an interview with the player. They printed this story on their front page. Menotti defended his player. "Maradona has come here to play football and not to give interviews. If he conceded to all the requests he's had for interviews since we've left Buenos Aires, then we'd have to open up a special office 24 hours a day, and there still wouldn't be enough time for him to give them all."

Argentina beat Eire 1-0 with a goal from Valencia, nodding in the rebound from a Maradona free kick after the number 10 had been brought down on a solo run. They completed their tour with a 5-1 victory over Austria in Vienna, in which Maradona scored a hat-trick and created the two other goals.

When the squad arrived back in Buenos Aires, Maradona confessed to having been feeling low before they had left for Europe two weeks earlier. "That tour did me a world of good because I was feeling very down before we left. Maybe it was all the publicity about the transfer to Barcelona, I don't know, but I was feeling very down. It's something I can't explain. Sometimes I just feel very down." It was a comment not picked up on at the time, but with hindsight makes interesting reading. Maradona was just 19 years old and already revealing his fragility to the press. It would be a saga which would fill a billion column inches and minutes of airtime over the next 30 years. Equally interestingly, he also said,

"We broke the tradition of Argentina teams going to Europe to play defensively. We went out to attack all the time, but the only thing that leaves a bad taste in the mouth is that we could have beaten England at Wembley, but God didn't give us it." Maybe God was saving his helping hand for another time.

The Argentina team arrived back in Buenos Aires on 25 May, Independence Day. The troops and flags were out, military parades dominating the news. The head of the navy, General Galtieri, saluted his men as they marched through the city centre. With inflation spiralling out of control in Argentina's failing economy, there would be a change at the top soon, Galtieri taking over the presidency from General Videla.

On page two of *Clarin*, a piece of news was printed that did not warrant reporting in England. The British ambassador in Brazil, George Hall, had released a statement expressing British Foreign Office disapproval of a recent bilateral agreement Brazil had signed with Argentina over some islands called Las Malvinas.

The official statement read: 'We don't know what these Malvinas are but believe it's a reference to the Falkland Islands. If so, these islands are under the possession of Her Majesty the Queen. Let there be no doubts about their sovereignty. We believe it is possible to solve this problem in a friendly manner. The Falklanders are an example of a people who wish to continue to be British and Her Majesty will never abandon a community that wishes to preserve its British identity.'

England 3 (Johnson 42', 47' Keegan 69')
Argentina 1 (Passarella (pen) 53')
Tuesday 13 May 1980. Wembley Stadium, London. Friendly. Attendance: 92,000
Referee: Brian R McGinlay (Scotland)

England: Ray Clemence (Liverpool), Phil Neal (Liverpool, sub 77'), Kenny Sansom (Crystal Palace), Phil Thompson (Liverpool), Dave Watson (Manchester City), Ray Wilkins (Manchester Utd), Kevin Keegan(c) (Hamburg), Steve Coppell (Manchester Utd), David Johnson (Liverpool, sub 77'), Tony Woodcock (Cologne), Ray Kennedy (Liverpool, sub 74') Subs: Trevor Brooking (West Ham, on 74), Trevor Cherry (Leeds, on 77'), Gary Birtles (Nottingham Forest, on 77')
Manager: Ron Greenwood

Argentina: Ubaldo Fillol (River Plate), Jorge Olguin (Independiente), Jose Van Tuyne (Rosario Central), Daniel Passarella(c) (River Plate), Juan Barbas (Racing, sub 54'), Américo Gallego (Newells Old Boys), Diego Maradona (Argentinos Jnrs), Santiago Santamaria (River Plate, sub 62'), Leopoldo Luque (River Plate), Daniel Valencia (Talleres de Cordoba), Subs: Carlos Ischia (Vélez Sársfield, on 54'), Ramon Diaz (River Plate, on 62')
Manager: Cesar Menotti

THE HAND OF GOD

WORLD CUP QUARTER-FINAL, THE AZTECA STADIUM, MEXICO CITY, SUNDAY 22 JUNE 1986

THE SHADOW of the TV gantry in the Azteca stadium covered half the pitch like a giant spider. Captains Peter Shilton and Diego Maradona stood in the burning midday sun, shaking hands with referee Ali Bennaceur of Tunisia. One hour later the same three men would be involved in one of the most controversial World Cup goals of all time (and Anglo–Argentine football relations would hit an all-time low).

England versus Argentina was by now a fixture which held so much significance for both sporting and political reasons. This was the first competitive meeting between the two countries since 1966. Despite the friendly relations surrounding the previous encounter in 1980, most Argentinians still believed they had been the victims of a cons-piracy that afternoon at Wembley 20 years earlier. Moreover, and more immediately, the shadow of the Falklands conflict hung over Mexico's Azteca stadium. Argentina believed the islands should be theirs and invaded on 2 April 1982, the last desperate throw of the dice by a military junta beset by hyperinflation and growing public discontent. They also believed that Britain would not defend their remote outpost and that 'our American friends' would be capable of persuading Britain to negotiate a peace deal over sove-reignty. They would prove to be wrong on both counts. As General Galtieri, an alco-holic, took to the presidential balcony, drunk on both power and whisky, seeking to whip the crowds gathered below into a patriotic fervour, they had the theme tune to the 1978 World Cup played on radio stations to invoke the spirit of that cheering, flag waving occasion. The crowd responded by chanting his name. It was a slow three-note football chant, a tune still common on the terraces today ('Rii-quel-meee', or 'Dii-eee-goooo'). In 1982, thousands of people in *La Plaza de Mayo* were chanting, *en masse*, 'Gal-tieee-riiiii, Galt-tieee-riii'.

Margaret Thatcher, Britain's prime minister, despatched a taskforce to the south Atlantic to ensure the invasion was dealt with swiftly. It was, although there was much pain and loss of life on both sides, Argentinian cruiser General Belgrano being sunk with the loss of 323 lives when allegedly steaming away from the British-enforced exclusion zone while the British landing ship Sir Galahad was mortally struck by Argentinian planes at Bluff Cove, killing 48 and badly injuring many others.

The Falklands War turned Osvaldo Ardiles's and Ricardo Villa's whole world upside down. For three and half seasons in English football the pair had been a tremendous success, the high point of which was Tottenham's 1981 FA Cup final victory. "Ossie's goin' to Wembley, his knees have gone all trembly," sang Chas and Dave with the Spurs squad on *Top of the Pops*, a sign of the midfielder's popularity. But it was Villa who shone in the Cup final replay, scoring two goals, the second a stunning solo slalom – an Argentine *gambeta* – through the Manchester City defence, voted the greatest Cup final goal of all time by the BBC.

On the day after the Falklands invasion, Tottenham faced Leicester in an FA Cup semi-final at Villa Park on their way to a second successive Wembley appearance. Villa was injured, but Ardiles played, his every touch booed by the Leicester fans. Conveniently for Ardiles, the semi-final was due to be his last game for Tottenham that season anyway, in accordance with a FIFA ruling that stated clubs must release players to their national squads 60 days before the World Cup.

Ardiles has often recalled how this period was the most terrible time of his life; the two countries he loved the most going to war. The following season he did not feel he could play in England, so spent a season on loan to Paris St. Germain, but then returned to Tottenham without any problems for the 1983/84 season. He had lost a cousin in the war.

Villa stayed in England during the conflict, but one year on from his famous Wembley goal, and with Tottenham in the final again, there was much debate over whether it would be right for him to play. The war was at its most delicate point; the Belgrano and HMS Sheffield recently sunk, hundreds dead. Tottenham manager Keith Burkinshaw received death threats and an armed guard was placed outside his door. Villa was set to play in the final, but the night before, decided that, with his country in a state of war, he could not appear in the English Cup final. The repercussions for his family in his homeland could have been fatal. The Argentine midfielder stayed away from Wembley, but when the match against QPR finished in a 1-1 draw, Villa appeared on the touchline at the replay and waved to the Tottenham fans, who cheered and chanted his name. Could that have happened to an English player in Argentina? "He wouldn't even have made it onto the pitch," says Villa.

All told 649 Argentinians were killed (1,068 wounded), and 258 British died (777 wounded) in the war. Argentina surrendered on 14 June 1982, while the World Cup was underway in Spain, although thankfully the draw kept apart the two nations on that occasion. After the surrender, Argentine radio refused to mention the name of the country in their commentary on World Cup games involving England – "the ball is with the centre forward of the team in white shirts" – although, intriguingly, they had no problem with Scotland, even cheering a Scottish goal against South American rivals Brazil. Four years later, while the rights and wrongs of the conflict, as with any global set to, could be debated long and hard, there was no doubt that, as the teams lined up in the Azteca, feelings were raw on both sides and that the situation was tinder dry, ready for an explosion, although no-one could have seen what would ignite it.

Seeking to focus on football alone, both teams had publicly done their best to play down the external issues before the match. The English FA secretary Ted Croker had led the way: "Sport and politics do overlap occasionally, but sport closes gaps more easily. It's a wonderful opportunity to build a bridge." Somewhat optimistically, Croker added, "We are convinced only good can come out of this match."

How wrong could he be?

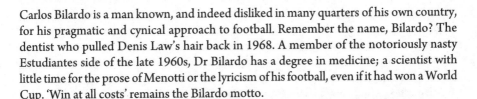

Carlos Bilardo is a man known, and indeed disliked in many quarters of his own country, for his pragmatic and cynical approach to football. Remember the name, Bilardo? The dentist who pulled Denis Law's hair back in 1968. A member of the notoriously nasty Estudiantes side of the late 1960s, Dr Bilardo has a degree in medicine; a scientist with little time for the prose of Menotti or the lyricism of his football, even if it had won a World Cup. 'Win at all costs' remains the Bilardo motto.

Bilardism versus Menottism. The two schools of thought are often discussed over a bottle of wine in Buenos Aires bars, although, in practice, the reality is more blurred. Menotti's teams have not always played in a free-flowing, attacking style and, in 1986, Bilardo had a certain Diego Armando Maradona in his team. No amount of defensive thinking could ever stifle this talent and the imaginative way he played the game.

Asked a few months before the World Cup if he had worked out his team for the finals, Bilardo replied, "yes, it will be Maradona and ten others". At 25, *el Pibe de Oro* (the golden kid) was in his prime and all of Argentina's play centred around him. "Give me 30 days," Bilardo had asked of Maradona when he visited him at his club side Barcelona in early 1983. "Dedicate yourself exclusively to football for 30 days in the summer of '86. Also I want to make you captain of the team." Maradona was so overjoyed to hear this that he burst into tears as he explained in his autobiography: 'Every trip I had been on, whether to Austria or New York, I had always bought captain's armbands, more and more of them. So when Bilardo confirmed I would be captain, Claudia [his wife] ran off to get 200 armbands that had been kept in a drawer, waiting for the right time to be worn.'

Coming from a shanty town on the outskirts of Buenos Aires, Maradona grew up living under a corrugated iron roof. His one toy as a child was a football, given to him by his uncle. He practised with it every day and slept with it at night. Even at the age of five Maradona showed extraordinary natural ball-juggling skills, and when he was ten, he was brought on at half-time at an Argentinian First Division match to entertain the crowd. At 15 he had made his debut for Argentinos Juniors in the First Division, and at 17, he had made his full international debut.

Maradona had disappointed at the 1982 World Cup in Italy, losing his temper and getting sent off in Argentina's final second round group match against Brazil after having been on the receiving end of some brutal close attention throughout the competition. He had learned from the experience – how to live with the constant kicking – and would not be making the same retaliatory mistakes next time round. Tight man-marking in the Spanish and Italian leagues had taught him how to escape the markers and draw the referee's attention to the fouling.

Despite the presence of Maradona, Argentina had struggled under Bilardo before the World Cup, not booking their place in the finals until the very last qualifying match. The Argentina manager had also faced severe criticism at home, including questions asked in Congress. Only personal intervention from AFA president Julio Grondona had prevented the sports minister having Bilardo sacked for bad results.

The knives were out, too, for England manager Bobby Robson, who had never been popular since England had failed to qualify for the 1984 European Championships, losing 1-0 at home to Denmark in the crunch qualifier. Previous managers, Ramsey, Revie and Greenwood had all taken their fair share of criticism, but the derogatory headlines that greeted Robson after every England defeat were of a more humiliating nature. 'PLONKER', said the *Sun*, urging the public to join the campaign to oust him by cutting out and wearing specially prepared lapel badges that said, 'Robson Out, Clough In'.

In a country that enjoys laying the boot into the national manager, Robson had got it worse than all three of his predecessors put together, but had battled on, resolute, and determined to prove himself when it may have been easier to resign and opt for a softer ride in club management where he had been very successful, building a team at Ipswich Town which had won the FA Cup, lifted the 1981 UEFA Cup and lived way beyond the expectations of a small provincial town club throughout his 13-year reign.

The problem with the England job was twofold. First, the people's choice to replace Ron Greenwood when he stood down after the 1982 World Cup had been Brian Clough, the phenomenally successful Nottingham Forest manager. Clough was also Brian Clough's choice and he had let it be known in no uncertain terms at the time.

Secondly, Robson took over from Ron Greenwood just when English football went into decline. Despite Greenwood's warnings back in 1980, by the middle of the decade the long ball tactics he had so forcibly warned about had taken a grip on the English game at every level, including the First Division, and yet, newspaper columnists and their mass readership, still basking in the glory of 1966, expected Robson to return England to where they believed was the country's rightful place, at the top of the international football tree.

The reality was that 20 years on from '66, English football was in a trough. Attendances in all divisions were at an all-time low and England internationals at Wembley were attracting crowds of barely over 20,000 even for crucial European Championship and World Cup qualifiers. Robson and his team were booed off after every unconvincing performance. "Even the prime minister does not get the pressure and criticism of an England manager," said Robson. "Some of the things written and said are completely out of order, but you just have to bite your tongue and take it."

Added to that there was an undercurrent of hooliganism accompanying every English trip abroad. When violence spoilt an England match in Paris in 1984, Robson warned, "I honestly don't know what the solution is but something very serious is going to happen soon." A year later came the Heysel disaster, with 33 Juventus fans dead at the European Cup final between their team and Liverpool.

Robson went into the 1986 World Cup with a 4-3-3 formation, hoping that Chris Waddle's wing play, and the tall centre-forward Mark Hateley, could unsettle opposition.

The problem with the system was that it was over-dependent on captain Bryan Robson who played a dual role in the three-man midfield. A player of incredible stamina, Robson was both the ball-winner in front of the back four, and also the spearhead of so many of England's attacks. If Bryan Robson was injured, there was not anybody else in the squad who could adequately replace him, and unfortunately for England Robson was not fit. He had dislocated his shoulder during one of the World Cup warm-up matches and no amount of painkilling injections could prevent his arm from popping out of its socket again and again. In the opening games, against Portugal and Morocco, captain Robson was not at his best, and, by his own admission, had been feeling 'groggy' from all the painkillers. "It's like going out after 20 lagers," he said.

Drawn alongside Poland, Portugal and Morocco, considered the weakest of the groups, England were expected to qualify comfortably for the second round, but they started poorly. Indeed, after two matches without scoring, it looked as if they were on their way out. A 1-0 defeat to Portugal was followed by a 0-0 draw with Morocco, an appalling match, in which Ray Wilkins was uncharacteristically sent off for petulantly throwing the ball at the referee over an offside decision. It was an utter disaster and the press let Robson and his team know it.

It was not only the British press who laid into the England team. Foreign journalists also lamented the fact that English players did not look comfortable on the ball, lacking the skill of the Portuguese, and even the Moroccans, and the defence of Gary Stevens, Terry Butcher, Terry Fenwick and Kenny Sansom, were particularly singled out for giving the ball away too cheaply. However, in true Alf Ramsey style, Bobby Robson was having none of it. He defended his players to the hilt, explaining that the energy-sapping conditions made the games in Mexico so tough, and he thought his men had performed admirably against Morocco after Wilkins was sent off. He was confident of beating Poland in the one remaining group game. With the press on their backs, the squad locked themselves away in their hotel rooms and a siege mentality developed.

Bryan Robson was ruled out of the rest of the World Cup after dislocating his shoulder yet again against Morocco and, with Wilkins suspended, manager Bobby Robson was forced to rethink his ideas for the last group game. He did so dramatically. Out went Waddle and Hateley as he switched from 4-3-3 to 4-4-2. In came little Peter Beardsley to partner Gary Lineker up front. The hard-tackling Peter Reid was brought in to complement Glenn Hoddle's graceful passing in the centre of midfield, while Trevor Steven would play on the right of the midfield, with young Steve Hodge on the left.

Suddenly the England team had shape and the players were in a formation they were more familiar with. England thrashed Poland 3-0, Gary Lineker scoring a hat-trick with a lot of assistance from the unselfish running of Peter Beardsley. England qualified for the last 16 by finishing second in the group. Hopes were raised again.

Their second round opponents, Paraguay, played to a typical South American rhythm, building from the back with short passes along the ground. For the opening half an hour, they outpassed England with fluid movement, forcing two good saves from Peter Shilton in goal. But England gradually found their feet and worked themselves into the match. Lineker scored on 32 minutes against the run of play, and, in the second half, the exciting and direct running of England's strikers gave the Paraguayan defence the runaround. Toothless Beardsley, especially, showed the world that some English players do have an abundance of skill to match the grit and grunt. He began to carve out chances for Lineker and, in the end, England won 3-0; Lineker grabbing two, Beardsley the other.

England's World Cup campaign was gathering momentum. After the Paraguay match, the English supporters in the Azteca stadium sang, "we're gonna win the cup" for the first time. Back home there was a growing belief in the new-look England team. But the next match would be the real test. England's opponents in the quarter-finals would be Argentina. A match loaded with political intrigue and on-pitch incident was now added to by the still-raw spectre of the bitter Falklands conflict. 'Bring on the Argies,' sang the England fans.

Argentina were on a roll, having cruised through their group. Maradona made all three goals in the first match, a 3-1 victory over South Korea, despite being repeatedly fouled. Jorge Valdano (2) and Oscar Ruggeri were the goalscorers. The Argentina captain was brought down ten times by the Koreans which led manager Bilardo to complain to FIFA about the standard of refereeing. The irony of Bilardo complaining about rough play was not lost, even in Argentina, but, in the context of the modern game, he did have a point. Referees had been told to clamp down on the tackle from behind. 'Let the ball players play,' was the instruction, but the Koreans had soon discovered they could hack Maradona at will and get away with it. The next day Scotland played Denmark and tactical thuggery came to the fore again when Klauss Berggreen went through Charlie Nicholas from behind, ending the Arsenal striker's World Cup.

Argentina drew their next game with Italy 1-1, Maradona scoring Argentina's equalising goal, flicking the ball past goalkeeper Galli after a neat one-two with strike partner Jorge Valdano. But, again, Maradona was singled out for special treatment. Valdano complained bitterly that the referees were not heeding the directive to watch out for the tackle from behind. FIFA's general secretary Sepp Blatter agreed and sent out a new instructions to all World Cup referees, scolding them for being too lax. "We wanted to see the ball players getting more protection – get tough with a stricter interpretation of the rules," demanded Blatter. The next day Uruguay's Jose Batista received the quickest world cup red card ever when he was sent off after just 40 seconds for a knee high tackle on Gordon Strachan of Scotland.

In their final group match, Argentina brushed aside Bulgaria 2-0, playing defensively, passing the ball around in midfield, without ever really breaking sweat, saving energy for future matches. Valdano and Burruchaga scored the goals.

In the last 16 Argentina faced Uruguay, a tough team who had won no friends in the competition. As well as lacking Batista (suspended), Uruguayan manager Omar Borras was banned from the bench against Argentina after calling a referee "a murderer" during a previous match. A single goal by Argentina centre-forward Pusculli, from a move that had begun with Maradona, decided the match, which was played in driving rain, thunder and lightning. The Argentina number 10 also hit the bar, had a goal disallowed for offside which perhaps was legitimate, and had gone on twisting run after twisting run. 'A virtuoso performance by the little wizard,' proclaimed the *Buenos Aires Herald*. By now it was becoming apparent that if you could stop Maradona you could stop Argentina, but the question was – how could you stop Maradona?

After the Uruguay match, Maradona said he would rather play England than Paraguay in the next round as "England let you play", but manager Bilardo warned that the "English are dangerous on crosses and centres". Already through to the quarter-finals, the Argentina squad attended England versus Paraguay at the Azteca stadium, all guzzling fizzy cola throughout the match. Bilardo spent the 90 minutes scribbling notes. One Argentine reporter, sitting behind him, noted that, by the end of the game, the notebook was so full of lines and arrows that he doubted that Bilardo himself would be able to understand them when he looked at it again.

Once England's third goal went in and it became clear they would be Argentina's next opponents, midfielder Burruchaga told the reporters, "They're big and strong and don't stop running. We will have to be careful when we go forward because they get forward so quickly, and we might have difficulty getting back." Olarticoechea agreed: "They're big and strong, but not an invincible force." Maradona had seen something in England's performance which had him licking his lips: "Their defenders don't like the ball on the ground, so we will keep the ball on the ground."

The two managers faced rigorous pre-match press conferences. "I'm only here to answer questions about football and I will not answer questions about politics, either about my country, or international politics," said an exasperated Bobby Robson. "It's going to be two great teams out there. We don't fear Argentina but we respect them. Maradona's a great player, capable of winning a game in five minutes. We'll see if we can control him." Famous last words.

Bilardo also warned journalists that he was not a politician and would not answer questions on non-footballing issues. A game of cat and mouse ensued; the press wanting to mention the war, the players trying to change the subject. A special meeting was held for the Argentina players in which they were told by the AFA to concentrate only on foot-ball and to think only of a sporting victory. Both associations hand-picked their most artic-ulate players to attend the FIFA-required press conferences to attempt to win the unwinnable war of words.

Jorge Valdano, the Argentine striker who would go on to manage Real Madrid, said, "Only idiots will confuse this great sporting occasion with politics. We have to find foot-ballistic motivating factors to approach this match and not confuse it with other strange elements as it appears a lot of people are doing. The 'Malvinas' [Falklands], and the sporting antecedent of that distant World Cup of 1966 in England, all these conflicting elements don't help the purity of the spectacle … Footballers are responsible for their actions and must go out and give a lesson to others on how to distance oneself from these hysterics. I have seen nothing to suggest that this duel could be anything other than sporting."

Back in England, 'IT'S WAR, SENOR' was the headline in the *Sun*.

Maradona cut one reporter short. "Look, the Argentina team doesn't carry rifles, nor arms, nor ammunition. We came here only to play football. How can I talk about war when only last month 30,000 Tottenham fans cheered me in Ossie Ardiles's testimonial? I'm tired of always being asked the same question. Look, we are in the World Cup, we have come here to play football not politics."

However, years later, Maradona would admit, "Of course, before the match, we said that football had nothing to do with the Malvinas war, but we knew a lot of Argentinian kids had died there, shot down like little birds. This was revenge. In the pre-match interviews we had all said that football and politics shouldn't be confused, but that was a lie. We did nothing but think about it. In a way we blamed the English players for everything that happened, for all the suffering of the Argentine people. I know it seems like madness and a nonsense now, but truthfully at the time that was what we felt. It was stronger than us. We were defending our flag, the dead kids, the survivors."

But not everyone in Argentina was backing their team to beat England. There was dark debate in the Argentine Congress. Eight Peronist senators demanded the withdrawal of the team. Humberto Maitara said that sport could not be divorced from politics, citing the example of South Africa where the rugby team were prohibited from playing as a show of support for the anti-apartheid movement. "Due to England having taken possession of land belonging to Argentina, a withdrawal of the team would be an act of demonstration of Argentina's permanent right over Las Malvinas and other islands currently in possession of the British government. It would not be appropriate to play the match while the British government continues its belligerent attitude towards Argentina," said Maitara.

Only a handful of senators backed Maitara's motion. The secretary of culture spoke to the house: "Our team must play against England and demonstrate its enthusiasm and talent and play with honour, win or lose." The general consensus of opinion within Congress was that if the team withdrew nobody would benefit. The centre for ex-soldiers in Las Malvinas suggested that white shirts be worn for peace with black shorts and socks for all those that had fallen in the war. They also asked the Argentina players to wear bracelets saying 'Las Malvinas son Argentinas' (The Falklands are Argentine). Neither happened.

Maradona was furious with the politicians for even daring to contemplate the team's withdrawal and he hit out with a typical trademark statement: "I can't understand how the senators and deputies can worry about a football match when there are far more serious problems they should be looking at in Argentina."

The England team were well used to pressure and big-game build ups; however, there was a new dimension to this match as Peter Reid explains: "The build-up to that game was mind-blowing, especially with it being over in Mexico, because loads of media had flown up from Argentina and they all wanted to ask us about the war. We were receiving the English papers a couple of days late, but days in advance of the game they were full of talk about the war, especially the tabloids. But we managed to steer clear of the subject on the whole. To me it was totally irrelevant.

"The political side of the game didn't even come into the equation for us. We were playing Argentina, the pre-tournament favourites, in the quarter-finals of the World Cup, in front of 115,000 people, in the capital city, at the Azteca Stadium, the venue for the final. Whatever spin anybody else was trying to put on it, the game couldn't get any bigger

Alumni, bastions of English sporting attitudes and fairplay, were made up of ex-pupils from Alexander Watson Hutton's English High School, including the four Brown brothers. They were Argentina league Champions nine times between 1900 and 1911.

Moustachioed giant of a goalkeeper Miguel Rugilo proved the hero of Wembley as Argentina held the lead for most of the match before succumbing to two late goals.

Stanley Rous, the English president of FIFA, is presented to the Argentina players before the first ever meeting between the two countries in 1951.

England players shake hands with Argentina President General Peron before the first of the two matches in Buenos Aires 1953.

Billy Wright and Norberto Yácono exchange pennants when England met Argentina at Wembley in 1951 as part of the celebrations of a Festival of Britain.

Left-winger Ernesto Grillo's astonishing 'Impossible Goal' which won the unofficial 1953 meeting.

The England team which beat Argentina 3-1 in the group stage of the 1962 World Cup. Back row, left to right; unknown trainer, Jimmy Greaves, Ron Springett, Ron Flowers, Bobby Charlton and Bobby Moore. Squatting, left to right; Bryan Douglas, Jimmy Armfield, Alan Peacock, Johnny Haynes, Maurice Norman and Ray Wilson.

(Left) No.17 Bryan Douglas, Blackburn Rovers' flying winger, attempts to take on Argentina's golden boy Silvio Marzolini in the 1962 group game.

(Below) Alan Peacock puts a chance wide as England dominate a poor Argentina side in Rancagua in 1962.

Argentina legend, Silvio Marzolini, who played against England at the 1962 and 1966 World Cups, and also starred for the rest of the world team against England in Stanley Matthews' testimonial in 1965.

El Rata, Antonio Rattin (no. 10), towers over German referee Kreitlein as he refuses to be sent off at Wembley. The game was delayed for 11 minutes and at one stage it appeared the Argentinians would walk off in protest. Instead Rattin wiped his hands on a Union Jack corner flag in disdain.

Geoff Hurst (not in picture) ghosts in to net a header from Martin Peters's cross in the 78th minute to win the game.

England manager Alf Ramsey stormed onto the pitch at the final whistle and refused to let England full back George Cohen swap shirts with Argentina's Mas. The image has become synonymous with the troubles between the two countries. Ramsey gave a curt post-match interview to BBC commentator Kenneth Wolstenholme following the tempestuous match in which he declared the Argentinians to have acted like 'Animals'. The epithet simply won't go away.

England defender Emlyn Hughes is 'helped' to his feet by Roberto Perfumo, Wembley, 1974. Roberto Telch looks on.

Goals from Frank Worthington and Mike Channon gained a 2-2 draw in this 'friendly' at Wembley in 1974. Here Colin Bell fires in a shot, with Frank Worthington in support. Bell's shot hit the bar and Worthington scored from the rebound. Roberto Perfumo is the defender.

Having just drawn with Brazil on their two game tour of South America, next was Argentina, and honours were even in this encounter too. England's goalscorer Stuart Pearson takes on Argentina captain Daniel Passarella at the Bombonera Stadium in 1977.

Anglo-Argentine relations reach an all-time high as Tottenham Hotspur manager Keith Burkinshaw shows off his two World-Cup winning midfielders; left, Ricardo Villa and, right, Osvaldo Ardiles, in July 1978.

Ron Greenwood (left) and Cesar Menotti (right) , both preachers of open attacking football, can't praise each other highly enough in the post-match conference after the thrilling and entertaining friendly that England won 3-1.

World Champions Argentina, including Maradona (far left) and Passarella (far right) prepare for the 1980 friendly at Wembley by training in Hyde Park amongst the totally non-plussed English general public.

Passarella nets a penalty, but the reigning world champions are well beaten in a Wembley friendly in May 1980. However, a young lad named Diego Maradona went close to scoring an astonishing goal, placing his final shot inches wide of the post. He wouldn't make the same mistake next time.

More 1980 action. Phil Thompson and Leopoldo Luque, with Dave Watson in the background.

Maradona leaves the field in Keegan's England shirt. The 19-year-old Argentine was given a standing ovation by the Wembley crowd.

The England team for the 1986 World Cup quarter-final against Argentina. Back row, left to right; Peter Shilton, Glenn Hoddle, Gary Stevens, Terry Fenwick, Gary Lineker and Terry Butcher. Front row, left to right; Steve Hodge, Kenny Sansom, Trevor Steven, Peter Reid and Peter Beardsley.

Diego Maradona writes his first headline of the quarter-final…

…sparking huge protests from the stunned England players.

Within minutes of the handball goal came Maradona's stroke of sublime genius. A goal which surpassed even the impossible.

Argentinians still revel in all manner of 'Hand of God' merchandise … and can even visit an interactive museum exhibit which allows them to recreate the very moment.

David Batty tumbles after being tackled by Sergio Vazquez (no. 2) in another physical, but this time forgettable, encounter in 1991.

Gary Lineker opens the scoring in the 15th minute of the 1991 game with his 40th goal for his country.

A streaker runs on to the pitch, which seems to signal the deterioration of the match.

The Argentinian players led by captain Oscar Ruggeri,whirl their shirts around their heads in a provocative gesture towards England fans at the end of the 2-2 draw at Wembley 1991.

Another tempestuous, dynamic and utterly captivating match: St Etienne, 1998. The World Cup second-round humdinger has already seen four goals, one from the boy named Owen, before David Beckham sees red after kicking Diego Simeone.

Goalkeeper Carlos Roa saves David Batty's penalty to put England out of the 1998 World Cup. This was the first penalty Batty had ever taken.

Strikers Gabriel Batistuta and Alan Shearer swap shirts at the end of an unusually forgettable friendly in February 2000.

Beckham's revenge. The England captain slams home the winning spot-kick … and then celebrates in front of the watching world as England force Argentina out of the 2002 World Cup with a 1-0 win in Sapporo.

(Right) Chelsea's Hernan Crespo celebrates scoring the opening goal in Geneva in November 2005.

(Below) Michael Owen returns to haunt Argentina with the first of two late goals which win the friendly for England. Unusually for Owen, both came from his head, meaning of the 19 goals England have scored against their old enemy from open play, an incredible 11 have come from headers.

from a pure football point of view. But I know the war was increasing that tenfold both in Argentina and at home. Even though we were thousands of miles from home, you could feel how massive it was to the whole country. We felt it intensely through the media and the fans that were out there with us."

Not all the Argentine press were seeking to set the powder keg alight. Others were more moderate. *Clarin* said, 'it's important everyone doesn't confuse the objectives. Those who search for strange ingredients in this match have misunderstood everything'. While *El Tiempo* magazine said, 'Argentina should concentrate on possession of the ball and not the islands. The match is exciting enough already just as a sporting event.'

However, some English tabloids could just not forget the war. As well as the *Sun*'s 'War' headline, the *Daily Mirror* ran an article saying that 'tanks and armoured cars were on standby in Mexico ready for the "grudge" match'. Geoffrey Foulkes MP complained to the Press Commission, claiming newspapers were making inflammatory remarks, converting the match into a new version of the Falklands war and trying to create new hostilities between the two countries.

To add to the pungent mix, in 1986 there were not two countries in the world with greater hooligan problems than England and Argentina. Naturally, the game was declared 'high-risk'. The Mexican police drafted in 20,000 officers, armed with batons for the occasion. Plain clothes police mingled with the fans and, outside the stadium, Mexican army soldiers patrolled the streets with automatic rifles.

The 5,000 English fans, exclusively male, draped in Union Jack flags with unlikely destinations written across the middle, had so far been reasonably well-behaved during the tournament, but their pre-match drinking and singing rituals the night before the big match, included charming little ditties like "Argentina, Argentina, what's it like to lose a war?" drunkenly screeched to the tune of Beethoven's ninth symphony until they were hoarse. This was filmed and relayed around the world, not going down at all well in Argentina. The Mexican police did not mess around, though, and went in very heavy-handedly with the batons.

Without doubt a number of fans from both countries saw the match as an extension of the war. Argentina's notorious Barras Bravas (hooligans) also had a large presence in Mexico. Organised gangs, dealing in mafia-like protection rackets and distortion, Las Barras often liaise closely with club directors and are handed free tickets for matches. The directors, in turn, need the hooligan groups' support and influence at election time at the clubs. Some of the Barras arrived in Mexico wearing T-shirts stating 'Las Malvinas son Argentinas' on the front, and 'Piratas' (Pirates) on the back. 'How could they afford to get there and where did they get their tickets?' asked *La Nacion*.

During Argentina v Uruguay in the previous round, a large banner displaying 'Las Malvinas Son Argentinos' had appeared and then quickly disappeared. The president of Mexico's World Cup organising committee had called police chiefs by walkie talkie, demanding it be removed. A Union Jack flag was burnt after the match – and that was even before the Barras knew for sure that England were their next opponents.

When it came down to it, all the talk of war got too much for England's excitable manager. Peter Reid recalls, "In the dressing room before a game Bobby was always hyper, but I remember before we played Argentina he was trying to calm us down, get us focused, telling us to forget about the politics surrounding the game, but then, his enthusiasm started getting the better of him because he badly wanted to win and he ended up going off on one ... He started telling us how we'd had good luck messages from the Queen and the prime minister, and how Maggie Thatcher had said we'd already won one war and now we could win another one and all that ... so much for forgetting the war! To be honest, we didn't pay much attention. We had enough on our plates with Argentina. We knew they had some very good players: Valdano, Burruchaga and, of course, the man everybody had been going on about, Diego Maradona. He had an outstanding touch, an incredible left foot and the ability to produce the unexpected at any moment."

Indeed the main football talk in England during the days leading up to the match revolved around how England should cope with Maradona. Should Bobby Robson assign a man-marker to him? If so, who? Could Peter Reid do it? But that would mean Reid would not be able to pick up any loose balls in midfield, his speciality. To apply a man-marker would disrupt the English system, which was based on patrolling zones rather than individuals. "I've got 24 hours to devise a way to stop Maradona," Robson admitted.

Ossie Ardiles, now retired from international football, predicted, "Argentina will win because they have Maradona. He's the vital difference between the two teams." Ardiles's '78 World Cup-winning manager Cesar Menotti agreed: "England have it right now because they have two points of attack, Lineker and Beardsley, but Argentina will keep the ball on the ground and feed Maradona – he's the difference between the two sides."

Sir Alf Ramsey, in his column in the *Daily Mirror*, said (with typically long memory), 'Rattin won't be around but Maradona will and he might give us just as much trouble. If we can tie down Maradona we can beat Argentina.' Sir Alf also wrote about 1966 and how he had never been allowed to forget what he had said, but 'Rattin had been the leader of the most undisciplined team I'd ever seen'. (He had met Rattin 11 years later in a 5-a-side match to celebrate the Queen's Silver Jubilee, and found him very courteous and polite.)

Howard Wilkinson was working for the English FA as a match observer and had watched all of Argentina's previous matches. "Take Maradona out and Argentina are a very ordinary side," he said, "but if he turns it on for just five minutes then we are in trouble." Very prophetic.

Glenn Hoddle was the English player chosen to face the press the day before the big game and he was characteristically bullish about England's chances, suggesting Argentina should be as worried about England as his side were about Maradona and his men. "We won't reshape the side just to man-mark Diego," said Hoddle. "We want to get to work on their back four, that's their weakness." He also mentioned that he had played alongside Maradona in Ardiles's testimonial and found him "very down to earth".

Bobby Robson refused to name his team until the day of the game and, in the end, elected not to make any specific arrangements for Maradona, reasoning that no method had worked so far, and to do so would mean changing England's formation and style of play. Robson's one change was to bring back Terry Fenwick, who had been suspended against Paraguay, in place of Alvin Martin in the centre of defence.

Bilardo, contrary to his adversary, was happy to talk tactics, as is his wont, revealing all his ideas and plans. Julio Olarticoechea would replace the suspended Garre on the left of midfield, but Bilardo was going to make one more significant change. Pasculli, the goalscorer in the previous round's 1-0 victory over Uruguay, would be left out in favour of holding midfielder Hector Enrique in a bid to outmanoeuvre the English. "You can't play against the English with a pure centre-forward, they'd devour him," Bilardo told the press, "and the extra man in midfield will give Maradona more room. Sincerely, I don't think the English will be used to a player like Maradona."

Bilardo, never more at home than when talking tactics and formations, today presents Argentina's Sunday afternoon football programme. In an almost comedy parody of himself, he previews matches armed with a whiteboard and coloured pens, passionately doodling, Rolf Harris style, as he fills the board with circles and arrows as if producing a work of art.

But did England not have a player with the talent to unlock Argentina's defence, which had not yet been put under severe pressure during the tournament, in Glenn Hoddle? "Hoddle is a good player and the English are dangerous when they get wide and put in crosses," said Bilardo before the game. "We've got to be careful on corners and free kicks. The two centre-backs will come forward for them. I ask our players to respect our scheme and to try and impose our game upon the opposition."

Like Ramsey in '66, Bilardo introduced a completely new tactical system at the 1986 World Cup that was copied by sides throughout the world after the tournament and during the following decade. His team lined up with only three defenders: Jose Luis Brown, the sweeper, Rugerri, who would be marking Lineker in this match, and Cuciffo, who would mark Beardsley. There were no full backs. The wide midfield players, known as 'laterals', had to cover the full back positions when the team was defending. (A version of the system was given the misnomer of 'wing back' formation in England, as, in Bilardo's original model, the laterals do not play as wingers – the wide sectors of the last third of the field are left free for the roaming strikers and the creative midfield playmaker to prowl.)

In an interesting cameo – part of the bridge-building Ted Croker had talked about – Bobby Charlton, who was working at the tournament as a commentator, went along to Argentina's last training session and talked openly with all the players, even joining in a little kickabout.

"Remember me?" enquired Argentina physio, Raul Madero, enthusiastically.

"I'm not sure I do," replied Charlton.

"Estudiantes versus Manchester United 1968, I was marking you!"

"Oh yes, that was a tough match," said Charlton diplomatically, recalling the night in Buenos Aires when he had his shin cut open in the opening minutes.

The day before the hotly anticipated contest at the Azteca, a Michel Platini-inspired France beat the Brazil of Socrates and Zico on penalties after a 1-1 draw in one of the all-time great World Cup matches. A not so classic game also took place that day. A friendly between officials of FIFA and the Mexican organising committee turned into a brawl. Referee Mario Rubio of Mexico, who officiated at Spain '82, sent off FIFA official Walter Hegz of Switzerland, and one player from the Mexican organisers. Neither FIFA nor the

Mexican committee published details of the match because of the brawl. When asked to comment, a committee official said, "I'm afraid it just got a little too serious."

But the real serious stuff had yet to begin.

High noon, Sunday lunchtime. The cavernous Azteca Stadium was 114,000 full. England wore their traditional plain white shirts, with light blue change shorts and white socks; Argentina, their change strip of dark blue shirts, black shorts, white socks. Rather than the TV gantry it seemed the shadow of the Falklands War towered ominously over the stadium.

Ali Bennaceur, the Tunisian referee, blew his whistle, and Argentina began to play possession football around the centre of the pitch, keeping it tight. Maradona, Batista and Burruchaga played short passes in midfield, Reid and Hoddle chasing them in the heat. It was slow. Neither side was going to take risks in the opening minutes; a time for weighing up the opposition. England, playing 4-4-2, had four across midfield, but Argentina had five, as Bilardo had planned, thus the early possession was Argentina's. Batista and Olarticoechea sat deep. Hoddle was covered by Giusti.

Peter Reid has strong memories of the occasion: "For all the difficulties of playing in Mexico City, with the heat, the humidity and the altitude, there's no denying it's a football-mad place and the atmosphere inside the Azteca Stadium was sensational," he recalls. "As you walk out onto the pitch, the noise, the Mexican wave going right round the ground, the colours – it really lifts you. Looking back, those are such great memories, memories nobody can take away from you, no matter what the result of the game. It was an utterly unbelievable experience, which I shall always cherish.

After nine minutes, the first breakout from the midfield huddle led to Maradona receiving the ball on the right, just inside the English half. He ran at the defence for the first time, forcing Fenwick to take him out with a crude foul. The Spurs defender was booked. Bobby Robson's reasoning for bringing back Fenwick after missing the previous match through suspension had been that Alvin Martin had been cautioned against Paraguay and the fear of a suspension might affect his performance against Maradona, but with Fenwick booked so early in the game, he was now vulnerable. Maradona took the free kick himself and bent it around the English wall, but Shilton was alert and parried for a corner.

Most of the play was in the centre of the park and Argentina had most of the possession, the words of manager Carlos Bilardo ringing in their ears: 'order, order, don't push too far forward.' They looked for Maradona every time, but the English players, with their zonal play, were watching him, three at a time surrounding the stocky little genius when he received the ball, 'like farmhands trying to shoo a bull away from the danger area,' said *The Times*.

Hoddle found some space for the first time on 13 minutes. He looked up, and sent a long ball forward for Beardsley to chase, but it was over-hit, and Pumpido, the Argentina goalkeeper, had it covered. Or had he? Pumpido slipped and the ball ran under his foot. Beardsley gave chase and beat the goalkeeper to the ball, going round him on his outside. It was a tight angle but the open goal was begging … Beardsley's shot hit the side netting.

Argentina's weakness was at the back. Brown and Ruggeri were thought to lack pace. If Hoddle, Trevor Steven and Hodge could get the ball through to Beardsley and Lineker, the England strikers could outpace their markers. But the through balls did not arrive. Argentina were controlling midfield and inexorably gaining the upper hand. After half an hour, Maradona split the English defence with a pass to Valdano down the right, but the lanky forward's cross was intercepted by Shilton before Burruchaga could reach it. Then Maradona went straight down the middle, three England players in close attention again as the Argentina captain shimmied to the left and shot, the ball deflecting off Fenwick for a corner.

Just before half-time Burruchaga turned and sent Maradona away. This time the number 10 whipped in a dangerous centre from the left but, again, Shilton's positioning and timing was perfect, cutting out the hanging ball before Ruggeri, on a rare sortie up the field, could connect.

The first 45 minutes of a tactical, closed game had passed without major incident. Like two boxers sparring, sizing up the opposition for the second half, neither team had been prepared to take risks.

The tension on the terraces exploded during the half-time interval when several skirmishes broke out, but they were dealt with by Mexican police batons. In England, it was Sunday afternoon and the national grid nearly collapsed as the nation put its kettle on for a half-time cuppa.

Likewise, the game erupted five minutes into the second half. Maradona received the ball midway inside the England half, slightly to the left. He comfortably swerved past Hoddle, cutting inside as he advanced towards the English penalty area. He played the ball across to his striking partner Valdano, who miscontrolled on the right-hand edge of the penalty area. Steve Hodge intercepted, but sliced his left-footed clearance high into the air, very high. The ball was coming down roughly on the penalty spot. Maradona had continued his run and now darted in from the blindside of the defence, and he and Peter Shilton rose to meet the ball together, the goalkeeper, with the advantage of using his arms, the favourite in every viewer's eyes.

Sergio Batista takes up the story: "I had strict instructions not to push forward, so I was behind the play, and I can honestly say I never saw the hand. But I knew something was odd, just the trajectory of the ball, the way it plopped into the back of the net. I ran towards Maradona and I could tell something wasn't right by the way the players were looking around."

The ball was in the back of the net, the England players were going bananas, screaming for handball, while Maradona was off, claming the goal, running towards his father and the Argentine fans with his left fist outstretched, without turning to look back at the referee. For Bobby Robson, it was not so much the handball that angered him, but the way Maradona turned away and celebrated. "That was the clever part of the cheating and that's what convinced the referee," the England manager said.

"Everybody who saw it remembers what happened," says Reid, "but I didn't see it! Honest, I didn't. As Hodgey flicked the ball back towards Peter Shilton from the edge of our area, I remember seeing Shilts coming off his line, but I turned away thinking he would gather it easily. I hadn't seen Maradona at all at that point. Then all of a sudden everybody's just gone up in arms, and I can remember Fen and Butch running past me, towards the referee, screaming, 'He's handled it, he's handled it!'

"Course, there's nothing anybody could do about it by then because the referee's Tunisian and he couldn't speak a work of English – and he'd already given the goal."

The incensed defenders plus Shilton chased the Tunisian official back to the centre circle, pointing at their hands, while Robson stood in the dugout shaking his head. Television replays clearly showed it was handball. Maradona had jumped with his arm above his head and flicked the ball into the net with his left wrist. The world knew it, even if not everyone on the pitch did. But the goal stood.

The Tunisian had been chosen to officiate this 'politically sensitive' match for geographical reasons, despite the fact he was quite inexperienced at international level. Due to the events of 1966, FIFA's referee committee had decided not to appoint a European nor South American. Of the rest, Bennaceur was considered the best available. In the referee's defence, the linesman, Bogdan Dotschev of Bulgaria, was not standing in the correct position and so had no view of the incident and could not correct matters.

Five minutes after the highly controversial goal and with tempers still remarkably high on and off the pitch, an England attack broke down just inside the Argentine half. Enrique picked up the loose ball and played a short pass to his captain. In one spinning back-heeled turn, Maradona left Reid and Beardsley for dead, and scampered into the English half. Without breaking stride, he cut inside Butcher, then beat Fenwick on the outside, the defender prevented from bringing Maradona down on the edge of the box due to having picked up that early yellow card and for fear of being sent off. Reid was still chasing but, even with the ball at his feet, Maradona outstripped the tiring midfielder for pace.

On he went, only Shilton to beat now.

Barry Davies was commentating for the BBC, his voice climaxing as Maradona scorched deep into the penalty area: "He's got Valdano to his left and Burruchaga to his right ... oh, you have to say that's magnificent!"

Victor Hugo Morales was screaming in Argentina, a famous commentary that has been replayed over and over again ever since: "GOOOOOOL, Maradooonnna, the greatest player of all time, what planet did you come from?" Morales then cried live on air, "thank you, God ... for football ... for Maradona ... for these tears ... for this: Argentina 2 England 0."

Peter Reid recalls watching Maradona pull off the 'goal of the century' at very close quarters: "I did see that goal!" he jokes. "Peter Beardsley and Glenn Hoddle lost it between them just inside Argentina's half and in a split second Maradona's picked it up and swivelled. He was now facing our goal. At that point, I thought, 'BOOM! I'll get him here,' but once he set off the moment was gone and I couldn't get near him. If it had been a January night at Goodison, pouring with rain, I'd have got him, or at least fouled him, but on that day, no chance.

"You know when you have a dream and there's a wind blowing against you? Well, I have a recurring nightmare about that goal and it's just like that. Every time I have that dream I think *I'm gonna get there* – I'm trying harder and harder, running faster and faster

– and every time I can't get near him. It's like the wind's blowing galeforce against me. Even when I see it now, I don't think about what a great goal it is, because all I can think about is how I just can't get there. I can't get it out of my head.

"But I don't blame myself, so to speak, because once he'd beaten me he well and truly beats three more players. First Fen, then Butch, and if you look at the finish, Shilts does well, because he stood up big for a long time and narrowed the angle. Gary Stevens was coming across from Maradona's left, Butch was coming in behind him, but he just waited and waited and waited, drew Shilts and knocked it in, all in one movement, calm as you like. You also have to remember the pitch was terrible. Bumpy, full of divots, and you couldn't just pat them back down because the pitch was rock hard. I was brought up on some dodgy Sunday league pitches and if you could play a bit, you could actually play on those, but this was like a cow field and Maradona could still play on it because of that touch of his. What a touch."

It was Maradona's greatest moment, the goal that carried him to god-like status in his own country. To score a goal of that quality, at any time, is brilliant, but to do it in a World Cup match against 'Los Ingleses' was fairy-tale. From inside his own half, with the ball sealed to his left foot, the stocky little Argentine had run at the English defence, twisting and turning all the way, six English players left in his slipstream, before sending Shilton the wrong way with a dummy, flicking the ball into the empty net with the outside of his left foot, despite Butcher's final, desperate attempted tackle. It was the fulfilment of the Argentinian dream – the perfect goal combined with the skilful Argentine artist who had left those awkward wooden English 'masters' standing in his wake. Those Englishman who, one hundred years before, had not let the Argentinians join their football clubs and told them 'football is played in this way'.

England had no choice but to go for all-out attack. They worked the ball forward and Peter Reid's header from Trevor Steven's cross was deflected wide for a corner. Two minutes later, Steven crossed again, but Beardsley headed straight into the hands of Pumpido.

Tapia came on for the tiring Burruchaga after 66 minutes, and Chris Waddle replaced the equally exhausted Reid. Waddle was fouled immediately. Hoddle took the free kick, and Pumpido pushed the ball around the post with his left hand. With 15 minutes remaining John Barnes was given his introduction to World Cup football, replacing Trevor Steven, leaving England with an attacking 4-2-4 formation, old-fashioned wing play; Waddle down the right, Barnes on the left. The introduction of the two wingers gave England the ability to get behind the 'laterals' and hit the bye-line to create opportunities from crosses. It also meant the Argentine defence would be playing on the turn, something they would not be comfortable with.

"We really feared Barnes," says Batista, "and we were pleased he wasn't in the original line-up." Barnes was well known in South America as two years previously he had stunned Brazil with a brilliant solo goal in a friendly in the Maracana stadium.

"Barnes's arrival meant England changed their formation," explains Jose Luis Brown, the sweeper. "It messed us up at the back. We had felt comfortable until then, but now we didn't know who should go with him. It really complicated things for Cuciffo. I remember he was shouting across to the bench, 'what shall I do, who's meant to be picking him up, should I do it?'"

Out on the left wing, Barnes ran at the Argentine defence, producing probably his finest ever 15 minutes in an England shirt. With no full backs in Bilardo's system, Cuciffo was pulled away from his marking duties on Peter Beardsley, and repeatedly turned inside out by Barnes. With ten minutes remaining on the clock, Barnes reached the touchline and whipped in a perfect cross for Lineker, waiting in the middle. The England striker lost his marker Ruggeri, pounced, and headed the ball home, 2-1. A typical Lineker goal, arriving at the right place at the right time, and taking his tally to six in this World Cup, making him the tournament's top scorer.

The English players ran back to the centre circle with the ball to get the game started as quickly as possible, but, in a swift counter-attack, Maradona and Tapia exchanged passes twice, and the substitute hit the post. Peter Reid was by now watching events unfurl from the England bench. "Barnesy was absolutely brilliant. He just kept beating their right-back and getting to the bye-line and from one of his crosses, Links got us back into it with a header at the back post ten minutes from time.

"A couple of minutes later he had an almost identical chance, but somehow it didn't go in. If that was on 'What Happened Next?' on *A Question of Sport* and you played the clip and stopped it as the ball came across, you'd say, 'Lineker scores' – no question. Nobody knows how that ball didn't end up in the net – Links included. Gary was in the net, the defender was in the net, the keeper was in the net. Everything except the ball.

"On the bench we were all up. 'GOAL! ... What happened there? ... Why isn't it in? ... he must have been fouled.' Watching it back, though, you've got to give the defender credit, because he just did enough to stop Gary getting there."

The England striker had looked certain to smash the ball into the open net from Barnes's swirling cross. England fans also jumped to celebrate – a two-goal comeback, extra time and it would be definitely England in the ascendancy and looking the better team. But somehow Olarticoechea's last-ditch tackle proved just enough.

At first, Maradona tried to deny he had punched the ball into the net, but when television evidence quickly proved he had, he coined, on the spot, the now infamous phrase: "The goal was scored partly by the head of Maradona and partly by the 'Hand of God'," he said. "The ball hit me, but I didn't do it on purpose and I even thought Shilton had knocked it into his own goal." A religious man, Maradona seriously believed that divine intervention had taken place. The rest of the world thought it was hogwash. Irrespective of how they had done it, Argentina had won. Celebrations went on all night in the centre of Buenos Aires; a cacophony of horn-blowing, and chanting of "Ar-gen-tin-a, Ar-gen-tin-a!"

Years later, Maradona revised his version of the first goal. "At the time I called it the 'Hand of God'. Bollocks was it the hand of God, it was the hand of Diego, and it felt a little bit like pickpocketing the English. No-one noticed at the time: I went for the ball with everything I had. Even I don't know how I managed to jump so high. I struck it with my left fist behind my head. Even Shilton didn't see what was happening, and Fenwick was the first one to appeal for handball. As I told a BBC journalist a year later, it was 100 per cent legitimate because the referee allowed it, and I'm not one to question the honesty of the referee, ha, ha, ha ... The rest of the world wanted my head, of course."

'CHEAT' was the front page headline in the *Daily Mirror*. 'The man they call the greatest footballer in the world handled Argentina into the semi-final with a blatant act of cheating.'

The *Sun's* headline was, 'OUTCHA', recalling its' 'GOTCHA' masthead at the sinking of the Belgrano during the Falklands war. 'The South Americans had gained revenge for the war four years earlier,' Britain's biggest-selling daily winced.

'It was an error by the referee,' admitted *La Nacion* without dwelling on it further. English bookmakers William Hill refunded stakes placed on a 1-1 draw. "In common with all England supporters we were stunned that Argentina's first goal, a blatant handball, should have been allowed to stand. We feel that the moral result of the game should have been 1-1, although we have, of course, paid out on the official 2-1 scoreline."

Bobby Robson seemed more philosophical than angry after the match, pointing his finger more at the officials than at the perpetrator: "We were beaten by one goal that was dubious and another that was a miracle. Maradona handled the ball into the goal, didn't he? It's a very bad decision in a very important match. You don't expect decisions like that in a World Cup."

Peter Shilton agreed: "Maradona was never going to get the ball, so he took a chance and punched it in. You have to rely on the referee and linesman to see it. They were not doing their jobs properly." Bryan Robson was less forgiving: "We were cheated," he glowered.

Skimming over all that had gone on before, all Carlos Bilardo wanted to talk about was the second goal, which he said was the best he had ever seen. The coach confessed that for only the second time in his life he was unable to stop himself jumping up and down for joy and shouting. (He didn't say when the first time was.) "Maradona has just confirmed he's the best player in the world, not only for his personal play, but for his work and sacrifice for the cause. What one has to praise about him is his contribution to the team," the Argentina manager said.

Maradona's striking partner Jorge Valdano reckoned that, "Diego had felt so guilty about the first goal that he had to come up with the magnificent second." Valdano was amazed when Maradona told him in the changing room afterwards that he had seen him on the other side of the pitch, calling for the ball. "That's impossible – I can't believe you were looking at me and you still scored that goal. What kind of superhuman are you?" Valdano had shouted at him.

Maradona also claimed afterwards that at the very end of his devastating run he had remembered the words of his young brother after the match against England at Wembley in 1980, when the seven-year-old had told him he'd been a fool to shoot before rounding the keeper at the end of his stunning dribble. Though, as with the first goal, Maradona revised this claim years later: "There was no time to think really," he said, "although maybe it was there in the subconscious."

So much has been said and written about the second goal, so many superlatives and comparisons to works of art that, perhaps it is best to quote the most authentic description of all, straight from the horse's mouth: "Whenever I see it again I can't believe I managed it. I started off from the middle of the pitch, on the right; I stepped on the ball, turned, and sneaked between Beardsley and Reid. At that point I had the goal in my sights, although I still had a fair way to go. I passed Butcher on the inside and from this point Valdano was a real help, because Fenwick, who was the last one, didn't leave my side. I was waiting for him to stand off, I was waiting to pass the ball – the logical thing to do. If Fenwick had left me, I could have given it to Valdano, who would have been one on one with Shilton. But he didn't. So I faced him, then threw a dummy one way and went the other, towards the right. Fenwick tried so hard to close in on me, but I carried on and I already had Shilton in front of me. I was on exactly the same spot I'd been on at Wembley that time in 1980, the exact spot! I was going to finish the same way but ... God, the Beard, helped me. The beard reminded me, tic ... and Shilton bought the dummy. So I got to the end and went tac, inside ... At the same time Butcher, a big blond guy, caught up with me and kicked me quite hard. But I didn't care, I'd scored the goal of my life."

The second goal has been replayed so many times that Fenwick, Reid and Butcher are household names in Argentina, three of the most famous England players of all time.

But while Argentina focused on the genius of the second goal, England was moving on from the obsession with the cheating surrounding the first one to ask questions about what might have happened had England been more attack-minded from the outset. 'The unavoidable verdict is that England, on the admission of their own tactics until the time they were two behind, had not the nerve nor the ability to risk attacking a suspect defence which by the end was having its inadequacies exposed by England's belated rally,' said *The Times*.

David Miller, also writing in *The Times*, put the blame on English league football. 'England look about as flexible as a sliding door, especially the back four, who had so much possession and knew not what to do with it. The traditional way for English footballers to get out of a jam is to hit a long ball and hope. The successful teams here in Mexico are playing their way out of a jam with a sequence of fluid triangles.'

Thirty-five years on, it was as if you were still reading the same complaints about lack of English flexibility that the sports pages of *The Times* ran after the first England v Argentina games in the early '50s. Miller even went on to blame English supporters: 'English football is not inherently inferior, but as Bobby Robson admitted after the defeat, the style in which football is played in the Football League inhibits the international team. The domestic game doesn't cater for sophistication. Crowds at home are fed a steady diet of goalmouth incidents of rugged determination and of ceaseless running. The idea of watching a sweeper tidying up behind a defence, of a line of five operating in midfield and of a lone figure leading the attack would be unpalatable to the English taste.'

True? Or snobbish rubbish from Miller? So many footballing arguments did the match produce. Gary Lineker, Peter Beardsley, Glenn Hoddle, John Barnes and Chris Waddle could hardly be described as inflexible and unsophisticated players, and four years on from this criticism, Bobby Robson's England would reach the semi-final of the next World Cup, losing out to West Germany on penalties.

Miller went even further, almost committing an act of treason by daring to defend Maradona's first goal: 'It was no more disturbing that Maradona handled the ball than it was, say, to see Fenwick apparently elbow Maradona in the face only nine minutes after he'd been booked for a foul on him. Cheating takes various forms. If you are organised specifically to stifle a single opponent, it is unrealistic to complain if on one of many occasions when he has you on the ropes he's given the benefit of an unfair decision." Are Miller's criticisms fair? Wasn't one of the arguments actually the opposite? – that Robson had not made specific arrangements to stifle Maradona and wanted his team, as much as possible, to play their natural game. Maradona had scored one illegal goal and one beautiful goal, but how much damage could he have done if he had been left completely alone?

Of course the other question was could England have achieved more if they had attacked from the start? In the last 20 minutes, Barnes had been rampant. How much damage could he and Waddle have done down the flanks if they had been on from the start, against a team that played with no full backs?

Maradona continued his one-man show in the semi-final. Against Belgium he scored another two quite brilliant goals in a 2-0 victory, the second of which was arguably better than his second against England. With majestic skill and an exhilarating change of pace, he picked the ball up outside the penalty area and slalomed his way through the whole of the Belgian defence before placing the ball to the goalkeeper's left.

Belgium had not just assigned one man to mark Maradona, but two. Manager Guy Thys explained afterwards, "We had to give two players the role of marking Maradona simply because one isn't capable of doing it on his own. It worked in the first half, but in the second half he escaped and punished us twice. He's incredible."

Back in an English TV studio, Bobby Robson defended his own tactics. "It's all very well for people to say that we should have put one man on him, but there is no-one in the world, let alone in the England squad, who is equipped to do the job. We would have wasted a player and disrupted our own system. Maradona is a little genius."

Ex-England manager Ron Greenwood, also in the studio, was asked how he would stop him. "I cannot see any legitimate method. I suppose you could take a small hand gun out there but you'd have to have huge bullets because he is so strong. And he's intelligent. He can work things out for himself. You can't legislate for talent like that. If someone is blessed with lightning speed and unbelievable control as he is, then you are helpless. He is a one-off, a joy to watch."

Not everyone was so generous in their appraisal, though. Sir Stanley Matthews, working as a commentator in Mexico, echoed the thoughts of many an Englishman in making it quite clear he would not be supporting Argentina in the final. Matthews felt Maradona had a duty to own up to the handball on the spot. "I am shaken by it," he said. "I know Maradona is a remarkable player, but it was immediately obvious to me that it was hands. I am sure the way Maradona ran to accept the crowd's applause will have removed any doubt which there may have been in the referee's mind. When Maradona took a throw-in against Belgium in the semi-final, and deliberately threw the ball to a Belgian because the throw had been conceded voluntarily when a Belgian player was injured and the crowd then clapped Maradona's sportsmanship, I could have throttled him!"

Argentina won the final against West Germany 3-2. The Germans assigned Lothar Matthäus to mark Maradona, 'the pair so closely attached they might have been a honeymoon couple on the dance floor', *The Times* observed. Although he did not score, Maradona was involved in all three of Argentina's goals. He was fouled crudely by Matthäus in the first half and from the free kick Jose Luis Brown nodded past German goalkeeper Schumacher. Brown had not expected to play in the World Cup, but injury to Passarella had given him his chance as sweeper. Criticised back home for being slow, he did not even have a club side at the time, but Brown's goal in the final capped off an unlikely dream every bit as extraordinary in its own way as Maradona's.

Maradona's pass supplied Valdano the second goal and then, after the Germans had pulled the game back to 2-2 from two corners (the old defensive weakness) in the last 15 minutes, Maradona's through pass fed Burruchaga, who ran through and rounded Schumacher to score the winning goal.

One week on from 'CHEAT!' the *Daily Mirror*'s front page headline was now 'KING DIEGO' – 'England have good reasons to feel that this magnificent little player cheated them out of the last four with a blatantly illegal goal, but we have all witnessed Maradona in action twice since that heartbreaking 2-1 quarter-final nightmare and he has proved without question that he is the greatest footballer on earth.'

Maradona collected the World Cup, cradling it as if it was his first-born. Was it his and Argentina's greatest moment? Probably not. It is always the match and the goals against England that are forever replayed and discussed in Argentina, remembered and celebrated far more than the final.

The players celebrated winning the World Cup in the dressing room by jumping up and down and turning the air blue with the rudest football songs they knew, before quickly returning to their hotel to collect their bags and fly into Buenos Aires for the victory parade. The players stood on the presidential balcony at *La Casa Rosada* (the pink house), the same balcony where Juan and Evita Peron and General Galtieri had made passionate speeches to the masses. With President Alfonsin at his side, Maradona spoke to the people and milked the applause of the cheering crowds.

"I lived the World Cup to the full," said Maradona years later. "It was an extraordinary success, but too much was made of it. We didn't bring down the price of bread. It's a lovely thought, that footballers can solve people's problems. I wish we could. The people were singing and honking their horns, but, to be honest, I couldn't get my head round it all. Grown men and women were outside my house for days afterwards. I guess it's about identifying with your heroes, you like what a bloke does and you want him to know it, but it was all a bit spooky – my family were forced to live under siege."

In the weeks following World Cup victory, after the celebrations had died down, Maradona locked himself in his house, claiming he just felt an enormous sadness and emptiness. Now the high was over, what was he going to replace it with?

No other footballer in history has come near to receiving the kind of idolatry Diego Armando Maradona has attracted: a kind of religious fervour that perhaps only the Pope, Mother Teresa and Princess Diana have matched on a worldwide scale. The year after the World Cup, Maradona's club side Napoli won the Italian league for the first time in their history and in the hot southern Italian city, as in poor parts of South America, it is not uncommon to still see photos of Maradona alongside the Virgin Mary.

It has never quite been understood in England, but his appeal in other parts of the world is not just for his footballing skills, but an ability to articulate and communicate. He uses metaphors and parable, and speaks in shanty town argot of the common people. The video of Maradona's 100 Greatest Goals sells well in Buenos Aires, as do any magazines and books that carry his picture, or an interview. 'The 1,000 best phrases of Maradona', many on non-footballing subjects, is a bestseller. One excerpt: 'The Pope's a good bloke,' says Diego, 'but they wanna get rid of that gold from the roof of the Vatican and give it to the poor.'

'So, is Diego Maradona the second coming of Jesus Christ?' asked Argentine writer Gustavo Bernstein, hopefully not too seriously in a book on Maradona's life. After drawing several comparisons he thankfully concluded that Maradona is not the son of God, or indeed in possession of any of the big man's limbs. Although, in flowery prose (the sort of thing Maradona would probably hate himself) Bernstein explained that Maradona's two goals against England represent the dichotomy of the two sides of the Argentine character.

Roberto Perfumo, the former Argentina captain, who is a trained psychologist, had this to say when Maradona the addict was at his lowest ebb in 2004: "The problem with Diego is that he's always been surrounded by people telling him he's God. In the end, maybe you do really start to believe you are invincible."

Perhaps Maradona could have done with Peter Shilton by his side when he embarked upon his journey of hedonism in the 1990s. Speaking in 1998, 12 years after the 'Hand of God' incident, the English goalkeeper was still hurting. "We all felt totally cheated and I still do. Everyone lost respect for Maradona. A lot of players chance using their hands to put the ball in, but Maradona didn't admit that. He said God had smiled on him. We didn't like that at all – that and the way he celebrated the goal as if nothing had happened. We thought he meant he had got away with it. Since then Maradona has had problems. He's let himself down with drugs and, as he is such a well-known figure, that hasn't done the game of football any good."

I make no excuse for dwelling on Maradona. He is a central figure in the history of England versus Argentina and the 1986 match is central to the story. The balance had shifted. A game that was already loaded with significance ended with a hotch-potch of emotions – tension, excitement, anger, revenge, joy, justice, injustice, a stunning goal and a deliberate handball.

Reid sums up English feelings, with his own personal anguish: "No matter what people say about Argentina being the better side and the genius of Maradona, goals turn games, and that game turned on a goal that should never have been allowed to stand. To go out on penalties – as the team would four years later – must be utterly heartbreaking, but to be beaten by a handball ... well, that's even worse. Almost worse than going to the World

Cup, getting walloped in the group stages and coming home early. Instead, we fought our way through adversity to reach the quarter-finals, only to be undone by a cheat. I still feel an enormous sense of injustice."

Twenty years after Ramsey's 'Animals' left Wembley devastated by the turn of events, now it was England's turn, with reason, to feel mightily aggrieved.

Argentina 2 (Maradona 50', 55')
England 1 (Lineker 80')
Sunday 22 June 1986. Azteca Stadium, Mexico City. World Cup Quarter-Final. Attendance: 115,000
Referee: Ali Bennaceur (Tunisia)

England: Peter Shilton(c) (Southampton), Gary Stevens (Everton), Kenny Sansom (Arsenal), Terry Fenwick (QPR), Terry Butcher (Ipswich), Trevor Steven (Everton, sub 76'), Glenn Hoddle (Tottenham), Peter Reid (Everton, sub 66') Steve Hodge (Aston Villa), Peter Beardsley (Newcastle), Gary Lineker (Everton), Subs: Chris Waddle (Tottenham, on 66'), John Barnes (Watford, on 76')
Manager: Bobby Robson

Argentina: Nery Pumpido (River Plate), Jose Luis Brown (Nacional), Jose Luis Cuciuffo (Velez Sarsfield), Oscar Ruggeri (River Plate), Julio Olarticoechea (Boca Jnrs), Hector Enrique (River Plate), Ricardo Giusti (Independiente), Sergio Batista (Argentinos Jnrs), Jorge Burruchaga (Nantes, sub 76'), Diego Maradona(c) (Napoli), Jorge Valdano (Real Madrid), Sub: Carlos Tapia (Boca Jnrs, on 76')
Manager: Carlos Bilardo

SPIT AND POLISH

WEMBLEY STADIUM, SATURDAY 25 MAY 1991

THE OLD foes nearly met in the 1990 World Cup final. "Imagine that," pondered manager Bobby Robson. "What a chance for revenge." It was not a great Argentina side either. Recovering from a bewildering defeat to Cameroon in the tournament's opening game, Bilardo's team had stumbled into the 1990 World Cup final via two penalty shoot-outs. In Italy, Maradona had been only 50 per cent fit, and striker Claudio Caniggia was suspended for the final.

Alas, it wasn't to be. England lost a penalty shoot-out after an epic semi-final against West Germany had ended 1-1.

The final proved to be an awful affair. The Germans won 1-0 thanks to Andreas Brehme's late penalty as Argentina, in a display of cynical football more akin to 1962 than the modern era, had Pedro Monzon sent off, the first man to be dismissed in a World Cup final. He was followed down the tunnel by Gustav Dezotti in the aftermath of the penalty winner on 85 minutes, leaving his pitiful team with just 9 men.

Bobby Robson had already been informed by the FA before the 1990 tournament that his contract would not be renewed once it was over. He moved on to manage PSV Eindhoven. During his eight-year tenure he had handled himself with dignity in front of some of the most vitriolic criticism a manager has ever received. "I was the victim of a circulation war between tabloid newspapers," Robson said upon leaving the job. "I only hope they treat my successor a bit better." They didn't, and that is putting it mildly.

Robson's replacement, the former Watford and Aston Villa manager Graham Taylor, would later be infamously turned into a turnip by the *Sun* amidst a deluge of ridicule after his side was knocked out of the 1992 European Championships by the Swedes. England then failed to qualify for the 1994 World Cup, lost a friendly to the USA and defeat in Spain turned Taylor into a 'Spanish Onion Head', to continue the vegetable metaphors. All that, however, was in the future.

In May 1991, three months after Saddam Hussein had surrendered at the end of the first Gulf War, Cher was number 1 in the charts with 'The Shoop Shoop Song' (it was in his kiss, apparently), her first UK chart-topper since the 1960s, while the world was being introduced to grunge music by Nirvana's 'Smells Like Teen Spirit'. The cheapest tickets at Wembley were £10, the most expensive £25, for the first meeting between England and Argentina since the Hand of God goal.

In England, Italia '90 is always remembered for Gazza's tears (the young midfielder cried upon receiving a rather harsh yellow card in the semi-final which would have kept him out of the final had England won) and is analysed as being a watershed, the turning point which helped football out of the abyss towards the coming Premier League megabucks era.

Many were the comparisons between Paul Gascoigne and Argentina's own wayward genius Maradona. "Daft as a brush," was how Bobby Robson described Gazza. "I told him to go out and play on the left, and he played on the right!" said the England manager after bringing the 22-year-old on as a substitute against Czechoslovakia at Wembley, two months before the 1990 World Cup. Gazza stole the show that night, scoring one and making two as England won 4-2. His club manager at Spurs, Terry Venables, saw similarities with Maradona both on and off the pitch; a close-knit, working class family background, coupled with a desperate craving for attention.

Gascoigne cashed in on his new-found fame after Italia '90 by recording a version of Geordie hymn 'Fog on the Tyne' – an upbeat, manic, dance along single, with a fists-in-the-air chant. It captured the mood of the nation and, thanks to a gurning appearance on *Top of the Pops*, Gascoigne reached number 3 in the charts.

But is the claim that Gazza, Italia '90 and all that revived the game in England entirely true? Though it may have begun the process, created the environment in which the Premier League could grow, particularly in terms of drawing in children and women, the change was barely visible to football fans just yet, even a full year after the so-called watershed. Attendances for England international home games fell even further after 1990, so much so that when the USSR and Argentina arrived for a prestigious end of season triangular tournament with England in May 1991, interest was so low that the FA had to give free tickets away to schoolchildren to boost the Wembley crowds.

Argentina's performance and utter negativity in Italy had been the nadir of Bilardism. So, when Argentina came to England in May 1991 it was with a new manager, a new team and a new outlook. Alfio Basile's appointment was seen as a nod in the direction of attacking football, a return to Menottism to a degree. Nicknamed 'El Coco' (the coconut) due to his large head, Basile, a man fond of whisky and cigars, was a bohemian broom that swept away nearly all of Bilardo's 1990 side. Of the young squad he was bringing to England, only goalkeeper Goycochea and new captain Oscar Ruggeri remained from the team that played in the World Cup final ten months earlier.

Maradona was not playing in the English Challenge Cup (the correct name for this tournament, not the Sir Stanley Rous Cup as has been so often reported) as the disgraced star had just started an 18-month ban from football after testing positive for cocaine in Italy. Also, three months earlier he had been arrested in a very public drugs bust. Beaming from ear to ear, the fallen idol had been escorted from his apartment into the back of a

Buenos Aires police car, live on Argentina TV. Somebody had tipped off camera crews that there was a big story to be had if they turned up at Maradona's place at 4am. Many saw these events as the end of his career. They would be proved wrong.

"We're going to England in search of experience," said 'El Coco' Basile. Central midfielder Diego Simeone, who had played in all three of Basile's first matches said, "This team's so young that, at 21, I feel like the veteran." Known as 'El Cholo' (The dark one, the nickname of his namesake who had played against England in '64), the hard tackling Pisa midfielder had been part of the 1990 World Cup squad, although he had not played in any of the games.

This time, the players would not be attending the FA Cup final as they were stopping off, *en route*, to play the USA, who were due to host the next World Cup finals in 1994. There had been complaints from some European FIFA delegates that the USA was not a 'sufficiently football-orientated nation' to host the World Cup, and there were even proposals for the finals to be changed to Germany, but 35,000 turned up at the Stamford University stadium, California, to watch Argentina beat the USA 1-0 thanks to a rare goal from captain Ruggeri, which was 10,000 more than were at Wembley, two days later, for England v USSR in the opening game of the English Challenge Cup.

On the day after the friendly the Argentina squad flew to Canada to change planes, and arrived in London late the following night, just as the final whistle went at Wembley as England beat USSR 3-1 with a goal from Arsenal's Alan Smith and two from David Platt, the rising star of English football, whose performances in the World Cup had earned him a transfer to Bari in Italy. Argentina immediately travelled to Manchester by coach, arriving in the early hours of Wednesday morning, ready to play the USSR at Old Trafford on the Thursday night, before again travelling overnight to London to play England on the Saturday afternoon. A tiring schedule.

The Argentinians were not the only ones who missed the FA Cup final. England's star player also missed it. Well, all but the first 13 minutes. In the days prior to the final Spurs manager Terry Venables had remarked upon the needlessness of a pre-match motivational team talk when Gazza was around. "He does it all for me," the Tottenham manager said. "He's so hyped up before games; singing, shouting, larking around, going up and encouraging every one of his team-mates that I really don't feel the need to add any more."

Perhaps Venables should have given Gazza a de-motivating talk instead, as what took place in the first 13 minutes of the 1991 FA Cup final was rather sad. Three minutes into the game the over-enthusiastic Gazza raced towards Nottingham Forest's Gary Parker and winded him with a karate kick in the stomach. In some countries it would have been a sending off, everywhere else it would have been a yellow card, but only in England could a referee – in this case Roger Milford – think a challenge of that nature was no more serious than a free kick.

Had Gascoigne been punished properly for the first foul, it might have prevented the disastrous second, ten minutes later. In a textbook example of the dangers of over-motivation Gazza made a needless two-footed lunge on right-back Gary Charles on the edge of the Spurs penalty area. Charles survived surprisingly unscathed. Gascoigne was stretchered off with torn knee ligaments. Not only would he miss the coming international tournament, but he would be out of football for more than a year, arguably never quite the same player when he eventually returned, having lost his electric burst of pace over five yards.

Gazza's knee dominated the news in the days leading up to the international against Argentina. He was meant to be transferring from debt-ridden Tottenham to Lazio for £5 million, but now the deal was off, or at least put on hold by Lazio for a year. There was a lot of discussion about the Cup final. Gazza should have been sent off for his two challenges, leaving his team with ten men, and substitute Nayim had come on and played well as Tottenham beat Brian Clough's Nottingham Forest 2-1 in extra time.

How would England fare against Argentina without their midfield conductor? Manager Graham Taylor was also without another creative influence, winger Chris Waddle, who was playing for Marseille in the European Cup final, so attention fell upon the great enigma, John Barnes of Liverpool.

Barnes suffered from a debilitating condition known as 'John Barnes Syndrome' – the inability to replicate club form in an England shirt. As a major part of the dominant Liverpool side of the period, and Football Writers' Association Footballer of the Year in 1988 and 1990 and PFA Player of the Year in 1988, he was one of the most breathtaking and dangerous attackers in the domestic game. Yet when he pulled on an England shirt he was never quite the same. Sure, he had had his moments. Against Brazil in 1984 he had scored a famous goal in the Maracana, dribbling from near the halfway line into the home penalty area before slotting home. He'd also created several chances in the 1986 World Cup quarter-final, but he was inconsistently dangerous. At least nowhere near as dangerous as his undoubted talent insisted he should be.

Other players have suffered from this mysterious virus over the years, but none quite as much as Barnes. He had over 60 caps, and yet, aside from the great goal against Brazil and the 15-minute cameo against Argentina in '86, the midfielder had done little when playing for his country. Even at Italia '90, he had frustrated so much that Bobby Robson dropped him for the semi-final against West Germany.

Why could he not do it for England? There were many theories. Running rings around average First Division defenders was a world away from international level, ran one train of thought. Another was that Barnes was always stuck out on the wing and tied down to rigid systems for England, never given freedom to express himself – apart from when rapping on the New Order 1990 World Cup hit single 'World In Motion'. Some even put it down to racism. Crowds for internationals at Wembley were low and there was a hardcore element among England fans. Barnes was often the target of abuse, but anyone who knew John Barnes knew he was above all that, and would not let it affect his game.

New England manager Graham Taylor knew Barnes well, having introduced him to league football at Watford, and he decided to sit down with the inconsistent winger before the matches against USSR and Argentina to try to get to the root of the problem. "We had an open and very frank conversation," said Taylor. "It was fascinating. We talked solid international football for two hours, and, in the end, he spoke far more than I did. John is extremely knowledgable and he feels that all the international midfielders who really influence matches, the real talents, operate from central positions." Was Barnes releasing pent up frustration at being constantly stuck out on the wing.

The choice of Taylor as England manager had not been unanimously welcomed. The fear, from the purists' point of view, was that Taylor's club sides played 'long ball', a euphemism for a style of play that involved launching high and hopeful balls into the opposition's penalty area. 'Into The Mix', was the expression. In its extreme form, tall, often cumbersome, forwards would try to nick a touch on the ball and a goalmouth scramble would ensue. It was not possession football. There was little building from the back, but an early release from all sectors was encouraged. Certainly Taylor's Watford team that rose from the Third Division to runners up in the First, had caused a fair degree of neckache among fans up and down the country, and, pre-Wimbledon, were considered the pioneers of 'route one' football. Taylor would argue that his approach was a positive one, and that his teams always attacked, with wingers.

The 'long ball' game was a scientific approach, the opposite of the blueprint Ron Greenwood had laid out for English football ten years earlier, and chief among the advocates of a direct approach was the FA's technical director Charles Hughes, who had his coaching theories carefully documented with statistics and charts. "There's nothing to learn from the Brazilians," he famously stated. "Teams must seek the quickest way of getting the ball into the areas of maximum danger." Hughes had had an influence in the appointment of Graham Taylor, although the technical director would later claim that Taylor did not implement his ideas correctly, and that he had never used the expression 'long ball'.

Taylor had been pleased with England's performance against the Soviets, but the low attendance disturbed the FA, especially as England had done well at Italia '90 the previous summer and were thus far unbeaten in eight games under Taylor (the new manager would only lose one of his first 20 internationals, against Germany 1-0 at Wembley). How many were going to turn up for Argentina v the USSR at Old Trafford?

The match which did not involve England was the first opportunity for another 'Hand of God' score to be settled. In a group game at Italia '90, Maradona had once again lived a charmed life as he got away with a handball in his own penalty area. No doubt, there would have been much greater interest had Maradona been playing in the tournament. A year previously, he had been paid 'a handsome fee' to turn out at Wembley for a 'Rest of the World XI' against England during the FA's centenary celebrations. The pantomine baddy's every touch had been roundly booed by the English public as he strolled half-heartedly around the centre of the pitch, so different from when the young 19-year-old Maradona had been given a standing ovation by the Wembley crowd a decade earlier.

As well as Maradona, manager Basile was also without young striker Gabriel Batistuta, and his Boca Juniors team-mate Diego Latorre, who were playing in an important Copa de Libertadores tie. Fernando Redondo, playing for Jorge Valdano's Tenerife in the Spanish league, was also unavailable, and Claudio Caniggia ... where the hell was Caniggia?

As if an echo back to 1974, when the Argentina manager did not know if and when some of his players would be arriving, Caniggia had not appeared at the Holiday Inn in Manchester. Frantic phone calls were made to Italy, but he was nowhere to be found.

Diego Simeone, who also played in Italy, reckoned Caniggia must be on his way as he had not played in Atalanta's last two games, wishing not to aggravate a niggling injury so that he would be fit to play for Argentina. But there was no sign of the lank-haired striker and he was sorely missed against the USSR as Argentina's slick passing cut through the Soviets in the first half, but they missed a number of good chances, converting all their possession into only one goal, another Ruggeri rarity. The USSR, inspired by winger Andrei Kanchelskis, who had six weeks earlier signed for Manchester United from Shakhtar Donetsk, equalised three minutes into the second half through Kolyvanov, and the match finished 1-1. Chenskov of the USSR was sent off a quarter of an hour before the end and Goycochea, Argentina's World Cup penalty hero, saved a spot-kick from Dobrovolsky, in front of an Old Trafford crowd of 23,743, made up almost entirely of schoolchildren on freebies.

"The ideal would be to play the way we did for the first half an hour, over 90 minutes, but that's not physically possible," said Basile, who noted how tired his players were at the end of the match. After all their travelling, and reaching the Royal Kensington Gardens Hotel in London in the wee hours of Friday morning they now had only 36 hours to recover for the match against England. "The fact that they water the pitches here is a huge disadvantage for us as well, it makes it very heavy," said the Argentina manager.

The players were very tired and the schedule for the Friday was a simple one – sleep all day. And why not? The £200 per night rooms were paid for by the English FA. The players who had played against the USSR got up in the early afternoon for a meal and were sent straight back to bed again. The players who did not play against the USSR did some light training in Kensington Gardens. Manager Basile, like Menotti in 1980, wanted to work on heading. However, since the last time Argentina had trained in the public gardens a sign had been erected saying, 'NO BALL GAMES'. After some discussion between manager and delegates it was felt that English laws ought to be respected, so they moved further down to another patch. *La Nacion* noted, once again, how non-plussed the general public were at the presence of the Argentine players in the park.

Despite this being the first meeting between England and Argentina since Maradona's 'Hand of God' goal, *La Nacion* noted a lack of excitement in England: 'Two great footballing nations, at Wembley, the cathedral of football, but you would hardly think there was a match on.' Perhaps taken aback by the way their team's first match in the supposedly prestigious English Challenge Cup had been played against a backdrop of echoes of screaming schoolchildren in a half empty Old Trafford, *La Nacion* concluded that, 'The English are far more interested in their own league than international football.'

Indeed so. The English press were concentrating on Gazza's knee, and the news that a group of leading clubs wanted to break away from the Football League to form a new, TV-driven, heavily sponsored Premier League. Most of the reporters were against the idea and 'greed' was a word that cropped up frequently in their articles.

The little publicity the match did receive centred around David Batty making his full debut after coming on as a substitute against the USSR. The combative Leeds midfielder was compared in England to Nobby Stiles. 'Oh No!' winced the Argentine reporters. Batty would be lining up in the centre of midfield alongside Geoff Thomas of Crystal Palace, another physical rather than creative influence. There seemed little doubt that England's plan would be to try and get the ball out wide, to Platt on the right, and Barnes on the left, with the overlapping full backs Lee Dixon and Stuart Pearce in support. The other change from the team that beat USSR was captain Gary Lineker returning in place of Ian Wright to partner Alan Smith up front.

Caniggia still had not arrived. "I don't know if he's injured or not," said Basile. "To be honest, I don't know what's going on, because he wants to play. The only thing I ask is that Atalanta tell us the truth." It emerged that the Italian side did not want Caniggia to play for fear of an injury – á la Paul Gascoigne – scuppering his big money move to Roma. In Caniggia's absence, Claudio Garcia played up front again.

Captain Oscar Ruggeri, whose medals now included World Cup winner, World Cup runner-up, Copa Libertadores winner with Boca Juniors and Spanish Liga winner with Real Madrid, would be renewing his old acquaintance with Gary Lineker whom he had marked several times while playing against Barcelona, and whom had lost him a bet by escaping to score in the '86 quarter-final. Ruggeri said, "England versus Argentina is a special game now. Of course, the politics influence it, but we want to separate that. We're a new team and we're very tired, but we don't want to make excuses. We want to win it."

Diego Simeone summed up the anticipation in the Argentine camp at playing at the home of football. "Playing at Wembley puts goose pimples on your skin," he said. "But we're not scared of anybody, the secret is not to let them have the ball."

Obviously without mentioning the Falklands, the official programme ran a friendly feature on the political leaders of both countries, explaining how John Major (Chelsea) and Carlos Menem (River Plate) were both keen football fans. It is probably fair to say that the extroverted Menem tended to voice his opinions on football more publicly than Major, although to do so was not always wise. Two days before England met Argentina, Boca Juniors had lost their Copa Libertadores match to Colo Colo in Chile, which led to riots and several public disorder arrests. President Menem addressed his nation regarding the grave situation. "Clearly, for those that understand football, the third Colo Colo goal was offside," he said knowledgably. "Before the ball was played through, the Chilean striker was beyond the last defender." However, the Chilean interior ministry disagreed and responded with a statement, claiming that Menem was 'completely wrong in his analysis of the situation'.

Back at Wembley, a reasonable 44,497 crowd turned up for the 3pm kick-off, double the attendance for England v USSR. However, the stadium was still only half full, the first time an England v Argentina match was not a sell-out. One of the formalities of England internationals in this era was the booing of the opponent's national anthem and, in this first match between the two teams since the 'Hand of God' goal, the booing was delivered with more gusto than usual.

Basile had spoken about his strategy the night before. "We must keep the ball from England and stop their advancing full backs moving up and down the pitch," he said. "I've put players who are good headers of the ball in the team to deal with the crosses." The opening quarter of an hour could not have gone less to plan for the Argentina manager. England were in control, with Batty and Thomas efficiently playing the ball wide early, particularly to the left, where Barnes, who had the beating of the full-back Vazquez and was well supported by Pearce, whipped in crosses.

England's first goal arrived on 15 minutes. Stuart Pearce took a free kick just inside his own half, launching a long ball, high into the penalty area, 'into the mix', a classic Taylor tactic. Gary Lineker peeled away from his marker, Ruggeri, diving low to head the ball inside the left post for his 41st international goal.

He was now just eight short of Bobby Charlton's record. 'An incredible goal,' said *Clarín*, with a mixture of resignation and admiration 'from a free kick inside their own half!'

It was also a very English goal. Forty years almost to the day since the two sides had squared up for the first time and little had changed about their styles of play.

Gary Lineker could never be accused of being a route one merchant, and Stuart Pearce's long balls were delivered with power and accuracy, defenders of Taylor's England would argue. And didn't cultured players like Glenn Hoddle and Bernd Schuster also hit long balls?

The pattern of play continued. England attacked from the wide areas for the rest of the half, Argentine defenders trying to snuff out the crosses. When they had the ball, Argentina played short passes in midfield, trying to move England's defenders around and create openings. Ironically, after his discussion with his manager, when he moved inside halfway through the half, Barnes was less effective than when he had been running down the left wing. Most likely this was because Argentinian defences are used to central playmakers and are set up to nullify any threat from that area of the pitch, with defensive midfielders sitting just in front of the defence, a tactic far older in Argentina than its modern fad in the Premier League.

Although most of the play was inside the Argentina half, there was little penetration from England, and few chances. Both sets of players were tired; Argentina, from all the travelling, and having played the USSR only 40 hours beforehand, and the English, after a long season of league football. There was little to inspire as the cagey game wore on. The crowd were quiet. 'A cold atmosphere,' said *Clarin*.

Five minutes before half-time, Barnes, back on the left, cut inside and hit a superb curling shot with his right foot. It was heading for the top corner, but Goycochea saved at full stretch. Argentina counter-attacked, a couple of neat, close passes between Simeone and Gamboa, and a defence splitting ball from Boldrini sent Claudio Garcia away. He beat Mark Wright for pace, but Caniggia's replacement shot weakly at David Seaman.

But a second goal arrived just five minutes after half-time. The gritty Batty won the ball in midfield and played a short pass to Thomas, who knocked it square to Pearce, moving up on the left. The left-back's deep cross sailed over the heads of those gathered in the penalty area and David Platt ghosted in, unmarked, at the far post. The ball flew into the back of the net like a missile. 'A spectacular header,' said *Clarin*.

Argentina defenders stood looking at each other, that old weakness exposed again. That now meant 11 out of the 16 goals conceded to England over the years had come from headers and crosses.

A substitution from either side followed immediately after the goal: Nigel Clough on for Barnes, and Argentine striker Antonio 'El Turco' (the Turk) Mohamed for Martellotto. AFA president Grondona had been criticised for organising too many games in too few days on this tour, and there was a worry that the players would tire in the latter stages of the match, which made England's two-goal lead seem impregnable. But strangely it was the home side who seemed to lose the initiative, not knowing whether to close the game down or continue looking for goals. The substitution of Clough, a striker, for Barnes, would suggest the idea was to carry on attacking, but the change upset England's balance, as they now had three forwards on the pitch and no wide player on the left. Was Clough meant to be playing deeper, behind the front two in the Argentinian *El Enganche* role?

England's second goal appeared to inject some life into Argentina. Simeone, a battler, found some extra stamina, and he and Gamboa began to move through the middle. On 65 minutes, Argentina pulled a goal back from an unlikely source. Mohamed, the substitute, took a narrow-angled corner on the right, and Claudio Garcia sneaked in at the near post to beat Mark Wright and catch Seaman off his guard. The first Argentinian headed goal against England ever.

Seven minutes later Mohamed took another corner, this time from the left. This time he floated it out towards the penalty spot, where defender Dario Franco powerfully headed into the roof of the net. 2-2. This time it was the England players who stood looking at each other. Two Argentina headed goals in seven minutes. What was going on? A dull match had suddenly sprung to life. A draw was still enough for England to clinch the Cup, but one more Argentina goal and it would be the visitors who lifted the trophy.

The most exciting moment of the game arrived soon after Franco's goal. A brilliant mazy run across half the pitch – by an Englishman. But this was not a Barnes or a Waddle dazzling with close control and hip swerve. It was a streaker, who had jumped the barrier and dodged the stewards. naked, but for the flag of St George draped over his shoulders, the man hared onto the pitch. Stewards gave chase and caught the patriotic exhibitionist around the centre circle. The flag was promptly re-positioned to cover the intruder from waist downwards.

The streaker's run seemed to spark off the deterioration of the match. Some of the Argentina players argued over where the drop ball should be taken from, trying to persuade Zoran Petrović, the Yugoslav referee, that play should resume from where the nude man had first entered the fray, which, of course, would have been to their advantage. But the referee correctly administered a drop ball from where the ball was at the time of the encroachment. Indeed, for such a light-hearted interlude to make such a difference to a match was remarkable. The game turned nasty just after the restart when Mark Wright made an ugly challenge on Garcia, whose reaction was melodramatic to say the least. In the last 20 minutes, play was continually interrupted by niggly fouls, kicks, pushing, and the surrounding of the referee. It was like 1966 all over again. *The Times* claimed Nigel Clough was showered in spit. Graham Taylor confirmed this after the match and gave more detail: "it was a right green, phlegmy one."

The previously subdued Wembley crowd, stirred from their slumbers by the streaker, now began to boo Argentina with more vigour. The game petered out, apart from the handbags at ten paces and lots of macho squaring up. At the final whistle the boos rang around Wembley. Some of the Argentina players took off their shirts, and swung them around their heads, enthusiastically and provocatively celebrating the draw as if it was a victory; and a few old wounds were mildly reopened. None of the players exchanged shirts because a new FIFA directive required that all shirt swapping take place in the changing rooms and not in front of the public. Gary Lineker collected the English Challenge Cup trophy to the sound of some half-hearted cheers from the now rapidly emptying Wembley stadium.

Graham Taylor was reasonably satisfied with his team's performance, and keen to play down the kicking incidents. "The discipline of the England team over the years has never been in question," he said. "Once again today, it was shown how disciplined they are. You have to remember it's a different culture and different ways of thinking. This is what the international scene is all about, it's what makes it so colourful. You've got to be able to cope with it."

Gary Lineker, with a sweeping national stereotype, said, "The Argentinians tend to get a bit excited but fortunately we just about escaped any major scenes."

The press on both sides begged to differ. Neither is shy of attempting to sell newspapers with a bit of controversy and both went after what headlines they could dredge from the last, niggly 20 minutes. The Argentinian press decried the English tackling as far too ferocious for a friendly match. The Brits, naturally, went with the phlegm incident. 'SPITTING IMAGE', said the *Daily Mirror*. 'Too much spit, not enough polish,' said the *Guardian*.

The Argentinians made a great deal of the streaker, while he was hardly mentioned in the English press. Maybe displaying your private parts in public was just another everyday occurence in the British Isles?

The *Sun* piled in, describing the shirt whirling as 'a highly provocative and distasteful episode', and saying the Argentinian players were 'Scum of the earth, thugs whose display of bad manners was a disgrace to their country.' Britain's most popular daily also roped in Sir Alf Ramsey to write a column. Ramsey didn't use the word 'Animals' but implied it, asking, 'Would you invite someone to dinner, knowing that he's going to spit in your face?'

Clarin voiced its disapproval at the way the Argentina players had exited: 'It's not easy to get a good result at Wembley and we understand their euphoria but, for our taste, the excessive ostentation of the shirts at the end was a provocative gesture towards the public. It's true they booed our anthem, and it's true that 20 years ago they fixed things in their favour, but it's not right to gloat when it goes well.'

Different countries, different cultures, as England manager Graham Taylor had said.

Argentina's players left for Buenos Aires immediately after the game. There was not even time for any shopping. Basile and his assistant Roberto Perfumo stayed on, though, as they had a personal promise to fulfil, a visit to the Vatican. Like Menotti before him, Basile stayed up half the night, propping up the bar at the Royal Gardens Hotel, holding court in a nocturnal *tertulia* with journalists, analysing the match and the tour. 'El Coco' was positively delighted. "I toast my team. It's not every day that you come back from two goals down in the temple of football. The fact that we scored two goals from headers didn't happen by chance. We had really worked on our heading."

England 2 (Lineker 15′ Platt 50′)
Argentina 2 (Garcia 65′ Franco 73′)
Saturday 25 May 1991. Wembley, London. Friendly. Attendance: 44,497
Referee: Zoran Petrović (Yugoslavia)

England: David Seaman (Arsenal), Lee Dixon (Arsenal), Des Walker (Nottingham Forest), Mark Wright (Derby), Stuart Pearce (Nottingham Forest), David.Platt (Bari), David Batty (Leeds), Geoff Thomas (Crystal Palace), John Barnes (Liverpool, sub 51′), Gary Lineker(c) (Tottenham), Alan Smith (Arsenal), Sub: Nigel Clough (Nottingham Forest, on 51′)
Manager: Graham Taylor

Argentina: Sergio Goycochea (Racing), Sergio Vazquez (Ferrocarril), Carlos Enrique (River Plate), Fernando Gamboa (Newells Old Boys), Oscar Ruggeri(c) (Velez Sarsfield), Claudio Garcia (Racing), Dario Franco (Newells Old Boys), German Martellotto (Monteray, sub 51′) Diego Simeone (Pisa), Ariel Boldrini (Velez Sarsfield), Sub: Antonio Mohamed (Huracan, on 51′)
Manager: Alfio Basile

THE HAND OF LETTUCE

SECOND ROUND, 1998 WORLD CUP, ST ETIENNE, FRANCE, TUESDAY 30 JUNE 1998

THE CHOICE of location is not a surprise. In the land of steaks the size of cows, where going for an *asado* (grilled meat barbecue) is ingrained into the culture, it is most unusual to find a meat-abstainer, let alone a vegetarian footballer. "This is a spectacular restaurant," says *La Lechuga* (The Lettuce) as he orders cream cakes to accompany the coffees. He insists there are plenty of other vegetarian eateries in Buenos Aires as well, although he points out that he is not a vegan, and lives on pasta and dairy products. "I think I'm more known as 'Lechuga' than 'Roa'. I never came across another vegetarian player in my career," says the extraordinary goalkeeper who has not eaten meat since the age of 20 and who played an integral part in Argentina versus England, 1998 vintage.

By the time the World Cup reached France '98 it had grown into a 32-team, one-month, television extravaganza, complete with lucrative sponsorship and advertising. "It was an extraordinary experience for me," explains Roa. "Here, in Argentina, the people live football 100 per cent. The whole country breathes and smells football, and nothing mobilises it with as much passion as the national football team. You know the whole country is watching you."

Ditto England. Both countries did indeed come to a standstill as kick-off between England and Argentina in the second round approached. Streets were deserted as shops closed down for the afternoon in Argentina, and in England, the AA reported that roads were 'extremely quiet' on the warm summer's evening, with an incredible 80 per cent reduction in traffic. Even the M25 was virtually empty at 8pm.

"Whenever England and Argentina play, it's a *clasico* [classic], because of the historic football rivalry," says Roa. "And I think it goes even further than that because of the *Malvinas*. Honestly, that's just the way it is. When you're on the pitch, you want to win no matter what, although for the players it's not about politics. I think this comes from somewhere else, and gives it a different perspective, but the player, first and foremost, concentrates on the match and winning. The political questions are secondary."

As thousands gathered around the Obelisk in the centre of Buenos Aires to watch the match on huge screens, a few Union Jack flags were burnt and an effigy of Margaret Thatcher went up in flames, even though it had been seven years since she had last been in power.

The English tabloids, which had offended many Argentinians over the years with their various stories, but who had seriously overstepped the mark with similar headlines during Euro '96, leading to a reprimand by the Press Complaints Commission, now adopted a more light-hearted approach. The *Sun* issued prayer mats, urging readers to place one knee on a picture of Maradona, and the other knee on a picture of General Galtieri, and then pray to God for help during the match.

On both sides of this divide memories were long. But a new chapter was about to be written, sparking a new controversy to add fuel to those older, smouldering fires. For what was about to unfold on screens the world over was a match that can be legitimately termed as one of the greatest World Cup ties of all time in terms of intensity and excitement. "There have been so many commentaries on this match," says Roa. "It was vibrant, emotional, heart-attacking. It had everything. All that can happen in a football match, happened in that match."

So much had changed in English football culture since they had last played Argentina. The advent of the Premier League, along with all-seater stadia had seen attendances soar, accompanied by a growing thirst for communal football-watching 'live' in pubs. It was also not just an exclusively male pastime anymore. Football was marketed as a family game. Gone were many of the hooligan problems in the domestic game, although the spectre of the yob still followed the national team abroad.

After the departure of Graham Taylor from the 'Impossible Job', as the Channel 4 documentary which filmed the final tortuous days of his reign was entitled, the FA had appointed Terry Venables to coach the team in Euro '96, the European Championships held in England. The tournament, and England's performance, had captured the nation's imagination and now that the team with 'Three Lions On The Shirt' had qualified for the 1998 World Cup, the flag of St. George draped from balconies and flapped on car aerials again. Face painting did a roaring trade and England replica tops sold like never before.

Changes had taken place within the FA as well. Thanks to some much-needed critical self-analysis in the aftermath of the disastrous 1994 World Cup qualification failure, Charles Hughes's long-ball dossier, which had been the FA coaching mantra for over 30 years, so derided by the likes of Ron Greenwood, was run through the shredder and tossed into the bin. The advent of the UEFA Champions League (as the European Cup had metamorphosised into in 1992) had highlighted even more the need for English club coaches to change their ways.

Chirpy Terry Venables charmed the nation through Euro '96, with talk of wing-backs and Christmas tree formations. 'El Tel' was seen as a modern sophisticate compared to Graham 'Turnip' Taylor. Especially in the eyes of the media, who loved him. The cockney coach had won the Spanish La Liga with Barcelona a decade earlier, acquiring respect back home, even though he was sacked after two and half seasons, and accused of playing 'long ball' in the Catalan capital. But his affable nature and the twinkle in his eye made Venables the darling of Fleet Street.

Many top managers have often agreed with the old maxim that it is better to be lucky than talented. To an extent, Venables had fortune. Firstly, he did not have to worry about qualifying for the finals as England were there by virtue of being the host nation. Secondly, unlike his predecessor, Venables was fortunate in that his appointment had coincided with a rich crop of youngsters coming through the ranks: Sheringham and Shearer, the 'SAS', were a finely balanced striking partnership: Sheringham the lean and subtle provider, a perfect foil for Shearer the powerful and prolific finisher. Then there were Gary Neville, Gareth Southgate, Sol Campbell, Darren Anderton, Steve McManaman, Paul Scholes, Jamie Redknapp; all had good technique on the ball, and the central midfield partnership of Paul Ince, in his prime, alongside Gascoigne, back to something approaching his impudent best having joined Glasgow Rangers, was as good as any on the international scene. They had been unlucky to lose, on penalties once again, to Germany in the semi-final. This time Gareth Southgate was the fall guy from the penalty spot, and he promptly joined 1990s spot-kick failures Chris Waddle and Stuart Pearce in a pizza advert. The nation loved it. The crowds were back. England were among the favourites for the 1998 World Cup, just over the Channel in France.

Venables was not staying, though. Some alleged murky business dealings had caught up with him and the FA dallied over offering a new contract. "I don't do auditions," crowed Venables, frustrated by the lack of support from inside the FA. He moved on.

If it was Venables' image the FA were worried about, then their choice of replacement was an odd one. Chelsea manager Glenn Hoddle had always been very open about his spiritual beliefs, and controversial opinions on life. One of Hoddle's first moves upon being appointed national team coach was to bring on board Eileen Drewery, a pub landlady and his spiritual mentor since a teenager. Amazingly, the FA agreed to give her a lucrative contract for a somewhat loosely-defined role. It was not obligatory for players to visit the 'faith-healer', but there was a feeling within the squad that it did help your selection chances. One young Arsenal player, Ray Parlour, not known for his metaphysical sensibilities, allegedly asked for a 'short back and sides' when Drewery placed her hands upon his head, and found himself out of the squad for the next match. However, Hoddle was an astute tactician, and, with the young guns maturing nicely, England qualified for the '98 World Cup, top of their group, above the Italians.

Both a by-product and catalyst of the English footballing boom was blanket coverage. Like in Argentina, even broadsheet newspapers now produced separate sports supplements, with radio stations broadcasting all manner of chat and discussion shows and phone-ins dedicated exclusively to football. As the England squad gathered for their warm-up matches in Spain they were constantly stalked by a media circus, always on the lookout for a good story. The headline writers were not to be disappointed. Five of the 27 players gathered in their La Manga base would not make the final squad, a cruel tradition (although, historically, the peripheral players were generally aware of who they were), but in 1998 nobody upon nobody was expecting Gazza, hero of Italia '90 and Euro '96, to be left out, least of all the player himself, who smashed up a hotel room in a rage.

Gascoigne's omission and subsequent tantrums remained amongst the first items of the national news for days as the country debated Hoddle's decision. Perhaps the midfielder had fallen foul of the coach's beliefs as he had been on the front pages a few weeks earlier, photographed drunk buying a kebab at 5am after one of his high-profile night outs with a couple of DJ friends, including controversial former Radio 1 breakfast show host Chris Evans, who was at the forefront of England's binge-drinking culture. For many, the gifted playmaker was still England's one and only truly world-class player. According to Hoddle, the player simply was not fit, and it had not been a difficult decision to take. "He's been treated like one of Pavlov's dogs," said sports writer Brian Glanville, in a reference to Nobel prize-winning scientist Ivan Pavlov's experimental canines, when the burning issue was discussed on BBC's *Newsnight* with Jeremy Paxman.

Without Gascoigne, the media spotlight fell on the Spice Boy. Manchester United midfielder David Beckham, 23, was the most promising player the country had produced since ... well, since Gascoigne. His right foot was capable of passing and crossing with pinpoint accuracy, and his curving free kicks were already legendary. Good-looking with floppy, bleach-blond hair, Beckham was already a tabloid favourite, even before he started dating Victoria Adams of the chart-topping all female pop group the Spice Girls. But now the couple were engaged they were front page regulars. Going out in front of the cameras dressed in a sarong just before the World Cup certainly caused a stir; the nature of Beckham's fiancé's work required the couple to court publicity.

Not everybody liked Beckham, though. There was a petulant side to his nature. He could lash out after the ball had gone, and his manner of gesturing back to opposing fans who goaded him in Premier League matches had not endeared him to supporters. "The signs of disciplinary problems are there and we need to stamp it out pretty early," said Hoddle of Beckham, after a qualification match against Moldova, and the manager caused shock number two when he left Beckham out of England's opening World Cup match, sending a message to the Boy Wonder. According to Hoddle, the player's "mind was on other things".

England beat Tunisia 2-0 with goals from Alan Shearer and Paul Scholes, a comfortable victory against mediocre opposition, but Romania would be a tougher test. The build-up was dominated by three contentious issues; the hooliganism which had once again reared its ugly head before, during and after the match in Marseille, the Beckham situation, and who should partner Shearer? Sheringham or 18-year-old Michael Owen? Experience or youth? Owen had become the youngest player to wear an England shirt in the 20th century, aged 18 years and 60 days, at Wembley against Chile four months earlier, and had impressed with his lightning pace in the warm up friendlies, but Hoddle stuck with the tried and tested SAS partnership against Romania.

Perhaps it should be Owen and Sheringham up front, argued some pundits. However, even though he was going through a barren patch for England, omitting Shearer, team captain, hero of Euro '96, and the star of the song, 'Walking In A Shearer Wonderland', which was being belted out the length and breath of the country upon closing time every warm evening that summer, was unthinkable.

England lost 2-1 to Romania. Gheorghe Hagi and the excellent Constantin Galca controlled midfield. It was not a good performance from England, and just to rub salt in the wounds, Moldovan and Petrescu, who both played in England for Coventry City and Chelsea respectively, scored Romania's goals, the winner coming in the last minute. Both Beckham and Owen had come on as substitutes. Owen's impact was immediate, injecting some badly-needed pace into England's attack. The young prodigy had appeared to have earned his team a draw with a goal in the 79th minute, just six minutes after being introduced, but Petrescu capitalised on a mistake by his Chelsea team-mate, Graeme Le Saux, to break England hearts.

Fortunately all was not lost. England needed just a draw from their last group game against Colombia. There was now a public clamour for Beckham and Owen to start. "It has always been in my mind to nurse Michael into this World Cup," said Hoddle. "You guys [the press] and the people at home can think what you want, but we always felt the time to play him from the start would come in this third game." But some of the press took that as a sure sign that Sheringham, and not Owen, would play against Colombia in Lens as a mistrust of Hoddle had developed. Journalists did not like the way he appeared to deliberately feed them false information, using them as part of some sort of psychological game he played with opponents, and neither did they like the way he spoke down to them from a lofty height.

In the end, Beckham and Owen were both in Hoddle's starting line-up against Colombia, in place of Batty and Sheringham. Beckham made more impact, curling home a trademark free kick on the half hour to add to Darren Anderton's opener in the 20th minute. For his part, Owen's pace had given the Colombians a torrid time. Like Beckham, he would keep his place in the team.

But who would England play? At one point that night, in the match played simultaneously in Paris, Romania were losing to Tunisia. But Viorel Moldovan scored again, equalising with ten minutes to go, which meant England finished second in the group and would face the winners of group G, Argentina.

1978 World Cup-winning captain Daniel Passarella had played under both Menotti and Bilardo, the two contrasting extremes of Argentine footballing philosophy, but he claimed to be a disciple of neither, and spoke of a 'third way'. Whether his team was more scientific or lyrical, one thing was for sure – Passarella was a strict disciplinarian. The stocky defender, known as the Kaiser, after German Franz Beckenbauer, the classiest defender of his generation, took over as manager in 1994 after Maradona's ephedrine-fuelled demise at the 1994 World Cup when the little maestro had been expelled from the tournament after testing positive for the performance-enhancing drug. Passarella said that he felt certain players within the national squad lead promiscuous lifestyles and that he was going to stamp this out with a strict set of commandments; there would be no drugs, no earrings, and any player wishing to be part of the Kaiser's squad would have to wear his hair short. Thus ended Fernando Redondo's international career overnight; the long-haired Real Madrid midfielder refused to visit the barber, while Claudio Caniggia, a Guns 'n' Roses fanatic, who plays rock drums and has a son named Axel, was also never selected by Passarella. Even Gabriel Bastituta was forced into international exile for 10 months. A compromise must have been reached with the Fiorentina striker, though, as 'Batigol', as his adoring fans dubbed him, made it onto the plane to France. Although Batistuta's hair could hardly be described as short, he had definitely had the ends trimmed.

Realistically, it was unfeasable that Passarella could have afforded to leave out arguably the best goalscorer in the world at that time. Even though Fiorentina were not one of Italy's top clubs, 'Batigol' had finished top scorer in Serie A three seasons running, with an assortment of poacher's goals from six yards, piledrivers from distance, and bullet headers. The 30-year-old had also scored a staggering 43 goals in 63 games for Argentina.

Playing in the free role, behind the striker, was the heir-apparent, Ariel Ortega, wearing Maradona's number 10 shirt. El Burrito's (the little donkey) favourite trick was to run at opponents, pause, and then accelerate again. He won a lot of free kicks that way, enticing defenders to dive in. Providing balance to the lightweight Ortega in midfield was Lazio's Juan Sebastian Veron, 'La Brujita' (the little witch – his father, Juan Ramón Veron, who had scored one of Estudiantes's goals against Manchester United in the 1968 Interconti-nental Cup final, had been nicknamed 'La Bruja' – the witch, because of a hooked nose). Alongside Veron was Inter Milan's Diego Simeone, known as 'El Cholo' ('the dark one', nickname of the 1960s player with the same name). Veron, 23, had a tremendous passing range, while Simeone, 28, was the only remaining player from the last match against England in 1991. Now in his prime, the captain knew all the tricks, and was well known to referees in both Italy and Spain where he had been the hard man in Atletico Madrid's 1996 league and cup-winning double team.

Not content with having two central, deep-lying holding midfielders (Almeyda and Simeone), Argentina played with a sweeper, Roberto Ayala of Napoli, and two central markers, usually Roberto Sensini and Jose Chamot, or Nelson Vivas of Lugano in Switzer-land. Seven of the Argentina first choice eleven played in Italy, the other four in Spain, so their play was intrinsically European-influenced. Their formation can be best described as a flexible 4-2-2-2, with Veron and Ortega playing behind Batistuta and Claudio Lopez, 'El Piojo' ('the flea', because of his bulging eyes).

Argentina had cruised through a fairly unthreatening group stage with a 100 per cent record, without conceding a goal, beating Japan (1-0, Batistuta), Jamaica 5-0 (Batistuta 3, Ortega 2) and Croatia 1-0 (Pineda). Batistuta had become just the fourth player in World Cup history to score a hat-trick in two consecutive World Cups, joining the illustrious company of Sandor Kocsis, Just Fontaine and Gerd Müller. But England manager Glenn Hoddle said, "Nobody has attacked Argentina yet."

Those old differences in playing styles remained. The Kaiser's Argentina played with little width, relying on threading the ball through the eye of a needle with intricate short passes down the middle of the pitch, while England would be looking for Beckham's long passes, and the wing-backs, Anderton on the right, and Le Saux on the left, to supply crosses to search out Shearer's head. But this England side also had the threat of the little-known Owen's pace through the middle.

England played a 3-5-2 formation. None of the three centre backs was a sweeper, but they played three in a line; Tony Adams in the middle, with Gary Neville to his right, and Sol Campbell on his left. In the middle of midfield, hard-tackling ball winner Paul Ince would play deep, allowing the Manchester United youngsters Paul Scholes and David Beckham to roam forward.

Leading up to the game captain Alan Shearer gave his thoughts on playing alongside a new strike partner. "I have to change the way I play slightly for Michael," said Shearer. "I have to drop deeper and wider and leave the last defender for Michael. I don't care if I score or not, as long as we win. And I'll settle for creating the spaces for Michael to run into. One thing I'm sure is that Ayala will have to come out quite away from his normal area, or Michael will have the space to run into and take advantage of his speed." Wise words.

Naturally memories of '86, the last World Cup meeting between the two countries, were revived. Hoddle, who at 40 was the youngest manager in the tournament, spoke about the famous 'Hand of God' game in which he himself had played. Mindful of the sensitivities, Hoddle refused to use the word 'revenge' as it was "a horrible term". Instead, he spoke of "redressing the balance" ... you mean revenge then, Glenn?

"Maradona wouldn't have scored the second goal if the score had been 0-0," Hoddle maintained. "He wouldn't have been allowed the space. The first goal was a sickening blow, but I don't think there was one of us who ever blamed Maradona for what happened. It was just instinct. It was the officials, and especially the Tunisian referee, who were the problem. This match is an opportunity to put right the injustice of '86 and get it out of our system."

The England manager could not agree with suggestions from Argentinian journalists that Maradona's goal had 'redressed the balance' following the acrimonious match in '66. "I think the blatant handball and what happened in '66 are miles apart," said Hoddle.

But young Michael Owen, who had 'the face of a college boy', according to *La Nacion*, did not mind using the word 'revenge'. And Owen had been just 6 years old when Maradona had handled the ball into the Azteca net. "I'll never forget the goal Maradona scored with his hand. It's still present in my memory and I want revenge," said Owen, while Shearer took a more light-hearted view. "That goal broke my heart and ruined my holiday with my parents in the Algarve, so we want revenge. I hope this time they talk about the 'Foot of Shearer' rather than the 'Hand of God', but really I don't mind how we score as long as we win, any part of the body will do including my arse – it's big enough!"

Tony Adams postulated that England had developed under Venables and now Hoddle, perhaps assisted by the influx of hugely talented foreign players into the money-spinning Premier League. "Other countries used to think we were strong, but very stupid," Adams said. "Now we have got the brains as well as the brawn." Daniel Passarella agreed. "England are much more tactically aware now. They have changed their tradition system of play, and they have great players in the centre and up front."

There were some problems between the Argentina players and their press. In a complicated dispute over a contract with a television company, the players were not giving

any individual interviews, but just turning up twice a week, the minimum FIFA requirement, for a collective press conference; 23 squad players, sitting together in a group,
passing a microphone down the line, and hardly bothering to answer the questions. In
1986, the Argentina players had been praised for their open and approachable manner by
the Press Association, but this time FIFA spokesman Keith Cooper reprimanded the AFA
for their players' attitude, asking for explanations and insisting on more cooperation in
the future.

The day before the second round tie against England they arrived for the obligatory
press conference an hour late, with security guards who, according to reports in Argentina,
manhandled some of the journalists and hit a photographer. Like pupils not wishing to
take part in an amateur school play they went through the motions of pretending to give
a press conference. "What memories do you have of the great match against England in '86,
where did you watch the match?" asked the first journalist. *En masse*, the players stared at
their feet, as the microphone was passed down the line, without emotion, and with minimal
answers.

As well as the dispute with the TV company, the players and, especially manager
Passarella, were annoyed with some of the press for printing false rumours about a positive drugs test. There was also a problem with well-known TV presenter Diego Fucks (a
common surname in Argentina), who the players wanted banned from the press conferences for negative things he had written, but FIFA had given him accreditation allowing
him to attend. Trouble at the press conference was calmed down by the presence of the
French police.

The Times ran an editorial discussing how England and Argentina were now friends
politically, partners in the Gulf War, with soldiers from both countries having fought alongside one other in Iraq, as well as both being part of the same peacekeeping forces in Bosnia
and Cyprus. On that Mediterranean isle, soldiers from both countries would be watching
the match together on a screen, each allowed one beer.

Having subdued the tension in the Argentinian press conferences, French police
turned their attention to worries about violence at the game itself. English fans had fought
running battles with locals in Marseille on the opening night of the World Cup, and there
had been 450 arrests in Lens on the day of England v Colombia. The Stade Geoffrey
Guichard, St. Etienne, with its 36,000 capacity was ludicrously small for a match of this
stature, and the French knew that thousands of English would be making the short trip
across the Channel without tickets. Argentina had been based in St. Etienne for all their
group games, so 12,000 Argentine fans were already in town before the English invasion.
These were two of the most supported teams at the World Cup, travelling Argentinians
taking advantage of the economic boom in their country to support their team. However,
each set of fans had only been given 2,000 tickets. As the Argentina fans had already been
in St. Etienne for the group games they had bought up most of the tickets sold by French
citizens on the black market. On the day of the match, it became apparent that the Argentinians outnumbered the English supporters by about ten to one.

There were a few incidents the night before the match, but generally the atmosphere
in St. Etienne was good and there were none of the problems that had accompanied

England's other games. Big screens were erected in the centre of the town for the thousands of fans, mainly English, who had failed to acquire tickets.

Inside the stadium, Argentines made most of the noise due to their sheer weight in numbers, banging drums, jumping and singing their famous song, 'He who doesn't jump is an Englishman', which had originated during the long wait before the 1953 match, but 'boy can the English sing their national anthem,' said *La Nacion*. 'The patriotism with which they greet the hymn is a sight to be seen. They don't just sing it, they shout it.' The other big English chant, repeatedly heard around the streets of St. Etienne was 'Ing-er-land, Ing-er-land, Ing-er-land', an updated, more drunken version of 1966's 'England (clap, clap, clap) England (clap, clap, clap)'.

In 'In-ger-land', the match was live on ITV, who ran its opening credits with images of Rattin's sending off in '66, Maradona's 'Hand of God' goal in '86, and Maradona's ephedrine-charged face running up to the pitchside camera in '94, all to haunting music, with the title Unfinished Business, written in bold letters over the St. George flag. There was no chance of anyone forgetting what had gone before.

In Argentina, five hours behind, televisions were allowed in schools and the workplace, while the thousands gathered around the big screen in the centre of Buenos Aires created a spontaneous party atmosphere, painted faces making a sea of blue and white becoming increasingly fevered in their anticipation as kick-off neared. Argentina TV channels ran a public health warning, advising what to do in the event of a heart attack. 'Not even the most sceptical could argue this was just another match,' said the *Diario Popular* newspaper. The tabloid *Cronica* tempered any remaining bad blood, writing, 'we don't speak of hate, but the pleasure of beating them. It's special for questions of history and not only football – it would be hypocritical to deny it.'

England wore all white, Argentina their change dark blue shirts and shorts, as they had in '86. Glenn Hoddle was worried about the bad karma. "I would have liked to have worn our red shirts," he said.

At 8pm (English time) on Tuesday 1 July, the match that had everything began. If all the range of emotions that football can provide could be condensed into one game then this would prove to be it.

It began in a blur. Only three minutes had passed when Owen received the ball in a dangerous position on the edge of the Argentine penalty area. Ayala, the sweeper, dived in quickly with a heavy tackle, but the ball fell to Le Saux, who whipped the ball across the goal from the left flank. Shearer slid in at the far post, and almost connected. If he had it would have been a certain goal. Thousands of pints of beer were spilt in the crowded pubs of England.

But before breath had been drawn, Ortega played a hopeful ball forward that Batistuta flicked on. It was going nowhere, but Simeone continued chasing. Seaman ran out of his goal, and with the ball running out of play, for some reason dived at it, catching Simeone's dragging right foot. The Argentina captain used his *viveza* (cunning) and exaggerated his fall. There had been contact, albeit minimal, but, with referees under strict instructions to apply the letter of the law, Denmark's Kim Milton Nielsen pointed to the spot. Seaman was booked. Batistuta blasted the penalty to the right. Seaman got a firm hand to it, but the shot was too powerful and cannoned in off the post. 1-0 to Argentina with just five minutes on the clock.

Four minutes later, Owen received the ball from a Scholes header on the edge of the Argentina penalty area and ran directly at goal. Ayala came across, but Owen was too quick. Ayala raised his arms, and pulled out of the tackle, but the England forward went tumbling over. Had there been contact? If there was, it was minimal, a brush at most, but the referee again pointed to the penalty spot.

Terry Venables in the ITV studio said at half-time that in his opinion it definitely was not a penalty. "Well, it's in the past now," said Carlos Roa. "It's not going to change whatever I say." Correct decision or not, young Owen had proved that he could fall as theatrically as any South American. His defenders would claim the tyro moved at such blistering pace that the merest touch could imbalance him, sending him tumbling. It certainly wouldn't be the last time it would happen, as Argentina themselves would discover four years later. Paul Ince was booked for trying to get Ayala booked. *Why was Seaman's foul a yellow card and not Ayala's?* he protested. Shearer blasted the penalty into the top right corner, giving Roa no chance.

"Owen was unknown to us," says Roa. "We really knew very little about him before the match. Passarella didn't say anything special about Owen in the team talk. He just said these players are very strong in character, and we spoke about the defensive column, Adams and Campbell, how strong they are, and Beckham's free kicks, but Owen was hardly mentioned. The only thing we knew about him was that he was fast, and that he could unsettle us – and boy, did he demonstrate it."

The game ebbed and flowed at speed. On the 15 minute mark, Ince tackled Lopez and passed to Beckham, who looked quickly up and knocked the ball through to Owen just over the halfway line. The 18-year-old, already haring towards goal, controlled the ball superbly, bringing it down from behind with his right foot, before accelerating off. He skipped past Chamot, and, with a swerve, left Ayala stranded like a rabbit in headlights on the edge of the penalty area. In beating the Argentine last line of defence, Owen had pushed the ball a few yards ahead of himself, to the right side of the penalty area. With Scholes approaching from the right with a clear shot on goal, Owen found a burst of speed, chose to get to the ball first, and finished the move himself with a perfectly-angled shot across Roa into the top right corner. It was a wondrous goal. England exploded, every pub in the country let out a deafening roar. From the early despair of conceding, England now led 2-1.

The experienced campaigner Tony Adams was playing at the heart of England's defence that night. He recalls, "That devastating run announced Michael's arrival in the world game. It's funny because at the time I didn't think much of it. I was excited because we'd scored, but rather than being a brilliant goal by Michael, I thought it was a weak goal from their point of view. He went around Nelson Vivas, who a year later was thrown out of Arsenal for messing up our league chances at Leeds. Ayala then gave him loads of room to go on and score. But Michael has done that to numerous players. Back then he was young, enthusiastic and he hurt people. Also, they didn't know who he was back then, but they do now. It's good to have a player you can spring on people in your team at a World Cup.

"Glenn had taken stick for not using Michael earlier, but I was in complete agreement with him. He eased him in and then unleashed him on an unsuspecting opposition and it paid off."

Adams is spot on. Argentina were not prepared for Owen. Action replays showed the fear in the defenders' eyes when the youngster ran at them. Even in slow motion Owen looked frighteningly fast. Shearer had also been right in his reading of Argentina's defensive set up. Ayala was playing so deep it had given Owen acres of space to run into.

"He was just so quick," says Roa, "and moreover, we had very fast centre-backs, but they just couldn't stop him. It was as if he was suspended in the air, but with complete control of the ball. A magnificent piece of play; precision and speed, leaving two centre-backs like Ayala and Chamot like that. As I came out he clipped it over me. I thought he was going to pass it to Scholes."

The goal was a 'masterpiece', said *Clarin*. Who would have thought it? An Englishman scoring a goal in the style of Grillo and Maradona against Argentina in the World Cup. The balance was being redressed.

A minute after Owen's incredible goal Ince hit a great strike that cleared the crossbar. Then Zanetti hit the bar at the other end as this tumultuous footballing fare gripped the watching world. On the half hour mark, Owen turned Vivas and shot narrowly wide. But now Ortega was coming into the game, floating to find space out on the right from where to inflict damage. The England players buzzed around him, reluctant to make a tackle for fear of committing a foul. For all Ortega's possession, though, Adams and Campbell dealt well with his crosses.

"I thought it was going to be very difficult for us to equalise," says Roa. "We were playing well, Ortega was starting to come into the play more, and at 2-1 down you started to see a different attitude on our part – we knew we had to give a little bit more."

On 38 minutes, England broke out in a counter-attack. Anderton crossed and Shearer won the ball in the air, nodding it back to Scholes, who had a golden chance to make it 3-1. His left foot shot went just wide. A costly miss.

A minute before half-time, Ortega, again in possession around the crowded English penalty area, threaded a pass through to Lopez, who received the ball with his back to Campbell on the edge of the D. The big centre-half only gave Lopez a slight nudge in the back, but it was spotted by the Danish referee, who awarded a free kick. England built a wall and Javier Zanetti stood on the end of it as Batistuta shaped up to take the kick, making everyone believe a strike on goal was inevitable. But Batigol submitted to the needs of the team and stepped over the ball rather than attempting to beat Seaman direct and Veron slipped the ball through to Zanetti, who had sneaked away from the wall. Unmarked for a split-second, the Inter Milan midfielder controlled the ball with his right foot and, in a flash, blasted it into Seaman's top right hand corner with his left. Passarella and the Argentinian bench leaped to their feet, as the players ran towards them in celebration of a well-rehearsed set-piece. "The free kick was a prepared play that went perfectly to plan," said Passarella afterwards.

"It was the last kick of the half, there wasn't even time to kick off," says Roa. "What a time to score!" The Argentina players walked off the pitch on a high. "It completely changed the atmosphere as we went in for half-time. It motivated us, especially as it was a free kick we had been working on during the previous weeks. It confirmed that we were doing things the right way on set-pieces, and for it to come off like that, against England no less, made it even better. I felt calm, above all else, at half-time, because we were level. We spoke about a couple of things, but we were calm, because we had equalised at an important moment."

It had been a breathtaking 45 minutes of pulsating drama and goals. In the ITV studio, an excited Bobby Robson remarked that Owen was a genius, and Ortega had touches of Maradona. It was the best game of the World Cup by far. As in '86, the national grid experienced a great surge in power during the break, around 12,000 megawatts, enough to make a million cups of tea, but anyone lingering over making their half-time cuppa missed the next significant piece of action, just one minute into the second half, as the match was turned on its head completely once again.

A loose ball was played to Beckham on halfway. The midfielder chested the ball down, but Simeone, clumsily, barged into the back of him. Both of them fell to the ground and referee Nielsen signalled for a free kick to England. The Danish official strolled over to show the yellow card to Simeone, who was levering himself up from Beckham, ruffling the Spice Boy's streaked blonde hair in the process. As he lay on the floor, Beckham flicked out his right leg and whacked it into Simeone's calf, under the nose of the referee. Simeone used his *viveza* for the second time, and exaggerated Beckham's kick by tumbling over backwards. Shearer and Batistuta hared over to the referee. There was a moment's confusion as not everyone had seen the incident. Simeone received the yellow card for the original foul, and then the 6 ft 3 ins referee brandished a red card at David Beckham, who looked at the card, turned and jogged off the pitch without protesting, a scowl of anguish on his face. Hoddle gave him a hard stare as made his way to the changing rooms. It was a horrible way to be proved right about Beckham's temperament.

Tony Adams says, "To me it's an incident that has been blown out of proportion. I played over 700 club games and 66 for England; things happen. The bigger the stage, the more it's highlighted. When you're in there playing, though, they're everyday things. People get sent off, but because it was David it was a huge deal. When incidents happen you don't dwell on them. Your mind just switches onto the game. 'We're down to ten men, this is what we're doing, let's get on with it. Let's shut up shop and try and grab a goal from a set-play.'"

"I don't think it was a controversial match, not in any way," says Roa. "The sending off of Beckham was a clear red card. He didn't have the right kind of mentality for this kind of match, at this time. He's a player with an extraordinary right foot – as he has demonstrated over the years – but, at that point, in terms of character, he wasn't at the level of this kind of match."

The dynamic of the game had shifted, but it was no less exciting. The next 45 minutes would bear witness to a magnificent display of tackling and defending from ten-man England, reorganised by Hoddle who rotated Owen and Shearer as front runners with the other dropping into midfield to supplement numbers. Tails up, Argentina came forward in wave upon wave of attacks, trying to thread the ball through the middle, but they struggled to deliver that final ball to the strikers, England's defence proving impossible to penetrate, the interceptions of Ince, Campbell, Neville and Adams timed to perfection.

A minute after Beckham's dismissal, a Shearer free kick shaved the bar, but a few minutes later Ortega's cross found Batistuta onside, in front of goal. It was a meat and drink scoring opportunity to Batigol, but the World Cup's top scorer tamely headed wide. On the hour mark, England's captain and centre-forward, Alan Shearer, cleared off his own goal line from Lopez.

Argentina made a surprise double substitution on 67 minutes, taking off the front two, Batistuta and Lopez, replacing them with striker Herrnan Crespo and tricky midfielder Marcelo Gallardo. The front two had not been receiving much service, so another man in midfield ought to count against a tiring midfield. Shortly afterwards Hoddle brought on Southgate for Le Saux on the left. "We had all the possession, all down the centre, but we couldn't reach the goal," says Roa. "First, because England didn't concede any space, but also because we didn't have the ability to look for alternative ways through. That's why we brought on Gallardo, to open up the defence and provide some variation to our play. We had only one thing in our heads – attack, score, play football, but the English centre-backs were like walls."

Argentina claimed handball as a cross hit Adams's hand in the penalty area, but Nielsen turned down the appeals. Another England substitution, Paul Merson for Scholes, shortly followed.

With ten minutes remaining, a well-worked England free kick saw Shearer's shot deflected off the wall and fall just wide. Anderton swung the resulting corner over, a mêlée of players jumped together, Roa missed the ball, and Sol Campbell nodded into the empty net. The England players were ecstatic and many ran in jubilation towards their manager on the touchline to celebrate. In the middle of their euphoria, they all failed to notice (as did many back home in England) that the goal had been disallowed. In a farcical scene, Hoddle and his staff desperately motioned for their players to get back on the pitch and join the game, which was still in play. Argentina had taken the free kick quickly and Veron was already running freely towards England's goal with half the English team off the pitch. Veron played the ball to Crespo in the English penalty area, but Anderton, who had managed to backtrack and cover the length of the pitch, slid in and saved the day with a quite brilliant tackle, stopping a certain goal. Television replays showed that Shearer's elbow had connected with Roa as they jumped for the corner. "He touched me. He jumped with me, but luckily the ref was there. 'You saved my life there', I said to the referee at that moment, but the TV replays show clearly that it was a foul. They were celebrating. These were moments of very high tension."

There had been enough drama already, but, following the ten men's heroics now there was to be the added tension of the Golden Goal rule – the first goal scored in extra-time would win the match.

A couple of significant substitutions took place. Before the match restarted, Argentina brought on Sergio Berti, River Plate's regular penalty taker, for Simeone, while, five minutes into proceedings, England took off Anderton, who could take penalties, for the more defensively minded Batty, who could not. At that moment, though, penalties seemed a long way off. Holding out was ten-man England's priority, with virtually every man back behind the ball. They occasionally broke out through Merson, or Owen, but when they looked up, they would find they were alone. "I remember Merson had a lot of speed, but everything was the same," says Roa. "We kept attacking, but without clear ideas, and without finding the spaces, because England were so good at the back. Only Owen, with his runs, worried me a little, but I think in extra time both teams knew it was going to penalties."

But not before some more controversy. As Chamot and Shearer jumped for a high ball in the Argentina penalty area in the first period of extra time, Chamot knocked the ball with his hand, but referee Nielsen waved play on. Once again the 'Hand of God' had been kind to Argentina. 'Chamot clearly did a Maradona', said the *Daily Mirror*. It was not as clear cut as in '86, however, and referee Nielsen later stated: "A player can't remove his arms before a game, so they have to be somewhere. There were a lot of arms going up and the ball hit the Argentinian player's arm. It was not, therefore, a penalty."

It was England's last real opportunity and the luck fell Argentina's way. At the other end, Argentina kept coming forward, but the English defending was magnificent. Neither side could come near to scoring the Golden Goal which would break the deadlock.

"I wanted penalties," says Roa, by now reliving the match moment by moment in front of me, leaving his cream cake uneaten, wrapt in decade-old, yet still fresh memories. "I wanted to be there. I had come from playing for Mallorca in the Spanish Cup final, which had gone to penalties, and I had done well. I felt confident."

The penalty shoot-out took place in front of the Argentina fans. It lasted 6 minutes and 54 seconds. Tense, nervous, hearts paralysed in both countries, with eyes almost incapable of watching as the players picked up their tired legs one by one. Shearer, Owen and Merson were obvious candidates for England, but Anderton and Scholes had been substituted, so were not eligible to take a penalty, and dead-ball expert Beckham, of course, had long gone.

Berti went first for Argentina and scored. Shearer equalised, cracking his second penalty of the tie into exactly the same spot, out of Roa's reach. The two goalkeepers crossed each other's paths, without making eye contact. "There is a bit of intuition, and a bit of looking in the eyes of the penalty-taker," explains Roa of his penalty technique. "They always say the goalkeeper guesses, but there's more to it than that. Nowadays, the goalkeeper looks at the opponent, above all in the way he runs up, how he shapes up to hit the ball."

Then, mayhem in England and torture in South America as Crespo, the Argentinian striker, missed, Seaman diving to his left to pull off a good save, a carbon copy of that which had won the 1996 quarter-final shoot-out against Spain in the European Championships. But immediately the balance was redressed as Paul Ince, who had declined to take a penalty in the Euro '96 semi-final shoot-out, missed as well, Roa replicating Seaman's save. "Obviously, I didn't know beforehand who would be taking the penalties," Roa tells me. "I didn't know much about the players, but you see some clues when they place the ball on the spot. Whether they look you in the eye, all these little things count for the goalkeeper. The player manifests a lot of little things in the way he walks, or if he pauses, it's all information to analyse and help you decide if you should go to one side or the other, or stay in the middle. I actually don't think it makes much difference if you know the player, because players don't always take the same penalty. There are goalkeepers who have good records for saving penalties, and others who have not – it's not luck.

"With Ince, I remember he took a very long run up, from the other side of where he hit it. I was thinking, *what a run up, he's going to smash this, not place it,* and I could see where he was going to hit it, so I dived to my left. He hit it right where I thought he would, and I stopped it – that wasn't luck."

Veron scored, but then came another hullabaloo as Roa protested about the placement of Paul Merson's ball on the penalty spot. Referee Nielsen eventually lost patience and cautioned the keeper, who admits to playing games with the England player, who was having to bide his time and hold his nerve before taking his spot-kick.

But hold it he did. Despite Roa getting his left hand to his shot, Merson scored, as did Gallardo, and Owen in succession, the young Englishman cockily rubbing his hands together in a celebratory gesture repeated across playgrounds and playing fields for years to come. 3-3 on penalties, both sides with one to go of the initial five. It was effectively sudden death.

Ayala placed his penalty low to Seaman's right, and scored. Surprisingly, up stepped David Batty for England to take the first penalty of his professional career. As he placed the ball on the spot, Roa bounced on his line. "The eyes of the world were on us, but all I was doing was concentrating on Batty," says Roa, "I was fixed on him. It's impossible to comprehend the enormity of what you're doing, you just have to shut everything out."

The two nations gasped for breath. In England, in one of the most tense moments in World Cup history, Kevin Keegan remarked to the 26 million viewers that this reminded him of a time when he was at Grimsby Town in a League Cup match ... "Quick Kevin," said commentator Brian Moore, "yes or no, will he score or not?"

"Yes," said Keegan, just as Batty hit a tame shot to Roa's right. The goalkeeper parried, and England were out of the World Cup. "I knew it would go to the right. You could just tell. I was studying him when he placed the ball and in the run up," the keeper tells me now.

A wild, whooping noise, a mixture of a scream and cheer was released from the centre of Buenos Aires. From hushed silence to shouts of joy in a single second. It triggered off all-night celebrations for the thousands gathered around the big screen and millions more around Argentina. 'He who doesn't jump is an Englishman' and '*Viva Lechuga*' (Long Live the Lettuce), they sang.

The Lettuce leapt and jumped and ran towards the Argentina bench. Manager Passarella ran onto the pitch and fell over in the excitement. He lay on the St. Etienne turf, rolling around, punching the air and screaming. "In the celebration, Passarella slipped and fell over, and everyone jumped on him. Very happy memories," smiles Roa.

In England, the pubs went from hushed silence to a different kind of hushed silence, as TV screens showed pictures of Batty walking back to the centre spot.

It had been one of the most exciting World Cup matches ever; Argentina had shown artistry on the ball, but England had demonstrated that tackling, timed to perfection, is also a highly-refined skill. Both had shown heart, commitment, passion and desire of their own ilk. Neither deserved to go out of the competition at this early stage.

Tony Adams recalls the devastation in the England dressing room in the immediate aftermath of the tumultuous game. "There was a lot of distraught people about I can tell you. Some were inconsolable," Adams says. "I admired Beckham for crying. I remember thinking I wish I could do that because it usually takes me about three years to come to terms with defeats in big football matches. Glenn was gutted. He was distraught, alone in the corner. We'd thought we had a hell of a chance. You win the lottery of a penalty shoot out and then who knows. It wasn't to be, though."

'HAND OF ROA' was the most common headline in Argentina. 'This time God used two hands, the hands of Carlos Roa,' said *Clarin*. 'Only the heart understands matches like this. The heart doesn't understand the tactics, nor the reasons. It's pure emotion. For the shirt of Argentina, for what the rival represents, and now the majestic stop of Roa allows us to celebrate again. We experienced all the sensations, all of them; joy, deception, tension.'

Owen was hailed as *El Pibe Maravilla* (The Marvellous Kid). 'Each time Owen started a run he was unstoppable for whoever was marking him,' said *Clarin*, but they highlighted Ortega as the man of the match. 'He's the Charlie Chaplin of the team, capable of removing the bowler hat from the Englishmen's heads, humiliating them with every dribble, leaving them by the wayside.'

"Both teams were brilliant," said Argentina manager Passarella. "My, how the English play! So much heart and courage."

In England, David Beckham's moment of madness dominated the headlines. 'TEN BRAVE LIONS, ONE STUPID BOY', roared the *Sun*. 'The pin-up boy ruined everything.'

Rob Hughes in *The Times* asked, 'What was in the head of the Spice Boy, who apparently believes that he has the licence to undermine a great team effort for his moment of wild self-indulgence?'

The *Daily Mirror* did not hold back in its condemnation either: 'It was an astonishing display of petulance, a foolish lack of self-control by the peroxide blond Beckham in England's biggest match for eight years. Hoddle had been right about his suspect temperament and lack of discipline.'

The *Daily Star*'s banner read, 'What an Idiot' and an effigy of Beckham was hung outside a London pub, while a Baptist church message board read, 'God Forgives Even David Beckham.' The midfielder had to go into hiding after receiving death threats and was continually booed the following season each time he touched the ball. The more cynical, looking back, might ponder the very public nature of the reporting which covered his 'hiding place'.

In the post-match press conference, Hoddle said, "We could not have asked for more from the players. Even with ten men we defended like lions. It's a night for us to be proud.

It is a bitter, bitter pill to swallow yet again. I don't know if destiny was against us. Everything went against us, but it is not a night for excuses." Asked about Beckham, Hoddle hung the midfielder out to dry: "The sending off cost us dearly. I am not denying it cost us the game." Beckham was sneaked out of the stadium with a baseball cap over his head, and the following day, aware that a hate campaign was gathering momentum, Hoddle appealed to the press to not destroy him: "We must not make him a scapegoat for what has happened."

Beckham issued a public apology through the *Sun*: 'This is without doubt the worst moment of my career. I will always regret my actions. I have apologised to the England players and management and I want every England supporter to know how deeply sorry I am.' Beckham had stood in the tunnel watching the last few minutes of the 'terrible tension' of the penalty shoot out. 'I kept thinking if I had been out there I would have been one of the takers.' He spoke of the subdued atmosphere in the dressing room after the game and how he had gone up to each of the players one by one and apologised.

Two days later, Hoddle said, "David has to learn from this and maybe this is what he needed to stamp that lack of discipline out of his game. The saddest thing is that we'll never know what we could have achieved. We'll never know whether, with eleven men, we could have gone on and won it."

It was the third time England had gone out of a tournament on penalties in eight years, and it became apparent afterwards that England had not practised taking them. Paul Ince and David Batty were taking penalties for the first time in their careers, but Hoddle defended himself: "You could never create the pressure of those nerve-wracking conditions on the training ground." Nevertheless, Argentina had practised theirs.

"If you'd asked me one week beforehand if I'd take a penalty, I'd have said not a chance," said Batty, "but the manager asked me and I felt OK, so I took it." Batty wasn't going to cry, nor dwell on it. "I slept fine," he told reporters the next day. "I've forgotten about it already." Would that millions of English fans could achieve such a feat. Newspapers reported that a 29-year-old man in Poole, Dorset had smashed up the TV set in his local pub after Batty's miss.

Daniel Passarella paid tribute to England: "We saw a typical English performance. What passion! There was so much character in their team and they played hard and tough. They are a very solid team with two outstanding strikers."

But his players did not display the same level of respect for their plucky, vanquished opponents. When the team coaches pulled out of the stadium, the England players claimed that the Argentinian players were goading them, whirling their shirts around their heads as their predecessors had in 1991 and singing. "We thought they were fans at first," said Hoddle, "but we couldn't believe it when we realised it was the players. That's a lack of respect, and it left a bad taste."

———————— ❖ ————————

Emotions can change quickly in a World Cup. Three days later, it was Argentina's turn to sit distraught on the coach, as Ariel Ortega went from hero to zero. Drawing 1-1 with

Holland, with four minutes remaining, Ortega was tackled in the Dutch penalty area by Jaap Stam. He appealed for a penalty, only to receive a yellow card for diving. The Argentina no. 10 reacted to a comment by Dutch keeper Edwin van der Sar by headbutting him, promptly receiving a red card. Two minutes later, while Argentina were still reorganising, a long ball from de Boer was beautifully controlled by Dennis Bergkamp, who scored a brilliant last-minute winner, turning Ayala inside out and clipping the ball past Roa, knocking Argentina out of the tournament.

"In Argentina, if you don't reach the final, it's always considered a *fracas* (failure)," says Roa, "but I think that win over England let us off a little when we went out in the next round. Football has these things, from very high to very low, very quickly, from moments of happiness to moments of sadness – that's why you've got to enjoy it when it goes well, you've got to know how to enjoy the good moments."

Back in Argentina, Passarella's team received some criticism for being too mechanical and European. Ortega, the hero just three days beforehand, was berated for his lack of discipline, although not with quite the same vigour as Beckham was copping flack in England.

One year on from the '98 World Cup, having finished third in the Spanish league with Mallorca, Carlos Roa shocked both his club and country by deciding, at the age of 29, at the peak of his career, to retire from football for religious reasons. As a member of the Seventh Day Adventist Church, he felt it was wrong to play football on Saturdays and wanted to dedicate more time to God. It was reported at the time that Roa believed, as some 'Apocalypse Cult' members did, that the world was going to end at the start of the new millennium, however this was never the case.

'I was really happy playing football, but I am seeking better things,' Roa told *Clarin* as he announced his retirement.'I asked God to give me the opportunity to play in the World Cup, and he gave it to me. I asked him to have a chance to play in Europe and he also gave it to me. I want to fulfil my promise to him and retire now.' Despite Mallorca fans holding up banners begging him to stay, Roa and his family went to live on an isolated countryside retreat in Santa Fe, where they meditated, studied the Bible and attended cows. "The reaction I met everywhere was one of incomprehension," he tells me.

However, after nine months of reflection on the retreat, Roa decided to return to football on condition that he did not have to play on Saturdays. Mallorca, with whom he still had two years remaining on his contract, welcomed him back with open arms. "Getting back into shape was tough. The hardest thing for a keeper is to get back his timing, and it was difficult to get back to the same level I had reached in 1998."

Due to Champions League qualification, Mallorca had to switch many of their league matches to Saturday, so Roa missed a lot of games. "My comeback at Mallorca was really tough, because the Spanish league is competitive and nobody was going to gift me a place in the team, so when the chance to sign for Albacete came up I didn't hesitate, even though it meant dropping down a division. I also spent five days on trial with Arsenal in 2002. Arsène Wenger wanted to sign me, but I didn't have a European passport. Strangely, my old Albacete understudy Manuel Almunia is now Arsenal's keeper, enjoying a privilege that I almost had.

"Everything was going really well at Albacete, but then God threw another crucial test in my path: testicular cancer. Being a Christian helped me, the strength of my faith enabling me to put up a tremendous fight. It's not something I can describe in detail, because you have to live with it to really understand what it's like. It was by far the worst experience of my life, but God sent me a sign telling me I was meant to carry on living."

Roa had chemotherapy in 2004 and returned to Argentina, where he made another comeback, playing in the Argentina First Division for Olimpo of Bahia Blanca from 2005 to 2007, before retiring, for good this time. "After the illness I now enjoy life day by day, and don't make too many long-term plans. After so many years of praying, the first lesson you are certain about is that, no matter how good or how bad things are, you must face them with your head up."

The Lettuce's abiding memory of the 1998 World Cup? "I always remember the looks on the faces of the crowd during the penalties. In those few seconds between each penalty, the faces can change from smiles to defeat. I have a clear image of the English people; smiling, concentrated, then suddenly destroyed, crying. They felt the colours of their country, they love the sport of football. There was this total silence during the penalties, including those celebrating the goal. They celebrated very quickly, between each penalty, and then returned to the silence, until the final one.

"After the game I spoke to a friend on the phone and he told me what had happened at home. When I made the save, Argentina exploded."

Argentina 2 (Batistuta (pen) 6′ Zanetti 45′)
England 2 (Shearer (pen) 10′ Owen 16′)   (Argentina win 4-3 on penalties)
Tuesday 30 June 1998. Stade Geoffroy-Guichard, Saint-Étienne. World Cup 2nd Round. Attendance, 30,600
Referee: Kim Milton Nielsen (Denmark)

Argentina: Carlos Roa (Mallorca), Nelson Vivas (Lugano), Roberto Ayala (Napoli), Jose Chamot (Lazio), Javier Zanetti (Inter Milan), Ariel Ortega (Valencia), Matias Almeyda (AC Milan), Juan Sebastián Veron (Sampdoria), Diego Simeone(c) (Inter Milan, sub 91′), Gabriel Batistuta (Fiorentina, sub 68′), Claudio Lopez (Valencia, sub 68′), Subs: Hernan Crespo (Parma, on 68′), Marcelo Gallardo (Monaco, on 68′), Sergio Berti (River Plate, on 91′)
Manager: Daniel Passarella

England: David Seaman (Arsenal), Gary Neville (Manchester Utd), Sol Campbell (Tottenham), Tony Adams (Arsenal), Graeme Le Saux (Chelsea, sub 70′), Darren Anderton (Tottenham, sub 97′), Paul Ince (Liverpool), David Beckham (Manchester Utd), Paul Scholes (Manchester Utd, sub 78′), Alan Shearer(c) (Newcastle), Michael Owen (Liverpool), Subs: Gareth Southgate (Aston Villa, on 71′), Paul Merson (Arsenal, on 78′), David Batty (Leeds, on 97′)
Manager: Glenn Hoddle

THE MEANINGLESS FRIENDLY

WEMBLEY STADIUM,
WEDNESDAY 23 FEBRUARY 2000

TWO MONTHS after the millennium celebrations the world was settling down to normal business. And 18 months after their World Cup classic in St. Etienne, England and Argentina met at Wembley for a not so memorable encounter. In fact it was a bit of a damp squib, in every sense, including the drizzly February weather.

With the number of World Cup and European Championship qualifying games ever increasing due to newly formed independent states in Europe and the single, large, ten-team group format in South America, the sporting public were beginning to realise that, despite the hype, international friendlies were fast turning into nothing more than glorified training sessions. Any number of substitutions could be made, and key players would either withdraw from the squad or suddenly contract muscle strains, before miraculously recovering in time to play for their club sides the following weekend.

Despite friendlies becoming increasingly meaningless, the media, as was their duty, tried to whip up some enthusiam for England versus Argentina, and a respectable 75,000 fans braved the rain to turn up at Wembley on a cold Wednesday evening, paying the same prices as they would for a more competitive match.

The obvious angle for pre-match publicity was to bill the clash as a personal grudge match between Beckham and Simeone, but that had fallen flat as the two players had already met and made up, hugging and shaking hands before Inter Milan versus Manchester United in the Champions League the year before. Indeed, rather than take the bait, Simeone merely remarked that Beckham was a great player who should never have been blamed for England's defeat in St. Etienne. This rematch did not make a great headline for those looking to reopen old wounds.

Beckham still managed to dominate the news, though. Three days before the international he had been left out of the Manchester United team having failed to turn up for training, and he was forced to watch the league match at Leeds from the stands. There were reports of an alleged deterioration in relations between the player and his manager Alex Ferguson, who did not think much of Beckham's wife.

The story was not only news in England, but half the world, and not just on the sports pages: baby Brooklyn had not been well, and wife Victoria had had an appointment in London to attend, so the man of the house had stayed at home to look after his son (without phoning in to say he wouldn't be at work).

In an early indication of how powerful an icon the young footballer was becoming, the story was discussed in gossip columns and women's magazines, both home and abroad. Conversely, while the player's indiscipline was criticised in sports columns, his actions were praised in other sections of the same newspapers; a role model for the new man. The Beckham-Spice PR machine pumped the caring dad angle for all it was worth.

Having reached an all-time low in the aftermath of the 1998 World Cup match against Argentina, the Beckham brand had been given a complete overhaul by the couple's image consultants, transforming Posh and Becks from hate figures into fashion models, with an adoring market in the Far East to exploit around the 2002 World Cup finals, which were to be held in Japan and South Korea.

Beckham's football had also continued to enthral as much as his clothes and tattoos. His sublime passing and crossing had contributed to Manchester United's treble triumph in 1999 (English Premier League, FA Cup, and European Cup titles), although flashes of the old temper could still surface from time to time. He had let down both his manager and image consultants with a dangerously high tackle on Nexaca's Jose Milan in the World Club Championships in Brazil a month before the friendly with Argentina, receiving another red card in a match beamed around the world.

Attempts to bill the friendly as a France '98 rematch were also diluted by the fact that both teams had different managers. Hoddle had been forced to resign in February 1999, although the comments that led to his downfall had actually been made a year before, hardly causing a ripple at the time. However, six months after the World Cup, and having irritated the press enough with his aloof manner and secrecy regarding team selections, not to mention an ever-growing spiritual entourage which now included 1970s TV spoon bender Uri Geller, some journalists felt it was time for the England manager to go. The issue of reincarnation, something about which Hoddle had spoken openly, was raised again, but was turned into a bigger story this time, and one that would inevitably see Glenn Hoddle fall on his bendy fork. In a telephone interview with Matt Dickenson of *The Times*, Hoddle was asked to explain again what exactly he had meant when he said that disabled people were paying the punishment for sins in a previous life. The England manager confirmed that he did mean exactly that. Even the prime minister, Tony Blair, joined the condemnation, leaving the FA with little choice but to dismiss Hoddle for his offensive views.

On the BBC's Saturday morning *Football Focus* programme Hoddle claimed he had been set up and misinterpreted. The interview gave him the perfect opportunity to retract what he had said, but he didn't. Hoddle has never retracted those comments, but oddly had no problems in securing managerial employment in club football at Southampton, Tottenham and Wolves, all of whose grounds have a special section for disabled supporters.

The FA desperately needed someone completely different. There was an obvious candidate in Kevin Keegan, a media-friendly, happy-go-lucky, chatty character, still bubbly, even without his 1970s perm. The Fulham manager was made caretaker, jointly managing England and his club on a short-term basis. But Keegan enjoyed the England job so much that he left Fulham to take up the post full-time in May 1999, much to the annoyance of Fulham owner Mohamed Al Fayed.

In complete contrast to Hoddle, Keegan read the the names of the players on the teamsheet with a big smile on his face the day before every England match, engaging in lengthy discussions with the press over his selections. But, by his own admission, Keegan's management skills were based on transmitting enthusiasm and motivation without a great deal of emphasis on tactics. Keegan's philosophy was a simple one; all out attack. "If it's a 0-0 draw in the Ukraine you're looking for, then I'm not your man," he said upon his appointment. Ironically, a few months later, England could have faced Ukraine in the Euro 2000 qualification play-offs, when 0-0 in Kiev, against the in-form Rebrov and Shevchenko would have been considered a good result. Luckily for Keegan, England drew Scotland instead and won 2-1 on aggregate.

The match against Argentina was the first international since those two games against Scotland the previous November, and the England manager was looking for signs of improvement after his players had produced a poor performance for the Wembley fans after winning the first leg 2-0 at Hampden Park.

Keegan had originally plumped for 4-4-2, but now switched to Hoddle's flexible 3-5-2 formation. It was the only way Beckham and Scholes, two attacking midfielders, could play together in the centre. The other big advantage was that the system required only one left-sided player instead of two. There was a dearth of left-sided talent in England. Against Argentina, the uncapped foursome of Steve Froggatt, Gareth Barry, Trevor Sinclair and 19-year-old Liverpool midfielder Steven Gerrard were all called into the squad in the hope that there may be some solutions to England's perennial problem down the left flank.

Froggatt, not even a guaranteed starter for his club, Coventry, never actually played for England as the left wing-back spot went to Jason Wilcox of Leeds, his first cap for four years. Kieron Dyer, the young Newcastle player, played as right wing-back, with Beckham, Scholes and Dennis Wise in the centre of midfield. In the absence of the injured Michael Owen, much to the relief of the visiting defenders, Emile Heskey of Leicester was handed his England debut, partnering captain Alan Shearer up front. The back three were Martin Keown, Gareth Southgate and Sol Campbell, with David Seaman firmly established as England's number 1 behind them. For all the tactical criticism of Keegan, it was a very balanced side and, true to his nature, a very attacking one.

Keegan read out the team the day before the match and entertained the media, inadvertently providing them with one of his classic quotes: "I'd say that right now Argentina are the second best team in the world, and I can't give higher praise than that."

Keegan was asked to justify the selection of Dennis Wise, who Manchester United manager Alex Ferguson had recently described as being "capable of starting a fight in an empty room". The Chelsea midfielder had been sent off six times in the previous 18 months, bringing his career total to 12 red cards, and he was also facing an FA charge for his involvement in a tunnel fracas after a league match against his old club Wimbledon. "I can't defend his disciplinary record," said Keegan. "The evidence is there, but it's the opportunity for a fresh start for him." Wise had been in outstanding form during Chelsea's Champions League campaign and had not actually been booked in a single European game. It was just domestic matches he was having problems with. "I've had a two-minute chat with him and I'm putting my trust in him," said Keegan. It was the diminutive, combative Wise's first match for England since 1995.

Argentina's new coach, Marcelo Bielsa, had taken over from Daniel Passarella immediately after the 1998 World Cup, following his success at Newell's Old Boys, where he had won the 1998 'Clausura' championship (since 1991, the Argentina season has been divided into two championships, the Apertura (opening), which runs from August to December, and the Clausura (closing), which runs from February to June). Bielsa kept the nucleus of Passarella's team; seven of the players that played against England at France '98 would be in the starting line up at Wembley. But there were other changes. Passarella's short hair and no earrings rule had been scrapped, and quite a few players celebrated their newly found freedom by letting their hair down, most notably Ayala, Ortega, Sorin, Pechittino, Burgos, and the now bearded Batistuta. If they stood together in a line they could easily have passed themselves off as a heavy metal band, and goalkeeper German Burgos of Mallorca (who had taken over from the 'retired', cow-tending Carlos Roa) was, in fact, the lead guitarist in a rock group, regularly playing gigs in Spain.

Long gone were the days when the Argentina players would fly into London all together from Buenos Aires and then spend a few days touring and shopping. Only 16 players were coming to England, arriving in three contingents two days before the match; Spanish-based from Madrid, Italian-based from Milan, with only Arruabarrena and Husein making the long trip across the Atlantic from South America.

Bielsa had promised the Spanish and Italian clubs that there would only be one very light training session, a game of football tennis with no physical contact, at Arsenal's training ground. Arsène Wenger and his players were training alongside, so no press were allowed in. Very different from the days when Argentina used to practise in Kensington's public gardens.

Is one day's preparation enough? manager Bielsa was asked. "We've had no matches between November and March and the only way to resolve this lapse was to arrange this game. It's not ideal, but there's no other way. I've scarcely time to work with the players, but I prefer this option to not playing at all."

Is it a pointless match? Batistuta was asked. "It's always worth testing yourself against the best countries in the world," Batigol said, but then gave the game away. "More than winning, what we're interested in is just finding a solid working block. That's the objective of this match," said the striker, virtually admitting it was being treated as a practice session.

Even though Bielsa was using roughly the same group of players, there were complaints in Argentina that the style of play was even more Europeanised than under Passarella; a pressing game that traditionalists did not like. *Could Batistuta and Crespo play together?* was the new debate. Bielsa thought not, and chose left-sided midfielder Kily Gonzalez alongside Ortega and Batistuta, leaving Crespo on the bench, something he was becoming used to.

Keegan reckoned that Ortega was still the dangerman even though *El Burrito* (the little donkey) was desperately out of form at Parma in Italy. "He goes all over the place and he's pretty much a free spirit," said Keegan, "but I've told my defenders that if they feel they need to go with him then it won't be a problem if Sol Campbell goes up the pitch to pick him up."

For his part Ortega tried his best to talk up the game, saying that there was never a small England v Argentina match and that he was thrilled at having the opportunity to play at Wembley before they knocked it down.

A new tradition in international friendlies was an Under-21 match the night before. An England team featuring Frank Lampard, Lee Bowyer, Jonathan Woodgate, Jamie Carragher, Danny Mills, Carl Cort and Joe Cole beat their Argentinian counterparts 1-0 with a goal from captain Lee Hendrie. Curiously, none of the young Argentinian players from that night ever broke into the first-team.

Five hundred Argentina supporters, mainly students living in Britain, were at Wembley for the main event, and they made themselves heard, so at least, this time, both national anthems received the now traditional Wembley boo.

A few hours before kick-off it was announced that Sir Stanley Matthews had died at the age of 85. There was something poetic about the legendary winger passing away on the day of an England international at Wembley. Matthews had gained the last of his 54 England caps at the age of 42 (he also played in 30 wartime internationals), though he never played against Argentina, missing out on the first meeting between the two countries in 1951 through injury. Both sides wore black armbands and a minute's silence was held in his honour.

As in that very first match England wore red shirts with white shorts, while Argentina wore their first choice sky blue and white stripes, with black shorts. Unusually, the two captains were centre-forwards, Alan Shearer and Gabriel Batistuta. Markus Merk was the first German to referee England v Argentina since 1966, although this did not seem to present any problems to the visitors. "I hope he's a strict referee," said Bielsa, though he probably did not want him to be quite as strict as Herr Kreitlein.

The match started at 8pm local time, live on satellite TV in both countries. England kicked off. A few short passes, before Wise found Wilcox on the left, whose cross was nodded on by Shearer at the near post, but Chamot headed clear. England's captain had spoken beforehand of his joy at teaming up with Wilcox again. The pair had won the Premier League with Blackburn Rovers in 1994/95, many of Shearer's goals coming from Wilcox crosses. England did indeed look good down the left-hand side in the first ten minutes, and enjoyed the lion's share of possession. Shearer shot high from 25 yards, and then headed a Beckham corner wide.

With quarter of an hour gone, Emile Heskey, receiving a neat ball from Wise, ran down the right flank at full speed. The Leicester player's cross was met at the far post by Wilcox, who shot into Cavallero's arms. Spurred on by the crowd, the muscular Heskey ran at the defence again, but this time down the left, sprinting past Sensini, Argentina's veteran defender. Heskey's perfect cross put Shearer through on goal, but the England captain was bundled over. Shearer jumped up and appealed for a penalty, arguing with the referee when it was not given. Replays revealed that Chamot had stuck out a leg and may well have tripped Shearer. England's luck had not turned since '98.

Between Heskey's runs, Beckham was booked for a studs-up challenge on Gonzalez and Arrubarrena was then booked for fouling Beckham in retaliation. The Manchester United player curled his free kick wide.

Beckham and Wise's passing was accurate and unhurried, but the pace of the match was slow, with Argentina offering little. *The Times* described Wise as 'clinging so tight to Veron that the influence of the Argentinian playmaker was negligible,' and therein lies a question. How seriously were the Argentine players taking the match?

Ortega tried to prove their hearts were in it, hitting an ambitious 25 yard drive … but it flew high and wide. He was booked a minute later for a blatant dive under a challenge from Dyer. The boos rang out once again around Wembley.

Sensini, a veteran of three World Cups, was struggling so much to cope with Heskey's pace and power that Bielsa substituted him on 35 minutes. Pochettino came on to mark Shearer, which released Chamot to move across to try and deal with Heskey. But still the Leicester forward continued with his direct running. Dubbed 'The Tank' by *Clarin*, Heskey glided past Chamot before unselfishly pulling the ball back for Scholes when he was in a better shooting position himself. Ayala intercepted and cleared. Undoubtedly Heskey had been the best player in a first half which had seen almost nothing of Batistuta, or indeed any Argentine attack.

Rio Ferdinand replaced Keown at half-time. A lot of expectation was pinned on the young West Ham player, a defender who possessed the ability to bring the ball out of defence, but he had little opportunity to display that side of his game as Argentina slowly began to creep into the game during the second half. Kily Gonzalez beat Dyer on the Argentina left and his shot was acrobatically saved by Seaman with one hand at the second attempt. Dyer was substituted for Phil Neville, but the passing became sloppier on both sides. Wise was booked for a foul on Gonzalez and Chamot saw yellow for a foul on Heskey as the game became stop start, dominated by the referee's whistle, but not for the reasons so many earlier editions had been.

A good chance came England's way on 70 minutes. Shearer received the ball with his back to goal on the edge of the penalty area and knocked it to Wilcox. Demonstrating the advantage of having a left-footed player on the left, Wilcox reached the ball as it was about to cross the bye-line and curled an accurate cross with the instep of his left foot to the far post. Heskey's goalbound header was inadvertently deflected over the bar off Pochettino's back. It was to prove England's best chance of the second half and Heskey's last meaningful contribution as he and Ayala clashed heads, resulting in the England player being stretchered off, receiving a standing ovation on his return to the fray. He would, however, be replaced by Andy Cole shortly afterwards amid a flurry of substitutions which rendered the remainder of the match limp.

Argentina nearly sneaked a winner at the death. Gonzalez, again progressing down the left, hit a shot which had Seaman beaten, but the ball flashed wide of the post. Cole had half a chance, but Cavallero saved comfortably and the boos at the final whistle were directed at the pointlessness of the game, rather than any sense of injustice.

This being England versus Argentina, there had to be headlines written. 'DECEPTION', ran the headline in *La Nacion*, although there was little controversy in the piece which accompanied the attention-grabbing masthead. 'Last night confirmed that diplomatic relations between England and Argentina are so friendly now that the two countries signed a pact of mutual respect and non-aggression yesterday in the most unlikely of places, a stadium of football. Thirty or so bureaucrats negotiated a bilateral treaty in which one team did very little (England) and the other almost nothing (Argentina). They agreed to a ceasefire on shots on goal. With matches like this it's better that they knock down Wembley as soon as possible.'

Other Argentine reporters described it as a 'match without ideas', with 'a lack of individual creativity' and 'an alarming lack of attacking power from two teams considered amongst the world's best, supposedly talented players like Veron, Ortega, Beckham, and Scholes were extremely disappointing.'

Claudio Cervivo, sports editor of *La Nacion*, confessed to having fallen asleep during the match, claiming that both teams had had a 'bad attitude' – only interested in completing the match in the required time, nine changes being far too many to provide any sort of spectacle.

Manager Bielsa described the match as a "worthwhile exercise", but back in Buenos Aires, ex-internationals were not so happy. Indeed they were downright angry. 1978 World Cup winner Omar Larrossa said, "The national team shouldn't use those tactics at Wembley and, with respect to their attitude, if the players don't want to play then don't play – there are plenty of others who will." 1986 World Cup winner Hector Enrique was not holding his tongue either: "It appears there's no pride in the blue and white shirt anymore and that offends me. I get the impression that some players just want to save their legs and avoid injuries and tiredness."

Maybe because the English press had been part-responsible for Hoddle's downfall, they were keen to praise Keegan's England. Or was it just that England had been so poor in their previous match against Scotland that the slightest crumbs of hope were celebrated? 'The future suddenly seems bright again,' said *The Times*. 'Assured, confident, poised England did enough to suggest that some form of success at Euro 2000 is on again.' However, the piece did warn that it was important not to get overexcited by this 'qualified success' as 'Juan Veron, Ariel Ortega, and Gabriel Batistuta had looked thoroughly uninterested in proceedings, but Keegan's side must take some credit for that'.

The piece continued, 'Heskey had left the Argentinian defence almost as disconcerted as they had been by Michael Owen in St. Etienne'. Good job they said 'almost'.

However, Matt Dickinson commented, with irony, in the same paper that, 'It just about sums up the illogical perversities of Kevin Keegan's reign that three months of inactivity should have done more to improve his team than three days of intense training ever did – perhaps the answer is just to turn up on the day before the match and let them get on with it.'

'A good, but not great match', said Henry Winter in the *Daily Telegraph* more guardedly.

Unconcerned, Keegan was characteristically bubbly. "Heskey was fantastic," he said. "They had to substitute Sensini because he couldn't cope with him."

And of his slightly controversial midfield selection? "Wise was fantastic," said Keegan. "He just came in and looked like he'd been there forever."

He didn't stop there. "England were fantastic," said Keegan, leaping to the assumption that his band of hard-bitten Premier League stars knew their footballing history. "I told the lads before the game to give a performance Stanley Matthews would have been proud of, and I think we did that."

Keegan's England gained another respectable Wembley result against South American opposition in May, a 1-1 draw with Brazil, but again the question of how seriously friendly matches were being taken was raised as the second half descended into a plethora of substitutions. But the real downhill slide began after England took an early 2-0 lead over Portugal in the opening game of Euro 2000. The Portuguese, led by the imperious Luis Figo, fought back to win 3-2 and England went out at the first hurdle after losing late on against Romania in the final group match, having beaten Germany 1-0 in between.

Keegan's renowned suspect temperament emerged once more after England had lost the final game at the old Wembley stadium 1-0 to Germany to get their qualification for the 2002 World Cup off to a dreadful start. The England manager resigned during a post-match tunnel interview, saying he had taken England as far as he could. "To be honest," Keegan admitted, showing the passion for his country for which he was equally loved and derided, "I think I'm a bit short tactically at this level."

England 0
Argentina 0
Wednesday 23 February 2000. Wembley, London. Friendly. Attendance: 75,000
Referee: Markus Merk (Germany)

England: David Seaman (Arsenal), Martin Keown (Arsenal, sub 46'), Gareth Southgate (Aston Villa), Sol Campbell (Tottenham), Kieron Dyer (Newcastle, sub 59'), Dennis Wise (Chelsea), David Beckham (Manchester Utd, sub 73'), Jason Wilcox (Leeds), Paul Scholes (Manchester Utd), Alan Shearer(c) (Newcastle, sub 78'), Emile Heskey (Leicester, sub 79'), Subs: Rio Ferdinand (West Ham, on 46'), Phil Neville (Manchester Utd, on 59'), Ray Parlour (Arsenal, on 73'), Kevin Phillips (Sunderland, on 78'), Andy Cole (Manchester Utd, on 79')
Manager: Kevin Keegan

Argentina: Pablo Cavallero (Español), Roberto Ayala (AC Milan), Roberto Sensini(c) (Lazio, sub 35'), Jose Chamot (AC Milan), Javier Zanetti (Inter Milan), Diego Simeone (Lazio), Juan Sebastián Veron (Lazio), Cristian Gonzalez (Valencia), Rodolfo Arruabarrrena (Boca Jnrs, sub 67'), Ariel Ortega (Parma), Gabriel Batistuta (Fiorentina, sub 57'), Subs: Mauricio Pochettino (Espanyol, on 35'), Hernan Crespo (Parma, on 57'), Nelson Vivas (Celta Vigo, on 67')
Manager: Marcelo Bielsa

BECKHAM'S REVENGE

WORLD CUP GROUP GAME, SAPPORO DOME, JAPAN, FRIDAY 7 JUNE 2002

2002. ENGLAND was in festive spirits; the Queen's Golden Jubilee and the start of the World Cup in Japan and South Korea in the same week. Times had changed, though. Perhaps indicative of how society had changed in the previous 25 years, there were no 1977-style street parties which had greeted Elizabeth II's silver jubilee. The official celebrations were condensed into a one-off Saturday night pop concert called the Party at the Palace. Brian May's windswept hair and guitar solo opened proceedings, a version of 'God Save The Queen' from the rooftop of Buckingham Palace, although there were no visiting fans to drown the national anthem with boos. May was described by critics as a 'spectacular Rock God', or 'Cheesy', depending on your taste. Rod Stewart, Paul McCartney, Cliff Richard, Phil Collins, Shirley Bassey and Dame Edna Everage all performed, but it was Ozzy Osbourne who drew the most enthusiastic applause from Princes Charles, William and Harry, whetting the nation's appetite for England's opening match against Sweden the following morning. Osbourne said it was the greatest moment of his career, although there was a minor controversy as some people had expressed displeasure at the prime minister's wife, Cherie Blair, for excessive dancing and singing.

Sales of Japanese wine were up 25 per cent thanks to the World Cup, and, in a now familiar ritual every other summer for a major international tournament, the St. George flag adorned shop windows and England replica tops were *de rigeur* fashionwear. World Cup wall charts 'Backed Our Boys' and the *Sun* gave away their 'traditional' England plastic bowler hats.

Despite the hype, or perhaps because of it, England's first match ended in huge anticlimax, like a nagging Sunday morning hangover.

'England had about as much sense of community as a rabble on the run. But at this level all the running has to have a point. England did not, and when Beckham left the field 17 minutes into the second half, the team's descent into chaos was already fully blown,' the *Independent* declared after the 1-1 draw with Sweden.

'Lack of Technique and Tactical Nous', said the *Daily Telegraph*.

'It's Not The End of the World, But It Just Feels Like It', was the headline in the *Sun*.

Pubs had opened early for the 10.30am Sunday kick-off, leaving fans with the rest of the day to stare into glass half-full pints of beer, pondering the reasons for England's collective second half malfunction. Five days later England were to face Argentina, unbeaten in 25 matches since the goalless draw against England at Wembley in February 2000 and joint favourites to lift the Cup with France. Even the most optimistic of Englishmen feared the worst. Astonishingly, even in England, more bets were placed on an Argentine victory than an English one, for a game which became the most gambled-on match in English football history.

Marcelo Bielsa's team was experienced and settled. Thirteen of the squad had been at France '98, including Gabriel Batistuta, hoping to emerge from the 2002 tournament as the World Cup's all-time top goalscorer. Most were very familiar to English fans, which only increased the fear factor. Veron, who was now at Manchester United, could devastate with his pinpoint passing; Diego Simeone, the warrior with 103 caps, ruled midfield; Ariel Ortega, the dribbler, could tear sides apart; captain Roberto Ayala and Javier Zanetti, both approaching a century of international appearances, were the the rocks on which the unbeaten run had been built.

Argentina had suffered only one defeat (away to Brazil) in 18 qualifiers, comfortably winning the South American group at a canter, while their Samba neighbours struggled and scraped fourth place. Morale was high. England were worried.

There had been a few minor if familiar complaints over the Bielsa style: 'Too European,' said the traditionalists. 'Too mechanical and scientific'. But there was an obvious reason for that. The run had been built on a team mostly drawn from those players signed to European clubs. While results were positive, Bielsa was able to resist calls for the in-form Argentina-based ball players: Saviola, Gallardo and Riquelme. So it was hardly surprising that there was a pragmatic European influence on style.

During the unbeaten run, Bielsa had played with one up front, generally Batistuta, despite having Hernan Crespo, Claudio Lopez, and Claudio Caniggia at his disposal. Caniggia, whose long hair and previous cocaine problems had given him no chance under Passarella's regime, was enjoying a surprising renaissance in Scottish football, first at Dundee, then Glasgow Rangers, and was back in contention at the age of 38.

The manager insisted that Batistuta and Crespo were incompatible together and, whenever Claudio Lopez played, it was on the left, rather than in his natural central striking role (where he had torn Spanish and Italian domestic defences apart with his pace while playing for Valencia and Lazio). And therein lies the old international manager's dilemma: does he pick players currently in form, or stick with the tried and tested? Although it had not affected Argentina's results over the year and a half period of the good run, at the end of a long, hard season many of Bielsa's key players were out of sorts at their clubs. Juan Sebastian Veron was a case in point. He had struggled to adapt to the speed of the Premier League following his £28 million transfer from Lazio to Manchester United. Or maybe it was his new team-mates who had failed to adapt to him? Alex Ferguson's original intention was to play with a lone striker, Ruud van Nistelrooy, with Veron and Scholes tucked in behind him, especially in European matches, but the United manager later abandoned the idea, returning to a 4-4-2 in which Veron did not fit into the established midfield quartet of Beckham, Keane, Scholes, and Giggs. Also, one of Veron's greatest assets, shooting and crossing from dead-ball situations, was made redundant at Manchester United due to the presence of Beckham, now one of the greatest strikers of a dead ball in the world. However, Veron's dip in form had gone largely unnoticed in Argentina.

Likewise Batistuta. Whisper it quietly, but spreading from Rome were the first suggestions that age was catching up with Serie A's most prolific striker of the last decade. But Batistuta's place in Bielsa's team was assured as the system revolved around him. Ortega, too, had been in poor form for Parma. After just one season, the Italian side were looking to offload their disappointing signing from Valencia, where he had also been below par the season before. However, the Batistuta–Veron–Ortega axis was such an integral part of Argentina's phenomenal run of results that leaving any of them out had not been contemplated. Add to that the fact that Simeone, injured for eight months, had only recently returned to Lazio's team, and his fitness levels were still not at their maximum either.

Going into the 2002 World Cup, hubris was so high that winning the trophy, it was considered, was going to compensate for the economic hardship the country was suffering. "It's true," says Juan Sebastian Veron, reflecting on events six years later, speaking to me at the training camp of his home-town team Estudiantes de La Plata, whom he rejoined in 2006 after eight years in Europe. "There was a lot of expectation on the shoulders of the players. As a group we felt that we were representing the people. It kind of got snowballed by the press, because of our incredible unbeaten run. By the time we travelled out to Japan we were going there to win the World Cup, to make up for all the problems back home, to make the people happy, and give the country back some pride."

England, like their manager, were a bit of a mystery. Following Keegan's resignation, the FA had continued their policy of appointing a manager who was the complete opposite of the previous one, in both personality and tactics, and the young chief executive, Adam Crozier, with no little advice from the FA's vice-chairman, David Dein, took the decision to bring in a non-English manager for the first time in the FA's 120-year history. Crozier was no stranger to change. A former employee of the advertising agency Saatchi and Saatchi, he had been hired by the FA to initiate reform and rid the organisation of its fuddy-duddy image. He had set about his task by immediately dispensing with the old FA blazers. Literally. Crozier also sought lucrative sponsorship and advocated a policy of spending to attract further investment. Projects included moving the FA headquarters from Lancaster Gate to trendy Soho Square, a multi-million pound training ground complex for national youth sides at Burton-on-Trent, and sanctioning the building of the new Wembley stadium. It was a radical shake-up, but ultimately one that saw the FA plunged into debt, resulting in cuts to grass roots football and lurching from crisis to crisis as first Burton was moth-balled and the cost of building the new Wembley spiralled out of control.

Sven-Göran Eriksson, the former Gothenburg, Benfica, Roma, Sampdoria and Lazio coach. Eriksson was a controversial choice for many reasons, the main being, of course, that he was foreign. 'It's a disgrace,' huffed the *Daily Mail*, and a host of English managers hit out, many put out at having been overlooked. Some felt that Eriksson's enormous salary, which made him by far the highest-paid international manager, was unjustifiable. Other voices of dissent raised fears over playing style. Throughout his managerial career, Eriksson's teams had played in a defensive, counter-attacking fashion. Anybody who thought he was similar in style to Frenchman Arsène Wenger, multi championship-winning manager of Arsenal was way off the mark. Previous England manager Kevin Keegan had more in common with Wenger's attacking philosophy than the new man.

Another concern was how Eriksson would cope with having to use the playing resources at his disposal. His success at domestic level had been based on spending heavily. His lavish purchases at Benfica had left the club in huge debt, from which it took years to recover. He had also splashed out at both Sampdoria and Lazio, again leaving under a cloud when the money dried up. Being an international manager was, of course, very different.

He was also known to follow the gold trail himself. Eriksson had been set to join Blackburn Rovers from Sampdoria in 1997, but reneged on the deal at the eleventh hour, preferring Lazio when they offered more money. However, in terms of trophies, no-one could argue with Eriksson's record: two Swedish championships and a Uefa Cup with IFK Gothenburg, three Portuguese league titles with Benfica, Coppa Italia victories with Roma and Sampdoria, and an Italian league and European Cup Winners' Cup with Lazio. His Lazio team had been based around the Argentines, Veron, Simeone, Crespo, and Lopez, all of whom he had signed.

Any doubts over Eriksson's suitability for the job were jettisoned into oblivion in September 2001 when England hammered Germany 5-1 in Munich. Michael Owen (3), Steven Gerrard and Emile Heskey scored the goals after Germany had taken the lead after 6 minutes (Carsten Jancker). David Seaman had pulled off an excellent save from Deisler when the match was still 1-1, but once England had gone a goal up just before half-time and the Germans had to attack in the second half, Eriksson's England kept hitting them on the break.

What was his secret? How had he managed to turn the shambles under Keegan into a tactically-astute team in such a short space of time? He seemed to do it all just by remaining calm, and believing in his undoubtedly talented players, who were christened the 'Golden Generation', including the likes of Beckham, Gerrard, Scholes, Ferdinand, Campbell and Owen. For a year after the famous victory over Germany, Eriksson was a national treasure in his adopted country. There was an air of mysticism about him as he cashed in by advertising classical music CDs and gave dry-witted interviews. Not since Alf Ramsey, briefly, in 1966, had an England manager enjoyed such popularity.

However, while Eriksson's counter-attacking tactics had worked a treat against the Germans, they were not so effective against teams that also played defensively. Like the Greeks, for example. Despite the result against the Germans, after the awful start under Keegan, England needed to win their last World Cup qualifier at Old Trafford on a sunny afternoon in October 2001 to be sure of topping their group and avoiding the play-offs, but when Greece went a goal up in the first half, England proved to be bereft of attacking ideas against a team that pulled every man back into their own half. Enter captain fantastic David Beckham, who produced one of the greatest ever individual performances in an England shirt. He seemingly single-handedly took on the Greeks in the second half, moving inside from the right, popping up across the whole of the midfield, including left wing, from where he delivered a series of accurate crosses. "Beckham is actually England's best left-sided player," remarked one commentator. Substitute Teddy Sheringham, with his first touch, flicked on a Beckham free kick with his head to score, but before the relief had even had time to sink in the Greeks retook the lead, taking advantage of more confusion in a creaking defence, a minute later.

Eriksson had named Beckham as captain the previous spring – a cynical marketing ploy cried some critics, but his performance against Greece, a landmark in Beckham's career, was an inspiration, and the reward for his non-stop running came in the 93rd minute.

Wise old head Sheringham exaggerated a slight nudge in the back – if there was any contact at all – and went down as if pole-axed 35 yards from the Greek goal. It was the type of dive that would normally have English blood vessels bursting with rage if perpetrated against them (the post-match pundits laughed it off). The free kick, in a central position, was perfect Beckham territory. The Manchester United midfielder's curling set pieces had been getting closer all afternoon, and he bent this one perfectly around the wall, beyond the goalkeeper's reach, into the top left corner of the net. The shaven-headed England captain, in his white shirt, with a single red line down the front left-hand side, ran towards the corner flag, arms outstretched in the crucifix position, and leapt into the air. By that stage England were sure that the 2-2 draw was enough as Germany were only drawing at home with Finland. England's players watched the final seconds of the game in Gelsenkirchen peter out. They were going to the 2002 World Cup.

Beckham's transformation from the the most vilified English footballer, following the sending off against Argentina four years earlier, to the most popular, was a remarkable turnaround. His never-say-die spirit against the Greeks encapsulated English values, and the photograph of the goal celebration captured the moment. But there was still one more pending fixture for his resurrection to be complete. When the World Cup draw was made in December 2001, Eriksson allowed himself a wry smile when England and Argentina were placed in the same group. He knew what it meant – a chance for revenge. The opportunity to get one back on a foe now as important to the English psyche as the Germans grabbed every headline, with writers, for the moment at least, ignoring the fact that, with Nigeria, the strongest of the African teams, and Eriksson's native Sweden making up the four teams, England had been drawn in the 'Group of Death'. Every World Cup has to have one.

Then the problems began to mount. In April 2002, three months before the tournament, Aldo Duscher, an Argentine playing for Deportivo De La Coruña against Manchester United in a Champions League quarter-final, caught Beckham with a late tackle and broke the metatarsal bone of the most famous foot in England. 'Good work, agent Duscher,' said Argentina sports daily, *Olé*. The following morning, every Englishman knew exactly where the metatarsal bone was, and how long it takes to heal. The great, living talisman of English football might not be able to play – Beckham's World Cup was in jeopardy, and it became a national obsession in England, a daily soap opera with medical updates leading news reports on every channel. *Will he, or won't he, make it?* everyone worried. Even Prime Minister Tony Blair expressed his concern.

By rights Beckham should have put his feet up and got himself right for the new season with Manchester United. But this was the World Cup, and more importantly this was Argentina.

The healing period had been timed and monitored and reported in minute detail. England's medical team opined that, even if the captain was unable to play in the first games, he should be fit for the later stages. Eriksson named Beckham in the final 23-man squad. While the rest of the squad ran and worked with the ball in training, Beckham watched from the sidelines, hopping on one leg on a mini-trampoline.

Beckham's miraculous recovery from the injury diverted attention away from the other members of the squad who would be missing. Reliable and experienced right-back Gary Neville was also out, as was Liverpool's midfield dynamo Steven Gerrard, with a groin injury. They would prove crucial absentees. Meanwhile Blackburn striker Matt Jansen, on standby, ruled himself out by having a motorcycle accident in Italy, which left him in a coma for six weeks. Kieron Dyer was doubtful and to avoid a Gazza-type situation Eriksson broke with tradition and named his 23 players before the warm up games. Trevor Sinclair was named as the lone stand-by man and flew to Japan with the squad, but when Dyer was declared fit, Sinclair travelled home again, despite being asked to stay. "It would hurt me too much just to be there for nothing, and I'd rather be with my family," he said, upon his arrival in London.

No sooner had the West Ham midfielder unpacked his bags, than midfielder Danny Murphy pulled a hamstring in Japan, so Sinclair once again put on the official England team blue suit, pulled on his brown boots and added to his now substantial air miles credit by flying back to Japan. Yet Sinclair's jet-setting was a mere sideshow compared to the real story of England's build up, at least as far as the tabloids were concerned. Sven-Göran Eriksson, the bald, bland, calm, classical music lover was having an affair with raunchy BBC weather girl Ulrika Jonsson. This had not gone down too well with feisty Italian girl-friend Nancy Dell'Olio, but was a gift from Sweden for the English tabloids. And the broadsheets. Many women previously uninterested in football now followed events surrounding England's World Cup campaign with closer attention, while stunned males wondered how on earth the 54-year-old had managed to pull Ulrika-ka-ka.

Argentina had more serious news to discuss. The country was bankrupt. After a decade of following IMF policies that had not worked, the over-valued peso, falsely pegged at 1 to 1 with the US dollar, was in free-fall. The economy had collapsed at the beginning of the year and there had been three separate governments in one week, three different presidents resigning. Bank accounts were frozen, and outraged ordinary people saw their life savings disappear. There were demonstrations and *cazerolazos* (the loud banging of pots and pans) outside banks and government buildings. Riots broke out, and there were reports of large-scale financial fraud. Amidst the all banging of kitchen utensils many Argentinans did what they often do in times of crisis and depression. They turned to football for a small piece of happiness.

"We were very aware we were representing the people," says Veron. "You could say it was an extra responsibility for us, but we were a very united group. Us Argentines, we are proud of our country and our flag, so when the country collapses financially, it not only brings hardship to the people, but national pride is hurt as well, so pride in our football becomes even more acute."

Although the tournament was jointly hosted between Japan and South Korea, each group was based in only one of the countries. The Group of Death was in Japan, and Sapporo, on the northern Japanese island of Hokkaido, would be the venue for the meeting between England and Argentina, who had opened their campaign with a routine 1-0 victory over Nigeria in Ibaraki, Batistuta becoming the first player to score in his country's opening game at three consecutive World Cups.

Any fears about hooliganism, especially the English variety, proved unfounded. Japanese police liaised with their foreign counterparts, and English hooligan specialists praised the Japanese force for carrying out an efficient operation, and for speaking English in their dealings with fans, which made them feel welcome. Distance and expense no doubt prevented many European hooligans making the trip, and certainly ruled out Argentina's Barras Bravas.

It wasn't only the Argentine hooligans who were missing. Not even their media outlets were able to send reporters due to the financial crisis. There had been 200 Argentine journalists at France '98, but only 30 travelled to the Far East. Argentina's J-village training ground was a ghost town, bereft of humming satellite trucks. Many 'live' radio commentators followed the action on the television back home – listeners unaware they were listening to commentators operating out of offices in Buenos Aires, making it difficult to justify travel expenses to future events. The crisis naturally affected the AFA as well. Manager Bielsa had not been paid for the previous eight months.

The toll from Argentina's victory over Nigeria had begun to mount. Captain and sweeper Roberto Ayala had stretched a muscle in the warm-up and been replaced by Bayer Leverkusen's Diego Placente. In Ayala's absence, Veron captained the team. Bielsa's high pressure, high tempo 3-3-3-1 was an attacking formation that required excellent levels of fitness. He always wanted the game to take place in the opponents' half, and did not use conventional full backs. In theory, there was not a lack of width as his idea was to create a constant creation of two v ones down the flanks, with wide midfielders linking up with two wingers. An obvious problem that could arise from the spaces left behind was the vulnerability to counter-attack, but, with good organisation and high fitness levels, this had not occurred during the 25-match unbeaten run.

For England, Beckham's substitution, as expected, on the hour mark to protect his still-healing foot had left the side without attacking ideas and unable to counter Sweden's equalising goal, scored by Niclas Alexandersson after Danny Mills's mistake. (Sol Campbell had given England the lead on 22 minutes from a Beckham corner.) "I felt tired, the foot was painful," Beckham said afterwards. He was replaced by Kieron Dyer, whose fitness was also not 100 per cent.

Neither of England's forwards (Darius Vassell and Owen) was a link man, and a large gap had opened up between them and the midfield, leading to a deluge of hopeful long balls, mainly drifting over the pair's heads, and easily dealt with by the Swedish defence.

England were missing the dynamism and passing of Gerrard in midfield, while Eriksson's failure to solve England's perennial problem on the left ensured the side lacked balance. Emile Heskey, by nature a striker, looked uncomfortable in the role against Sweden. At this stage Eriksson was reluctant to use either Trevor Sinclair, who was right-footed, or Joe Cole, on the left. The latter, he reasoned, although undoubtedly talented, did not have the experience, nor discipline, to play on the left side of a (rigid) 4-4-2.

Many observers noted a distinct lack of leadership on the field once Beckham had departed. "We haven't started as well as we hoped," explained the captain. "In the changing rooms we were down, but we shouldn't be as we didn't lose. This draw obliges us to beat Argentina and we will do it." The war of words was beginning.

The 'stand out' group match, the game that the whole world of football had been looking forward to since the draw was made six months earlier, had arrived. There were five days between the opening games and England versus Argentina and the media used them to the full. Inevitably, most of the build up revolved around David Beckham. As captain and the most recognisable sportsman on earth, he was obliged to give the most interviews and attend the most publicity shots. His designer, bleach-blond mohican became the height of fashion in the Far East, copied by thousands of fans. Of course it was the re-encounter between Beckham and Simeone that captured the imagination of the English public. On the morning of the match, *The Times* led with a picture of the two adversaries. 'The Rematch: Simeone v Beckham Reflects 100 Years Of History', it said on its front page, a testament to how big the fixture had become. The last time England and Argentina had met in the group stages of the World Cup, in 1962, the preview in *The Times* had consisted of one paragraph on the inside of its sports pages.

'Cunning' was the new buzz word. Eriksson had spent 14 years of his career working in Italy. Simeone, Veron, Crespo and Lopez had been under his tuition at Lazio, so he was familiar with the Latin ways. It was clear that this was something he had discussed with the England players.

"I think we will have to use a bit more cunning," said Beckham in a thinly-veiled reference to Simeone's actions in France. "They are cunning players. If they use things to get an advantage then they will do that. England are not as cunning as that, but we will see. I wouldn't expect our players to play certain tricks, but you never know. We are not cynical enough. That has always been the case of England. Players were too honest."

Michael Owen agreed: "I don't think you should cheat, but I think you should be clever. I'd go down for a penalty. If you go down without being touched that's cheating, but you can try to make someone foul you by enticing them to get a ball and then getting a toe in. If they bring you down it's not cheating, is it? It's clever. It's drawing a foul out of them." Some English coaches and officials were horrified to hear this coming from the mouth of England's star striker. As Glenn Moore of the *Independent* wondered, 'this is where the ambivalence creeps in,' and asked, 'where does gamesmanship become cheating?'

He would soon be given the opportunity to discuss this theme in far more detail using a specific and crucial match incident.

Beckham was asked if, given the chance, he would score a goal with his hand as Maradona had in '86? "Yes ... no ... I don't know," he replied. "I won't get sucked into any retaliation this time. I would walk away now. The red card four years ago changed me as a person and as a footballer, and it's been rewarding for me to win over the people through my football on the pitch. I could have done interview after interview and talked my way around it, but I've just gone out there and worked hard and tried to get to where I am today."

'Revenge' was a perfectly acceptable noun in the England camp on this occasion. In fact, it was a key word as Eriksson appeared to be using past incidents as motivational techniques. The Argentine shirt-whirling on the coach four years earlier was fast developing into a main talking point before the match in Sapporo. Was the England manager reminding his players of the hurt they had felt? "Their whole bus was pounding," remembered Teddy Sheringham, "and I could have no more incentive than to be pumped up for this game to get revenge. I can't remember any other professionals doing what the Argentinians did on that coach. It's one of those things that lives with you and is my lasting memory of France. It riled a lot of our players. We were upset at going out of the tournament and you can't really react to what they were doing at the time. But you put it down in the little notebook at the back of your head and hopefully, it comes back to hurt some of them."

Beckham agreed: "I was in bits after the game because of all that had gone on. They were jumping up and down with their shirts off, swinging them around their heads and banging on windows. We felt humiliated anyway because we were out of the competition, and down enough as it was. To see that upset us a lot ... One of the most upsetting parts was that they could behave like that when we were all standing there with our families. After all that I don't think we'll need any team talk on Friday."

Clear enough, but both Veron and Roa do not understand what all the fuss is about. In Argentina jumping up and down and celebrating on the coach is normal, they say. "We were just celebrating like we always do after winning," says Roa, "and then we saw the English coach next to us, and I know it's been said that they thought we were goading them, but it wasn't like that at all. It wasn't meant to be taken like that. The Argentine is very open. We manifest our feelings in this way. I don't know how to explain this to you, but it's a misunderstanding between the cultures. In Argentina, you see players and fans swinging their shirts above the heads all the time, but the England players took it badly. Beckham spoke to Veron about it, and Seba explained it was nothing. It was a question of interpretation. They didn't undertand this thing, how the Argentine player is."

Even in the modern world, when so many barriers have been broken down and players on opposing sides would become club team-mates, the age-old cultural divisions remained.

Eriksson, a master of deflecting provocative questions in press conferences, an important requirement of the England manager's job, was keen to play down any suggestion that Argentina players were dirty. "I'm sure they are very focused. I coached some of them while I was at Lazio, and I know they are professional, so I don't think they are thinking about tricks right now."

Eriksson had the art of saying very little down to a tee, but not quite as well as his counterpart, Marcela Bielsa, who had a policy of not giving interviews to anyone. Except the *Daily Star* that is. Having turned down countless invitations to speak to his own country's press, Argentine journalists were most upset that it was to an English tabloid that their manager chose to give an interview. Their tempers were calmed when it emerged that the *Star*'s exclusive had in fact been completely made up.

It didn't stop there. On the day of the match, the *Sun* ran with the headline, 'We'll Cheat Your Boys Again Say The Argies', based on a few quotes from some Argentine ... supporters. Not players or coaches. All part of the pantomime and build up. Juan Sebastián Veron found himself in the unusual, and awkward, position of playing against the country where he played his club football – the first time this had happened in this fixture as Ardiles had opted out and Villa had been injured in 1980. Trying not to offend his fellow countrymen when talking to the Argentine press, Veron said, "I know that everyone will now be talking about me playing in England, but I don't look at it as me facing them, as much as I look at it as me representing my country. I have no feelings about the English people. My one concern is for Argentina." Inevitably, 'VERON: I FEEL NOTHING FOR THE ENGLISH PEOPLE', was the story in England.

The Sapporo dome was an indoor stadium, the pitch on an air bed. The match was classified as 'low risk' due to the absence of Argentina supporters. FIFA had sent 3,000 tickets to Argentina, but 2,000 had been returned as fans could not afford them. There were some small pockets of ex-pat Argentines, banging drums and singing 'he who doesn't jump is an Englishman', but Japanese outnumbered foreigners by four to one in the 36,000 crowd (6,000 below capacity), the vast majority supporting Beckham's England, or just Beckham.

One Argentinian who probably could afford a ticket, but would not be there, was Diego Maradona. Japanese authorities refused him entrance due to his cocaine conviction. FIFA also refused to allow the AFA to retire the no. 10 shirt as a homage to their legendary hero, but the Argentines used their *viveza* (cunning) to get around it by giving the 10 shirt to their third choice goalkeeper, Banano. "At least this time, the Argentina number 10 will be allowed to use his hands legally," quipped FIFA president Sepp Blatter.

Eriksson had not wished to dwell upon the match against Sweden. To prepare for Argentina the players had been sent on golf or fishing trips, and shopping in Tokyo. His style was always to relax before key games.

In Argentina, where the kick-off was at 8.30am, children were advised to arrive early at school where they would be allowed to watch the match. "It's not that we're not going to work, but we're being flexible with the timetable," said the head of the teachers' union.

Several Argentine companies provided big screens, and even laid on a World Cup breakfast for employees. Checkout girls in supermarkets dressed in the national blue and white football strip, and the government called for tolerance from employers for football-related absenteeism, at least for two hours, anyway. The governor of Buenos Aires, Eduardo Duhalde admitted, "it will be inevitable that one will be working with one's ear near a speaker or screen."

In England, it was the longest lunch break as the 12.30pm kick-off time saw companies laying on free food to avoid a wave of employees throwing sick days off. "The smart firms have incorporated the tournament into their businesses and human resources plans and will suffer less as a result in the long term," said Richard White, managing director of recruitment firm Resource Management. "Everyone is caught up in the excitement surrounding the England team and if firms go with the flow just for a couple of hours they will reap the benefit when their employees return to work." Even at the Old Bailey, jurors were given two hours off in a rape case. "We all know that a football match, one which three-quarters of the population will be watching, is on television, so I will find out if there is a television set to watch it on. If not I will think of other places nearby," said Judge Simon Goldstein.

Despite that, the centre of economic research said one in five workers took the day off in England and that the absenteeism would cost the country £750 million in lost output and productivity. Chiltern trains cancelled eight services into Marylebone because of 'driver shortages' and Connex South Eastern experienced 'disruption due to short term sickness'.

Sales of Argentinian wine fell by 16 per cent in the days leading up to the match, English supermarket chain Safeway said, while demand for mouthwash and fresh breath products increased dramatically on the morning of the match, purchased by fans aiming to watch the match in the pub but not wanting the boss to know where they had been.

By noon those pubs were crammed, many requiring a ticket. ITV's opening credits ran with the same clips they had used in 1998; the haunting music, Rattin arguing with the referee, Maradona's goals, but now Beckham's red card was added as well, before the title 'PAYBACK TIME', over the St. George flag appeared on the screen. Over on the BBC, John Motson was obsessed with lunchtime food: "Revenge is a dish best served cold," he said.

With the bore draw friendly at Wembley two years earlier having produced little to guide either coach, or set of fans, as to what to expect and where any threat might come from, Argentina took the field as narrow 11-10 favourites.

With all the talk about Beckham and Simeone, few paid attention to the fact that Ayala, the experienced Argentina captain, had failed his fitness test, so Mauricio Pochettino would stand in, assigned to check Owen's runs. Bielsa also made another change; midfielder Kily Gonzalez for striker Claudio Lopez. More bodies in midfield. One of Gonzalez's tasks would be to cut out Beckham's crosses at source.

To counter Argentina's strategy, Eriksson flooded his central midfield. The back four remained the same: Mills, Rio Ferdinand, Campbell and Ashley Cole, with Seaman in goal, but Nicky Butt, who had not been fit for the opening game, lined up alongside Owen Hargreaves to form a central defensive midfield screen. Scholes moved out to the troublesome left, with Beckham on the right. Emile Heskey, free from the shackles of the left midfield berth, would partner Owen in attack, in place of Darius Vassell, providing bulk and a far better foil for his Liverpool strike colleague.

Another variation on kits; for the first time, both teams wore their second strips; England in red shirts and white shorts, Argentina all dark blue. For old time's sake, the Argentina national anthem was booed by the 8,000 English fans, while the Argentina fans whistled through 'God Save the Queen', but sensibilities had gone way beyond taking umbrage at such run of the mill, minor insults. Fans had mingled well in bars, playing football and drinking peacefully before the match. The Japanese police reported that the crowd was impeccably behaved. One Argentine banner of 'Las Malvinas', and an English one saying 'No Surrender To The IRA' were quickly taken down.

Sensibly FIFA had selected the best referee in the world, Pierluigi Collina, the man with the harshest stare in world football, to officiate. The bald Italian with the piercing blue eyes would stand no nonsense and the players knew it.

Finally the much-hyped game was on. Hargreaves and Butt stuck tight to Veron and Simeone, and Scholes cut inside from the left to offer further protection in the middle. The tone was set early on when Batistuta went in very strong on Campbell, but Collina did not signal for a foul much to Campbell's aggrievement. The Italian did halt the play when Butt caught Simeone though, the referee giving the England midfielder a mean stare. Was that an early indication that the ball was rolling Argentina's way?

Although sitting deep, the English midfield passed the ball around well, with Heskey dropping to collect, but on three minutes a very significant incident occurred. Hargreaves, moving forward, was caught in a clash between Pochettino and Owen. It was actually Owen who kicked Hargreaves's calf. England's Bayern Munich midfielder limped on, but on 18 minutes was forced to depart. Trevor Sinclair, who had flown home two weeks previously, came on to play on the left of midfield, with Scholes moving into the centre in place of Hargreaves.

The pace was fast, on an entirely different plane from the 2000 friendly. Zanetti took the first shot of the match, a long range drive that was easy for Seaman. Then, Argentina worked a move on their left. Sorin backheeled to Gonzalez, who drove narrowly over.

Every good and bad pass was greeted with nervous cheers and boos in pubs and bars on both sides of the Atlantic. Bielsa's men were unable to get their passing game going, as tigerish England matched them in every department. The gaps between the three bands of England's defence, midfield, and attack, so evident against Sweden, had been closed. Argentina looked to isolate Gonzalez against Danny Mills, with Veron trying to spray the passes, but Butt closed Argentina's conductor down well.

It was a tough affair. Batistuta, tearing around, appeared to catch Beckham with his elbow, but the referee did not see it. Whether it was deliberate provocation or not, Beckham rose above it. However, when Batigol made a rash challenge on Ashley Cole, Collina, without hesitation, showed him the first yellow card of the match.

The enforced substitution had actually given England more shape, and a greater attacking edge, with Sinclair providing pace on the left. When Veron made yet another stray pass, Heskey snapped it up, and fed Butt, who released Owen with an excellent through ball. Owen held off a challenge from Pochettino and fired a shot through Samuel's legs that beat goalkeeper Cavallero, but came back off the post.

On Argentina's right, Ariel Ortega and Ashley Cole were having their own personal duel. Determined not to let Ortega run at the English defence as he had in '98, the Arsenal left-back, lauded normally for his attacking virtues, proved that first and foremost he was a strong defender by producing some timely interceptions. However, when he sycthed down Ortega on the halfway line on 26 minutes, Collina brandished another yellow card.

The tension and determination was unlike any other World Cup group match. Veron, denied of all space, was struggling. He had been unable to set the rhythm and one over-hit pass went straight out of play, much to the astonishment of the Argentine supporters. Veron shrugged and shook his head, but minutes later Gonzalez volleyed narrowly over the bar, reminding England how dangerous Argentina could be.

Beckham had spoken about being cunning before the game and he, in particular, was trying to gain free kicks. One dive in the penalty area was laughable. Collina delivered a frosty stare as he waved play on. On 38 minutes Beckham and Gonzalez clashed, the England captain's elbow catching Gonzalez, who was left with blood coming out of his nose. Collina, again, signalled play on. Revenge or an accident?

Scholes was revelling in being in the middle, his natural position, at the heart of many of England's moves, switching the direction of play. Two minutes before half-time, Scholes fed Sinclair on the left. The substitute neatly poked the ball through to Owen on the edge of the penalty area. Pochettino moved across, but Owen remained rooted to the spot for a split second, drawing the challenge, just as he had said he would, before swivelling inside. As the England striker swayed to the right, heading past Pochettino's outstretched leg, the Argentine defender tried to move out of the way, but contact was made with his left foot. Owen tumbled down and the referee, without hesitation, pointed to the penalty spot. Surprisingly, there was little protest from the Argentinians.

It was a cunning penalty, almost Argentine in its manufacture. Owen had drawn his opponent into making the contact and exaggerated his fall. 'Even as Pochettino was trying to withdraw the offending foot, it took on a life of its own in the manner of Dr. Strangelove's siegheiling right arm,' David Lacey said in the *Guardian*.

Asked before the World Cup who would take penalties, Beckham had replied that he would have to discuss that with Michael Owen, but there was no question over who this one was for. The script demanded it was Beckham.

As he stepped up and placed the ball on the spot, goalkeeper Cavallero walked up to him and pointed, offering advice as to where to place the ball. Beckham ignored him as Collina dealt with the miscreant, but then it was the turn of Beckham's old nemesis, Diego Simeone, to stroll over for a quick chat. Simeone tried to shake Beckham's hand, but Butt and Scholes, alert to the gamesmanship, ushered the Argentine out of the penalty area.

Beckham breathed deeply, focusing solely on the ball while the waiting world held its breath. His red shirt and shining mohican caught the lights of the Sapporo dome and the flashes of several thousand cameras from the crowd. The man who had not even been sure if he would be playing in the World Cup, the man who had redeemed himself from footballing ignominy, put four years of hurt into one kick. It was hard, low and straight down the middle. Cavallero shifted his weight to his right and was unable to recover, so stuck out a forlorn leg to try to stop the ball. But nothing could prevent the unstoppable force entering the net.

The zip of ball on net triggered an almighty roar from Beckham, from fans inside the stadium and from the millions watching across England. Somehow Beckham's personal journey had become the English football fan's. England identified with their captain and had willed him to recover from his foot injury just so he could savour this moment. And they could lap it up with him.

Most importantly the goal came immediately before half-time, allowing England respite and 15 minutes with the coaching staff to plan their approach to the second period.

During the break, John Motson continued to make allusions to food, mentioning lunch no fewer than 11 times. Well, kick-off had been at chow time. "He became convinced we were all eating back in England," said Danny Baker, who also observed that Argentina appeared "to have modelled themselves on Led Zeppelin circa 1973". Maybe that's why Veron, the only shaven-headed Argentine, was taken off. As the teams came out for the second half, the Argentina captain was missing, replaced by Pablo Aimar. It had been one of the worst halves of Veron's career, 45 minutes that he has never been allowed to forget, accused by some in Argentina of taking bribes from the English.

Having won that penalty, Owen, as in '98, continued to scare the Argentine defence, who backed off every time he received the ball. Running onto a through ball, he turned inside Placente, and flashed another shot across the goal. A minute later, as England looked to ram home their advantage, Heskey's shot was blocked, but the rebound fell to Scholes whose volley was brilliantly saved by Cavallero.

Eriksson made a tactical switch, taking off Heskey and replacing him with wily 36-year-old Teddy Sheringham. Almost immediately England put together the move of the match. Seventeen consecutive passes; Owen, Scholes, Butt and Sheringham stroking the ball around in a marvellous demonstration of one-touch football, culminating in a Sheringham volley that hit goalkeeper Cavallero.

In contrast, Argentina, despite having most of the possession, made few inroads into the final third of the pitch. The twin pillars of Ferdinand and Campbell, who would both be selected for FIFA's team of the tournament, stood firm, accompanied by some magnificent tracking back from Butt. With half an hour remaining, Bielsa took off Batistuta and replaced him with Crespo, like for like, quickly followed by replacing Kily Gonzalez, who had little change out of Danny Mills, with Claudio Lopez.

As the match entered its nervous last 20 minutes, it was reminiscent of the second half at France '98, when Argentina attacked in waves. Aimar was the danger man, dribbling down the right, while his team-mates packed the penalty area. One Aimar shot from range flew just over the bar, but Eriksson's system, with its deep-lying defence, was designed for this type of situation. Waiting for the counter-attack, Sinclair on the left was the outlet. For all Argentina's possession, it was still England breaking out and creating chances.

A superb piece of defending from Campbell blocked Zanetti, who was clear through on goal, and English hearts were in their mouths when Seaman somehow scrambled away Pochettino's downward header from Aimar's cross with a brilliant save off the line. A curious phenomenon was taking place: clocks were ticking slowly, almost backwards, in England, while in Argentina the minutes were flying by at lightning pace.

With ten minutes remaining Eriksson made another tactical substitution, taking off Owen for defender Wayne Bridge. The Southampton full back took over left midfield, with the specific task of plugging Aimar's runs, while Sinclair moved across to England's right. Eriksson had switched from 4-4-2 to 4-5-1, with Sheringham the lone striker, although the Tottenham man was spending more time in his own half than in the opposition's. With ten Englishmen behind the ball, Argentina could not pass through the cramped space to Crespo, and they showed a reluctance to shoot from outside the penalty area. They tried to carve out chances but the English bodies packed inside their own penalty area repelled all boarders.

Then, suddenly, a chance. With five minutes remaining, Rio Ferdinand, who had given a masterclass in the art of defending, slipped. The ball ran loose. Panic in England. Crespo closed in for the equaliser, but this time Danny Mills became the saviour and cleared. The right-back, whose mistake had led to Sweden's goal, had, like the whole of the English defence, hardly put a foot wrong in this game. It was a minor redemption for him, eclipsed by those of Beckham and the England team in general.

England's first victory over Argentina for 20 years, and their first in a World Cup since 1966, started the party back at home. And it continued all Friday afternoon and evening. By 6pm town centres were full of happy revellers. In London, Paul Gascoigne, live on the BBC, dressed in an England top, climbed on top of one of the lions at Trafalgar Square to conduct the chanting of '1-0 to the In-ger-land'. The next day, a 'statue' of the England captain was raised in the square, marking his rise to sainthood.

'REVENGE', ran the single word headline on the front page of London's *Evening Standard*, on the streets within an hour of the final whistle. On its front cover was a picture of Beckham running, arms outstretched at 90 degrees as if he was about to take off after dispatching the penalty.

"It doesn't get any sweeter than this," admitted Beckham. "As a football nation we've been waiting a long time for that result, and it was definitely the most satisfying goal I've ever scored in my life. I wanted to put the ghost to rest after my World Cup was turned upside down four years ago. I don't normally get nervous when I take penalties but this time I was. I just ran up and hit it as hard as I could. I was trying to blank Simeone out. There were a few antics going on, which we knew there would be. He came up to me and was trying to shake my hand. Butty and Scholes stepped in between us, and that's the last I saw of him. Also, the keeper was telling me where he wanted me to put the ball down. I didn't look at him. I didn't make eye contact with him and I didn't let him distract me from what I had to do."

The following morning's papers were full of the best resurrection since Lazarus. The *Daily Telegraph*'s Paul Hayward said, 'Beckham four summers ago had been held up by some commentators as everything that's wrong with English society. Now he appears to be everything that's right.'

'BECKHAM PUTS THE WORLD TO RIGHTS', declared Matt Dickinson on the front page of *The Times*. 'In an extraordinary evening that felt not so much like a football match as the righting of the wrongs of history, England beat Argentina, their most dearly beloved enemy in sport ... Beckham wakes this morning with his halo brighter than ever.'

Others were less descriptive. 'YEEEEEEEEESSSS!'screamed the *Daily Mirror* on its front page, stamped across a picture of Beckham tugging his shirt and screaming. 'UP YOURS, SENORS', said the bold headline in the *Sun*. 'There is something deeply satisfying about knocking the smug look off the Argentinians' faces,' their editorial sniggered.

La Nacion ran a resumé of the things the English press had written: "'Up yours Senors', accompanied by a picture of a clenched fist, probably meant to say Up yours, Señors," pointing out the typographical error that would have passed almost every England fan by. It also reprinted the *Daily Mirror*'s back page of a photograph of a sad Batistuta on the bench under the title, 'Don't Cry For Poor Argentina, The Truth Is We Never Loved You', and quoted Jane Ridley's report comparing 'the long-haired and sweaty South Americans to the fresh faces of our lads'. Every day there are diplomats working to forge better relations between the two countries but, overnight, their work could so easily be undone by a football match.

Revenge, payback and exorcism were three of the most frequently used nouns in the English media. Little time was devoted to the obvious discussion of whether it had been a penalty or not. ITV commentator Clive Tyldesley commented upon Owen's penalty tumble: "I am not quite cynical enough to suggest that after years of failing to beat them England are at last joining them. But greater exposure to the different cultures around the Premier and European club circuit is teaching our boys a thing or two their fathers may not have approved of." Most papers chose to skim over the details of how Owen had won the crucial spot-kick, concentrating instead on the fact of England's victory.

Interestingly, especially given the reaction which would have inevitably ensued had the incident happened in the other penalty area, there was little bleating from the Argentines about the penalty incident. Diego Simeone merely looked at the bigger picture: "We had the ball for most of the match but lost because of one moment from Owen. He's so fast."

Despite all the headlines about Beckham, it had been a stoic team performance, in which the captain's contribution in open play had been peripheral. Scholes, Butt and Cole were singled out by many as the men of the match. The left-back's attacking qualities had never been in doubt, but defensively he had come of age in this match, winning the personal duel with Ortega. Alongside Cole, Rio Ferdinand and Sol Campbell had been assured and commanding at the back. Trevor Sinclair, the man whom it had taken two attempts to reach the World Cup, had made a big difference, charging up and down the left. Indeed, it could be argued that the biggest single contribution to England's success by Michael Owen was the tackle that forced Owen Hargreaves out of the game.

Tactically, Eriksson had had a good game, his stock rising once again. He was praised for bringing on Wayne Bridge, seamlessly switching from 4-4-2 to 4-5-1. 'To survive in tournaments like this you need to be able to play two systems well,' wrote ex-England manager Graham Taylor, 'because even in the dying seconds opponents of Argentina's quality will never resort to the long ball.'

In Argentina the autopsy had begun. 'WHY US?' asked *Clarin*. 'The team didn't function, we didn't control the play, we were too mechanical, and Veron couldn't read the game. The collective movement was not good and Ortega didn't receive any passes.' Argentina were accused of playing in an 'unaesthetic style'. 'The team plays that way precisely because its ingredients are in Europe and because, fundamentally, this is the manager's way of thinking,' *Clarin* complained. It had, after all, warned of the risks of taking on the Europeans at their own game.

Veron admitted he had been a shadow of himself: "I've been two months without playing and carrying a tendon injury. I was more or less OK, but for 5 or 10 minutes the pain returned, but that doesn't serve as an excuse. I didn't play well and I'm the first to recognise that. The coach makes the changes, he's the decision maker. We knew that if they scored everything would be much tougher, and that's what happened. England played as they wanted, with counter-attacks and long balls to Heskey and Owen. We didn't have space to play and that made things hard for us."

Veron's father tried to explain his son's and the team's disappointing performance: "Eriksson knows very well how the Argentina midfield works and he dealt with that perfectly. The English have adapted their style due to the influence of foreign players in the Premier League. Historically, they always attacked, but in this match , when they had to do it, they positioned themselves well at the back."

Manager Bielsa tried to defend his strategy: "We deserved a draw. Our breakthroughs were down to our skills and England's chances were down to our mistakes rather than their skills."

Batistuta was reflective: "I wasn't happy with my own performance. I don't know what was missing. All we know is that in the last two games we haven't created clear chances on goal, but I don't know if that has anything to do with the system. I was surprised I was taken off because we were losing, and I thought another attacker would be useful."

Five days later, the discussion over whether Batigol and Crespo could play together was rendered academic. While England were earning the point they needed to qualify for the knockout stages in a dull goalless draw against Nigeria, Argentina only managed a 1-1 draw with Sweden and were out. Despite Argentina dominating, and having 20 clear chances on goal, Anders Svensson gave Sweden a shock lead from a 40-yard free kick. Crespo equalised three minutes from time, scoring on the rebound as Coventry City's Magnus Hedman saved Ortega's penalty, but the favourites were out.

Batistuta, substituted again, cried on the bench, and Veron, who had been left out, but came on in the second half, slumped to the turf. "I'm absolutely devastated," said Veron. "This is the worst moment of my life. We had hoped to win the World Cup as a present to the people of Argentina. We would like to apologise for our failure." With that 'Batigol' retired from international football.

"It's something we can't explain," said Crespo, "not because we want to make theatre, or feel sorry for ourselves, but really it's how we feel. Really, it hurts so much, equal or more than it hurts the people. The thing that hurts most is that Argentina football is going to find it difficult to find a group like this one, so united and identified with the people. It really really hurts."

During the game Argentina's other big name striker, Claudio Caniggia, had become the first ever player to be sent off in the World Cup Finals without having actually played in a single minute of it. "I just cussed," he revealed, "and the referee thought I insulted him. It's going to be very difficult to overcome this. Not even the most pessimistic thought this was going to happen."

The nation was baffled. Argentina did not play badly, but they did not score. Was it just bad luck? Veron said they must stay calm and proud, because they had given their all, but as the day continued it became clear that he, just as David Beckham had four years earlier, was going to bear the brunt of most of the criticism, based on his poor 45 minutes against England. It's the blot on his very successful career. He, too, suffered booing in Argentinian grounds and has even been accused of taking bribes. "I don't mind constructive criticism, but when it's made with bad intention, that is not right," explains Veron, sadly, five years later.

La Nacion believed it knew the 'reasons for the *fracas* [failure]'. 'It cost us enormously to resolve the matches where opponents play 4-4-2. The three matches were similar in that not one of the opposition confronted the rival face to face and tried to attack us. We were impotent in the last 25 metres and the opponents' defences didn't make mistakes ... But Argentina just repeated its mechanical strategies; there were no dribbles, no *gambetas*, no subtle touches and changes of direction and we never put Batistuta and Crespo together ... Also there were too many players out of form and only in the team due to their past. There was no-one like Kempes in '78 or Maradona in '86 ... No-one could question Bielsa's professionalism, honesty and dedication, but his conception is too cerebral, systematic and he cut off a quota of lyricism that could have served the team more'.

Maybe because England v Nigeria had been so dull, Argentina's shock exit actually relegated the news of England's qualification to the inside pages of the tabloids the following day. The *Daily Mirror* ran a computer montage of the Argentina players lined up in a defensive wall, carrying handbags. 'ARGENTINIAN TRAGEDY – DON'T FORGET YOUR HANDBAGS, DEARS', was the headline. 'England is laughing at us,' bemoaned *La Nacion*, although it pointed out that the picture had been doing the rounds on the internet the previous day, and had originated in Argentina, photoshopped by a disgruntled fan.

'THIS WAY TO THE DOOR, SENOR', said the *Sun*, who quoted Teddy Sheringham: "We are very pleased to see them out," he said. "It's just a shame we weren't the team to deliver the final blow".

❖

Having finished second in the group, England's next opponents were Denmark. The same starting eleven (but with Sinclair for Hargreaves) won convincingly, 3-0 (Ferdinand, Owen, Heskey), all the goals coming in the first half. Suddenly, England was dreaming; the no-hopers who drew with Sweden were now being spoken of as candidates to win the World Cup. Unfortunately, the small hurdle of Brazil stood in the way.

In a now, increasingly familiar routine, the nation rose early on Friday 21 June for the 8.30am (English time) kick off. There was a general understanding in most companies that employees would be arriving late.

A 50,000 crowd gathered in Shizuoka, the majority enthusiastic Japanese, and the match could not have started better for England. Halfway through the first half, Scholes played a ball to Heskey, who hit a long ball, a poor ball, for Owen to chase. Lucio had it covered, but the Brazilian centre back tried to bring it down on his thigh, miscontrolled, and provided Owen with a perfect pass to chase. The England striker chipped the ball over goalkeeper Marcos. Now England really was dreaming.

Eriksson's men held on well, but in the 4th minute of first half stoppage time, Beckham jumped out of a tackle on the halfway line, thinking the ball would go out for a throw, but Kleberson kept it in play. With the English midfield pushed forward, Brazil had a break; Kleberson skipped past Scholes, releasing Ronaldinho through the middle. In a three against three situation, Ronaldinho swept past Ashley Cole before passing to Rivaldo, who stroked the ball past Seaman and inside the far post.

Five minutes after the break, Scholes gave away a free kick, 40 yards from the England goal. Seaman organised his defence, expecting a cross, but Ronaldinho, spotting the goal-keeper off his line, tried an audacious shot on goal. The ball hung in the air, while Seaman flapped. It drifted over his head, but under the crossbar, into the top corner of the net. England were handed a lifeline when Ronaldinho was harshly sent off for a clumsy tackle on Mills, but Brazil kept possession, giving the impression that it was they who had the extra man as England resorted to long balls, as they had done in the 2nd half against Sweden. There was no attempt to adjust tactically to the new circumstances, no substitution of a defender for a more creative, attack-minded player to make the numerical advantage count. Eriksson took off Sinclair for Dyer, on the left, like for like, while England's back four stood flat in a line, marking one forward. The Brazilians were content to leave Mills unmarked as the extra man, watching the right back carry the ball across the halfway line and into their half, where he had little idea how to use it, except to hit hopeful high balls. Vassell (for Owen), and Sheringham (for Ashley Cole) came on for the last ten minutes, but there was a lack of passion and tension in the 2nd half, as the game petered out into nothing. England went out of the 2002 World Cup with a wimper in front of a silent crowd.

Beckham, who had a poor game, had only been 75% fit according to assistant manager Tord Gripp, but England could take heart that they lost to the eventual winners; Brazil beat Turkey (1-0) in the semi-final and Germany (2-0) in the final.

'At least we'll always have Paris as they said in Casablanca. At least we'll always have Sapporo. Remember when England beat Argentina.' (Simon Barnes)

Argentina 0
England 1 (Beckham (pen) 44')
Friday 7 June 2002. Sapporo Dome, Japan. World Cup Group Match. Attendance: 35,927
Referee: Pierluigi Collina (Italy)

Argentina: Pablo Cavallero (Celta de Vigo), Diego Placente (Bayer Leverkusen), Walter Samuel (Roma), Mauricio Pochettino (Paris St.Germain), Juan Pablo Soria (Cruzeiro), Javier Zanetti (Internazionale), Diego Simeone (Lazio), Juan Sebastián Veron(c) (Manchester Utd, sub 46'), Cristian Gonzalez (Valencia, sub 64), Ariel Ortega (River Plate), Gabriel Batistuta (Roma, sub 60'), Subs: Pablo Aimar (Valencia, on 46'), Hernan Crespo (Lazio, on 60'), Claudio Lopez (Lazio, on 64')
Manager: Marcelo Bielsa

England: David Seaman (Arsenal), Danny Mills (Leeds), Ashley Cole (Arsenal), Rio Ferdinand (Leeds), Sol Campbell (Arsenal), Nicky Butt (Manchester Utd), Owen Hargreaves (Bayern Munich, sub 19'), David Beckham(c) (Manchester Utd), Paul Scholes (Manchester Utd), Michael Owen (Liverpool, sub 80'), Emile Heskey (Liverpool, sub 54'), Subs: Trevor Sinclair (West Ham, on 19'), Teddy Sheringham (Tottenham, on 54'), Wayne Bridge (Southampton, on 80')
Manager: Sven-Göran Eriksson

GAME OWEN

GENEVA, SWITZERLAND, SATURDAY
12 NOVEMBER 2005

2005. HURRICANE Katrina devastated the USA, Gordon Brown and David Cameron eyed the leadership of their respective political parties, Argentina president Nestor Kirchner announced the repayment of IMF loans as his country's economy stabilised and the Iraq war entered a difficult phase, without any sign of an end game. In mid-November Westlife's cover version of 'You Raise Me Up' spent its second week at number 1, just holding off Madonna's 'Hung Up', a track that sampled Abba, and would soon top the charts.

Three years on from Sapporo new faces had appeared on the international football scene, most notably Juan Román Riquelme, Carlos Tevez and Wayne Rooney, extremely talented footballers who had emerged from rundown inner-city ghettos to carry the hopes of their nations through to the 2006 World Cup. However, the latest Argentinian wonderkid, 19-year-old Lionel Messi, was suspended for this friendly against England, having been sent off for a clumsy challenge within 47 seconds of his international debut, a world record, against Hungary.

Arranged on an official FIFA international match date – the day of the World Cup qualification play-offs – this match in neutral Switzerland between two already-qualified teams on a weekend of no league fixtures received the full treatment in terms of build up and coverage. With the tournament just seven months away both managers were under a degree of pressure following recent lucklustre performances. "We are taking it very, very seriously," confirmed Sven-Göran Eriksson, promising not to spoil the spectacle with a flood of irritating second half substitutions, as he had done in previous friendlies. Argentina manager Jose Pekerman felt the same: "It's an excellent test for us, the type of opposition we must measure ourselves against if we want to achieve something at the World Cup."

The match kicked off at 17.45 Swiss time, which was late afternoon in the English autumn, a sunny spring midday in Argentina, but there was a new social phenomenon in both countries; groups of people, huddling together, outside pubs, cafes and pizzerias, inhaling like outcasts; the recently passed smoking bans were in place in both England and Argentina.

Once again, the Argentine team bus was the centre of controversy. *"Vamos a ganar a los putos Ingleses"* (we're gonna beat those English whores/pooftas/transvestites) sang the players at the top of their voices, rocking the coach from side to side as it pulled into the stadium in front of the international press. The culture clash was underway. What the Argentines would consider a bit of banter and a sing-song caused offence to those who wished to be offended. Outraged, sensitive English tabloid journalists sought out the UN peace envoy, Adolf Ogi, for his comments. "This is totally unacceptable. I will be asking the Argentine authorities to explain the incident," said Ogi. The United Nations in Geneva had billed the match as the match of peace. It had not got off to the best of starts.

The *Guardian* described the scene: 'The Argentina players arrived abusing the English fans with words and derogatory gestures, and the compliment was soon returned with choruses of "What's it like to lose a war?" and "You'll never take the Falklands".' The *Sun* described the songs as 'risible homophobia', while the *Daily Mirror* wrote of 'foul-mouthed abuse that turned the air blue on their team bus; they kicked and punched the windows as well as shouting obscenities about England players.'

The English press revelled in their role of playing up the antagonism, converting the fixture into one of mock nationalist stereotyping, with pantomine goodies and baddies. Not to be outdone, Argentina sports daily *Olé* also did its best to heat up the match. 'In England, in the build up on TV, the most-repeated is the 1-0 in Japan. Perhaps they don't have a video of Mexico '86? Or perhaps they don't show it because it includes a trick goal – a player can't dribble past so many rivals in ten seconds without cheating?'

Pedestrian, static, *un pecho frio* (cold-hearted/passionless) … or an exquisite football genius? Nobody divides opinion in his homeland quite like Juan Román Riquelme. It's not just the way he plays, but what he represents; *El Enganche* (literally, the Hook, or Link), the free man, who, bereft of defensive duties, drifts behind the strikers – a throwback to the old days, the playmaker who stops and puts his foot on the ball, *la pausa* (the pause), as it's called in Argentina. Is there still a place in the modern game, with all its emphasis on physique and speed, for the laidback character who likes to play the game at his own tempo?

With Riquelme, it was almost as if he deliberately took languidness to new extremes, making no concessions to directness and pace as a matter of principle. Argentina's 1986 World Cup winner Jorge Valdano summed him up thus: "If we have to travel from point A to point B, most of us would take the six-lane highway and get there as quickly as possible. Riquelme would choose the winding mountain road, the beautiful scenic route which takes him six hours instead of two."

The "Last of the Mohicans" was how Mexico's 2006 World Cup manager Ricardo Lavolpe described Riquelme. The words of the former Argentina goalkeeper, who had been a member of the 1978 World Cup-winning squad, did not go down well in the Riquelme-adoring quarter of his home country. "The problem with playing with an

'*Enganche*' is that you have to build the team around him, and who else is there apart from Riquelme these days?" argued Lavolpe. "If he's unavailable, or having an off day, then the whole thing falls apart." Lavolpe was not alone in his views. The pro/anti-Riquelme debate had replaced the old Menottism versus Bilardism arguments among Argentina's cafe philosophers and street corner coaches.

In reality, Riquelme, at 27, had always been around the fringes of the national team. His had been the absence most felt by the purists when they bemoaned Bielsa's mechanical and European style of play in the aftermath of the 2002 World Cup disaster. Born into the poor provinces of Buenos Aires, 1 of 11 children, Riquelme was always going to be compared with Maradona, especially as he had followed in his footsteps; that well-trodden track from provincial dust pitches to Argentinos Juniors youth team, then on to Boca Juniors, where he was hero-worshipped, before a big money, but ultimately unsuccessful, move to Barcelona.

The comparison doesn't end there. In one match, rich in symbolism, the River Plate versus Boca Juniors *superclasico* of October 1997, a podgy, static Maradona was having no influence in what turned out to be his last ever professional appearance. With Boca 1-0 down, Maradona was substituted at half-time and his replacement, the relatively unknown 18-year-old Riquelme, ran the game in the second half as Boca came back to win 2-1. That half-time substitution is seen as representing the moment when the old master handed over the baton to the new leader. However, in terms of style of play, the players were quite different. At Boca, Riquelme was the star of the team that won the Copa de Libertadores twice (2000 and 2001) and beat Real Madrid in the 2000 World Club Championship, but he became a pawn in a political game upon moving to Europe in 2002. Under-fire Barcelona president Joan Gaspart needed a prestige signing to appease fans for the loss of Luis Figo to Real Madrid two years earlier and to counter Madrid's Galacticos signings of Zidane, Ronaldo and Beckham. But Dutch Barcelona coach Louis van Gaal, famed for his straight lines and rigid systems, had no place in his team for a free spirit like Riquelme and said so, much to the annoyance of his president. After 30, mainly disappointing, appearances for Barcelona, generally in an unfamiliar left-sided role, Riquelme was loaned out to newly-promoted Villarreal, a town with a population of just 47,000, and a stadium that held only 23,000.

There was new money at Villarreal, though, and the arrival of Chilean coach Manuel Pellegrini from River Plate, along with Riquelme's Argentine compatriots Sorin and Figueroa, and the Uruguayans Diego Forlan and Sebastian Viera, saw this tiniest of Spanish clubs finish third in La Liga and qualify for the 2005/06 Champions League. Surrounded by team-mates and a coach on his own South American wavelength, the Boca Juniors play-maker reappeared. Román, as it said on the back of his shirt, was at the fulcrum of most of Villarreal's play as they knocked Everton out in the Champions League qualifiers, and, after two goalless draws with Manchester United, progressed from the group stages at the expense of the English club. (They later disposed of Rangers and Inter Milan, both on away goals, before eventually losing to Arsenal 1-0 on aggregate in the semi-final, Riquelme missing a last minute penalty.) Going into the match against England, Riquelme was at the peak of his form, and arguably the best midfielder in the world.

A change of national manager had also worked in Riquelme's favour. Marcelo Bielsa, tired, had stood down not long after Argentina had lost to Brazil in the final of La Copa America in the summer of 2004, and his replacement, the low profile Jose Pekerman, was a dyed in the wool Riquelmista. An average midfielder for Argentinos Juniors, the small, neighbourhood club that has remarkably produced so many of Argentina's best youngsters over the years (Maradona, Batista, Redondo), Pekerman, after retiring, began coaching some of the 11- and 12-year-olds at his old club; kids like Riquelme, Juan Pablo Sorin, Esteban Cambiasso, and Fabiano Colocini. The AFA put him in charge of Argentina's youth set up in 1994 and his reputation rose when the Under-20s won the World Cup for their category three times, Qatar 1995, Malaysia 1997 and in Argentina in 2000. In celebration Pekerman named his three dogs Qatar, Malaysia and Argentina. The class of 1997 was the most celebrated of all, earning plaudits around the world for the dazzling football they played. Pekerman would stick to the same formula once in charge of the senior side, i.e. indulging Riquelme and building the team around him.

Under Pekerman, Argentina qualified comfortably for the 2006 World Cup. They topped the 10-team South American group, having sealed their place in Germany with four games remaining by pulverising Brazil 3-1 in Buenos Aires in June 2005. In a majestic first half display, Riquelme ripped the Brazilian defence apart, scoring with a bullet shot from 30 yards, and setting up two for Hernan Crespo as Argentina chalked up a three-goal lead within half an hour. However, as always with Riquelme, there were detractors. Argentina were uninspiring in their remaining qualifying matches, and also took a 3-0 hammering from Brazil in the Confederations Cup final, the now traditional World Cup rehearsal tournament that takes place in the host country a year before the actual event.

"Before they said Argentina played too fast, now they say it's too slow," said Riquelme, responding to his critics before the England game. "It's true we haven't played well lately, and clearly we have to play better, but there's still enough time before the World Cup. There are skilful players here. The team will appear at the right moment and this game against England will be a strong test for us, a chance to show what we can do."

Did Riquelme believe individual performance was more important than the tactical side of football? "Both things count, but I've never changed my thinking. For me, football is a game. I always want to enjoy myself on the pitch. I have always played this way."

In contrast to Riquelme, who had taken his time establishing himself in the national team, the player upon whom English World Cup hopes were pinned had burst onto the scene overnight. Born and bred in Croxteth, Liverpool, of Irish descent, Wayne Rooney had made his Premier League debut for Everton in August 2002. Two months later, five days before his 17th birthday, he had spectacularly announced his arrival with a phenomenal swing of his boot, lashing the ball past David Seaman from 30 yards for a last minute winner, which ended reigning league champions Arsenal's long unbeaten run and made Rooney the youngest scorer in Premier League history (since surpassed by James Milner and then James Vaughan).

At 17 years 111 days, Rooney became the youngest player to play for England (the previous record was held by James Prince of Clapham, who had made his debut in 1879. Arsenal's Theo Walcott broke Rooney's record by 36 days in May 2006). Rooney then became the youngest ever scorer for England when he found the net against Macedonia in a 2004 European Championship qualification match. He was outstanding in the finals tournament in Portugal, which precipitated a £23 million transfer to Manchester United.

Rooney operated as a 'second striker', running at defenders at pace, scoring and creating. Ironically, the young Englishman's stocky build and in-bred drive and passion gave him more of the features of Argentina's all-time greatest player than any of the young Argentines who had been burdened with the title of 'New Maradona'.

Rooney's England striking partner Michael Owen summed up the teenager's exuberance before the big match against Argentina. "He's just so confident. He can give the ball away and then pull another rabbit out of the hat. As he grows older he will probably understand a lot more, and have a bit more realisation of what football's all about, but at the minute it's a positive for him because he has no fear. When he drops and is not marked he can turn with the ball and anything can happen. He can beat people, take a shot, play people in. He is incredible in those occasions."

But did Rooney have the discipline to survive at the top level? There was a natural aggression to his play that sometimes crossed the line into violent conduct. A few months after his league debut for Everton a dangerous challenge had resulted in a red card at Birmingham, soon followed by a fifth yellow and a four-match suspension. While he had settled well at Manchester United, scoring and laying on some stunning goals, not least a hat-trick on his debut against Fenerbahce in a Champions League group stage match, temperament and disciplinary issues constantly bubbled under the surface. Two months before the match against Argentina Rooney was sent off against Villarreal in the Champions League for sarcastically applauding Kim Milton Nielsen (the referee who had shown Beckham the red card against Argentina in 1998). Rooney's tantrums caused the English Schools Football Association to drop him from a guest appearance, claiming he was not a good role model for young players.

It was becoming an issue and Argentina were bound to try on the gamesmanship. "There are going to be many teams that try to wind Wayne up, but he can handle it," said England captain Beckham. "Wayne plays with a lot of passion and that's why some of the things happen to him in games. When you are frustrated and angry, you react. In a way that's a good thing." Beckham himself had tarnished his heroic image in recent months, receiving two red cards as he appeared to be slipping back into his petulant old ways. Could the old master take the young gun under his wing and help him mend his ways?

Riquelme was happy to ramp up the rivalry when asked about Rooney's temper. "He is a kid with great fight, but that is not always enough. You need intelligence as well as fight to win matches. When we [Villarreal] played Manchester United Rooney lost his nerve and that ended in disaster for them. You cannot afford to lose your temper in the World Cup and that is the key to victory in modern football."

But England coach Eriksson insisted, at least in public, that he was not concerned, saying, "You want to finish these games with 11 players, but I am not worried about Wayne. I will speak to all of them before the game with Argentina. It's really important we behave, play good football and are organised and calm. We must think of it as a World Cup match, and in those games you must finish with ten outfield players." Both Riquelme's and Eriksson's words would make interesting reading with hindsight, especially considering the manner of England's 2006 World Cup exit.

Against Argentina Rooney was likely to be singled out for close man-marking, the type of special attention he was not so accustomed to in the Premier League. Veteran defender Roberto Ayala was looking forward to the confrontation. "To mark Rooney will be a new experience for me. Neither of us will avoid a tackle, and we both enjoy having the ball in the air. He is young, but I have more experience. We will see who is singing victory songs in Switzerland."

While Rooney's importance to England was undoubted, it was the role of his striking partner Michael Owen that was becoming increasingly open to question. More and more top European club sides were opting for formations that featured only one striker in a specialist role: Didier Drogba (Chelsea), Fernando Torres (Atletico Madrid), Peter Crouch (Liverpool) and Zoltan Ibrahimovic (Internazionale) played with their backs to goal, bringing others into the game, often teeing up goalscoring midfielders with opportunities as well as carving out chances for themselves. Was tactical evolution leaving behind the old penalty box goal-poacher? From Jimmy Greaves, through Gary Lineker to Alan Shearer, England teams had always found a place for the centre-forward who did little but score, but managers like Jose Mourinho and Rafael Benitez were bringing new, some would say, 'defensive', ideas to the English game.

Owen's club career had declined since moving from Liverpool to Real Madrid in the summer of 2004. In an ill-thought out signing by Madrid president Florentino Perez, Owen found himself surplus to requirements amongst the Galacictos. "I asked for a lamp but they bought me a sofa," said frustrated manager Jose Antonio Camacho, when Owen signed. "It's a very nice sofa, but I've got four already and really wanted a lamp." Fifth choice, Owen moved back to England a year later, signing for Newcastle for £23 million, where niggling injuries had prevented him making much of an impact.

Argentina's main striker Hernan Crespo was also suffering from the changes in tactical thinking. Now back at Chelsea, after a year on loan at AC Milan, Crespo often found himself on the bench, while Drogba played as a lone striker in manager Mourinho's scheme. But Despite his lack of football, Crespo's strike rate for Chelsea was good, and he had been impressive in his season at Milan. Often forgotten amid the euphoria of Liverpool's magnificent comeback in the 2005 Champions League final was that Crespo had scored two typically instinctive goals in the first half.

Carlos Tevez, 21, was another youngster from poverty who had trodden that familiar path from precarious housing and shanty-town *proteros* (dust pitches) to Boca Juniors, followed by a big money transfer, while still a teenager. In Tevez's case his lucrative move was not to a European team – his economic rights were controversially bought by a business group, MSI, who loaned him to Corinthians in Brazil, a club with whom they had an economic partnership. The £11.5 million fee was the most expensive in history between two South American clubs, but who were MSI and where was their money coming from? Amongst suspicion of Russian mafia money-laundering a government investigation was launched in Argentina. MSI also paid £8 million for River Plate's Javier Mascherano, whom they also lent to Corinthians. Whether or not Boca Juniors president Mauricio Macri, the current governor of Buenos Aires, and his River counterpart Jose Maria Aguilar, were able to use their political influences in the murky connections between football and politics in Argentina is unknown. The investigation was dropped, amidst much suspicion. Later in Brazil, the MSI group were charged and found guilty of money laundering and illicit association after a Federal Police Operation called Perestroika investigated corruption at Corinthians.

At Corinthians Tevez won the Brazilian championship and the South American player of the year for the third year running. His status as one of football's emerging superstars was no surprise to those who had watched him grow up. "Tevez is the biggest explosion in Argentine football since Maradona," is legendary youth coach Ramon Madonni's description of the kid from Fort Apache.

Madonni, 62, can proudly reel off the names of the 70 professional players he has discovered, "Redondo, Riquelme, Cambiasso, Colocinni, Sorin, Gago...", but is under no doubt as to who he considers the best of the lot. He first saw Tevez play when he was eight years old. "He was just different, but when I say different I suppose I mean he was just better than everyone else. He was playing for Santa Clara, the team from Fort Apache, against my team El Parque, who were the best in the area, but he ran us a merry dance that day. He played just as he does today, running all over the opposition's area, beating everyone. He had lots of aggression and chased everything. So we invited him to join El Parque, which was a kind of Harlem Globetrotters team that didn't play in a competitive league, but concentrated on forming players and working on their skills."

Fort Apache is not actually the real name of the isolated ghetto that lies four miles to the north of the centre of Buenos Aires. A journalist first coined the phrase after a shootout in front of the local police station in the early 1980s and it has stuck ever since. Most of the 30,000 inhabitants of the 22-block labyrinth are descendants of indigenous Indians from the interior of Argentina and bordering countries. It is a self-contained community with its own set of codes, and a shocking crime rate. "Carlitos was a great kid, always well behaved," Madonni tells me. "All he wanted to do was play football. He never missed a training session once. We loved him and so did all his team-mates because he gave his all in every single match and inspired everyone around him.

"I remember that when I first took over at Boca we had a match against All Boys and Tevez started on the bench for them. We were winning 1-0, but then he came on in the second half and scored two. When he got the winner he ran over to the bench and started doing that Cumbia [Colombian music style] dance thing in front of me, grinning away. I said: 'What? You want to dance with me?' And he took my arm and started swinging me around ... That's Tevez for you."

John Terry, 25, and Frank Lampard 27, the two footballers of the year in England, were now an established part of Sven-Göran Eriksson's team, and their Chelsea teammate, Joe Cole, 24, was at last fulfilling the accolades that had been bestowed upon him as a teenager, proving in the Premier League that he did indeed have an end product, and was not just a keepy-uppy showboater. Steven Gerrard, 26, Rio Ferdinand, 27, and Michael Owen, still only 25, were now experienced world class players. In theory, the 'Golden

Generation', the burdenous phrase Adam Crozier had bestowed upon them, were now reaching their peak.

Some old halos had fallen, though, or at least gone a bit skewiff, since Sapporo. When David Beckham had slammed home the penalty against Argentina in Japan he was at the peak of his popularity. Marketed as the perfect man; handsome, rich, caring husband and loving father, it was a level of idealism impossible to maintain. Highly publicised extra-marital affairs had dented his golden crown, but on the pitch things were not going so well either. The recipient of a flying boot during one of Alex Ferguson's infamous hairdryer blasts, Beckham paraded a cut above his eye to the press the following day. It was part of a deeper rift between player and manager and precipitated a move to Real Madrid at the end of the 2002/03 season.

Cynics scoffed that the pin-up England captain had been bought only to sell shirts, especially in the Far East, as part of President Perez's Galacticos policy. Beckham had not played badly for Madrid, but neither had he set the world alight in the manner that many felt a £20 million pound player, with his superstar billing, should. Combined with this inconsistent club form, Beckham had also had some indifferent games for England. He became the first England captain to be sent off, against Northern Ireland, having already damaged his reputation a year earlier when he made a dangerous tackle on Ben Thatcher of Wales, only to admit that he had done it deliberately, to receive a yellow card, so he could serve a suspension against the minnows of Azerbaijan four days later, a match he knew he would miss anyway as he had pulled a muscle. Clever? Not when you tell the world and his wife in the papers the following day.

What had happened to the English values of sporting behaviour and fair play? The England captain was forced to write an explanation to the FA and apologise to the country. There was even debate over whether Beckham, now 30, was worth his place in the team. Never the fastest player, he was losing some zip and young pretenders to his berth on the right side of England's midfield had emerged in Shaun Wright-Phillips, Aaron Lennon and Kieron Dyer. Also his move abroad had taken him out of the English spotlight. One man ever loyal, though, was his international manager. Perhaps Eriksson could empathise with all the negative publicity, for if Beckham's popularity was slipping slightly, then Eriksson's had dramatically slumped. Sven, once a synonym for calmness and mystique, was now a byword for calculated sneakiness. Despite being under contract with England, behind the back of the current incumbent Claudio Ranieri the Swede had held a secret meeting with Chelsea owner Roman Abramovich about taking over as manager of his club, set up by super-agent Pini Zahavi. Eriksson's reward for this manoeuvre was a whopping £4.2 million pounds a year contract extension with England, taking him up to 2008.

The money was double the amount of the Italian job, the next highest paid in international football, and four times as much as the German, French and Dutch managers earned. The Argentina and Brazilian managers took home about a tenth of Eriksson's wage. Around this time, Paolo Maldini Snr, who had managed Italy and Paraguay at World Cups, remarked that international management was really just a part-time job. He was seconded by Guus Hiddink, who successfully combined managing PSV Eindhoven to the

Dutch championship while qualifying for the World Cup with Australia. It begged the question, what exactly did Sven do? He did not even take the coaching, which was organised by Middlesbrough manager Steve McClaren, while the £4 million-a-year man watched from the side.

If his image was tarnished by the Chelsea incident, then it was comprehensively dragged through the mud and across the front pages of the tabloids when news of an affair with Faria Alam, an FA secretary, broke. The England manager kept his job, but details of his sexual exploits made pornographic reading when the secretary, whose initials ironically spelt FA, sold her side of the story with the help of Max Clifford to the *News of the World*.

Eriksson's image had plummeted a long way since the 5-1 drubbing of Germany three years earlier, but things would not have been so bad for him if the football was ticking along smoothly. However, at the 2004 Euro championships, Eriksson was heavily criticised for negative tactics. His team, seemingly, had only one way of playing – to sit deep in a rigid 4-4-2 and wait for the counter-attack. It worked for 89 minutes in the opening game against France, after Lampard scored in the first half, but after constant French pressure, and a Beckham penalty miss, the dam finally broke in added time when France scored twice. England comfortably beat Switzerland 3-0 and Croatia 4-2 – Rooney the outstanding player, scoring two in both matches – but lost in extra time to hosts Portugal in the quarter-final, again after taking the lead in the first half, but defending deep after the loss through injury of Rooney and inviting their opponents to attack for the rest of the match.

In the 2006 World Cup qualifiers England had not impressed either, and the criticism reached a crescendo when England lost 4-1 to Denmark in a friendly in August 2005, quickly followed by an uninspiring win in Wales (1-0) and a shock defeat in Northern Ireland (1-0) in the qualifiers. But narrow victories over Austria (1-0) and Poland (2-1) at Old Trafford in October saw England through as group winners. Eriksson was always at pains to explain that there were no easy games at this level and the team had achieved their objective by qualifying, but it brooked nothing with the press. While England failed to entertain the public, Eriksson was accused of lacking passion. The England manager was even criticised, presumably by people who had never seen how Sir Alf Ramsey conducted himself, for not jumping up and down to celebrate goals. The most serious criticism though, was that Eriksson was a fraud, recycling old English-style tactics, like IKEA taking MFI's ideas and selling them back to the English. And then there was always the money. What *did* he do to justify his enormous salary? Without question Eriksson needed a good performance against Argentina.

As did Beckham, who was captaining England for the 50th time. Before the game the skipper pondered on his controversial relationship with the South Americans. "I really don't know what it is about me and Argentina. In my first season at Real Madrid, every tackle, every booking, any problem turned out to be an Argentina player, which was bizarre. I haven't got a problem with Argentina players, so maybe you should ask one of them." To mark the occasion Adidas give Beckham a pair of boots with the names of his children, Brooklyn, Romeo and Cruz, stitched in gold, plus the names of the two countries.

England were suffering from depleted resources. Full backs Gary Neville and Ashley Cole were both out, so Luke Young of Charlton and Wayne Bridge of Chelsea deputised.

Ledley King of Tottenham would be given the job of stifling Riquelme's talents in midfield, although not strictly as a man marker. Like Bobby Robson, with Maradona in 1986, Eriksson wanted a pressing game in zones, with King as the holding midfielder, even though he played at centre-half for Tottenham. The other newcomer was young Tottenham goalkeeper Paul Robinson, in goal, who pledged never to grow a pony tail like former England number 1 David Seaman, who had cut his off for the Bobby Moore Cancer Fund charity that week.

With Lampard in the middle, it was Gerrard's turn to play the square peg in round hole role on the left of midfield in Eriksson's 4-4-2. Up front, the Owen/Rooney partnership was set in stone, with polemic Peter Crouch on the bench. The 6ft 7 ins striker had so far, three months into the season, scored no goals since his £7 million transfer from Southampton to Liverpool, and had been booed when appearing for England against Poland at Old Trafford.

For Argentina, Tevez would partner Crespo up front, the classic Argentine 4-3-1-2 formation; Riquelme as the one, the *Enganche*, with a licence to roam horizontally across the final third of the pitch. Tevez could not wait to play with his idol. "At times you need a little time to learn where to place yourself with Riquelme, but this will come with matches."

Tevez's Corinthians team-mate, midfielder Javier Mascherano, was injured, as was Manchester United defender Gabriel Heinze, who seriously damaged his knee against Villarreal, so Martin Demichelis, the Bayern Munich defender, would make his international debut alongside Inter Milan's Esteban Cambiasso, a double 5, as it is called in Argentina, two holding players, to counter balance the free-wheeling Riquelme.

At the back, the old guard of Ayala and Samuel played in the centre, alongside right-back Zanetti, now playing his fourth match against England, and equalling Simeone's record of 104 caps. Boca Juniors' goalkeeper Roberto Abbondanzieri was the only Argentinian-based player in the starting line up.

The kits were different yet again. This time, England wore their traditional first choice: white shirts, navy blue shorts, white socks. Argentina sported dark blue shirts, white shorts and blue socks.

Riquelme took instant control. He let fly with two fizzing shots from the edge of the area in the first five minutes, forcing two good saves from Robinson. Even in those opening exchanges it was obvious that King was struggling. When Riquelme drifted out to the left, should he go with him? Should he man mark? The problem was that Tevez, the second striker, was dropping deep to link with Riquelme, but neither Terry nor Ferdinand were going with him. King was outnumbered. 'Hard as King tried, the Spurs defender never managed to shackle his man,' wrote Joe Lovejoy, in *The Times*. Riquelme was improvising, finding space. Subtle, clipped passes. He played a measured through ball to Tevez, who shot from close range, and Robinson saved with his feet.

All the early play was in England's half, but when they broke into their first attack on six minutes, Owen headed Rooney's through ball into the back of the net. The referee had already blown, correctly, for offside, but it was an early sign of the potency of the Rooney/Owen partnership, and how quickly they could break.

John Terry blocked two more goalbound shots in the first 10 minutes, and Maxi Rodriguez hit a 15-yard volley from Zanetti's low cross, which again produced an excellent save from Robinson. On 12 minutes Argentina thought they had scored when Ferdinand turned Rodriguez's cross into his own net, but the own goal was disallowed for a slight push by Crespo on Robinson. It was debatable, but the luck on this occasion had gone with England.

The first 20 minutes contained so much good football and excitement that it was like a tribute match to the thrilling 1998 World Cup clash. That this encounter was still scoreless was mainly due to Robinson, but as the half progressed England's counter-attacks became more frequent, with Beckham peppering Argentina's half of the pitch with accurate diagonal passes from the right flank for Rooney and Owen to chase.

Lampard headed wide of the far post from a Beckham corner, and, on the half hour mark, a breakthrough nearly arrived. Gerrard's perfect pass found Rooney tearing towards goal. As Abbondanzieri raced out to close him down, the English scamp audaciously chipped him. The ball hit the post. Two minutes later, Rooney went on another powerful run that left Demichelis sprawling behind him, but this time it came to nothing.

Quality football, with a real buzz to it. This was no friendly, not in the modern sense of the word, as the previous encounter had been. The tackles were flying in, hard but fair, and, unusually for an England v Argentina international, 30 minutes had passed without a player being booked, nor even being spoken to by the referee.

Perhaps Rooney was trying to do too much. He tried to take the ball off Beckham's foot, and, in the confusion, Riquelme, drifting back, picked up the loose ball and was away. Suddenly England were caught too far up the pitch, in the same manner as when they had conceded Brazil's equalising goal in the quarter-final of the 2002 World Cup before losing 2-1.

Riquelme covered 10 yards with the ball before slipping a pass to Tevez, who sharply turned away from Gerrard and fed Rodriguez on the right. The Argentine midfielder comfortably beat Bridge again, and his low cross bounced off Ferdinand. Crespo reacted quickly to knock the loose ball into the goal with his left knee from five yards. Few could argue that Argentina's lead was undeserved.

Five minutes later, without time to pause for a breath, Gerrard hit a long pass to Rooney, which Ayala intercepted. But instead of clearing, the defender uncharacteristically skewed the ball up into the air. Beckham reacted the quickest. Running into the penalty area, he headed the ball backwards and down for Rooney, who was completely free and blasted it low on the half-volley into the far corner of the net with a superb finish.

A pulsating first half, with so many talking points, and, unusually in this fixture, all of them about football, came to an end when Crespo nearly restored Argentina's lead right on half-time, but his header produced another fine save from Robinson.

According to Bobby Robson, the experiment with King had not worked. "You can't be too harsh on Ledley, though. He is being asked to go from being Tottenham's centrehalf to an international midfielder. The two roles are completely different. As a central defender you get tight on the guy you are marking and concentrate on him. In midfield you have to be aware of all the dangers around you. And the runs Riquelme was making, with Carlos Tevez coming deep, gave him all sorts of problems."

Eriksson made one change, bringing on West Ham's Paul Konchesky for the rusty Bridge at left-back. Rather than sit back and let Riquelme dictate, as he had in the first 30 minutes of the first half, England appeared to have been instructed to take the game to Argentina.

Eight minutes into the second half, against the run of play, England gave away a free kick in a dangerous position, just outside their penalty area, slightly to the left. Samuel and Ayala trotted up from the back as Riquelme stood over the ball, weighing up the situation. It was within his striking range and he ran up to the ball as if about to shoot. Instead he floated a chipped cross over to the back post where Samuel was standing all alone. The Inter Milan defender met the ball with a cushioned header. It drifted across the goal, past Robinson, Ferdinand and Terry, dipping into the far corner of the net. Ayala rammed it home to make sure. The England players stood looking at each other. Poor marking. 2-1 to Argentina.

Eriksson acted positively, taking off Ledley King for the attacking Joe Cole, who took up a position on the left of midfield, allowing Gerrard to move into the middle. With Cole in front of him, offering more width, Konchesky had a natural outlet down the line, and the pair combined well.

As England came forward, trying to salvage the match, the often-questioned Gerrard and Lampard combination in the middle of a 4-4-2 began to click and worked well for a period. Lampard, Beckham and Joe Cole all took shots from distance, and every time Rooney and Cole ran at their opponents, the Argentine defence looked decidedly uneasy. Cole, playing for a place in Eriksson's World Cup starting line-up, had the beating of full back Zanetti, who was more comfortable in midfield, or as a wing-back, rather than a traditional full back.

After 70 minutes of fast-paced, end to end action, it was no surprise that legs became heavy. Argentina made their first substitution, Sevilla's Javier Saviola for Hernan Crespo, and four minutes later, Pekerman was forced to take off Ayala, who had taken a knock in a challenge with Rooney. Coloccini replaced Ayala as Argentina tried to retain possession in classic style with short passes in the middle of the pitch. Riquelme, clearly tiring, adopted a more pedestrian pace, curtailing his forward runs, but the holding midfielders, Cambiasso and Demichelis, kept the ball well, inside their own half.

Tevez was limping, so Pekerman replaced him with Inter Milan striker Julio Cruz for the final ten minutes, and it was at that point that Eriksson decided to play his Joker. *El Grandote* (The Giant), as the Argentinian commentators called substitute Peter Crouch, replaced defender Luke Young, as the normally conservative Eriksson threw caution to the wind. Gerrard went to right-back and Rooney dropped into the midfield, while Crouch took his place up front.

The Ayala-less Argentina defence pointed at one another and tried to reorganise around England's changes, but two minutes later Pekerman had to make yet another substitution, his fourth in 14 minutes. Riquelme retired from the match with muscular fatigue, replaced by Lucho Gonzalez.

England were in the ascendancy and a trademark Beckham free kick produced a brilliant double save from Abbondanzieri. Rooney had followed up the original kick, and the

Argentinian keeper, reeling backwards, somehow managed to tip the ingenious chip over. 'Wayne Rooney's chip, the sheer audacity of it, was living proof that true genius shoots at things nobody else sees. What must the rest of the world think of him, this maestro from the land of spirited runners who came dripping in perspiration?' oozed *The Times*.

Chances were still aplenty. As much as Argentina tried to take the sting out of the game, the never say die English spirit urged its players forward, none more so than makeshift right-back Steven Gerrard, who ran down the wing with four minutes remaining. The Liverpool player swung over a cross. Coloccini went to mark Crouch, the perceived dangerman, tightly. Joe Cole rose in the middle of the area, but got nowhere near the ball. But who was that at the far past? Unmarked, Michael Owen, Argentina's chief tormentor of the last decade, a player who had been a peripheral part in the preceding 86 minutes of play, headed home the equaliser, across Abbondanzieri to save the game for the English.

In keeping with the ebb and flow of this classic fare, Argentina responded by going on the attack, but there was no Riquelme and Tevez to open up England anymore. As the match entered the final minute a gap appeared. Cruz was sent through on goal and Gerrard made a last-ditch tackle, bringing him down. "Penalty!" screamed the Argentines, their bench all on their feet appealing. It would not have been a 'proper' Argentina v England match without a true moment of controversy, but Swiss referee Philippe Leuba waved play on. To add insult to Argentina's considerable injury, the ball was moved straight down to the other end, Demichelis made an error and Abbondanzieri had to make another reflex save, this time from a Beckham backward header. So much incident in the last ten minutes.

But it was not over yet. As the match entered the last minute of added time, Joe Cole cut inside Zanetti, and ran towards the Argentine penalty area. Coloccini, the centre-back, moved towards Cole, gesturing to Cambiasso to cover Owen. There was a clear lack of synchronisation in the Argentina defence. Before Coloccini could reach Cole, and before Cambiasso could get across, the England substitute sent over a high cross. Samuel was the only Argentina player in the penalty area with Crouch and Owen, two against one. All eyes were on Crouch as he stretched for the cross, but the 'Giant' was somehow outjumped by Owen, getting in front of his man, even if it was his strike partner, to head the ball home for an incredible, breathtaking last-gasp winner.

Sportsmanship has never been top of the bill when it comes to England versus Argentina matches. And this one was no different. At the final whistle Jose Pekerman behaved impeccably, saying "very good" in English three times to Eriksson, but AFA president Julio Grondona was less forgiving: "The result was unjust. It was a clear penalty on Cruz and if the referee had given it, obviously it would be a different result," he complained. His refrain was not repeated much in Argentina, however, where the press were more concerned with the shortcomings of their own team rather than the referee.

'GAME OWEN', said a stunned *Olé* on its front page in computer game graphics, a play on 'Game Over', above a big picture of Abbondanzieri lying flat on his back, with the ball in the back of the net, and Owen turning away in celebration. 'To have the woman of your dreams in your bed, close your eyes, only to wake up and find yourself speaking with the pillow, that's exactly the sensation that the national team experienced when Michael Owen celebrated again. It wasn't just an empty sensation, but also one of bewilderment, incredulity, failure, and vulnerability – at least it was a friendly and not a World Cup match. If this happens in Germany, we'll cut our veins with an *alfahor* [typical Argentine biscuit].'

'FOUR FATAL MINUTES', cried *Clarin*. 'The England goalscorer has the face of an Angel but the spirit of a Hatchet man.' 'A HARD PUNISHMENT', said *La Nacion*, 'but that's the way the best strikers in the world are – cold, lethal and without mercy.'

The mood was conversely upbeat in England and there was plenty of gloating going on. 'YOU'RE NOT SINGING ANYMORE', said the *Mirror*, in reference to the Argentine arrival at the ground. 'UP YOURS SENORS', said the *Sun* on Monday, still without an ñ on its keyboard. 'We Silenced Argie Poof Chants', it proclaimed. The *Mail on Sunday* marvelled at how, 'England plucked victory from the jaws of defeat.'

Reminiscent of Desmond Hackett on Jimmy Greaves in 1962, Rob Hughes in *The Times* likened Owen to a burglar. 'Missing in action for all but two minutes of a compelling spectacle, Owen gave a reminder of his enduring qualities. Quite how he does it, nobody knows, but his brace of goals stolen in the cold night air here were full of alertness and hunger and deliberation. It is totally beyond belief for here is this comparatively small man, who at 5 ft 8 ins, was like the pimpernel to the Argentinians last night, stealing in behind their backs to head in, not once but twice, from all of seven yards. They knew he was there but they couldn't stop him.'

With over 30 attempts on goal, the match had been bigger on incident and excitement than the whole of the qualifying campaign, 'a routing for those such as Sir Alex Ferguson, who claim that international football has been usurped by the Champions League as the pinnacle of sport,' declared Matt Dickinson in *The Times*.

Dave Walsh wrote in the same paper, 'It was supposed to be friendly but that was a laugh. If England played Argentina at bridge, you would advise the participants to wear shin-guards. The wonder of last night's game was that it could be so competitive, so sporting and so damned entertaining.'

The *Guardian* agreed, purring, 'this friendly made competitive matches look a sham', while *La Nacion* said, 'Welcome to the first level of international football.'

"It was a great match and a great result," concurred Sven-Göran Eriksson, heaving a silent sigh of relief that his players had got him out of another lashing by the tongues of the watching scribes. Eriksson explained why there would always be a place for Michael Owen in his team. "He can sleep for 89 minutes, but you know the goal will come. He can be quiet, and then, suddenly, boom, he's there." Of Rooney, Eriksson said, "He can do everything. He was even winning headers against their centre-backs, which was incredible. He is the complete footballer and he's still 20. That's not bad!"

Owen and Rooney had not actually combined much during the match, but that is not to say they did not complement each other, as Owen expanded upon after the match. "The great thing about our partnership is that we dovetail really well. Every one of his strengths is totally opposite to my strengths. We are opposites and when you are opposites you tend to gel quite quickly. He has got virtually everything. My game is not Wayne Rooney's. My strengths are not coming off and linking play. My strengths are seeing opportunities, knowing where a ball is going to, sniffing out a chance, scoring. I clear out of the way for him because he is better than me in the hole, so why do I want to drag defenders into it?"

Suddenly, thanks to two late goals, things were looking up for England and the usual tide of optimism at a good performance in the World Cup finals in Germany began to rise, fuelled by the manager. "It's my best squad yet, it's more mature every time it comes together," said Eriksson, doing a passable impression of Alf Ramsey 40 years earlier. "If we don't have injuries we can win the World Cup."

What had really impressed the pundits was the way England had attacked in the second half. "The good thing for the neutrals is that positive football seems to be back in vogue," said Bobby Robson. Another ex-England manager, Graham Taylor, shared his opinion. "England are at their best when they attack positively and aggressively – yes that approach can leave them open a little bit, but this is the way we tend to play our football in this country and I still think we are better adopting that approach than becoming defensive-conscious."

More of this please, was the rallying cry of the tabloids, veering from one extreme to the other, now calling for a traditional English 'up and at 'em' approach, the exact tactics for which Kevin Keegan had previously been criticised. The *Sun's* chief sports writer Steven Howard led the charge, with some forthright views: 'Backbone, indomitable spirit and a refusal to die that has always been the hallmark of the great sides of the past. Thankfully, gloriously, we were England's England and not Eriksson's England ... far too long the talent at England's disposal has been held back by Eriksson's inbred pessimism and negativity. Far from moving on from that night in Munich and allowing his players to express this talent, he put them in a straitjacket. His natural reticence has held his team's progress in check ... In Rooney, Owen, Lampard and Gerrard, England have players who are at their best when they take the game to the opposition ...We should play to our strengths. That, more than anything is a determination to get forward and put the opposition under pressure. We possess neither the inclination, the finesse nor the patience to play the slow-burn tactical game that was Eriksson's hallmark in club football.'

The goals and the second half display were genuine reasons for Englishmen to feel positive about the forthcoming World Cup, but, on the cautious side, it had not escaped Eriksson's attention that England had failed to prevent Riquelme controlling the match in the first half. "If you want to take him out you have to go man to man on him and I don't want to do that. He is a fantastic footballer. He hasn't got pace, but when he has the ball it's impossible to take it off him."

Ledley King himself was the first to admit he had found it tough going. "It was difficult. Even though Riquelme seems to play the game at his own pace, you still can't get near him, which is strange. There were times when he drifted out and dragged me with him, which left spaces for others."

Frank Lampard said, "For us to beat one of the best teams in the world was huge. We had to contend with a different style of play – we didn't come up against anything like that in qualifying. Their technical ability and the use of the player in the hole who can move the ball around you and hurt you were a challenge we had to deal with and I thought we coped well. When you come up against players like Riquelme in the hole, who are a bit special, you learn that you cannot play the straight four across the midfield. You need a bit of depth to cover players like that."

Rio Ferdinand was also impressed with the Argentina no.10: "Riquelme is one of the best players I've ever played against."

In the *Independent*, James Lawton wrote, 'England can go anywhere from here. They can go to the mountain top and truly compete when it matters most, or they can slide back into another breakdown of cohesion and self-belief, as they did in the Far East in 2002 and Portugal in 2004 when all the strength and the promise of England dwindled to nothing in the World Cup and European Championship. They can touch the stars – or they can scrabble in the dirt.'

The frustration for the Argentines, who always see matches against England as a clash between two different interpretations of how the game should be played, was that they believed their way had been on top until the late goals. 'It was a dispute between styles of the English tradition of the long balls and European aerial play, and old school Argentinian football. And *La Nuestra* [our way] was clearly superior until the accident at the end. This defeat hurts. For the way we lost and for the rival,' said *La Nacion*.

Certainly Ayala's departure with 15 minutes remaining had been a big loss for Argentina as the big defender had been dominant in the air. Now, in those frantic final few minutes, two more English headers had taken the figure to an incredible 11 headed goals scored out of the total 19 goals conceded from open play by Argentina against England in all matches between the two countries. All the worse then that it was pint-sized Owen who had jumped to it and finished the crosses. "That hurt," conceded Jose Pekerman. "They hit lots of crosses and filled up the area with people – that's logical – and we couldn't control it, but I'm treating it as something isolated that didn't correspond to the rest of the match."

Captain Sorin said, "The balance was very positive until the last five minutes, but the two goals leave us with a lot of anger. It's a merit of theirs, for their persistence, and a lack of concentration on our part, to leave Owen free. We're really annoyed about it."

Three days later, Argentina had another friendly, in Qatar. When they arrived at the airport, greeting them next to the duty free shop was a giant cardboard cutout of Michael Owen advertising watches.

Argentina 2 (Crespo 34' Samuel 53')
England 3 (Rooney 39' Owen 86', 90')
Saturday 12 November 2005. Stade de Genève, Switzerland. Friendly. Attendance: 29,000
Referee: Phillippe Leuba (Switzerland)

Argentina: Roberto Abbondanzieri (Boca Jnrs) Roberto Ayala (Valencia, sub 74'), Juan Pablo Sorin(c) (Villarreal), Javier Zanetti (Internazionale), Martin Demichelis (Bayern Munich), Walter Samuel (Internazionale), Juan Roman Riquelme (Villarreal, sub 84'), Maxi Rodriguez (Atletico Madrid), Esteban Cambiasso (Internazionale), Carlos Tevez (Corinthians, sub 80'), Hernan Crespo (Chelsea, sub 70'), Subs: Fabricio Coloccini (Deportivo de La Coruña, on 74'), Luis Gonzalez (Porto, on 84'), Julio Cruz (Internazionale, on 80'), Javier Saviola (Sevilla, on 70')
Manager: Jose Pekerman

England: Paul Robinson (Tottenham), Luke Young (Charlton, sub 80'), John Terry (Chelsea), Rio Ferdinand (Manchester Utd), Wayne Bridge (Chelsea, sub 46'), Frank Lampard (Chelsea), Ledley King (Tottenham, sub 58'), David Beckham(c) (Real Madrid), Steven Gerrard (Liverpool), Wayne Rooney (Manchester Utd), Michael Owen (Newcastle), Subs: Paul Konchesky (West Ham, on 46'), Joe Cole (Chelsea, on 58'), Peter Crouch (Liverpool, on 80')
Manager: Sven-Göran Eriksson

EPILOGUE

IN ARGENTINA, one man turned up with impeccable timing before the 2005 match against England. Remarkably. He should have been dead by this time. All the articles of a year or so beforehand had read like obituaries. They were accompanied by pictures of a fat, drug-addicted ex-footballer with dyed blond hair, bloated like a beached whale. They bore no resemblance to the player who once led his country to World Cup victory. But all those predicting his imminent death had overlooked one thing. Diego Maradona's career had always been a series of spectacular comebacks.

Drug free and the host of a prime-time television programme, the most striking aspect of the new Maradona was his appearance: he had weighed nearly 19st but now was a little over 11st, his weight at the 1990 World Cup, a remarkable advert for the gastric by-pass operation that involves shrinking the stomach by stapling it together so it rejects pizza and steak and chips, which formed the basis of the old Maradona's diet.

Maradona's top-of-the-rankings TV show, *La noche de 10* (the night of the number 10) was a two-hour extravaganza in which he sang, danced, ball-juggled and talked about himself, amidst much hugging and tears. His interview with Pele was particularly poignant. The two greatest players of all time, sat together for half an hour, chatting about football, poverty and cocaine. "I was nearly dead you know," Maradona told Pele, desperately struggling to hold back the tears, "it was only my daughters, the love of my daughters that saved me." Even though he had not taken drugs for a year and a half, Maradona lived with his parents and still considered himself an addict. "My recuperation isn't overnight. The ghost of the drug still follows me."

Amazingly, Maradona's comeback even included football. Not only was he playing again in charity matches, but AFA president Julio Grondona offered him a position within the national team, in a nebulous role described as a cross between team motivator and adviser to coach Jose Pekerman. Maradona turned down Grondona's offer: "I don't think it's the best moment to join the team. I don't want to get in anyone's way." Not for now maybe, but Grondona hinted Maradona would be a future national coach.

❖

The 2005 match proved to be a microcosm of Argentina's World Cup, six months later. Like the first half against England, Riquelme and the team dazzled in their opening games, a 2-1 victory over the Ivory Coast followed by a majestic display of passing and movement against Serbia which Argentina won 6-0, and had the world drooling. The second goal, one of the World Cup's greatest, the ultimate team goal, contained 24 passes, with Riquelme at the heart of the move, before Cambiasso drove home Crespo's back-heel. With six strikers in the squad, Argentina had an embarrassment of attacking riches, the outstanding Saviola keeping Tevez and Messi on the bench, although both had come on in the second half to score a goal each against Serbia.

Argentina rested players for their final group match v Holland (0-0), before the second round tactical showdown with Ricardo Lavolpe's Mexico, a fascinating match which Argentina won 2-1 thanks to a spectacular extra-time winner from Maxi Rodriguez. But, after starting brightly and taking the lead against hosts Germany in the quarter final, Argentina ran out of steam. As in the friendly against England, injury and fatigue set in, and Pekerman was forced into making unplanned substituions. He took off the tiring Riquelme for defensive midfielder Cambiasso. With Michael Ballack inspiring the comeback, Germany's pace and dynamism forced an equaliser and took the match into extra time and penalties. This time it was German goalkeeper Jens Lehmann who was the penalty shoot-out hero. He had a note stuffed down his sock, handed to him by his coaches, a list of where each Argentina player normally places their penalty, and he checked it before each player stepped up, saving from Ayala and Cambiasso as the hosts went through. Pekerman spent most of the post-match conference, as he had done against England six months earlier, trying to explain his substitutions. The lasting image of Argentina's 2006 World Cup was Lionel Messi cutting a forlorn figure as he sat on the bench, an unused sub in the quarter final defeat. Pekerman resigned almost immediately, and a few weeks later Riquelme also announced his retirement from international football. He was sick of all the criticism. It was making his mother very ill.

England's World Cup never quite got going. Beset by off-the-field distractions – a bodged attempt to secure the services of Portugal manager Phil Scolari to take over from Eriksson after the tournament, and wives and girlfriends (WAGs) partying in the relaxed atmosphere of England's Baden Baden base. Although if the football had been more gripping, the WAGs might not have attracted so much media attention

Having beaten Paraguay (1-0) and Trinidad & Tobago (2-0) in unconvincing performances, England drew with Sweden (2-2) – Joe Cole's brilliant curling volley into the top corner was a rare bright moment in a match that saw Michael Owen injured after four minutes and out of the tournament. In the second round, an extremely laboured performance against Ecuador produced a 1-0 win from a second half Beckham free kick, but by the end of the match he too had joined England's casualty list, and was out of the World Cup.

English hopes of beating Portugal in the quarter final were severely dented after an hour when Rooney's indiscipline, much talked about before the 2005 friendly against Argentina, boiled to the surface. He was sent off for stamping on Ricardo Carvalho, a harsh decision perhaps, like Beckham's in '98, but by the letter of the law, a red card offence. The referee Horacio Elizondo was Argentinian. That was noted in the English media, although this proved a mere distraction to the main event of slaughtering the coach Sven

Goran Eriksson. Thanks in no small part to Portugal's blunt strike force, England had held onto 0-0 for the remainder of the match and extra time, before another penalty shoot-out heartbreak; Lampard, Gerrard and Carragher all missed from the spot.

England's 2006 World Cup campaign lacked the excitement and thrills of a big match against a team like Argentina or Germany, and is not a tournament that will live long in the memory of the nation.

Alfio Basile, who had been in charge from 1990–94, returned as Argentina manager. *El coco* successfully completed his first task by managing to persuade Riquelme to come out of international retirement. In the 2007 *Copa America*, Argentina sparkled through to the final, with Riquelme, Messi, Crespo, Tevez, and a rejuvenated Juan Veron, recalled for the first time in five years, playing intricate passing football. But when they met the physical strength of Dunga's Brazil in the final, they were outfought and outplayed in a humiliating 3-0 defeat. The 2010 World Cup qualifiers also turned into a nightmare for Basile. The ageing, gravel-voiced manager stood down halfway through the eighteen-match schedule, unable to get his ideas across to the 'playstation generation'.

England's Steve McClaren fared no better. Eriksson's ex-assistant began his ill-fated reign as manager by leaving out Beckham; it was meant to signify a new beginning, but England regressed, failing to qualify for the 2008 European Championships. In the last qualifier, a shambles of a match at a rain-soaked new Wembley, England lost 3-2 to Croatia. McClaren was christened the 'Wally with the Brolly' by the tabloids before being sacked.

Could the English and Argentinian football associations' choice of replacements have been more different? Italian Fabio Capello was handed a multi-million pound contract and asked to bring order and tactical discipline to the England set up. This the former AC Milan, Roma, Real Madrid and Juventus manager did by banning WAGs, agents, mobile phones, and even tomato ketchup from the England camp. Tactically, he embraced Emile Heskey as a battering ram centre-forward, whom the attacking midfielders – England's great strength – could feed off. Rooney and Gerrard, playing behind Heskey, were given the freedom to drift and interchange, especially on the left side of the pitch, thus overnight solving the problems in that area. He recalled Beckham, but now more as a specialist cameo substitute, and Capello was fortunate that Theo Walcott, the surprise, but unused, addition to Eriksson's 2006 World Cup squad, was now coming of age. Unleashed on Croatia, the young Arsenal winger scored a hat-trick in a marvellous 4-1 away victory. This time it was Slaven Bilic's turn to smell the coffee, and England booked their place at the 2010 World Cup at Croatia's expense by hammerng Bilic's team 5-1 at Wembley.

Meanwhile Maradona brought madness and chaos to Argentina. His time as manager had arrived. Perhaps to try and balance out their bizarre appointment, AFA sensibly, but somewhat naively, appointed 1986 World Cup winning manager Carlos Bilardo as general manager alongside Diego as a soundboard for advice and tactical know-how. But Maradona soon let it be known that he was nobody's patsy and would not be listening to anyone. He rejected AFA and Bilardo's choice of coaches and appointed his own inexperienced staff.

Maradona made his debut as manager in November 2008, a friendly in Scotland, where he is revered as a hero for what he did to the English in '86. He was given a magnificent reception at Hampden Park by almost everyone. The exception was Scotland's assistant manager Terry Butcher. "I'll never forgive him," said Butcher in the official pre-match press conference. "It's not nice when you lose a World Cup quarter-final under those circumstances. I was selected for the drugs test with Gary Stevens and Kenny Sansom and ended up in the room with Maradona and two of his pals. Our World Cup was over and they were celebrating. It could have been a war-zone in there but it wasn't. I wasn't next to him, if I was I might have done something. He was playing it very cute because he said he headed the ball, not handled it. Not that I could speak Spanish but he indicated through sign language that he put his head to the ball rather than his hand. It's very hard to forgive and forget in the circumstances."

Argentina beat Scotland 1-0 and Maradona twisted the knife afterwards, when asked in the post-match press conference if he had shaken Butcher's hand. Maradona retorted, "Who's he? Who is Butcher? I shook hands with Burley, the Scotland manager after the game. Who is Butcher?" He then burst into a wide smile.

But the laughing did not last long. Maradona was unable to halt the slide that had begun under Basile. There were some alarming errors in defence as Argentina continued to lose important World Cup qualifying matches, including a 6-1 thrashing in the altitude of Bolivia; "Every goal was like a stab through my heart," Maradona depaired. By then he had lost Riquelme, the prickly midfielder retiring from the national team yet again, unhappy with Maradona's comments on the radio about his play during a Boca Juniors match. The manager had broken certain 'football codes', according to Riquelme, although he later insinuated there was something more than just the radio comments.

Qualification went to the wire, and only an injury-time winner by 35-year-old substitute Martin Palermo in torrential rain at home to Peru allowed Argentina to go into the last match, four days later, still with a chance of automatic qualification. Palermo's goal was greeted by a drenched, but ecstatic, Maradona running onto the pitch and launching into the greatest belly-flop in sporting history outside of swimming pool events. A potential disaster was still in store though, as Argentina faced the old enemy Uruguay in Montevideo in the last match, both teams needing a result to qualify and avoid the play-offs. There was even the prospect of complete elimination depending on other results.

But Argentina won 1-0, and Maradona released all his pent-up frustrations by jumping up and down and chanting with his players in the centre of the pitch, before venting his spleen at journalists with some quite vulgar remarks in the press conference – "you lot can suck on me, and keep on sucking on me" (among the most printable), he told the press, for which he earned a three-month ban from all football by FIFA.

Translating slang is not easy, and it may well be that Maradona's words sound worse than they are in another language. That was how Kia Joorabchian, Carlos Tevez's representative, saw it when the Manchester City player called Manchester United and England full back Gary Neville a 'moron' and a 'boot-licker' (literal translation 'sock sucker') on Argentine radio. Joorabchian claimed the insults were lost in translation. "If you use slang terminology, that slang terminology translated word for word may not sound as it would in context," he said. The spat had come about after Neville had responded to Tevez's cupped-ear goal celebration in the 2010 Carling Cup semi-final between the two Manchester teams, by showing the Argentinian his middle finger. Tevez himself had been upset by comments Neville had made in the media that backed Alex Ferguson's assertion that Tevez was not worth the 25 million (pounds) City had paid for him after his two year loan period at Old Trafford had come to an end.

To cover the complex and drawn out Carlos Tevez and Javier Mascherano transfer sagas to, and within, English football would require a whole new book – and one that might have difficulty getting past lawyers – but during his four seasons in England, Tevez had won the hearts of the supporters at every club he had played for – West Ham, Manchester United and Manchester City – and was even able to celebrate both the Premier League and European Champions League trophies he won at Manchester United in 2008, draped in an Argentinian flag. Like Ardiles and Villa before him, Tevez had been a positive ambassador for his country.

The *News of the World* claimed that Gary Neville had 'PREVIOUS ARGY-BARGY' when it came to 'spats with Argentinians'. It attributed quotes to Veron, recounting a story from his time at Man Utd, when he invited Argentine rugby players Agustin Pichot and Felipe Contepomi, who were playing in England, along to United's Christmas celebrations. "I took a microphone and started to sing 'Let's Go Argentina' and then Neville started to sing for England. So I hit Neville on the head with the microphone and there was a big fight between me, Pichot, Contepomi and the English. There was blood everywhere. When I came home, I had loads of scratches and my shirt was ripped." Whether the tension was as real as presented by the Sunday tabloid, or whether the incident was just hi-jinks that got exaggerated, Neville's feelings were no doubt still raw after being in the team that lost to Argentina on penalties in the 1998 World Cup.

And meanwhile, away from the football, the old issue, the one that dies down for a while, but never goes away, resurfaced again. Over the previous decade or so, there had been sporadic diplomatic spats over issues such as fishing and flights from the Falklands to mainland South America, but, in February 2010, when the British government gave the go-ahead for British companies to ship drilling equipment to the Falklands and its surrounding waters, to begin exploring the region for oil, Argentine edginess reached new heights.

President Cristina Kirchner signed a decree that demanded all vessels apply for permits to pass through Argentina waters. She made a show of it, signing the law live on TV, accompanied by a trademark Eva Peron-style passionate speech, reiterating Argentina's claim for sovereignty of *Las Malvinas*. It was perhaps more of a political gesture rather than a practical measure, as the British ships and rigs could use other ports in the region, and neither did the decree state the would-be punishment for any transgressing boat.

While British prime minister Gordon Brown and British diplomats tried to play down the issue – "it's perfectly within our rights to do this, sensible discussions will prevail", he said, the *Sun* newspaper seized upon an opportunity for headlines: 'ARGIE BLOCKADE ON FALKLANDS' and 'NEW FALKLAND BATTLE BREAKS OUT', the tabloid declared and it spoke of 'a re-run of the 1982 conflict'. Britain's biggest-selling daily cited a routine voyage of HMS *Scott*, a deep-water survey vessel, as evidence that a new taskforce had set sail. All this was reported back to Argentina, where the story was the main television news and front page in all the papers. When questioned over the defence of the islands, Gordon Brown replied that "all necessary precautions had been taken."

Argentina has never renounced its sovereignty of the islands, and in the aftermath of the latest row, it promised once again to take the issue to the United Nations and urge UN general gecretary, Ban Ki Moon, to pressure Britain into negotiating the future of the islands. Then, on the day of the general election in Britain (6 May 2010), it was reported that a British Company had struck oil for the first time in the Falklands. Argentines reacted with groans of dismay, followed by protests from President Cristina Kirchner's government.

And so the world awaited the next meeting of the two rivals with bated breath. There could be a possible clash at the 2010 World Cup in South Africa as the two countries would meet in the quarter final if one won their group and the other finished second. In theory, that should not happen as the draw was kind to both squads, handing them supposedly easy groups that they ought to win, but with Argentina's erratic form under Maradona, and England's traditional propensity to make hard work of the group stage, the prospect of another mouth-watering knockout clash cannot be ruled out.

If they were to meet some interesting ingredients from past matches are likely to be there. Although David Beckham ruptured an Achilles tendon while playing for AC Milan in March 2010, ruling him out of the tournament, England manager Capello has asked him to join the squad in a coaching role. The former captain will take a seat alongside Capello on the England bench in South Africa, helping out in training and acting as an intermediary between players and staff. Beckham, red card fully forgotten after ramming home the penalty that decided the 2002 World Cup meeting, had also captained England to victory in the exciting 2005 friendly. He would no doubt be a focus for Argentine revenge should the two sides meet in South Africa. However, Michael Owen is not part of Fabio Capello's squad as the striker, still only 30, has struggled with a series of hamstring injuries and lack of form since the 2005 friendly. Argentina will breathe a sigh of relief over Owen's absence after all the damage he has inflicted on them in the three games he has played against them.

Without doubt, the Argentine player who would most see an England v Argentina World Cup rematch as a chance for revenge is Juan Sebastian Veron. Booed in his own country after his dreadful first half performance against England in the 2002 World Cup, even accused of taking bribes from the English, Veron has reinvented himself back home in Argentina and is a national treasure once again, the South American footballer of the year two years running in 2008 and 2009.

When, for this book in 2005, Veron's father, Juan Ramon, spoke about Estudiantes' *Copa Libertadores* triumphs in the late 1960s and their Intercontinental Cup win over Manchester United in 1968, he reckoned something like that could never happen again to such a small town club. "The economic realities of the modern game simply do not allow for it," he said. But, incredibly, history did repeat itself. In 2009, Estudiantes de La Plata, inspired and driven by Juan Sebastian Veron, lifted the *Copa Libertadores* to become champions of South America again. They also won the 2008 Argentinian 'clausura' championship. In December 2009, Estudiantes faced European champions Barcelona in the final of the World Club Championship in the United Arab Emirates, a match taken very seriously by both clubs, but sadly did not get the coverage and recognition it merited in England. Estudiantes took a first-half lead through Mario Boselli, and were only a minute away from winning the trophy before Pedro equalised for Barcelona in the 89th minute, and ironically it was an extra-time winner from Lionel Messi that broke Argentinian hearts.

By now, Veron had firmly re-established himself as an integral part of the Argentina national side. The whole crowd rose to chant his nickname 'Bruja, Bruja' in the qualifying match against Brazil in September 2009, a stark contrast to the boos he received after the 2002 World Cup, and like Beckham in 2002, Veron would view a victory over England as the final act of his redemption.

But for Terry Butcher, Peter Shilton and all Englishmen who still felt bitter about '86, what better an array of stars could have been set up for avengement should the two teams meet in South Africa? Carlos Bilardo, manager in 1986, is now technical director, and Hector Enrique is one of Maradona's coaches. It was Enrique who played the short pass to Maradona, back in his own half, before the number 10 set off on the stunning run that produced the wondrous second goal against England in '86. "I provided the assist", Enrique often jokes. And then, of course, there is Maradona himself, now the manager. Twenty-four years on, how the English would love to wipe the smirk that still descends upon his face whenever the 'Hand Of God' goal is mentioned.

A purely hypothetical scenario at the time of going to print, but if both teams were to win their group (or both finish second) and then progress all the way through the tournament, they would not meet until the final. 'Imagine that', as Bobby Robson had said back in 1990. The tantalising prospect does not bear thinking about. With Maradona as Argentina manager, it would be the celestial football scriptwriters' dream, the ultimate football showdown – all that would be lacking is Rattin and Ramsey. But you could guarantee the match would produce some sort of controversy somewhere. It always does. England v Argentina is, quite simply, the greatest Inter-Continental rivalry in the world.

BIBLIOGRAPHY

The main sources for this book were newspapers as I wanted to tell the story through the eyes of the players, and the press at the time of each match.

In Argentina, I chose the most widely-read newspapers:

La Nacion
Clarín
Cronico
Critica
La Razon
Olé
Buenos Aires Herald
El Grafico sports magazine

In England I have used a wide range of newspapers from the broadsheets to the tabloids. *The Times* features a lot as it was there, with its football coverage, from the beginning with the very first match in 1951 and I have followed that through to the present day, but I have also sourced and taken quotes from all the British dailies from the *Guardian* to the *Sun*.

Books

Passion of the People? Football in South America: Football (Critical Studies in Latin American Culture) Tony Mason
The Ball Is Round; A Global History Of Football (Viking) David Goldblatt
Soccer in Sun and Shadow (Verso Books) Eduardo Galeano
Historia de Futbol Argentino (El Grafico)
Fuimos Campeones, La Dictadura, y El Mundial 78 Ricardo Gotta
Hecho Pelotas Fernando Ferreira
Soy Diego (the autobiography of Diego Maradona) Diego Maradona
Ossie's Dream – My Autobiography (Bantam Press) Osvaldo Ardiles
1966 and All That (the autobiography of Geoff Hurst) (Headline) Geoff Hurst
My England Years (Headline) Sir Bobby Charlton
Don't Shoot The Manager (Boxtree) Norman Giller
The Story of the World Cup (Faber & Faber) Brian Glanville
Argentina: An Economic Chronicle. How one of the richest countries in the world lost its wealth Vito Tanzi
Inverting the Pyramid Jonathon Wilson

Neil Clack writes on Argentinian and South American football for the *Independent*, the *Independent on Sunday*, and the *Sunday Herald*, and covers English football for the Argentinian sports newspaper *Ole*. He is a regular contributor to he West Ham fanzine, *Over Land and Sea.*